Reverence

Reverence

[handwritten inscription and signature]

Janet Sassoon

Library of Congress Control Number:		2013918508
ISBN:	Hardcover	978-1-4931-1216-6
	Softcover	978-1-4931-1215-9
	Ebook	978-1-4931-1217-3

This book was printed in the United States of America.

Rev. date: 11/25/2013

To order additional copies of this book, contact:
Xlibris LLC
1-888-795-4274
www.Xlibris.com
Orders@Xlibris.com
132295

Contents

Dedication

To my husband, John R. Upton Jr.,
for his encouragement and enthusiasm
have made this book possible.
Last of all, to Mother (deceased).

$\mathcal{P}$*reface*

I have attempted to write this book to give the readers an idea of what happened to me in my quest for a career in the art of classical ballet. Thus it is a journey from my childhood into adolescence and beyond, always growing and changing. You will follow me into the world of ballet and share my passion for not only its art but also its human side with the good times, those of humor and those of tragedy. You will be with me as a choreographer creates a new ballet and then join me in a dressing room filled with nerves and excitement. I have attempted to write about these events as I remember them, honestly and to the best of my ability. Due to my many travels, some of the sequences and dates may be a bit inaccurate, but the facts are true. Having experienced so much, I hope that you will feel the same magic for my art, which filled me with such joy, passion, and love. As these will stay with me forever, I only hope that what is contained within these pages will remain with you, dear reader.

Acknowledgments

I would like to express my sincere appreciation to Kenneth Rexroth (deceased) and Llowelyn Chin Capalla in their assistance.

Also, my special thanks to Iris Bass for editing my manuscript.

Reverence

from the Latin reverentia

1. A feeling or attitude of deep respect, love, awe, and esteem as for
something saved; veneration.
2. A manifestation of this, specifically an act of respect or obeisance
as a bow or a curtsy.
—*Webster's New Twentieth-Century Dictionary*

In the world of classical ballet, the word *reverence* has more than
the above meanings. It is demonstrated in many ways throughout your
entire life of dance. You start by physically using reverence, in the form
of a curtsy or a bow. As a very little girl, even before learning ballet, I
was trained to curtsy to my elders; I also curtsied after a piano lesson or
any other kind of instruction. Then came ballet class, where from the
very first day we were expected to curtsy to our teacher, one by one, as
we exited the studio. This became automatic, as much a part of my life as
brushing my teeth.

As time passed, reverence became a much more involved act,
emotionally as well as physically. I developed reverence for my art: for the
places where I worked, for the teachers who trained me, for my fellow
dancers and choreographers, for many other members of company and
theater staff, and for the composers and instrumentalists who created
such beautiful music for me. Last and not least, I developed reverence
for the audience. These elements did not come together all at once: they
interlaced internally over the years as I thought about my passion for my
work, my love for dancing, my gratitude for what talent I possessed, the

good luck that occasionally came my way . . . and the ever-astounding fact that the initial small curtsy I had made to my first dancing teacher had somehow led me to bow upon all the great stages of the world. Performing ballets and making reverence nightly were what I always did with all my heart.

1

Childhood

One of my first childhood recollections is of sitting on the lap of a spider. I was seven years old, and had been chosen from the littlest girls' class of the San Francisco ballet school to be an elf in the opera *Falstaff.* The spider was ballet dancer Russell Hartley—in later years, he would become a beloved friend—and we were seated below the stage at the War Memorial Opera House, waiting for our act 3 entrances. That evening was the beginning of life for me.

Even before the audience had seen me, I was already thrilled by my experiences in this new magical place: the world of backstage. The downstairs area of the opera house had seemed like an underworld filled with strange and wonderful creatures. My first glimpse had been that of a dressing room filled with light-surrounded mirrors. Costumes had hung everywhere—gauze, tulle, silk, velvet—and diamondlike crowns. It was as if I had found a cave filled with the jewels and riches from a forgotten kingdom. And I had been allowed to touch and look at everything. I had watched a dresser try to make a costume fit, and another woman who seemed to know everything and everybody. Later I was to learn that this lady, Mrs. Goldstein, ran the dynasty known as Goldstein's Costumes, located on Market Street. But to me, those fabulous clothes had been the product of fairyland seamstresses.

My fitting had been fairly easy: I was given a clingy small chiffon dress, which she had directed someone to pull off a rack high above all the other racks of costumes. Mrs. Goldstein had smiled now and then and was very kind to me, even though she appeared much more forceful toward her adult colleagues. Completely familiar with her stock, she seemed to know exactly what would look best on each body or fit with a minimum of alteration. I adored my costume, my very first. I felt as if I had truly become an elf.

Once I had been dressed, I had visited a room beneath the stage where the musicians had gathered to tune their instruments. Not all had been doing this. Some had been pacing the floor or just chatting with the dancers and extras. All had been dressed to enter the pit. I had loved their coattails and shiny black shoes. I had also loved violins, even at seven, and had been pleased to be able to identify a melody after having heard only a few strokes of the bow.

I had also seen a room devoted solely to makeup. In there was the most beautiful-looking man I had ever seen. He had a mass of white hair and heavy eyebrows that tapered to a point—a Mephisto with shiny eyes. This was Everett Mason, longtime makeup artist with the San Francisco Opera. Mr. Mason had sat me down in front of the mirror and had smiled while applying to my face first a base makeup, then a lot of powder, finally rouge and lipstick. He actually did very little as, being so young, I did not require much makeup and, too, he knew that I would be moving in a blue light that would obscure any other colors. Nevertheless, getting a taste of his vast store of cosmetics made me feel very professional.

After I had seen these bewitching rooms, I had been taken upstairs where I stood in the wings, waiting to take my first steps upon the great stage. My heart thumped until I thought it was louder than the music. Suddenly, my knees did not seem to belong to me, but my mind was clear with what I had to do. I was to run onstage while Falstaff slept under a tree. This character was being performed by the formidable Salvatore Baccalone. He looked quite stout. I had been instructed to dance around him while the chorus backstage sang in Italian "*Pizzica, pizzica,*" which meant "Pinch him." This was precisely what I was there to do; during my dance I was to poke him now and then.

My cue came. To my delight, once I had left the wings, there was even more magic: the stage was dully blue and dark . . . but I was in a light that moved with me! I found this so remarkable that I moved with precision, as if challenging the light to obey me. Then, because of Falstaff's girth (which I *thought* was padding), I poked and prodded very much, to my great satisfaction. But I began to realize that this padding was actually Mr. Baccalone, who started to make growling sounds when my poking got too severe. He then "awoke," raised his body on one elbow, and sang an aria. As I was to learn later, singing in that position is very difficult, even without at the same time suffering the mischievousness of a little elf!

Soon, after doing my worst to Mr. Baccalone, I heard a voice from the wings saying, "Ballet girl, ballet girl, offstage," and so I slipped around the tree and disappeared. By that time, I really *was* a creature of the forest. I had become transformed and transported by the same make-believe that had done such wondrous things to time and space. I felt as though I had found a great new friend in this place called the stage.

My introduction to theater had captured all the magic I had only dreamed about. Physically taking part in all the backstage activities and then stepping upon the stage itself had allowed me to enter, totally, a world that had gone even beyond my imagination. On that unforgettable night, I realized that I could *become* a story, not just a listener to it.

It had been my destiny to have been chosen out of a class of many little girls to be that elf. The next few years were spent attending daily classes at the San Francisco Ballet School.

I shall never forget my very first day. I was to enroll as a beginner. My heart pounded as we approached the ballet school, then located at 236 Van Ness Avenue, down a block and across the street from the opera house. As we entered the building, we were met by a long staircase—and an elderly woman with a kind face. As she enrolled me in the first-girls' level, she told my mother the school's dress code: what I was to wear to class and where I could buy my first pair of soft leather ballet shoes. She explained the latter were to be white and that I was to sew elastic across the top to hold them on. No ribbons, which were reserved for toe shoes.

Sitting everywhere were long-limbed older girls whose hair were pulled back tightly. Their individual perfumes mixed fragrantly in the air. The students were dressed in leotards, wool leggings, and "gymps" (a typical ballet classroom dress made of chiffon, which somewhat resembles a Greek tunic). The girls were darning toe shoes, reading, or drinking tea. I wanted so much to be a part of them! What fascinated me was that they were all so *sleek*. There was an atmosphere, an aura about them even as they were just being themselves, not dancing, that made me adore how they looked and behaved. Once I had been enrolled as a student, I watched everything the girls did, and I must say that many of them took me on, helping and encouraging me.

The school as a whole became a special home to me. Each day, being welcomed by the elderly receptionist and ascending the stairs, I passed a pair of French doors that opened out from the large main studio where we took class. On occasion, when the receptionist would step in to call the roll, I would quickly sneak behind her to peek into the big room beyond the doors, to see what was going on with the company dancers. On the other side of our studio was another room, for the ballet mamas waiting to take their children home. Some would knit, some would gossip, some would chat of other things, and all would speak about how wonderful their respective daughters were (almost all; my mother did not do this as she had been raised to observe great modesty).

Behind the mothers' waiting area were the general offices of the faculty and of the three Christensen brothers who were at the helm of the San Francisco Ballet. They had a wonderful lineage as instructors: They had trained with Stefano Mascagno*, a pupil of Giovanni Lepri*, who had himself been the pupil of Carlo Blasis*. They had also worked with another great teacher, Luigi Albertieri*, ballet master of the Metropolitan Opera. Additionally, Willam had studied with Mikhail Fokine*, Harold, and Lew at the School of American Ballet.

Farther along was a hallway where we would stand to warm up for class, opening to a girls' bathroom, a boys' bathroom, and separate dressing rooms for the male and female students. There was also a wonderful spiral staircase in the hallway, leading up to the company girls' dressing rooms. My eyes always followed the steps up whenever I passed them. It seemed to me the stairway to heaven.

My first classes were held in a small studio that looked out onto Van Ness Avenue. As I faced the barre, I could see Commerce High School and its football field, on which now stands Davies Symphony Hall. I was supposed to be concentrating, not looking out the window, but every once in a while I would hear the sounds on the avenue and glance down or watch rain as it fell. But, for the most part, I had no time for dreaming.

I must honestly admit that the traditional positions with which we began were not difficult for me. I was lucky to possess a natural turnout, and they came easily to my body. Also, my mother had already shown me the five basic positions of the feet as she had had the chance as a young girl to study ballet with a Russian teacher who had been in Pavlova's company. Only later was I to realize the difficulties other children faced when entering this profession.

My first class was for children, of course, and taught by Dean Crockett, who seemed to have great patience, which was good as I was painfully shy. But my shyness left me when I became engrossed in trying to do what he asked of me. Day after day my world consisted of standing at the barre with my feet turned out, head tall, back straight, bending, pulling, stretching, trying to master the groundwork of the technique of classical dance. There was no way to quicken the process of training one's limbs to be strong and supple, of making the ankles raise one off the floor with power and yet with ease. I quickly learned that one's feet should always be beautifully pointed and that one went far with good feet; I took to massaging mine in hopes that they would point more easily. I even tried to sleep with books hidden under my covers, atop my feet, to force my toes down—until, to my chagrin, my mother discovered (and ended!) this nightly practice.

While my class was in session, I longed to belong to another class, an advanced one, which was scheduled for that same time. It contained fewer girls—around fifteen—who possessed notable talent. I was allowed to watch it one day and was told that I would be allowed to join it soon. From that day onward, I dreamed of nothing else and endeavored to make my body worthy of membership in that elite.

By then, going to ballet school had become my sole reason to exist. There is no passion like that of a small child as it carries little or no sense of reason, only a great need and conviction that, unrepressed, pours out as if by sheer instinct. By such determination, I finally was allowed to enter the advanced class. But my joy soon turned to despair as I seemed not only its smallest child but also far from its best.

This class was taught by Harold Christensen himself, the first of the brothers who had chosen not to have a performing career in favor of becoming a teacher. Alas, despite his heritage, Harold seemed only interested in *demi-plié* (a half-bend of the knees) and turnout and blonde girls. I was all too aware that he had his favorites and that, with my jet-black hair and Middle Eastern Jewish looks, I was not one of them. As for turnout, he emphasized extreme turnout, not particularly from the hip but from the feet, which in later years could in fact cause damage. But we didn't know that as his students. Nothing mattered except that our feet were turned out. Very often, when Harold demonstrated our steps, his own foot positions were so extraordinary that we little girls would ask him to pull up his pants' legs. We wanted to see his knees, which we were certain were bent to achieve so exaggerated a turnout. Of course, Harold didn't like our teasing one bit, and though he was quite serious, he also teased us a great deal in turn, in ways that were quite cruel to a small child.

I also found, during this period, that my body would be tied up in knots from the strain of our work. When outsiders would come in to teach, I was fine—my body flowed easily with the movements. But when Harold led the class, we repeated movements too many times. In spite of my slight physique, I began to notice that I was building unnecessary muscle. Obviously, people need to develop the proper muscles in order to be able to dance and to obtain the strength for jumps. However, good training is so very important that it must not be over-exaggerated at an early age. Listening to my body, I sensed that some of my training in this class was not quite right for me. As I learned Harold's interpretation of classical technique, I also became acquainted with defiance. The resilience of a determined young child is not to be taken lightly. I was able to fantasize how I would find expression of my love of dancing through my work, and this kept my spirits high.

Every day, my mother brought me to school and waited patiently to take me home in all kinds of weather, worrying about my being cold or hungry or both (later, Gene Compton's Cafeteria, on our way from the streetcar, would become a regular stop, where my mother would nourish me with custard or Jell-O, though even a taste of their many cakes was forbidden). My father, meanwhile, looked upon my classes as some childish desire I would eventually outgrow. My brother and sister made fun of and mimicked me yet quickly came to my defense if some other child attempted to do so. I knew I was small, thin, and not pretty, that I looked very foreign alongside more all-American girls' looks and ways. And in Harold's class I had learned that someone might not find a dancer attractive, however well she might dance.

I now had a new goal. During this period, I would often catch glimpses of the company class as they took class or rehearsed. I would stand at the doorway and be filled with hope and yearning to do what they were doing. Among them was a man who seemed like a wizard to me: one minute, he was a swan, the next, a magician, then a young girl. Whatever he was, he was the dancer in command there. This was Willam Christensen, eldest brother of the Christensen clan and the director of the San Francisco Ballet, who had danced the Orpheum Circuit and also with Ballet Caravan. I sometimes imagined that he noticed me in the doorway, and I would feel exhilarated.

Then the day came when Willam became the teacher of our class. Never had I tried so hard, every muscle pushing and straining. But I realized that he wished something else from us than had Harold. Willam wanted us to dare *more* in our technique: to make it do more than we thought possible. He wanted us to turn many turns, challenged us to jump higher, and made us pour with sweat. Then, when we thought we had understood the lesson, he proclaimed that we were all dumb because we didn't "dance"! We never answered him back, of course. He wanted us not only to dance steps but also to *feel*, to dance from our hearts. Miracle of miracles, he saw how much I loved this work and, I felt, began to understand *me*. I never spoke, I only danced. I bloomed as I felt my way toward excelling for the sake of excellence and not just for his approval.

During this period of my life, I was dedicated only to dance. School, friends, and even family came after dance. Although I loved my music studies and Hebrew lessons, I felt that half my hours in ordinary day

—

school had become a waste of time, spent on subjects that would never help me to do what I *wanted.* I ached to be released from what I felt were nonessential features of my schedule, such as gym, lunch, or study period—to me, a total waste of three hours each day! It was at this point that I entered into a private war with the Dean of Girls, who insisted that the Board of Education would not excuse me from such periods to enable me to spend those hours dancing.

Since I had reached the seventh grade (I had skipped sixth grade), I was obliged to switch from grammar school to a junior high school within my district (in California, elementary school ended at sixth grade). Neither of the two private local junior-high schools would allow me to miss a single day of school for performances. My only alternative would have been private tutoring. And so, until I could enter Lowell High School, I was to spend the next two years on a rigid schedule of classes at junior high, followed by my daily dance lesson.

To my great joy, during this period, my daily dance lessons continued to be taught by Willam. He would often call me to the front of the class and ask me to demonstrate a group of steps or a "combination," as we called it, that he had just given to us. It was obvious that I was one of his favorites.

During this time, Willam was struggling to make the San Francisco Ballet a company of national, not merely regional, importance. His energy was limitless. During the opera season, he was on constant call as a choreographer—he seemed to make up the gavotte for *Don Giovanni,* the processional march for *Aida,* or the Spanish dance for *Carmen* in only a few minutes, and under unbelievable circumstances. Chaos invariably erupted during the opera season. There were, without fail, ongoing fights between directors; a "turf war" mentality prevailed. Nonetheless, Willam remained effective.

He began using me in every opera ballet that he could. The season was a wonderful training ground for a dancer, during which I had the opportunity to learn about music and conducting and to hear great artists. The general director then was Gaetano Merola; Kurt Adler was choral director; and the conductors included Fausto Cleva and Erich Leinsdorf. I had the opportunity to watch and listen to such singers as Ezio Pinza, Lily Pons, Bidu Sayão, Jan Peerce, and Kirsten Flagstad. What an incredible education!

The future seemed bright and full of hope, but suddenly one day I became weak and ill. The doctor was called, and after an examination and tests, he declared me very anemic. He ordered that I receive iron shots every day and a complete rest—absolutely *no* dancing. I cried very dramatically, announcing that he might as well let me die of anemia as he was surely causing me a slow death by not allowing me to dance. Indeed, in spite of the rest and injections, I was not improving as I should have been, and after much pleading and the passage of a few months, he conceded to permit me to return to my work upon my promise to eat and rest properly. I soon became well and stronger than before. My one worry was that I had lost my place, that I would no longer be one of the best in class.

Once I had resumed my full schedule at school (which I only just tolerated now), dance lessons, and performance, I felt as though I did not have enough hours in the day. My class had progressed to working in pointe shoes, which I loved most of all: I felt that this was the true art of a dancer, pointe work. To raise oneself with ease and yet with strength was a great and exalting challenge.

By this time, the conflict between my ballet studies and my academic schoolwork had become intolerable. Academically speaking, I was a good scholar and had succeeded in leaving junior high early to enter Lowell High School in the ninth rather than in the usual tenth grade. It was then the most difficult public high school in northern California, where pupils were very competitive to maintain scholarship levels and high marks. But the length of time I was expected to physically spend each day in the school building had become a problem. In desperation, I took matters into my own hands.

Even before my first term at Lowell began, I knew what I had to do. I felt very small and insignificant as I entered the building, and my breakfast caught halfway down to my stomach. It amazes me even now that I had the nerve to put my battle plan into action. I had rehearsed all night what I was going to do and say.

I strode to the office of the venerable principal of the school, Mr. Stevens, and knocked on the door. As I was ushered in, I looked straight into his eyes, rattled off my name, and said that I needed his help. He had known my brother, who had graduated from Lowell and held high honors in the ROTC. With that to go on, Mr. Stevens said a few words of welcome and added that he expected good things from me. But nothing could have prepared him for my proposition, and it was to his credit that he allowed me to fully state my case, which I had worked out in detail. If I took all my subjects in the morning, I suggested, I could be out of school by 12:30 pm, eliminating gym, lunch, and study periods. As for gym, I would agree to bring a letter from my ballet school stating that I was getting my physical activity with them. I would eat on the bus while traveling to the ballet studio. And I swore that I would retain honor roll grades without needing a supervised study period. He listened with amazement as I explained that my whole life depended on the hours I gave to dance and that, since I was certain that this was what I wanted to do with my life, my school should aid me in every way that it could instead of holding me back. I also asked him to come to the opera house to see me dance. With that last bit of bravado, I closed my case. My conviction had indeed won him over, and he made a promise that I could finish my school years under the conditions I had described, being as I had made so definitive a decision as to my career.

Unfortunately, not all my teachers at Lowell took to this idea. Rehearsals and performances created absences; although I kept my grades up, I was away from school more and more. One teacher would greet me sarcastically, asking me if I was visiting the class that day. Another, my poetry teacher, looked sympathetically at my tired face and would dismiss me to the library on the pretense of my looking something up, whispering under her breath for me to close my eyes there and rest. She had a soft spot for me as she loved to attend dance and would look for me onstage at the opera, and also she admired the poetry of Siegfried Sassoon, a distant relative of mine.

In ballet school, my classmates and I were also now participating in not only in operas but also in the San Francisco Ballet itself: Christmas performances of *The Nutcracker* followed by a short season of other works. I remember dancing in a ballet called *Blue Plaza*. The music was by Aaron Copland. The costumes and scenery were designed by Antonio Sotomayor, a truly gifted artist; he was extremely kind to me, a true gentleman with Old World manners. Jose Manero, a member of the company, collaborated with Willam in creating authentic Mexican steps based upon Manero's knowledge of Mexican folk dancing. It was great fun to perform. Sally Bailey and I portrayed donkeys: At the end of the ballet, a tourist came upon an idyllic Mexican scene and asked the dancers and bystanders to pose for a photograph. In the last two seconds, as the tourist was to snap the picture, Sally and I ran in and struck a donkey pose. Flashbulb, blackout, curtain! Last but not least, we were there!

I loved Saturdays best. This was when we took regular dance class, pas de deux class, and also character dancing, the latter thanks to Willam's own interest in it. We were lucky to have started so young with character work; it is not easy to pick up later in one's career. Willam's instruction to us was developed from what he had learned from his own teachers, who had taught csárdás and mazurkas from classical repertory. He added to this other forms of folk dances.

I loved this class. We looked spiffy in our long skirts and character shoes, which had small heels on them (for a young girl, it was a thrill to be wearing shoes with heels!). Class began with a character barre. This was quite difficult as we remained in a bent-knee position while raising and lowering our heels and stamping our feet. Our calf muscles ached every Sunday morning. Jose Manero gave us classes based on authentic folk dancing from Mexico, and we were also taught by an incredible man, Guillermo del Oro, who though trained under Maestro Cecchetti gave us not a classical class but one in Spanish dancing. He had been a partner of the great flamenco dancer La Argentinita, Encarnación López Julvez.

Then came pas de deux class, in which we were taught to work in partnership with male dancers. Although we did not take class with the ballet company, our partners for pas de deux class were company members brought in to work with us. I always got chosen right away. One of the male leads was Peter Nelson, a wonderful dancer and an incredible partner; he was a good instructor, making sure that I was using the right muscles as we worked. Another good partner was Joaquin Felsch. What wonderful luck we had in the men who started us on our way!

We also prepared a dance demonstration to exhibit to invited family and friends the class's progress for the year while also giving us the chance to gain experience performing before an audience. Most of the program consisted of ensemble work by the class, with few solos; if I recall correctly, the company also danced something at the end to make the point of what we aspired to. We were all given white organdy tutus: a simple bodice, with a skirt of several layers of ruffles, all in very good taste. This was our first step in the magic of dancing in any kind of tutu, however modified.

This performance was held in the Marine's Memorial Theater, a perfect size for family and friends. Although we had participated in ballets and operas, we were petrified at the thought of doing this. To present a *class*, in all its in stark, exposed motion, in front of an audience made us very nervous; we feared even something so simple as a *grandplié*—a deep full bending of our knees—would prove a literal downfall! As I stood waiting to go on, I wondered what I was doing there. Willam checked us out, and before we knew it, the curtain opened.

There we were, twenty girls in tutus, our heads bowed, little white flowers on the side of each identical chignon. The audience applauded even before we took one step. Willam announced combinations for us to do, speaking loudly enough for the attendees to hear the names of the steps as well, and somehow we got through them.

Then came three different solos, one of which was mine. Willam had choreographed for me a wonderful dance to the music of Walton's *Façade*. It was a highly stylized piece, physically as well as musically. Willam nodded to me to come onstage, and I began to dance my heart out. A few minutes into it, I could hear laughter. *Oh, dear,* I thought. I must have done something wrong. Jumping off from the unanticipated mood I sensed from the audience, I used that energy to make the ballet slightly comical, as a deliberate act. And suddenly, I felt I had found the expression that went with the music and the steps, which I had never realized while not receiving audience feedback during my learning of it! It was a wonderful success, and a wonderful lesson.

Then it was over. I accepted my very first bouquet, of roses, and—stunned—took my bow. I could hear Willam saying to the audience, "This is her first bouquet, and I have a feeling she will get many more in her life." I hugged the flowers to me as I left the stage.

Those fleeting moments of exhilaration fueled my desire to a new height. It crystallized what I had felt from my very first experience of being onstage as a small child and has mattered since through my entire life: I already realized that I loved the *actual working toward* the perfection of whatever I attempted. But, on that first night of solo work in a small theater, I understood that the focus of my work and passion, my goal, was to deliver that acquired or attempted perfection to others. This was my calling, almost religious in feeling. I felt that if I were to dance with all my heart, God would help me give something to others. In dance, nothing is left behind—it flashes by in a moment, never to be recaptured again. The magic of a performer occurs in the moment when the motion is given and received. Even a video, as we have now, is just a record once the act is completed. My awareness of the importance of the live audience in the very nature of the art was truly a revelation.

Once that evening was over, we continued to work every day at the studio, as usual. We were proud that the performance had not only just shown off our individual efforts but also that of the school. Even though in today's world the studio would seem lacking in facilities and luxuries, it was such an exciting time for us to be there. We weren't working for money; we were working to fulfill a dream. Sometimes we even bought our own rhinestone earrings or whatever the school's budget could not afford. Imagine, if you can, this expanse of incredible people, some staff members working part-time at other jobs in order to live, coming together to rehearse at 8:00 pm sharp, building with their hearts and souls the single dream that the San Francisco Ballet would mature to become a permanent fixture of its city and the world.

Now our hard work began. We were told that we would have, as a guest teacher, Madame Julietta Mendez. Madame Mendez was a pupil of the great teacher Mascagno*, and she had been Willam's teacher. We were all very excited and took special care to pull our hair back tightly, that our pink silk stockings were spotless for our first class. And this was not just girlish expectation. When this extraordinary lady entered the studio, I had my first experience of that sublime aura that only accompanies a great teacher. There was an instant hush as she walked over to our pianist and spoke a few words to him. Her aura was such that she held our complete interest without even trying to make an impression. Dressed in black silk pants and top, she made quite an entrance. Her hair, jet-black, pulled back in a bun, rested neatly at the nape of her neck. Her black eyebrows were penciled in the spidery arch so reminiscent of the style of the thirties. Her feet were encased in black satin slippers. She looked almost Chinese. She held a very long cigarette holder; as we were to discover during class, she would not smoke but would use it as a baton or to gesture dramatically when she was not pleased with us. It seemed a part of her personality.

Her classes were structured with great intelligence, paying attention to the order in which the barre work was given. Only later in my dancing life did I become aware of how harmful it could be to a dancer's muscles to not observe a proper order throughout a lesson. So many teachers are guilty of choreographing their exercises rather than maintaining a strict order based upon a class's proficiency in working with an increasing vocabulary. Also, Madame Mendez demonstrated more with her upper body than with her legs, the mark of a good teacher. Students need to learn to express style and feeling at this stage of training. She was the first teacher to place so much attention in the involvement of one's entire body in the dance—something we think of as the Russian school of training. This training seemed so right for my body, and indeed, later I would eventually place myself in the hands of genuine Russian teachers. I loved her teaching method and did it well; she, in turn, gave me much of her attention and would kiss me at the end of my classes, telling my mother that I would go far. Madame Mendez was a vital influence at that time, giving me the much-needed encouragement to keep my heart set on a difficult career.

Willam, too, gave me new confidence when he selected me to be one of the blackamoor slaves in *Aida* in the upcoming opera season. This meant not only performing in San Francisco but also going on tour with the company! My dream was becoming a reality!

The terminal of Third and Townsend streets. We were to be there at 7:00 am in order to board our train and depart for Los Angeles, Portland,

and Seattle. Five younger girls were going, in addition to myself, so we had a chaperone who was to guard us at all times. Still, to this day, I will never understand how my father agreed to such an arrangement. But then, he didn't really have much of a chance to object; everyone else thought it was marvelous that I should have such an opportunity to work amid such illustrious talent. I could not believe that, all day and all night, I would be involved with dance and with people who were a part of it. I was bursting with sheer joy!

I had never been on a train before, let alone away from home. I wanted to appear grown-up and more worldly: I hated my braids and wished that I wasn't so inexperienced about travel. I watched everyone else to make sure that I was doing all the right things. We six little girls tried to grasp all this new behavior in which everyone engaged in. Although we already knew many of the people, it felt as if we had joined a strange band of gypsies.

We had our own train, the San Francisco Opera Special. What a different atmosphere from that of rehearsals! Even the most serious staging directors and musical conductors acted as if they were about to embark on a holiday cruise—everyone seemed to be preparing for a great party. This struck me as strange, and it was not until much later that I comprehended that while touring is hard work, it is also an escape from the everyday world. On tour, the company enters into its own bubble of work, travel, and being together as happily as possible. It was also interesting to see the entire company all together. The singers were all ages and sizes, and the musicians looked a bit like their instruments. The ballet dancers were the best looking, to my eye. We all looked like what we were. Everyone liked the dancers, especially Willam or Mr. C, and treated us with great respect. I think Mr. C loved touring most. He seemed like a schoolboy on holiday, fascinated by everything.

I don't remember how I eluded the chaperone, but I spent as much time as I could in the club car, drinking ginger ales and listening to Mr. C tell of the days when he had toured as a dancer in the Orpheum Circuit. Around me, some played cards, some drank, and there was constant eating; I overheard many languages, especially Italian. Everyone told stories, and I was completely enchanted and awake, soaking it in.

And so the days passed: arriving at our succession of theaters, making up, taking class, performing, eating, sleeping at a hotel, laughing, adults playing like children. I didn't know then that all tours would not be as easy and carefree. A particular point of which I was unaware was that this was an *opera* tour, not a *ballet* tour: on this tour, everyone was delighted to have half a dozen little girls along. (I had tons of homework to do, and gleefully

—

distributed some of it to singers and musicians; even Mr. Pinza took one assignment—which he failed! That teacher never knew she had flunked the great Ezio Pinza in American History!)

Our first stop had been the Shrine Auditorium in Los Angeles. It was to be a memorable performance, in many ways. To begin with, a circus had been there just before us, and we were greeted by the smells the animals had left behind!

We were assigned dressing rooms—there on the door, written in chalk, was "Sassoon," along with five other names. In my own, albeit shared, dressing room! Not just a large room used by all the anonymous extras! Now I was really part of the company! With stars in my eyes, I looked forward to looking like a glamorous dancer in the opera *Aida*.

I was just unpacking my case when a knock on the door summoned us all upstairs. We reported to the stage manager, who told us to report to Makeup. There was my Mephisto, Mr. Mason, with his jars and tubes. He handed the other girls and me sponges and a pot of greasepaint and told us to apply it to each other: not only on our faces but also on our limbs. Our dresser attired us in our costumes: a tiny bralike top and small bikini-like pants trimmed in gold.

We were a sight, but we certainly did look like the theatrical stereotype of that time, little black slaves, with our dark greasepaint and curly black wigs. Onstage, we started our dance and in one point were to dance in twos, as we had rehearsed. At that moment, however, we were now unrecognizable to each other! Nobody knew who anyone else was, to pair up with the correct partner: there was bedlam for sixteen measures! Luckily for us, the dance built up to sufficient frenzy that we somehow got through it, ending with our familiar practiced movement of falling to our knees and lowering our faces to the floor, as if salaaming to each other. Then we spent the next five minutes sitting back up on our knees while the opera continued. To my horror, during the salaam, my wig had slipped, and of course once upright again, I was supposed to remain motionless—a black slave with a white forehead. Everyone on stage around me was trying very hard not to laugh but seemed on the verge of absolute hysteria. For the first time in my then-brief career, I couldn't wait to leave the stage, thankful that I couldn't be identified. This was the fastest exit I'd ever made!

Our troubles were not yet over. We then discovered that the Shrine Auditorium did not have adequate facilities for showering. It was impossible to remove the body makeup with cream alone, and so we decided to conceal ourselves in our makeup robes and return to the hotel as we were. The clerk at the Figueroa Hotel gave us a bewildered look as he handed us our keys.

While in Los Angeles, we enjoyed one free day. Of course, we wished to see and do everything! Two of the first violinists received permission from my chaperone for my friend Sally Bailey and me to join them on an outing for ice cream. Even the drive to the ice cream parlor was an adventure: As we drove down Wilshire Boulevard, I glimpsed one restaurant that looked like a hat—the famous Brown Derby Restaurant, a favorite of the stars. Then, farther along, was another restaurant that looked like a Dutch windmill. It was so vastly different there than in San Francisco that I felt as if I were indeed in a foreign country!

Our destination was a drive-in ice cream parlor that had advertised the largest rainbow sundae in the world. Furthermore, they claimed that anyone who could finish one would get a free hot dog and another sundae!

This restaurant had a sign that was a giant neon sundae, beckoning us to the challenge. I was only eleven, and Sally was two years younger than myself; we had both had little experience with self-moderation. We insisted on ordering the famous sundae.

Well! The sundaes were brought to us, and looked exactly as named. My eyes grew large as I tried to count all the syrups and the different flavors of ice cream that comprised the "rainbow." The waitress who placed mine in front of me shook her head as she walked away—I was rather small for my age; Sally was taller than me but thin as a toothpick! We attacked our sundaes with great bravado and gusto. This was, after all, a forbidden item on a dancer's diet.

The start was quite delicious, and I consumed the chocolate, vanilla, and strawberry ice cream. I glanced at Sally, who was already on the peach and blackberry, followed by marshmallow sauce and the pineapple sorbet with pineapple sauce. She was almost winning the race! I think, had I not looked at her, I could have gotten the fruit down, but I hit the obstacle of discovering there were actual slices of peaches to conquer before reaching the ice cream beneath it. Scarcely chewing, I bravely let the fruit slide down my throat without tasting it and immediately regretted it. That was the end of the line for me. My stomach felt terrible, and the thought of never eating "forbidden fruit" again became established in my mind. I was further tortured, though, by the sight of Sally finishing her ice cream and devouring her free hot dog! As a further insult to my pride, I was forced to excuse myself and run to the ladies' room where, thank goodness, I lost most of my rainbow. To this day, whenever I see a rainbow, I remember almost eating one!

—

One other escapade, which was a touring-season tradition, was a party held at the Figueroa Hotel after the last performance. The hotel provided a wonderful buffet, and it was held in their ballroom. Everyone was obliged to go: the stars, chorus, stage directors, orchestra, conductors, dressers, carpenters, makeup and costume people, and the dancers. Unbeknownst to all of them, from the first day of rehearsals, two dancers had been in charge of taking note of any unusual incidents, interesting remarks, or mistakes in English (in which the latter were constant due to our vast number of Italian, German, or other foreign staff). The entire ballet would then appear on the night of the banquet in the "Opera Folly," as we called it, putting all those notes to good use. We made fun of everyone, including the stars—all were fair game, from Ezio Pinza's pinching the ballet girls' bottoms (which occurred if one got too near him), to the long train of Lily Pons's costume having become stuck on a piece of scenery just as she was trying to sing her glorious aria in *Lakmé*. Naturally, we exaggerated beyond belief any directors' remarks, choristers' mistakes, or anything else pertaining to the season. For the dancers, this offered the perfect opportunity to act outrageously, using up all that excess energy that we had built up during the run. Everyone laughed, nobody was offended. It was pure theater fun. I often wonder if our sheltered lives and intense concentration upon our physical career gave us ballet dancers a particular need—and ability—to blow off steam by playing pranks. On that trip, this ability was only just awakening in me, and I joined in with the company's recreations of the mistakes and mishaps that had occurred during rehearsals. The future was to prove me a natural comedienne and horrific prankster while on tours!

We left Los Angeles and headed north to Portland. Oddly enough, though I kept a diary, I wrote nothing in my journal about this trip. I only remember looking out of the train window, watching the most beautiful landscape pass by. Because of my work, I did not ordinarily have time to be with nature on a leisurely basis. Consequently, I truly valued and needed the sight of trees or the ocean. It always gave me a sense of peace as well as a certain strength to survive the intensity of my existence. I had no one to share my thoughts with, and in spite of great comradeship, I felt very alone.

2

The Best Is Yet to Come

There was no question, my desire to dance was a total passion that could not be deterred. My father, whom I adored, never encouraged me. On the contrary, he fought me every step of the way. Had it not been for my mother who pacified him, I would never have gone as far as I did.

His reasons were sound but fell on deaf ears. In spite of the fact that Willam would always bring me home after rehearsal, Father did not approve of my late hours or of my total dedication to dance, which was all too apparent. As he saw it, he had offered me life on a silver platter, and I was not accepting it. He desired that I would go on to a college education and a social life with people my own age; his dearest wish was that I would then marry and give him many grandchildren. In spite of his British upbringing, in his mind and in his heart, he still had a Middle Eastern outlook (ours was a Sephardic Jewish family) regarding women and the stage.

This is not to suggest that he was a narrow-minded man. He was curious about everything; there was nothing he would not have attempted. His interest in people kept him broad-minded; he mixed easily with bankers, diamond merchants, and people in show business, loving it all. This broad-mindedness, however, excluded a theatrical life where his daughter was concerned.

As rehearsals and the opera season continued, I was certainly not living the life of the average twelve-year-old schoolgirl, and I knew my father would not endure this situation. Everyone can vividly recall the watershed incidents in one's life as if they happened yesterday. The

—

31

following, above all else, is what *I* remember as it was to determine the course of my whole life:

One night I returned home shortly after 1:00 am after a performance at the opera house. I put my key in the lock of the front door, slowly entering so as not to make a noise. There stood my father, who had stayed up awaiting my arrival. I knew I had to meet his challenging eyes. He announced that no daughter of his was to live like this. He continued, and all I knew was that something beyond myself caused me to understand that what happened in this next moment would decide my fate. When I found my voice, it was strong, and had my heart and soul in it. I looked back at him, my gaze unwavering, and I told him that I could not live without dancing. If he were to forbid me, I would find a way to do what I must without his help or money, even if it meant scrubbing toilets. There was a dead silence as the two of us faced each other. I don't know what I expected, but I did know that I had to make my stand then or forever hold my tongue. He walked away from me without a word.

To this day, my awareness of that defiance remains one of the most difficult moments in my life. I had been raised with great love and respect for my parents, and I adored them greatly. My father had probably protected me too much, but he had given me love, comfort, and luxury. Never had I spoken to him like that before.

The next morning, everything seemed normal. At breakfast, I kissed him good morning, as was our custom. Not a word was mentioned of our previous night's confrontation. We had an unspoken moratorium. I knew he was a smart man who possessed incredible determination, and now I had shown that some of that was in me too. He loved me enough to understand that I needed to do this, no matter what the consequences. He may also have gained a new measure of respect for my having fought so fiercely for what I believed.

I had an older brother and an older sister. My sister, Celia, and I were at extreme opposites in our tastes. The middle child, she was extremely outgoing and pretty and made friends easily. She possessed a very big heart, especially toward animals. When we were young and went on family outings to the country, Celia often disappeared. We just needed to inquire whether a horse or farm was nearby, and there she would be found—having made friends not only with the barnyard creatures but also with their owners, who had been immediately taken with her. They would inevitably invite her to come back to visit them and the animals anytime.

As time passed and our interests diverged, I was becoming an oddity not only to my siblings but also to my schoolmates. I was "different," a burden that is not easy to carry when one is young. As I advanced in my world of dance, I began to withdraw into it, becoming somewhat secretive and private about it with my brother and sister, and also at school. It seemed to be the only way I could protect myself. In retrospect, I can see I did not receive emotional support, with regards to dancing, from anyone in my family except from my mother—and yet, at the time, I was not completely aware of this as I had had enough support and encouragement from within my own ballet world. I think, too, my having had a very close and happy family life as a young child gave me a great deal of stability, which was to help me later on in my career. At this point, I was still able to participate in most family events and holidays.

Before the bombing of Pearl Harbor, my father already feared a war with Japan. His response was to purchase an almond and apricot orchard in Los Altos, south of San Francisco—to build a house far away enough from the city that we could move there if war actually came to our mainland as well as have a summer house. He indeed built the house, which had two bedrooms and bathrooms, a living room, a large kitchen, and a dining area. French doors from the dining area opened onto a large sleeping porch, which was very popular during that era. This room was glassed-in during winter, but its screened sliding windows could be completely opened in the summer, allowing us to fall asleep gazing at the stars and moon while we were cooled by the evening breezes. During the day, the several beds on this porch served as comfortable couches, and this was where we gathered to have most of our fun.

As time passed, my father cut away the hill rising behind the house and created a wonderful cascade of plants flowing along a stairway that linked a trilevel garden. The main level of the house was filled with flowers of every variety. I remember the smell of jasmine, and we enjoyed the fruit from the garden's pear and peach trees. Around the path were rose trees and oleander bushes. We were warned never to eat the oleander leaves or to even put them to our mouths as they were poisonous.

On the second level, my father built a large structure on top of our garage, for my brother. It had a hideaway bed, a bathroom, and a small kitchen. This is where Meyer could entertain his friends and play his records to his heart's content. Since it was high up, the view was breathtaking, and one could see all the way to the huge zeppelin hangars at Moffitt Field. This level was named the Rose Garden as it featured roses planted in formal arrangements.

The next level up was the vegetable garden, which served us well all summer. We harvested string beans, tomatoes, cucumbers, and most other summer delights. This garden produced a great deal, and we gave much of it away to our neighbors.

Last of all, Father couldn't resist building a gazebolike structure in the garden nearest to the main house. It had a built-in barbecue and rotisserie and a small kitchen.

A gravel driveway lined with cypress trees and rose bushes stretched from the bottom of the entrance road all the way up to the garage, with an additional large gravel pathway that led to the front door of our house. On both sides of this formidable driveway was the apricot orchard, lined all along its perimeter with almond trees. In the spring, the combination of white and pink blossoms was stunning.

On the very edge of the property, facing the road, was an archway that had probably been the original entrance to the orchard. It had a lovely old railing where we would sometimes sit as we waited for my father's return from the city as he had to commute during the summer.

My family was to nickname the house the Sassoon Winchester Mansion, after the strange house in San Jose that had been built by an eccentric family who continually added rooms to their home. They had nothing on us! Working on our house and its surrounding property truly became my father's greatest pleasure. He created, out of a simple orchard, a small paradise. He loved the land. Often, he rode the tractor around the grounds out of the sheer pleasure for machinery and soil.

My mother coped remarkably when my father would say, "I've invited a few people for Sunday dinner." He thought nothing of asking twenty people to drop by. We did not have permanent help as they weren't easy to find, but luckily we did have assistance when we really needed it. Having company over meant preparing huge platters of salads, fruit, rice, and every imaginable garden vegetable, and we had divine pies all from the produce of our own fruit trees (we also sold our apricots, so this was still a "working" orchard). The "chef," my father, was always the one to put the chicken on the barbecue after my mother had done all the marinating.

Los Altos was then very small and quiet. The entire town proper was only one block long, and had a great drugstore with a real soda fountain. My father bought the property next to it, enlarging the town to two blocks by adding a medical building and two other buildings for offices and stores.

The town had a wonderful train station. Often we would go to San Francisco by train. It would stop twice and then end up at the Southern Pacific's Third and Townsend street station. But soon the time came that my visits to our orchard home had to end due to my increasing commitments to dance. After the summer, I found myself back in San Francisco with little extra time except for the daily routine of school and ballet. I had no social life at all as evenings were spent rehearsing and performing with the opera, which was solidly in season from September through December.

3

The Nutcracker and Classes

Once the opera season was over, we went back faithfully to training for the ballet. Willam was going to choreograph a full-length *The Nutcracker* ballet. There was a great deal of anticipation in the air. Everyone at the school knew that we would each be part of it regardless of how small each role might be. The ballet school waiting room quite suddenly seemed to contain a virtual avalanche of "mamas." Their theory seemed to be that if Mr. Christensen saw them there every day, it would influence his casting choices. (The role of the Sugar Plum Fairy was to be danced by our teacher, Gisella Caccialanza, the wife of Lew Christensen, who was then away in the army.)

Finally, the day arrived when the cast list was posted on the board that contained announcements about rehearsals, schedules, and parts. Along with my immediate dance classmates, I was to be one of the Sugar Plum Fairy's pages. But, farther down, in larger letters, my name appeared again, alongside that of Alton Basuino, one of the boys in the older class. It stated that I was to dance the role of the female Russian Doll. That was quite a big fish to have caught! The two Russian Dolls appear in the first act as a gift beneath the Christmas tree. They are wheeled out in front of Clara and her friends, to much oohing and aahing and to the delight of the audience as well. I was aware that Alton and I would dance a charming pas de deux in which it would be difficult to retain the doll-like rigidity of our bodies and a lack of facial expressions. This was to be a wonderful lesson for playing some future Coppelia!

Underneath the school, there was a large space that was used to store costumes and scenery. This was where Russell Hartley (you will recall he was my spider friend at my debut!) spent a great deal of his time as in addition to being a dancer who would appear in this production as Mother Buffoon, he was also responsible for painting the scenery, sewing the costumes, and building the props. Since the company was severely lacking in funds, he did not have a permanent assistant. At the time Earl Riggins, whom I have mentioned as helping Willam in business matters, was spirited away from his official duties at every chance to assist Russell. Also, every dancer who was not busy with classes and rehearsals would go downstairs for a fitting or just to offer help. And with minimal instruction Russell allowed us to color in the scenery—he might hand one of us a brush and say, "Paint here, just stay inside this line."

Once in a while, he would take me along when he went to J. C. Penney's on Market Street, where we would rummage in the fabric remnant bin. Great treasures were to be found there for fifty cents and up. Russell would always find something and hold it up in triumph. In truth, at first I would only see a rumpled piece of cloth until Russell's voice proclaimed, holding a piece of red velvet with some embossed design, "That's it! The Cossacks' hats!" Our safaris to Penney's, flea markets, and antique stores were to give me a terrific education; to this day, such treasure hunting remains one of my greatest passions. But it will never be as exciting as it was in that quest to create a full-length version of Tchaikovsky's *The Nutcracker*. Those moments were themselves golden nuggets that I collected without even realizing it.

I was learning my craft from the bottom up, and I do mean the bottom. Gisella, who was teaching our class, was, for me, a vision of perfection. She had lovely legs, beautifully proportioned with the rest of her body. Thin, not gaunt. Large eyes that lit up. Most importantly, this was my first opportunity to see someone who had a completely different training from ours, of the upper body. Only later, after my own training in the Cecchetti method, did I understand that nothing occurs by chance. Maestro Cecchetti had himself trained Gisella in that which in her lessons he handed down to us. In spite of her work in George Balanchine's company, Ballet Caravan, her classes were completely different from any others we had had so far.

Since most of our training had been based on the ideas of the Balanchine School, we had until now concentrated on the lower body and on technical achievement, unless we were being taught by Willam, who wanted us to dance with our hearts as well. However, we did not use our upper body and arms until we took class with Gisella. From the beginning, in the Cecchetti School, this is taught from the very start so that it becomes second nature to dance with the entire body. Gisella started us at the barre, using all the *port de bras* (literally "carriage of the arms"—arm positions) appropriate to our leg positions. When we finished doing all our exercises on one side, we would end by closing our feet in a perfect fifth position (in which the feet are tucked closely parallel, pointing in opposite directions), raising on our demi-pointes (the balls of our feet), and—in perfect tempo with our music—turn to restart the exercises on the other side. In other words, with Gisella, we never broke from the continuity of the music to change sides. It was a step up to being more professionally trained. The whole class was thus conducted in a strict ballet format, which enabled us to build our concentration while also extending our physical strength and endurance. At the beginning, this new style of training was not easy. But Gisella's classes were invaluable as we were still young enough to allow her to instill the Cecchetti fundamentals that we had been lacking.

We also now had exercises that we knew would be repeated on certain days (this does not mean that the entire class was duplicated). Thursday was the dreaded day of challenge and shame for us all. An exercise that has stayed with me to the end of my performing career, and that is known by every professional dancer with a certain amount of training, appeared regularly on Thursday. This was the *quatre pirouette,* meaning four turns, done in one of the four ballet positions, starting from the fifth position of the feet. The principle of this exercise is to gain control over your body before you even *get* to the placement of the first turn. Then we were to execute this exercise successively doing only one turn in each position. Over the next two or three years, we were to build toward doing four revolutions in each position and eventually on full point. Two turns done well was considered very good. Interestingly enough, I have become known for giving this exercise frequently in the classes I have taught; it is always greeted with a groan. As a student, I had found it a challenge and hoped that as I handed it down to others, it would inspire dancers to do more, to not be afraid to try what they might not accomplish easily.

Gisella was a sympathetic teacher but also had a positive nature that stated, without a doubt, we could do whatever we set out to do, and she truly sought unregimented solutions that would work for us as individuals. At that level of our schooling, we were already learning pointe work, and our class would always conclude with exercises performed on pointe. Again, Gisella was very helpful in putting me into a very sound regime that worked well for me. I had strong feet and, at the beginning, felt the American toe shoe was too unnatural and too hard on my feet. Gisella suggested an Italian shoe that I could obtain from London: Porselli's. That was to be a wise choice. They were flexible, and so I could take all of my classes in them, mounting on pointe where and when it felt natural to do so.

During the ballet season, rehearsals and classes were combined in each day of our work. There was also considerable activity in the dungeon below. If someone had a rest period, he or she would go down, to be handed a paintbrush or a needle and thread. People ran to and fro, everyone helped.

My love affair with dance increased with the constant proximity of those I so admired: beloved friends included the lovely Jocelyn Vollmar, who was to dance the Snow Queen with Joaquin Felsch as her Snow Prince; Celina Cummings, Joaquin's wife, who would have the lead in *Waltz of the Flowers*; this incredible creature named Onna White, who was to perform the Arabian Dance. Christensen had a way of attracting others like himself, with prodigious talent. Others I looked up to included Lois Treadwell, Rosalie Prosch, Sally Whalen, and Peter Nelson. He sometimes chose me as his partner for pas de deux class, which consequently gave me much confidence for dancing a pas de deux. Overall, the company dancers were truly generous to the younger members of the cast. This became the glue that held our impossible dreams together.

The production was a team effort in every way imaginable. Even the adult dancers availed their spare moments to help in any capacity in which they could. I even saw some of the older girls stuffing tickets into envelopes. And Earl Riggins, Willam's right-hand man, threw us flyers and said, "Go out and take them everywhere!" With all this monumental effort, *The Nutcracker* indeed reached the stage on December 24, 1944, at the War Memorial Opera House (its first full-length performance in America).

Opening night. All of us were excited as we entered the theater, checking to make sure that our costumes, shoes, and props were ready. We did not have the luxury of dressers or wardrobe staff, except for those fellow company members who had volunteered to help.

I remember so clearly the wonderful magic of the first act, when all the bargains from J. C. Penney's looked like a million dollars. Every lady of the company who was portraying a lady looked like a born aristocrat. It suddenly struck me how elegant our staging was.

I was made up to have red cheeks and enormous eyes, and my Russian Doll costume was red velvet with white fur at the collar and cuffs. My partner was made up and costumed in the same scheme; together, we looked as if we were right out of Stravinsky's *Petrouschka*.

At last, our moment came. We were pushed out from beneath the tree and presented to the children at the Christmas party. All the sighs! As if admiring real dolls, the children tried to touch us. It was quite difficult to hold still. Then our pas de deux music started, and we danced our parts with great conviction. As we finished, both the real audience and the children onstage applauded. We could hear children in the auditorium asking, "Are they real?" I felt very pleased as this meant that we had been convincing.

We then changed costumes, and I became a Snowflake. If I were asked to choose the one early performing experience that made me fall totally in love with this profession, it would have to be that scene—its score and its atmosphere. Music is what motivates one to dance, and that music is sublime. The entrance of the Snowflakes was truly magical. We had little hoops that were lit up with sparkling lights. As we entered into that famous blue light that I so loved, all the audience could see at first were lights moving and flickering. Slowly the stage lights came up, and there were twenty-four sparkling flakes and the Snow Queen with her cavalier. Then the music began.

No sooner were we finished being Snowflakes than we had to leave the land of snow behind and change for our next entrances, as Pages. We were not glamorous here—we looked as though we had come from the ballet *Schéhérazade*. We had yellow and red turbans and puffy pants. However, this role allowed me to stay by Gisella's side the whole time she was to dance. I remember to this day, standing next to her backstage as she was warming her feet and letting out her nervousness (later, I was to understand, myself, this kind of nervousness). She held my hand, and I think that I would have done anything for her. I would hold her shawl for her, in readiness, to keep her from getting cold. My love for her was really special, even once I became an adult.

We performed *The Nutcracker* for several weeks and became quite seasoned performers. This was our real beginning as San Francisco Ballet. I remember Russell telling me that the whole production was done on $500. The full-length *Nutcracker* was to become a San Francisco tradition and was always so well received that it helped the company survive through those years. As I look back, I think how lucky I was to have been just a little piece of that extraordinary original production.

After *The Nutcracker*, we continued to work very hard. Classes became even more strenuous. Gisella went back to New York; my memory is not clear whether Lew was back with us or had returned to the New York City Ballet. Now we had Ruby Asquith, Harold Christensen's wife, who was also a ballerina in our company; she taught our pointe classes. She was a wonderful inspiration to me as an actress. Her *Coppelia* was delicious; she changed her face and style of moving according to each variation she was dancing, which was very difficult for a ballerina to do as each variation changed so much in character. I have always thought that *Coppelia* takes a backseat, so to speak, to what people regard as the truly great classical ballets. But in reality, the title role is an enormous challenge to any ballerina, not just for her acting but also for her ability to conquer the steps of the various variations and to have the stamina to perform those variations one after the other.

At this time, I was working very hard myself. Often, Willam would have me learn whatever he was choreographing. My technique became very strong. I had a very easy and high jump. My feet were my main attraction; they moved quickly and sharply, as if I were dancing on hot coals. Turns were not in themselves difficult for me, but I was not a natural turner. I turned slowly. (I was able to hold the end of a pirouette before descending. Pirouettes are taught this way in the Russian School to gain control; it is very difficult. Nureyev and Baryshnikov used this technique, and it is now seen more often, especially as done by male dancers.)

I loved allegro and adagio—each held a different challenge: my body was learning to do the fast beats and longer combinations of allegro, while at the same time I had to obtain the control to do a long adagio without faltering. This process was reversed continually every day, until my body began to form into a finely tuned instrument that could anticipate what I was trying to do and correctly respond.

Willam constantly remarked that I seemed naturally at home in the classical style, but I was still too young to understand his meaning. Later, when a critic wrote that someone should revive a Maria Taglioni or Fanny Essler ballet for me, it became apparent that whatever God gave me was a bonus! I had a classical instinct and style, which was natural for my body.

4

San Francisco Civic Ballet

We continued daily classes with Willam and were pushed much faster to attain a classical technique. Classes were difficult but always exciting. Allegro (quick, lively) work was studied and made even more difficult with the addition of beats (legs beating together or crossing) to as many jumps as could be added. To me, beats were a very individual skill, and only some of us were able to master them. I loved these movements the best and excelled at them. At that age, I was much more of an allegro dancer and jumper than I was a lyrical dancer.

Meanwhile, there were rumors in the air that we were to do two seasons under the auspices of the city, which was funded by them plus private donations. The enterprise was to be called the San Francisco Civic Ballet and would feature guest ballerinas and *danseurs nobles* as well as guest choreographers and conductors other than our own beloved Fritz Behrens. We were also to have a manager and dance expert from England, a man who was very well known at the time for his reviews and knowledge of ballet. This was Irving Deakin, who arrived accompanied by his wife, Natasha.

The formidable Adolph Bolm, a veteran performer of both the imperial Maryinsky and Diaghilev companies, arrived to join the new company. It was a great honor for us as he had been the first director of the San Francisco Ballet. He was no longer a young man—already sixty-three—but possessed a style I had never seen nor danced before. He would be choreographing a piece for us, and again we crowded to the call-board. My name was down for the first rehearsal.

Duly respectful, I was a bit shy and nervous about working with Mr. Bolm. He had watched class and thus personally chosen his dancers. I felt honored to have been picked as I was then still in the junior ballet class. But my delight turned to agony as I learned my first steps. They were very harsh movements, awkward to my body, and *demi-caractère* in style. I had to jump in the air with my legs bent and my feet flexed. This was brutal. I went home to my mother and cried, thinking that I was not doing well and that I was ill-suited to these strange demands. Years later, I could see the influence of Nijinska's *Les Noces* in Mr. Bolm's choreography and only then appreciated what this early exposure had added to my experience.

Mr. Bolm required expression in these strong movements, believing that there was no such thing as truly abstract—in the sense of meaningless—dance. I found my expression through the music and strove to perform even these peculiar steps with all my heart.

As a choreographer, Mr. Bolm had a great facility in demonstrating clearly what he desired of his dancers: both the character steps and also the more classical movements that appeared later in his ballet. He was anything but old and possessed an energy that seemed endless, preferring to work in long stretches nonstop instead of taking (or allowing) pauses. Watching him, one could imagine how he had been in his Ballet Russe days, and with what power he must have danced in *Prince Igor*. Such glimpses of this strength were our great treasures: he was a piece of living history, right out of the pages of the ballet books I had read so ferociously. His very presence began a chain to which I would add links as I made my way through the world of dance.

The company was rehearsing its first two programs. The British-born Anton Dolin and Alicia Markova were to be guest artists along with members of their own company, which they called the Markova-Dolin Ballet (this predated by two years another troupe that they were to form, the Festival Ballet, to become the London Festival Ballet). We were to dance *Giselle* with Markova and Dolin. Jocelyn Vollmar (who was to dance Myrtha) and Willam had gone down to Mexico City where Markova and Dolin, then on tour with their company, were performing the second act so that they could study the choreography before the troupe came up to San Francisco. Meanwhile, we rehearsed the ballet with another bearer of the Diaghilev flame, Marie Rambert, who came to San Francisco expressly to show us the traditional act 2 choreography for the corps de ballet.

She was truly a character, and I thought her unique. Willam and I had coffee with her, and as we were strolling down Van Ness Avenue (one of San Francisco's largest streets), she suddenly did a cartwheel. We were delighted. She then gave a "Humph" and continued walking and chatting as if nothing unusual had happened. For me, it was a great giggle as not only was she in her seventies then, but it was so . . . un-English of her. I think that was more unusual than her age!

Giselle was the first full-length classical ballet, aside from *The Nutcracker*, that I had ever danced. I was mesmerized by the rehearsals and, in my mind's eye, learned all of Giselle's variations, even without the presence of the principals at rehearsal. Of course I couldn't resist attempting to dance the leading role, in secret, when I was by myself.

Our first rehearsal with Markova was a disaster. It appeared that we could do nothing as she wished. Either we were standing too close to her or there were problems when she and the corps danced together. We had to stop continually so she could address comments to Dolin, whom she addressed as Pat. She never voiced her remarks directly to us but told Pat to have the girls keep their distance, and so on. Since we all spoke English—indeed, despite her stage name, Markova *was* English—I thought this very affected. It registered in my memory, and in later years, I often thought how uncomfortable it must have been for the entire company to have to work in such a manner.

As a dancer, Markova conveyed a very ethereal image when she moved, which was quite effective from the audience's point of view. Yet I was to find her first act less moving, less emotionally touching, once I began to see other ballerinas in the role. It was the second act in which she really excelled, creating an unearthly aura that affected us all as we watched her.

As we almost never left the stage during act 1, I learned so much by observation. I dreamed of dancing its Mad Scene myself one day. When I was at home, using a hanger as a stand-in for the sword, I would rehearse all that I had seen Markova do. One afternoon, my mother walked into the living room just as I was about to plunge the hanger into my heart, my hair loose and my feelings focused upon dying tragically. Mother abruptly stopped the performance, calmly announcing dinner. She was not shocked by any of this, but my brother and sister of course started to tease me, with feigned dramatic outbursts of their own.

While we rehearsed act 2, Russell Hartley, who was designing and fitting our costumes as Wilis (the ghostly spirits of maidens who had died of unrequited love), used me as his model—another thrill. We met between rehearsals and rest periods. The first Wilis tutu Russell put on me possessed an airy long white skirt made of tulle. There were also droopy tulle sleevelets kept on by elastic on the upper arm to add a softness to the arms. Russell was frantic to complete the many identical costumes and was always running to Penney's for tulle or other necessary elements.

We worked out the correct hairdo for the ballet: a classical bun with the hair at the sides draped across our ears. This is an unflattering coiffeur for some faces, but for me it remains the epitome of how one should look in this ballet.

As the production took shape, we began to look more and more like a genuine corps de ballet. I was to be the first Wili of the corps to step onstage, a great responsibility as I was to set the style for all those entering, one by one, behind me. What a difficult feat for twenty-four girls to assume an identical style not only with regard to overall posture, head, eyes, arms, and legs but also with line and emotion!

Markova and Dolin had brought some wonderful dancers along with them: Royes Fernandez, an up-and-coming young dancer who was to indeed go on to become a *danseur noble* with American Ballet Theater; and Bettina Rosay, a very slight, petite dancer with great charm, who was partnered by Oleg Tupine in the Black Swan pas de deux (I learned her choreography for this, of course, for later!). It was very exciting to have such dancers in the company.

Our conductor for most of that season's programming was Robert Zeller, from neither the Markova-Dolin troupe nor San Francisco but New York City, where, though young, he had already achieved a great reputation as a ballet conductor. I had a great admiration for him. I adored most of the conductors I was to work with, and many returned the sentiment, becoming very attached to me during my career.

The Civic Ballet was also going to perform a piece called *Parranda*, choreographed by Willam to a score by Morton Gould, who was to conduct his own work for us. I was chosen to dance as one of the Mulattos. The sets and costumes were designed by Antonio Sotomayor, an elegant, charming gentleman who was very kind to me and loved the fiery temperament I displayed in this ballet.

The dress rehearsal date finally arrived for this very disparate pair of programs. The first program was largely given over to Dolin and Markova's company, except for Adolf Bolm's *Mephisto Waltz* (in which I had to wear a heavy, rather hideous costume that made me feel like a milkmaid—anything but glamorous). The dress rehearsal for the Bolm ballet went very well. Then came *Giselle,* and next we proceeded to *Parranda.*

We had had only one general rehearsal with orchestra for this. Now, Mr. Gould himself took the podium to conduct his own score. All proceeded as we'd rehearsed previously, when suddenly, during the finale, where the entire company formed a giant conga line, we were taken by surprise. Mr. Gould, with a surge of energy, had decided to double the tempo and raise the volume. We—and the musicians, who hadn't been prepared for this either—struggled to keep up with him.

We were left breathless by the end but were bursting with the sheer joy of dancing. The dancers all came forward to applaud Mr. Gould, and the musicians tapped their bows and other instruments on their music stands. The composer modestly accepted our enthusiasm for his success in having pushed us to our fullest capabilities. The conga had been so contagiously exciting that if our own feelings about it were any way to pregauge an audience's reaction, we were in for an exciting finale during the actual performance. The only question was, could we do it again?

As we had no time for additional rehearsals, every dancer in the company had to meet that challenge by mentally retaining the quick pace, rehearsing ourselves with our brain. It would not do to cheat on steps—they had to be articulate, even though tripled in speed from how we had originally learned them. When we came to perform this, everyone was so seriously concentrated within their inner minds and on their bodies, determined to make a success of it, that the joyousness of the music and movement almost made us laugh as the finale began. The exhilaration of moving at such high speed in a trained, technical manner was freeing, and our enjoyment indeed overflowed to the audience. In such a moment, there is a very special tingle throughout the entire house; audiences over the world, once they have tasted it, long for such moments, when everyone unites in spirit to become totally one—not with the performers, but with the performance. We, as artists, try to achieve that state nightly, to be taken outside ourselves to a level that makes us one with our audience. Only sometimes, as with *Parranda*, does everything come together with such a level of sheer exuberance.

On November 11 and 12, 1947, the San Francisco Civic Ballet tried its new wings. The first night belonged to Markova and Dolin's visiting company, with the exception of Adolph Bolm's *Mephisto Waltz*. The program included *The Lady of the Camellias*, which was well received by the audience but which to me seemed a slight ballet, lacking a full corps, and generally not really fulfilling what choreographic potential I sensed would do its story justice. The Black Swan pas de deux was first rate, and Bettina Rosay and Oleg Tupine deserved their ovation.

Next came the *Mephisto Waltz*, whose harsh choreography was explained in the audience program as being in a "stylized, symbolic manner inspired by the paintings of Hieronimus Bosch, Albrecht Dürer, and Brueghel in their great works depicting the Dance." Although I did not understand the importance of this work, the audience loved it, and it served to showcase the San Francisco Ballet element in this new

—

company—what physical strength it had for such dynamic choreography and what caliber of training had been achieved by a largely American, not European, troupe. What an important event this evening was for the San Francisco Ballet, even though the program had been dominated by works for the Markova-Dolin company.

The second night, the program opened with *Fantasia*, choreographed by Nijinska to music by Schubert and Liszt. This was danced by the Markova-Dolin Ballet. But then, the evening was given over nearly entirely to the San Francisco Ballet in its first-ever production of *Giselle*. Although Markova and Dolin danced the leads, our company dancers were in the other main roles, and of course the ballet utilized our corps. In act 1, there was such good projection in every character role, with strong expression by everyone. We could thank Willam's coaching and belief in us for this.

In act 2, Myrtha, queen of the Wilis, proved the perfect role for Jocelyn Vollmar, again demonstrating what first-rate dancers the company possessed. As for the corps, we simply *had* to shine. We had to be perfect because we were dancing a ballet that was well known to theatergoers as well as to balletomanes. We couldn't relax for a second. There was one moment especially, once we had filed on and filled the stage, when all twenty-four girls had to stand absolutely still in arabesque. This was our true test. Not one leg could falter. All extended limbs needed to remain at the same height; all heads and eyes had to stay fixed. No one dared to breathe, and I am sure I was not alone in praying that my leg would not shake, not the least reason being that even the slightest quiver would prove notoriously contagious! The position is very difficult to hold even when alone, and needing to do it as part of a larger picture was an excellent lesson in forcing me to conquer any show of nerves onstage. It was the proverbial trial by fire, but what training for the future! I didn't realize it at the time, but these performances planted in us magical seeds of experience that would begin our artistic growth.

When the curtain lowered on act 2, it was clear that we had made a success. Excitement filled the air as the audience returned to their seats for *Parranda*, which would close the evening's program on an exuberantly upbeat note. Mr. Gould increased the tempo in the finale as he had in rehearsal. We were all so relieved that *Giselle* had gone so well that we all "let ourselves go" in the rapid conga, dancing with a genuine joy that manifested itself directly to the audience, who returned that heady feeling in full force when the curtain lowered. As it was a premiere, in these curtain calls, everyone in the company came onstage: director, choreographer, conductor, designer. What the audience didn't see in

—

such situations is the happiness of the dancers—really, a flood of every imaginable emotion—as they wait for their creative team to come onstage with them and say to them what they will. I love these moments after a premiere. One's nerves are so alive as one listens for any word that might give you a clue as to how to improve something for the next performance, trying to remember all that is said in spite of all the commotion. Hugs and kisses, well earned, will be forgotten the next morning when, at ten o'clock, class starts again. But the right word, spoken at the just right time just after the curtain closes, might touch you forever.

There was a song at the time whose lyrics went something like this: "The love bug will bite you if you don't watch out; and if he bites you, you will sing and shout." I was obviously badly bitten.

One special event of the company's second program was to be *Les Sylphides,* which is set to a score by Chopin. This would be taught by John Taras, a protégé of Balanchine's who had already choreographed his own ballets and was obviously greatly gifted. At this point in his career, he was not only working closely with Mr. Balanchine and New York City Ballet but had also begun working with Ballet Theater (later called American Ballet Theater). Aside from being extremely musical, Mr. Taras had the advantage of having been a pupil of the work's original choreographer, Fokine, and thus was probably one of the few people who could stage *Les Sylphides* as Fokine had conceived it. I was very excited to be learning this ballet from him as it is one of the greatest works in the classical repertoire; and as I expected, he demanded that we fully understand and replicate the style of Fokine. When I see *Les Sylphides* today, it has lost the Fokine nuances, yet it endures—the sign of a true classic.

Once again, the participants were handpicked from class. I was to be a demisoloist, which meant that I danced one of the two girls at the beginning and in the grand entry as well as doing corps work. I thus enjoyed a bit more status than just being in the corps plus it allowed me to have a few moments of wonderful pointe work as nearly a soloist.

I loved the rehearsals, where Mr. Taras explained how Fokine set many of the steps in opposition to the position of the head. In classical ballet, the head normally follows the line of the *arabesque* arm. This unusual opposition in *Les Sylphides* is one of the ways that Fokine heightened the air of fragility about these almost unearthly dancing creatures.

Russell Hartley was making our costumes, those for sylphs similar in many ways to the gauzy creations he had sewn for the supernatural Wilis. Again, I loved being his guinea pig at the fittings. As he placed the lovely, ethereal wings on my back, I remember prancing as if I were indeed going aloft, testing how my arms might work with the wings. Wearing a costume immediately gives one a feeling for the role, for a dancer perhaps even more so than for any other performing artist. On a dancer, it becomes second skin. I felt it almost a religious act: once in a costume, I was inside my role, whatever it might be. This costume made me feel so light and airy. The floating quality of the skirt, the way it seemed to expand with even the slightest motion (and I learned discreet ways of allowing my hand to brush against the tulle, to sustain that illusion of airiness) made me seem even more unearthly.

There was so much for me to learn, but I took it in stride. Mr. Taras taught us our steps in great detail. It was a pleasure to work with him, precisely because his musicality and sense of precision were so demanding. Somehow I felt that there was an important connection between us. Being in this ballet was an important event in my life.

Mr. Taras could often be sarcastic, even cutting, but even this I found rather enjoyable as he had a great sense of humor, and his comments had that Noel Coward quickness of mind that combined humor and sarcasm in a way one could only admire.

It was clearly apparent that I worshipped him, and when I began joining him for coffee or a snack, he opened up to me: He had decided even while a child that he wanted to be a dancer. His mother had died when he was eight or nine and his father when he was fifteen. He had been fortunate to have been befriended by a kindly couple who had taken him into their lives and given him the financial support to study ballet. All this, I learned in bits and pieces as we were en route to coffee. I remember he once said, rather abruptly, "This dance life is hard," and turned his shoe to show me the sole, which was commencing to wear out in a small, thin circle. Was this to help me understand what lay ahead of me, or was this just his strange, naughty humor?

My immediate reaction to his disclosures was that I had been so lucky that my parents could afford to give me a comfortable life as well as the financial backing for my studies. I had always been aware of this and had never taken it for granted. It is certainly a chance matter, who and what one's parents are, and I had been blessed for all they had provided and continued to support. At the theater and in class, I had always been very sensitive, and so very few of my colleagues knew anything about my personal or home life. Nor did I know much about theirs. This was considered private, and questions never came up. Ballet was a great social equalizer in this way. Nor did my mother or father push me toward dance as "stage parents" so infamously meddled with their children's lives. On the contrary, my father was not at all happy about my choice to pursue a

—

profession that he felt could cause me hardship and heartache with little or no financial award. But that problem would only rear its head later. At this time, I was still contentedly living at home with the normal conflicts any artistic adolescent might face when leading a life so different from that of her average high school peers.

On our breaks, Mr. Taras and I also "talked shop," of course. In one of those conversations, I said that I thought the variations in *Les Sylphides* were not technically difficult. He said, "Good. I expect you to understudy every one of them." I had already danced the mazurka, alternating with Jane Bowen, and had understudied the waltz. But I had never even attempted the prelude, for it was not something that was natural to me. I got his message loud and clear and consequently put in many hours of practice learning his entire choreography, which I quickly discovered was indeed difficult, after all—the correct head and arm positions especially proved to be anything but easy. Even the very stamina required for the ballet was a new experience for me. Mr. Taras took my assignment seriously: as I rehearsed each and every variation, I received many corrections. To have been so challenged to conquer that combination of technique, style, and stamina in a single piece was a kind of revelation for me—anything *but* a punishment! I enjoyed this experience immensely . . . but I also learned never to open my mouth again! In a few years' time, this initially sarcastic directive came to be one of the most valuable pieces of advice I ever could have received. And, in later years, teaching and coaching this ballet became one of my greatest loves. As a consequence of having learned everyone's variations in addition to my own, I was able to give so many valuable corrections to others, especially concerning style. For that, I must thank, too, the incredible knowledge of Mr. Taras, his direct passing along of what he had himself learned from Fokine.

Once we had learned *Les Sylphides*, Mr. Taras needed to leave for New York; however, he would be back in a few weeks to start rehearsals with us on a new ballet that he would choreograph. For now, we were to continue to concentrate on *Parranda, Mephisto Waltz*, and *Giselle*.

Throughout this period, the San Francisco Civic Ballet enjoyed close contact with our angel, Jerry (Geraldine) McDonald, who was later to marry and become Jerry McDonald Bodrero. She was an extremely elegant lady, American born and bred. Tall and slender, she had clearly been a great beauty in her younger days and still retained a distinction and attractiveness, with incredible grace and good manners. I admired her ability to put anyone at ease immediately. (This is a sign of a true gentleman or gentlewoman, and the true reason for etiquette!)

She was never far away, always there to help the San Francisco Ballet, which she had made her pet project. She truly cared about us and frequently came to watch us in class and at rehearsals. I was fortunate to be invited to her home for tea or dinner, and began to build what became a great friendship with her. She became something of a patron to me, encouraging me, always excited by my progress. She obviously had every belief that I would succeed as a dancer and even remarked to Willam, "There's gold in them there hills," a prophecy I never forgot. It was so inspiring to have this great lady believe in me. And she did not merely provide morale to the company. Besides extending her graciousness to us all, she often reached into her purse to ensure that Willam's bills would be paid. She must never be forgotten for the role she played in the history of the San Francisco Ballet as she alone was the financial sponsor of the 1947-1948 San Francisco Civic Ballet season.

5

Tamara Toumanova

We now began rehearsals for *Swan Lake*. Because time and space were limited there, we were unable to rehearse solely at the school. For some of our rehearsals, we relied upon Polk Hall, a recital auditorium located three blocks away. It was housed in the same building as a German restaurant called the Rathskeller, and we found ourselves learning our steps amidst the pungent odors of bratwurst and sauerkraut, two of my least favorite foods. Be that as it may, we were hard at work there and eagerly awaiting the arrival of our next guest performers. I had read about Tamara Toumanova, who had been one of the baby ballerinas of the de Basil branch of the Ballet Russe during the early 1930s. She was to dance the lead in our *Swan Lake,* partnered by Danish-born Paul Petroff (*né* Petersen) as well as in *Coppélia* and in many other excerpts from the classical repertoire.

One afternoon, we were deep into rehearsals of act 2, trying to space the movements and patterns of the corps, under Willam's direction. It was late and we were tired.

Without warning, the door opened and a full entourage entered, led by Irving Deakin, Tamara Toumanova, Paul Petroff, Mama Toumanova, Mrs. McDonald, and George Baker, the president of the Ballet Association. But I never noticed anyone but Toumanova—she was the most exquisite creature I had ever seen! We were all thus affected; it seemed the room was suddenly filled with electricity. The excitement she generated simply walking in, in her elegant street clothes, was extraordinary. Nobody was tired anymore but stood expectantly at attention as she came toward us to be introduced. We spontaneously burst

—

into applause the moment she stopped walking. She flipped her hand, saying, "Oh no, I will change quickly," and rapidly exited, fur coat and all. In her wake, all I could think was, *Was this a dream?* I had just come face-to-face with the woman to become my greatest influence, my role model, someone who represented to me everything a ballerina should be.

Willam called a pause to our rehearsal, until her return. Then she reappeared, looking even smaller in her practice clothes. She was olive skinned with aquiline features and enormous brown eyes, her face delicately chiseled to perfection. Her arms and back were very Russian; her size was perfect, not emaciated or even thin, just the body of a beautiful woman with soft curves and beautifully sculpted legs and feet. Her hair was still down. She wore pink tights and a deliciously fashioned and quite unique white top that she tied around her waist, with a crocheted border around the neck and sleeves. Over this she wore a short white classical-practice tutu of the lightest tulle imaginable. Toumarova excused her tardiness; her plane had been delayed. As she spoke, she twisted her hair into a small bun on top of her head. My eyes grew larger by the second as I absorbed every movement she made.

We abandoned *Swan Lake*, the company dismissed, all but Toumanova and the six dancers who would portray Coppélia's friends. I was one of those six. She explained to us the beginning sequence, and we commenced to dance the first part along with her. Suddenly, she stopped and exclaimed, "Why are you so far away from me? You are my friends! Come closer. This is only a tutu. You can touch it. Be more with me, not separate. We are all together, dancing—not me and then you!" My first thought went to our previous guest, Alicia Markova, who had complained that we were too close!

This was the beginning of a wonderful rehearsal. Toumanova watched us perform the six friends' individual variations, which took finely tuned technique and precision. I tried to be very clear technically even while I also felt such joy bubbling up inside of me as I danced. We stopped after we had rehearsed two hours; Toumanova was very pleased with us. We were now free to go; she and Mr. Petroff would stay to go through their first act, "Wheat" pas de deux. She went over to the rehearsal pianist to discuss tempos; Mama Toumanova and others in the entourage were still seated on the other side of the room, chattering volubly. Willam stood by the piano, explaining where everyone else would be onstage when they were to dance the pas de deux. Instead of leaving the room, I seated myself in the opposite corner, trying to make myself inconspicuous, busying myself with taking off my toe shoes.

At last, Toumanova started but not before requesting that the small bouquet of wheat be brought to the next rehearsal. Willam asked his right-hand man, Earl Riggins, to make a note of it. The pianist began to play, and all conversation ceased. There wasn't another sound to be heard. It was that divine time in late afternoon as light slowly fades; only the streaks of the remaining day joined us in the rehearsal hall.

As Toumanova moved, Petroff seemed to anticipate every *arabesque*, partnering her without effort. There was no clutching at her waist; indeed, he seemed barely to hold her. As they did each *arabesque* pose, he echoed each line of her body with his own, mirroring her every movement with ease. This made the end of their combined motion sustain its beauty so that the audience would register the conclusion of the phrase.

As Toumanova danced, she expressed herself not only through her body but also from the heart. She danced full out. Every expression on her face, even her breathing, was a part of her dancing. I felt my face dampen with tears from the sheer beauty of her dancing. When she finished, her small entourage and I burst into applause.

She acknowledged our applause but then immediately walked to the pianist like an ordinary human being to make corrections. Yet there was a quality about her that stayed and made a deep impression on me. As I was to discover, her aura was genuine, not manufactured—it was a virtual impossibility for her to move without expression.

When she retired to the dressing room to change, I stayed in my corner, putting on new toe shoes that I wanted to break in before going home to prepare them for future rehearsals. Out she came and, putting her tutu down with her bag, approached me and said, "Very good girl." She asked my age and responded, "Good, good." She ignored the waiting entourage that had resumed its chatting and, taking hold of my hands, asked me to do a *relevé*—a gradual rise from flat foot to full pointe—in the shoes I had just been trying out. But first, Toumanova checked my toe shoes for herself, telling me never to put my foot into a too-small shoe, that they should fit comfortably while my feet were flat on the floor. She advised me to pour hot water inside the toe box for a moment before putting on a new pair of shoes. This would allow the glue and satin of the toes to soften and take the shape of my foot. Walking and doing a few *relevés* (rises on point) in the dampened shoes would also help them to take on the shape of my feet. I would then take the shoes off and allow them to dry, which only took a few minutes. Another quick way to condition new shoes was to use rubbing alcohol to wet them as it evaporated faster than water, but I preferred the less odiferous water method.

Asking me to do a *relevé*, Toumanova felt the heels of my shoes, which I had bought ready made to a standard size. They gaped slightly below my ankle, and she told me that my heels were too narrow for the shoes and suggested that perhaps I should now start to order shoes custom made to exactly fit me. She further advised a long vamp for the toe and a slightly higher cut on the heel. Toumanova also told me that "Mama" would teach me how to sew on the elastic properly and, most important, how to darn the toe with crochet cotton. She explained that besides helping to make the shoes last longer, darning also minimized the sound of a new toe shoe onstage.

I don't remember breathing during all of this but obviously must have been. She then kissed me on both cheeks and said, "Good, *doushka*" ("dear") to me. All this time, she had kept everyone waiting to hand down a part of her art—to me! She picked up her tutu and gave it to me, asking if it would be too much trouble for me to take it back to the studio with me for our next rehearsal, to leave it in the office for her. Would I mind? I would *die* for her, let alone carry her tutu! With this, we said our good-byes; none of the above had escaped the entourage. As they left with Toumanova, Willam turned toward me and said, "See you shortly for class, *baby*," a term he sometimes used when addressing me. He wore a big smile on his face as if he was verifying all the belief he had put into pushing me forward, far beyond my years. "If there were 'baby ballerinas' in the Ballet Russe," he seemed to be saying, "why not in the San Francisco Ballet?" After all, I had been steadily primed for ballerina roles since I was fourteen.

I changed and gathered together my bag and, of course, that most precious tutu that had been left in my care. I was the last to leave Polk Hall that evening. As I left, I looked about the now-deserted rehearsal space. For the first time, the sour scents of bratwurst and sauerkraut did not even exist for me. I marched down Van Ness Avenue toward the school, clutching the tutu to my body so tightly that I could smell the last whiffs of Toumanova's perfume still clinging to the cloth. My steps seemingly fell on air; I moved as if I were still in a world that had belonged, for those few moments, to me alone, that could never be shared with anyone else, except perhaps Toumanova herself. Everything else seemed very distant. For me, there was only dance. A dream was becoming reality.

My arrival back at school did not go unnoticed due to whose tutu I was carrying. A class was just about to start, with Harold teaching. I quickly changed and joined my colleagues. Harold eyed me, and I sensed I was to become his target. Sure enough, he addressed me: "Miss

Toumanova, if you would step forward to dance in the first row." I could feel the tears well in my eyes and my face flushing red. Eyes down, I took my place. His sarcasm continued. Harold advised me to use less expression and less force. These remarks and others obviously implied that my brief encounter with Toumanova that afternoon had somehow affected my movements. I was puzzled and hurt by what he said. Clearly, one cannot instantly change what one has been given by God; what I was exhibiting in class was how I had always danced. Toumanova's influence had only been to clarify my feelings about dance; any accidental resemblance should only have been a compliment to me and certainly not a fault, being as she was such a great artist. This was, in fact, not the first time that Harold had tried to subdue my natural spirit. I went home crying and told my mother what had occurred. She listened patiently and gently calmed me, softly saying that I should feel very happy if I resembled someone like a Toumanova. She advised me to reply to Harold's, or anyone else's teasing, with a simple "Thank you, how honored I am."

I swore that day that I would leave San Francisco as soon as I finished school and that I would seek teachers who wanted expression and artistry, not just technique, height, and blonde hair.

Not all my teachers were as exasperating, of course. When he was not busy with other matters concerning the season, Willam continued to teach class, and he was just the opposite of Harold. If anything, I now progressed under his tutelage in leaps and bounds because Willam's words as he'd left Polk Hall that memorable afternoon continued to ring in my ears.

Often, Willam would ask the whole class to advance to the front of the room, and then he'd ask one of the dancers to do a sequence as the others watched. He wanted us to learn from each other. More and more, he began to select me for these demonstrations; moreover, he allowed me to use my own style that was not like anyone else's.

Each dancer had something the others didn't. I loved these moments in class, when we showed what gift we uniquely possessed. Other colleagues whom I recall were called upon to demonstrate included Nancy Johnson, especially in adagio, and Jane Bowen, who had a particular ease, a very soft approach.

John Taras arrived from back east, as promised, to choreograph a new ballet for the company. The music for *Persephone* would be the Symphony No. 1 in E-flat Major by Robert Schumann. There were to be eight couples plus six girls, with Jocelyn Vollmar and Richard Burgess as leads. It was thrilling for me to again be selected as a soloist, this time as one of those six girls. Our costumes were simple: fitted close to the body, they were of the lightest chiffon, making us feel as if we were ourselves weightless.

In this piece, we were required to dance a lot. The ballet began on an exhilarating note: I was the first to enter with a great jeté and then another, followed by the next soloist, and so forth. We never stopped all the way through the first movement because we carried the melody. We flew across the stage in intricate patterns that required very quick footwork—a style influenced by Balanchine but totally Taras in spirit. Everything we were asked to do was extremely musical, and while we danced with a clean and exact technique, we also found a joyous sense of release in our movements as the lyrical score carried us along. Of all the ballets I had been in to date, this was the first to satisfy me both technically and musically. I had found a friend in this style of dancing: it demanded strength in addition to technique, and the movements that Mr. Taras had choreographed could not help but coax expressiveness from us.

To be working with him again was such a thrill. He would show us a step very quickly then turn around and say, "Do it," thinking we had caught it all and exactly as we'd been shown, which was of course impossible. Then he would inform us that it hadn't been quite what he had done. It was amazing, how he was able to keep the tiniest detail in his head. Instead of feeling pressured, we rejoiced in the challenge of getting it right. If we got a "Good" by the end, it was immensely satisfying. Our rehearsals went quickly as this ballet was just full-out dancing for dance's sake, without a storyline (despite its mythological title).

Persephone was scheduled for the second part of the Civic Ballet season, to take place across four evenings: on February 5, 6, 7, and 8, 1948. What a difference from our November season, when we had had to contend with the Markova-Dolin Ballet sharing our bill—it was a total climate change from British cold to Russian warmth! Toumanova, partnered by Petroff or sometimes by fellow guest artist Michel Panaieff, would appear in *Coppélia*, the Black Swan pas de deux, and the *Nutcracker* pas de deux.

To me, these two artists were the heart and soul of classical ballet, and it was a priceless experience for me to watch them rehearse—and to rehearse in their presence—every day. The reciprocity was palpable to all concerned: I never missed a single one of Toumanova's rehearsals, and she never missed watching, or helping, me.

On the night of our dress rehearsal for *Coppélia*, Toumanova's husband arrived from Los Angeles. Casey Robinson, a very distinguished and beautiful white-haired man, was a well-known Hollywood film writer.

—

He was such a gentleman: polite, gentle, and very sweet to me. Everyone attended this rehearsal: the ballet company's board of directors, Jerry McDonald—of course—Irving Deakin, and the entire company staff.

All commenced well, and Toumanova was brilliant in the various dances that Swanilda does when she pretends she is the doll Coppélia obeying her master. Everybody was riveted.

Then we came to act 3. I had a solo as one of the friends. Having just donned new toe shoes, I slid on the hard floor. Even though I did not fall, I was devastated. I continued, trying not to show how upset I was. Finally, when we had a break, I took the opportunity to go into the ladies' room to wash up a bit and have a good cry! In sailed Toumanova, tutu and all, saying, "Darling, you cry. I fell in Covent Garden. You only slipped. I told my husband you have so much talent. I like you very much." She took me by the hand, and I tried to hold my head high as we walked back into the studio. I felt so tender and loving toward this incredible artist who was so kind and giving to a young dancer with stars in her eyes and dreams in her head.

Nothing had prepared me for the most important and unforgettable dancing that was still to come. On the program was the grand pas de deux from *Don Quixote,* set to a score by Minkus. Toumanova and Petroff were to rehearse the opening pas de deux, both variations, and the coda. Toumanova donned the special *Don Quixote* practice tutu that Mama had made (actually, Mama made all of Toumanova's tutus). The tutu had piano wire inside, to hold it out into a true circle. The piano wire was quite supple and would give if Toumanova leaned against it. She always wore this skirt so that she could feel the correct distance from Petroff during partnered turns or the work's dramatic balances *en pointe* and how the shoulder lifts would work—details the audience would never think of as needing precision planning of *costume.* Actually, it is an art in itself, to dance in any style of a tutu. Their bodices are almost always boned and, as in *Don Quixote,* might be made of tight, heavy velvet, which has little give. Sometimes a dancer wearing a tutu needs to use all her back muscles just to move and bend.

As always, Toumanova danced full out at this rehearsal. For her variation, she always held a fan. During a previous rehearsal, she noted that I was watching and said, "Try to learn." I was elated as this variation is wonderful, very quick. But learning the steps was one thing and the fan another. After certain steps, one had to open the fan, on another step, to close it, and always with a dramatic *snap!* This all required great dexterity; I ended up going to Chinatown to buy inexpensive fans to practice with, for many broke until I had mastered the timing and correct use of this deceptively simple-looking prop! At that time, I never envisioned that this pas de deux would become one of my signature roles. (I also didn't know that I would someday take class with our production's choreographer, Mikhail Obukhov, who had styled it after Petipa's original.)

Finally, our opening night arrived. The first program on our four-night bill was a curtain-opener, *Gift of the Magi*, based upon the O. Henry story. It was staged by Simon Semenoff, with Ruby Asquith Christensen and Roy Fitzell as the leads. The cast was very small and the plot simple, but it was a very touching and beautiful little ballet, a jewel. Then came a condensed version of *Swan Lake*, listed on the program as a "choreographic poem in one act," restaged by by Willam as based upon the original choreography by Marius Petipa and Lev Ivanov.

The overture began. Of all the ballets in the world as one stands backstage waiting to go on, that music immediately touches one's soul. Years of dancing would never change that feeling for me. We stood in the wings, kicking each other's rear end with our knees—our way of wishing luck—wringing our hands, rising on our toes, waiting impatiently as if racehorses for the bell to ring.

At last, the curtain rose, and each girl immediately transformed into a swan. We danced the entrance of the swans, and then the prince appeared. We all quivered in perfect form. Then, as if a bolt of lightning had struck the stage, out came our swan queen with a great jump and *arabesque* balance. When the queen started her pas de deux with the prince, the corps divided and formed a line on either side of the stage. The prince has a friend called Benno, and in the original choreography for this pas de deux, there is an important sequence where the queen does a great *développé*, unfolding one leg high into the air and drops backward into Benno's arms; he then returns her to the prince. This particular element has been cut for years, and I think it's a pity. Willam retained it for our production. The production concluded with the prince dancing with us only to collapse in despair as the wicked sorcerer, Rothbart, spirited the majestic swan queen away, across the lake.

As the swan queen, Toumanova was a dream, her natural beauty breathtaking. Her face was radiant, changing in expression as the swan's emotions shifted: warm when she revealed the woman hidden by evil magic within her, steely when she faced Rothbart. Never again would I see such a vividly felt *Swan Lake*. Toumanova provided me with a prototype for the swan.

When the curtain came down, the ovation was incredible; Toumanova stepped forth to bravoes well deserved. There were many white Russians in San Francisco in the 1940s, some of them fanatical balletomanes. That night they saw, finally, what they remembered from Russia. What an exciting evening!

Following the intermission would be the *Don Quixote* Pas de Deux. I changed into my robe and stood by the wings, eager not to miss a single second of it. Toumanova was nearby, warming up, testing her shoes; and she handed me her shawl. Then she took her place onstage behind the lowered curtain. Her partner was Michel Panaieff, who stood directly behind her. When the music began, the curtain rose to show the two figures still, heads down. Then three chords and the dancers raised their arms and heads as the audience applauded. Toumanova's (Obukhoff's) version contained a great many balances. She excelled in this. It was uncanny how she could hit each one without wavering, a feat for any ballerina. Hers were phenomenal. The pas de deux concluded in a coda that was a tour de force for both dancers, and again the audience went mad. I was so elated that I found myself crying. I had little time to react, though, as I needed to dance in the last ballet of the evening. I handed Mama Toumanova Tamara's shawl and fled to change costumes before I could even speak to her daughter coming offstage. We closed the program with *Parranda,* guaranteed to leave the audience in a good mood, not that we needed have any worries about the house that night.

I took off my makeup and packed my bag with my tights and shoes then headed to Toumanova's dressing room, where I found her surrounded by admirers. When she saw me, she said, "Janet, come take a rose," and gave me a kiss. With that rose, I took home every second of what had happened that evening.

We returned the next night for a different program. *Blue Plaza* was first; the donkey role served as my warm-up. Next was the ballet we had all looked forward to dancing, *Persephone.* We hurriedly changed into our costumes, that barest flutter of chiffon, and then we stood in the wings as Schumann's "Spring" Symphony began with the curtain down. On a particular musical cue, the curtain slowly rose, and then the first melody was my entrance cue. I ran in, executed my first jetés, and heard the audience applaud!

The décor for this work provided us a huge space, and the stage opened to its greatest depth. The ballet seemed to fly by; I was in sheer heaven, dancing with utter abandon. It was fantastic to dance so much and to demonstrate such technique. We received many curtain calls.

We each received a small bouquet of flowers from Mr. Taras. Inside mine was a card from him, which I have carried for many years. Now, the faded writing is barely visible. Mr. Taras was quite content, but we still got corrections.

We continued to dance spiritedly the following night, the *Coppélia* premiere. We had a superb cast: Toumanova as Swanilda, Panaieff as Franz, and Simon Semenoff as Dr. Coppélius.

The week just flew by, and then we had to say our good-byes. Mr. Taras left for other commitments in New York City. He told me, when I grew up and he was directing somewhere, that I should look him up. This was my greatest desire: to work with him again.

Toumanova suggested that, on my school holidays, I come to Los Angeles to work with Bronislava Nijinska, who was her teacher. We hugged, and I fought back tears. Panaieff also conducted classes in Los Angeles; I promised too to come and attend his.

And so we said good-bye to the Civic Ballet's first season. It should have continued as a company, but economics forced us back to our regular schedule as the San Francisco Ballet. We needed to participate in the opera season and also at an outdoor summer performance to be given at Stern Grove. This would be an open-air production, performed on a stage in a eucalyptus grove.

Stern Grove had been given to the city of San Francisco by Rosalie Stern in the early 1930s in honor of her husband, Sigmund. Later during that decade, free-to-the-public performances began to take place there every summer. When I first danced there with the San Francisco Ballet, whose appearances were one of the highlights of the summer season, the very performance space was a challenge in itself: no dressing rooms, except for temporary partitions; and exactly one toilet, yards away, to which we often had to trudge through mud, as San Francisco summer weather was invariably uneven. Even the stage was damp—one chanced one's life there. I cannot say it was wonderful to perform there, but when the sun shone, filtered through the eucalyptus leaves, it felt like a special blessing. This venue was hard on the audiences too as many of the people who had not succeeded in snaring picnic tables (where they watched the show as they ate) had to sit on the ground. Particularly treacherous to dancers was any manifestation of fog. No sooner had we warmed up than in seconds we became cold again, our legs literally freezing up on us. But there was an advantage to braving the elements there: Willam always gave the younger dancers a chance to do a solo, which pushed us younger ones forward. That experience, and even needing to learn to work in such unstable and primitive conditions, hastened a future reward for those who managed to shine regardless. I have learned that, since my dancing days at Stern

Grove, the stage facilities there have progressively improved, though the weather continues to be a gamble.

Very soon after we had appeared there, we had another engagement at the Hollywood Bowl. Despite my doubts about that venue, this single performance proved to be enchanting. The Bowl was filled. We danced *Les Sylphides*, a perfect choice for under the stars; Willam's newest ballet, *Danza Brilliante*; and also *Parranda*, which was of course a great success.

With the end of summer came my last year of high school. I counted the days until June 1950. Our graduation ceremony was held in the opera house—how amusing to enter down the aisle on the other side of the footlights instead of dancing! Between my ballet studies and the fact that I had skipped a grade when in junior high school, I felt little in common with my fellow graduates. Still, graduation was a serious matter, as it meant I would need to decide what next to do with my life.

On graduation day, I wore a lovely lavender organdy dress. When we took off our somber graduation gowns worn on top of our own clothing, we girls looked the picture of youth, energy, optimism—and very pretty. When the ceremony ended, we threw our mortarboards high into the air though we had to return them and the gowns to the rental agency. We kept the tassels.

After briefly joining my parents, I walked across the street to the ballet school, sensing that perhaps one day my training there would also soon draw to a close for me. This one day felt so life changing.

Willam was there and remarked upon how pretty I looked. When I replied that I had just graduated from high school, he appeared to be taken aback: Where did that little elf go, all of six years old, now replaced by a young lady of nearly seventeen? I stood there, regarding him with great love and admiration. We both knew that the time was imminent when the fledgling would leave its nest.

During the next months, I began to take class with Guillermo del Oro, who had a small studio on Bush Street. He had set the dances in *Carmen* for us during the opera season, to great success. He used to teach Spanish dance in the company's school, but now he had this studio on his own. A mild man with impeccable manners and old-world charm, he had a certificate from Enrico Cecchetti himself.

At his studio was a terrific pianist, a Mr. Paniagua, who was to eventually play for the San Francisco Ballet School as well. Mr. del Oro had taken him on when the entire company of the Spanish production *Cabalagata* had found themselves stranded in San Francisco. Whenever

I walked into the studio, Mr. Paniagua would always manage to insert a phrase from the *Don Quixote* pas de deux into whatever he was playing.

Prompted by Toumanova's encouragement, I also went to Los Angeles during every available holiday to work with Nijinska. In addition, I took classes with Carmelita Marracchi, a fabulous teacher, and I liked Madame Bekefi, who taught at the same studio. I also loved my studies with Michel Panaieff, with whom I became great friends—we enjoyed a mutual admiration on society. He was unique, and anyone who was anybody could be found at his classes.

Although there were so many good teachers in Los Angeles at that time, as I gathered opinions from dancers and teachers I met, there seemed to be no doubt that Europe would be a far more advantageous destination for me than remaining in the United States. In my studies, I had observed that the focus of American schooling was becoming more and more athletic, to the exclusion of traditional aesthetics derived from the old-world masters. I knew I could never be content dancing merely toward a goal of technical proficiency. I felt more from the inside needed to be developed and expressed and wished whatever style I possessed to remain based in a classical schooling.

I was torn over what to do. Lew Christensen had returned to San Francisco and had taken over our classes there. He choreographed a ballet for three of us plus a corps de ballet, which we performed in Nourse Auditorium, behind the present-day Davies Symphony Hall. At that time, I had such a good rapport with Lew. I could pick up his choreography quickly—as with John Taras, he would give me steps and ask, "What did I do?"—but I could replicate them (it is advantageous for a dancer to have this capability to pick up an entire sequence; it enables the dancer to become a choreographer's dream—translation: workhorse!). My rapport with him, and his support of my work, was pulling at my heart. But I had a dream, and that dream was Paris.

Not only had the City of Light captured my heart when I was still a child, but I also loved everything French. Although I couldn't speak the language, still I bought every French magazine then available in San Francisco. I also kept up with current dance news, following which companies over there were the best and where they were located. Plus, all the Russian ballet teachers who dated back to the Imperial Theater were teaching there; indeed, it seemed a mecca for everyone connected with the arts. The more I reviewed my options, the more I was certain: I *had* to find a way to get to Paris. But how?

6

The Voyage

It was decided that I would study in Paris—ballet professionals presented a united front to convince my father to give me that chance. Edward Caton, ballet master of both the Ballet Russe de Monte Carlo and of American Ballet Theater, and Dimitri Romanoff, regisseur of American Ballet Theater, gave him exactly the same advice: it was important for me to go to Europe when I was so young because of my potential in classical and dramatic ballets. Ballerinas who were dramatic in style were not then in vogue in America; instead, a cooler technique was desired, in the Balanchine vein. Luckily for me—I was not at all physically suited to the Balanchine mold—in Europe, teachers stressed personal artistic growth and not just the polishing of technique. Both of these men believed that if my natural instincts and stylistic gifts were allowed to develop rather than being quashed for the sake of becoming merely another technician, I would one day return and be accepted in the States as a truly exceptional, classical ballerina.

At that time, I had been taking classes with Guillermo del Oro, in addition to those I was obliged to take with the San Francisco Ballet. The next decision was that I would begin my studies under the tutelage of Leo Staats, who was deeply connected with the Paris Opera, first as a dancer (from the age of ten!) and for the last several decades as a choreographer. He now had a school of his own. Mr. Del Oro felt that it would be wisest for me to begin training with Monsieur Staats. We wrote to Leo Staats, and to my great joy, he accepted me and said he was looking forward to my arrival. My father, satisfied that I now had a definite commitment from my new teacher, contacted a business associate in Paris, who arranged for

—
63

me to stay at Pension Muette, in the sixteenth arrondissement. There, I was to be chaperoned by two ladies, the older appropriately named Madame Grande and the much younger, probably in her forties, named Madame Garnier. They, and my lodgings, came highly recommended. Madame Grande was the owner of the establishment, which was how a widow of a certain class was able to receive a good income. As I would discover, she understood her position perfectly. Madame Garnier, however, would be more or less in charge of my comings and goings; she would oversee my progress in French and make sure that I got to ballet class. For all this apparent guardianship, my actual experience was to be more like the ballet *La Fille Mal Gardée* (The Badly Guarded Girl), but my father could hardly have predicted that when he booked my accommodations.

Eyes shining, I commenced to shop for my trip. First, my parents and I went to Malm's Luggage Store, where I was allowed to choose my very own luggage. There in the corner, I spotted a white calfskin steamer trunk and, alongside it, a smaller, matching cosmetics case. The trunk was outfitted with everything I might want or need: hanging space for short dresses, other compartments for long dresses and ball gowns. I immediately pictured how I would greet Paris with this white calfskin trunk bearing my initials in gold.

Next, my mother decided that I needed a warm coat. We settled on the most beautiful and expensive model, in pale pink. To wear at fancy occasions, I picked out a polka-dotted organdy dress; my only long dress, though, was to be my graduation dress, which was strapless, with white lace over peach silk and with a bow that tied in the back. Of course, I also packed everyday plain wool skirts, sweaters, mittens, hats, and gloves.

I also needed a passport. It was only the year before that I had become an American citizen. Since I had been underage at the time, I had not been required to take any test but had been granted citizenship as both my parents had become U.S. citizens. My mother, who originally held a French passport, upon marrying my father had automatically become a British subject, resulting in all three of their children being registered as British subjects. As dual citizenship was recognized between Great Britain and the United States, I would retain my British citizenship upon becoming an American citizen. The only stipulation was that I enter the United States using my American passport. I loved my passport and all it stood for: not only for my official citizenship in the "land of the free" but also my newfound freedom to travel all on my own beyond American shores! This little book thus became my most precious possession.

I was now ready to embark on this voyage that had started in San Francisco. My parents would go with me only as far as New York to ensconce me upon my ship.

We were to travel east by rail on Western Pacific's *California Zephyr*. It was an incredible train, with superb accommodations. My parents had a suite; between their bedroom and my own bedroom and bath was a lovely sitting room. Breakfast was served in the sitting room (although my father on occasion sometimes went instead to the train's dining room for a bit more excitement). The suite always had fresh flowers; and as I look back upon it, we were served extraordinary meals: fresh fruit and vegetables, perfectly greaseless fried chicken, homemade desserts such as strawberry shortcake and baked apple, and wonderful waffles and pancakes. We experienced the elegance, comfort, and luxury of traveling with great style and pleasure: back then, the trip to New York took five days. Little did I know that this magnificence of journeying by train would be a passing glory, never to return.

Time seemed to pass quickly. We read and played cards or simply enjoyed the view. My father and I found the "dome car" a real treat. It had a domed glass roof that enabled us to view with awesome perspective woods that we passed through and to gaze up at the stars amidst a landscape where there was not an artificial light in sight. But even back in our suite, my nose was always glued to the window, fascinated by the sheer expanse of America. I loved how dramatically and completely the landscape could change, sometimes right before my eyes, or overnight, when we would awake to yet a new view. It was quite thrilling to a young girl. But, too, the vastness began to overwhelm me as it began to sink in that I was ultimately going to be so very far away from home. Of course, I never let on that I was feeling a bit frightened. Despite my fears, I devoured my books about Paris, wanting to assimilate into its culture as quickly as possible.

We finally arrived in New York. After nearly a week on the train, walking on solid ground felt as if we were rocking from side to side! Before I was to join my ship, we spent a few days in the city and also visited Connecticut to see one of its senators, Joseph Neil, who was a friend of my father's. In Connecticut, I saw lovely countryside with beautiful homes, many with horse ranches.

The day came when we went to the pier where the French Line docked: my parents and one wide-eyed girl trying very hard not to say, "Don't leave me." Of course I would never lose face by saying such a thing, but I was only a hairbreadth away from it. Everything was very gay on board—a band playing, visitors and passengers alike celebrating the ship's upcoming departure. As I presented my ticket as the sole traveler of my family, the officer looked astonished and then took charge of me as if I were the only passenger boarding. I was escorted and introduced—in French, of course—to a steward; off went my luggage, and we followed. I was going cabin class, because my parents were not traveling with me (for a ballet student, though, that was big-time). I was to share my cabin with a French lady who lived in New York but who went to Paris every few months, where she would always stay at the Ritz Hotel—something that was to turn out to be very fortunate for me.

My parents and I took a quick tour of the other accommodations on board the *Île de France*, which was a beautifully appointed compact vessel. On the upper deck, the steward took care of booking me a table in the dining room for the second seating, and he also arranged for my deck chair, complete with red plaid wool blanket. Even before I would be living in Paris, I felt as if I had entered a new world, one that would affect the rest of my life. Everything seemed a fairy tale.

Suddenly, a whistle blew. At that moment, my heart sank to the soles of my shoes, and my joy turned to sheer panic. Then, even more frightening, was a voice over the loudspeaker, announcing, "All visitors, please clear the ship." In my great desire to dance and imagine my possibilities, I had thought of everything except the reality that I would now be truly alone. Not many sixteen-year-old girls were traveling abroad then, even with their families, and certainly not on their own. I clung to my parents, trying not to sob, but cry I did—as did they. Again the whistle blew, and it sounded to me like the voice of doom. As they abandoned me to my fate, my mother and father tried to give me courage, assuring me that all would go well and that I would soon be off on a marvelous adventure.

They left the ship, and I managed to find a spot where I could still see them on the pier. It seemed like an eternity before the vessel cast off. Streamers were being thrown all around me, and people waved hankies joyfully as I used mine to wipe away tears more than to wave it. Slowly, the *Île de France* left New York behind. My voyage really began then as I gazed at the sea as we drifted away from the sight of land—a life's journey that would ultimately take me not only to France but also to many other places of the heart and soul, even as I would physically visit foreign lands: from France to England, Belgium, Holland, Germany, Sweden, all of South America, Japan, and Hong Kong. Even then, I recognized that this was a day to remember as I hugged my pink coat to me and descended to my cabin.

There, I found my lovely French roommate unpacking with practiced ease and hanging dresses, leaving on her bed those that would need to be sent for ironing. I watched her and proceeded to copy her actions as I unpacked my own belongings. I hurried to lay my crushed graduation gown on my bed so that it would be taken for pressing at the same time as her garments—with, I hoped, *her* instructions, in French. She seemed to be absolutely charming and motherly and, gently asked me, in English, if I needed anything. I burst into tears. I wanted to say, "I need my father and mother," but of course I didn't. Still, she understood that I was frightened to be traveling on my own. We sat on our beds, and she offered me a consolatory glass of champagne (the French never think it is unwise for a minor to have a sip or two). It indeed cheered me up: this was the Paris I'd dreamed of—champagne, the Tour Eiffel, La Place de la Concorde, and the Paris Opéra. Suddenly, I was filled with excitement, telling her my plans to study and one day join the greatly esteemed ballet company called Le Grand Ballet du Marquis de Cuevas, whose headquarters were in Paris when they were not on tour. She was fascinated by my disclosures as she knew about this troupe. She told me that not only was the company adored in France but also that it was also famous the world over. Upon hearing this, I expanded upon my plans, explaining that I was to study all the classical variations with this and that well-known ballet teacher in Paris. Now I was in my element, speaking about my dreams as the champagne warmed up that terrible pit I'd felt in my stomach.

We were interrupted by a knock at the door. It was a steward, who rattled in French to my roommate. My lovely lady gave him my gown along with her own clothes that needed ironing, issuing her instructions in her own tongue. I couldn't understand one word; however, at that point, nothing fazed me. I had found a cocoon of comfort, and my head was reeling with my renewed anticipation of Paris and what I would do there. I knew that I would be working very hard there, morning till evening, dancing with all that was in me, filling every hour with all I had, to attain my dream of becoming a ballerina. Looking back now, I can see I was asking for the world, but, oddly enough, at the time, I never once thought that this couldn't happen. Ignorance is indeed bliss, and bliss was truly what carried me forth from that moment.

On our first night out (as the last night), passengers did not need to dress formally for dinner. Madame Blanche, as my new friend was called, selected for me one of my plain silk dresses that had a sweet ruffle as its only ornament. I looked very young in it, even more so with my hair pulled back into a ponytail with a ribbon around it. Suddenly, we heard a gong as a steward informed all the passengers on each of the ship's levels that the *deuxième*—the second dining shift—was commencing. Madame Blanche knew the ship quite well as she had traveled on it before, and together we walked to the dining room located several decks below our cabin. It was really quite marvelous, this first stroll. My lady friend and I passed ornate antique mirrors and, at the end of one of the decks, came upon huge beautiful flower arrangements set upon lovely narrow tables. We also passed a paneled smoking room and bar that connected by a sweeping staircase to a large salon. I had no idea a ship could be so vast. This was my first conscious experience of being aboard an ocean liner as when I had traveled for forty-five days from the Dutch East Indies to San Francisco, I had been only eighteen months old, and I remembered nothing of that trip.

When we reached the dining room, the maître d'hotel greeted us. He made it his business to know every passenger's name on first night as well as where each was to sit according to his great master plan. I was to share my table with several officers and three other people.

The menu placed before me was unbelievable. Luckily, the entries were in French on one side but in English on the other. Still, it was problematic. Firstly, I was very much unaccustomed to foods that went outside the dietary laws of my Jewish religion. Secondly, being Sephardic made it even more difficult; I was primarily acquainted with the traditional (Middle Eastern-style) Jewish dishes relating to my family's background. French cuisine was a mystery to me. Finally, the waiter helped me decide on my first shipboard dinner. A glass of wine was poured for me with each course. I had never before drunk wine with meals although my parents had served it to adult guests at dinner parties. Believing my sophistication had fooled them, I didn't realize at the time that the ship's French waiters would have served wine to even a ten-year-old. Ah, the French, already pushing the buttons that would awaken me to the wonders and deliciousness of the world!

Throughout dinner I was held rapt by every new sensation and detail, trying to take in and remember all that was happening, moment by moment. When the time came to retire to my cabin, I was delighted to find that my roommate was lightly snoring away. I was extremely modest, so grateful for her state of oblivion, I undressed, put on my nightgown, and got into bed. My prayers were said quietly, and then a stream of requests in which I asked God to help me followed. How much faith I seemed to bestow on God.

I lay awake, digesting that very long first day. This was not an uncomfortable insomnia; on the contrary, I loved the sound of the sea and the magic of being snug in my comfortable bed, listening to that and the creaking of the ship. Eventually I drifted blissfully and mercifully off to sleep.

The next morning, my priority was to find a space where I could do my ballet exercises to keep my body prepared for what lay ahead of me. The purser was extremely kind and explained to me that the ship's theater had a stage where, at 11:00 am, I could use a chair or ladder as a barre and work to my heart's content. However, I had to wait until that time because before eleven, Monsieur Robert Cassadesus would be practicing the piano, and no one was permitted to enter the theater while he was at the keyboard. Mr. Cassadesus was an internationally acclaimed pianist. It struck me as odd that even such a great artist felt the need to practice every day just as I felt that I shouldn't miss a single day of my own studies. Thus began the wonderful romance of my sharing the same space with the likes of Robert Cassadesus. I would always arrive one hour before my scheduled time and crouch at the back of the theater, listening and learning how a great musician practices each day. It was sheer magic, and I took this as an omen of what Paris was all about, a consciousness that to absorb art should be a natural part of my daily life and that it was as it should be, that Europe should feed my soul. It was as if I took my first step into heaven.

Sadly, after my first practice session the following day, I noticed the ship, rather than rocking from side to side, was rolling. Anyone who has ever been seasick knows that this rolling is deadly. Indeed, I was forced to bed, feeling very unglamorous and wretched! My steward and Madame Blanche held my head as I lost all that was in me. I lay there thinking surely I would die (another common sensation of seasickness). Although at that age I was quite able to endure more than others—as ballet is a good training ground for self-discipline, for holding up even when one is in pain—I must admit that all I wished was to be somehow lifted from my rolling bed and suspended in space, to not move an inch. I was pampered and never needed to ring or ask for anything. Tea, broth, toast, and rice appeared in my cabin at appropriate intervals, and eventually I could face ingesting them. All that could be done was to set me back on my feet, and indeed I continued with my barre exercises even while my world queasily rippled around me. When I ventured above deck for a post-illness stroll, grasping the railing to walk in a straight line, I even found myself able to enjoy the delicious air and taste of the sea bestowed on one.

I returned to my covert appreciation of Mr. Cassadesus's piano playing. Or was my presence so secret? After a few days, Mr. Cassadesus was passing near me on deck and stopped to speak with me. I stuttered how thrilling it was for me to meet him. He said that he had seen me practice and that he was impressed with my discipline to work in spite of my malady. Again, I stammered, what an honor it would be for me to hear him play. As he walked away, he slyly smiled and said, "Chère mademoiselle, try sitting up straight in your chair as I practice, and you will enjoy the music so much better than when you crouch in your seat." Dear God, he knew all along that this strange creature had been hiding and listening to him practice every day!

As we neared the end of our voyage, Madame Blanche informed me that the night had come for our dressing in formal black tie, for the "captain's dinner." I must say that the level of elegance, even for those of us in cabin class, was very high in those days. I could hardly wait for evening as it would give me a chance to wear my only long dress, which had, until that time, remained in the care of our steward. I found the gown hanging in my cabin exactly when I needed to get ready. Its organdy skirt had been puffed up gloriously, ironed to perfection. It was a dream. I looked very pale, and my lovely fairy godmother applied just a hint of color to my cheeks. And then I stepped into my strapless dress. Madame Blanche hooked me up as I held the bodice close and then stood back to appraise the effect. I immediately took on the role of model, raising my arms. To my horror, I had lost so much weight from my bout of *mal de mer* that my dress slipped off and dropped to the floor! Disaster! Panic! Tears! What was I going to do? Madame Blanche subdued my sobs and assured me that by the time the gong rang for second seating, my dress would fit me. And, before I knew it, the gown was in its proper place again—as my roommate sewed me into it. How many more times would I experience this, a costume being literally sewn onto my body. But this was different. My evening gown had a slightly boned bodice, shaped to the small breasts that would fill that space. But with the illness, I'd lost what I'd had. We ended up filling the boned area with lambswool, which I had tons of as this is what I used to pad my toe shoes.

At last, I was sewn and stuffed, so to speak. Madame Blanche snipped off the hanging portion of the ribbon that tied in a bow, creating a lovely more-mature-looking belt effect. She used a piece of the ribbon remnant to fashion a small bow for my hair. In spite of my recent illness, I looked and felt like a princess. Plus nobody else of my age on the ship was traveling alone. In fact, nobody in cabin class *was* my age, solo or accompanied! As Madame Blanche, protégée in hand, escorted me into the dining room, I felt very nervous—praying my dress would not betray me, feeling all eyes turning in our direction. The maitre d'hotel commented, "Mademoiselle, très jolie," and I floated to my table on his compliment. This was exactly what I had often fantasized about: being a part of an elegant and real outer world to match the one that lit up and danced inside me. When I was finally seated, having shaken hands with or nodded *bon soir* to each other person with whom I was to share the table, I was graciously received. I sensed that everyone was pleased with the *petite fille* who was already on her way, possessed of a bit of French chic. That childish bow on my dress, thank God, had been removed. (What a horror I feel to this day, when I see a lovely young woman at a cotillion being presented to society with a bow or bustle-like gathering of fabric on her behind. Indubitably, it is a fat girl, who should never be put into a dress with a bow at the back.)

My first lesson in style was learned and stored away for future use. After this gala evening, only one day and one night remained. I spent my final day on the ship trying to fit in everything: people asking me to join them for tea or to meet them before or after dinner, juggling my mixed feelings about closure on this, the first chapter of my journey. I felt a curious mix of anxiety and heady enthusiasm.

My health had improved; I was bounding back to feeling more myself. I was aware that my world among the friends I had made on board was but a temporary safety net: in two days, I would arrive at Le Havre and then board a train for Gare Saint Lazare. However, I felt braver now than when I had left New York; my spirits were high and I thought of nothing but dance.

The practical side of daily life in a foreign country whose language I could not yet speak was still unimaginable and far from my thoughts. Instead, I dreamed, slept, and read what pertained to my romantic notion of *Paris* (a word whose magic remains for me even to this day, some fifty years later).

As I look back on that trip, I think that my capacity for intense enthusiasm was so great that it not only conquered my fears but also gave me strength and determination, a kind of trust that could not be conjured up merely by conscious effort. It was this—later to be labeled *passion*—that had filled me from when I was a child. It was this that carried me through many a performance, giving me also the endurance that grew with time. This passion never faltered through the years of good or bad, joy or suffering; it burns within me still.

When my final day on the *Île-de-France* arrived, Madame Blanche helped me to prepare small envelopes, which she provided, to contain small amounts of cash for the steward and all those who had served me faithfully throughout the trip. That was a small and special lesson in courtesy when I was at an impressionable age; to this day, I never travel without small envelopes in which to leave tips. It just seems so much more ladylike not to have to baldly hand over money for services rendered. Everyone should have a Madame Blanche in her life!

My fairy godmother and I promised to call each other, exchanging telephone numbers and addresses. At Le Havre, I was to be separated from her. On my train, I was again in second class, but it was quite lovely, separated into beautifully appointed compartments that seated three on each side, our luggage neatly stacked on racks above our heads. I had a window seat and noted that there were even lace doilies for where each passenger would rest his or her head. Such details, though, did not divert me from my new sense of feeling alone, now that I did not have Madame Blanche by my side to rely upon. I concentrated upon looking out the window at my new country.

My first vision of France was of the area close to Le Havre, an important harbor. Outskirt towns slowly came into view. I was shocked. Nothing in my reading had prepared me for what I had imagined would be a jubilant entrance into the City of Lights. It had never occurred to me, being so young, that the French countryside and towns alike retained the raw scars left by World War II. This was, after all, 1950; the war had been over for several years. I was horrified to see from my train window burned-out shells of what had been farmhouses, some barns only partially inhabitable, the other half reduced to charcoal; machinery abandoned on fields; small patches of land and manmade structures alike fought for life. Iron overpasses and bridges still leaned, forming mind-boggling, grotesque images. These outskirt towns had obviously been hit for having been situated so near to Le Havre, home of transportation depots and factories. As we progressed toward Paris, the level of devastation lessened, but still there were reminders of what had taken place.

Had a child been innocently walking to school when this or that bomb fell? Where had I been when children my age had been killed or had to watch as parents were separated from them or, as I was later to learn, even shot or tortured before their eyes? I'd truly had no idea that France would appear so ravaged by the war. Surely the fields should have been filled with the famous French poppies and not this devastation, I was riveted, aghast.

It's not that we in the States had been unaware of the war. My parents spoke in whispers about the atrocities that they had heard about against all peoples, but especially against Jews. Jewish communities all over America knew what was happening; many people had been asked to sponsor refugees to guarantee their entry into America, and we had prayed for those who were suffering under the tyranny of war. The words had moved me, to be sure, but it was only when I saw such evidence with my own eyes that I understood the full impact of what had happened. And even then, little did I know what cards would be dealt to me, involving probably the most important choices that I would ever have to make in my career.

—

When the outer district of Paris came into sight, I began to feel that old excitement again. My father's friend would be at the station, holding up a sign with my name on it so that I could find him. When the train halted, the luggage that had been stored above my head was handed out the large windows, which were pulled entirely open. I descended to the platform in my handsome pink wool coat. It had not occurred to me that what with the deprivations from the war, I would be surrounded by people in the somber colors of navy blue, black, and brown. I must have stood out like a lit-up Christmas tree though I didn't fully realize this at the time.

Suddenly a voice said, "Mademoiselle Jeanette Sassoon, s'il vous plaît." Well, I caught the "Sassoon" part and looked around wildly. There stood Monsieur Mercier, my father's business associate. He graciously handed me flowers and personally escorted me to 32 Rue de Boullanvilliers, where the Pension Muette appeared to be a nice residential building. Monsieur Mercier was as lacking in English as I was in French. Still, he was able to make me understand that he would keep my father informed via teletype (this was before the age of faxes and instant, easy-to-place long-distance telephone calls; one could wait for hours for a phone call to finally go through). I was placed in the hands of Madame Garnier, who was quite pretty. Did I have any immediate sense that Monsieur Mercier seemed especially attentive to Madame Garnier? Oh well, time to investigate this later. At long last, I had *arrived.*

7

My First Steps

Once I was settled into my room at the *pension,* I had barely enough time to do anything but wash my hands and face as it would not do for me to appear late for lunch on my very first day. When I entered the *salon* (the large common area for guests used as a living room), I saw Madame Grande seated at her desk. She had white hair that was upswept in a fashionable style that totally suited her and wore a black dress with a high lace collar and long sleeves—also trimmed with lace—and very sensible heavy-heeled shoes. It all seemed the very epitome of a painting of a French interior one might find at a museum—it was French to the point of looking like a stage setting of a room in France. Of course, I was *in* France, so I oughtn't to have been so surprised to face such a scene!

In all my dreams of my new life abroad, I had given little thought to what everyday living would be like. Madame Grande welcomed me, offering her hand as she rose, observing this new addition to her world. She spoke only a few words of English but managed to assure me that Madame Garnier would soon take me in hand and that I would learn to speak French. Even as she said this, the magnitude of my utter ignorance of that language started to frighten me. Why on earth had I assumed that I would be conversing in English here? In my preparations for this trip, I had not learned a single French word, not even *yes.* It suddenly sank in that although I was in one of the nicest residential areas in Paris, few people in such a neighborhood were likely to speak English in those days. On the streets as I'd arrived, there had been virtually no tourists in sight. I am sure that instead of seeming reassured by her words, I must have looked very small; and my eyes, which were naturally quite large, must have become the size of spotlights! I was terror stricken by my sickening apprehension that I could neither understand others nor be understood.

Onward we marched into the *salle à manger* (the dining room), where people were already seated at several tables. Madame Gamier introduced me to all and then considerately placed me at a table where there was a nice-looking man in his twenties, dressed in a very English manner that stuck out almost, but not quite, as much as my own American-ness did. It was if I had discovered gold. He immediately addressed me in very elegant English, introducing himself as Richard Griffith. He was in Paris to settle some business matters. Richard represented an international firm that would eventually merge with another company and become very large and successful. The postwar years were a time of rebuilding in every field; Paris especially was becoming the center of a new Europe. Richard couldn't have been kinder or more caring. He told me that his wife would be coming as soon as his office was set up and that she was expecting their first child.

As we spoke, lunch arrived: what I was to learn was typical French home cooking. How unfortunate I was at the time to not be old enough to be at ease with the variety of foods that were to be presented to me at the *pension*. Also, I needed to maintain my discipline to a dancer's diet: healthy amounts of fruit, vegetables, and protein. On my first day, the first course was a salad of sliced tomatoes with slivers of white onion, dressed with oil and vinegar. The others took a piece of that deadly French bread that I so adored, and sopped up the oil and vinegar with great gusto. In France, I was to grow accustomed to the sight of people even in restaurants and bistros wiping their plates clean with a piece of bread. But for me to have done so would have felt sinful, against all I had been taught as far as good manners were concerned. I didn't do it then, but now I adore doing it and just always hope no one notices!

Also staying at the Pension Muette was a family with a five-year-old boy who spoke both French and English. He became my official translator. What shame I felt that a five-year-old had mastered two languages while I, despite my parents' fluency in a multitude of languages between them, had grown up totally uneducated in foreign tongues.

When lunch concluded, Madame Garnier approached me and informed me that I had an appointment with Monsieur Staats. It being a Saturday, there were no classes that afternoon, but he had set aside the time to meet with me to discuss my curriculum. Before I left for his studio, Richard invited me to come with him the next day, when he would acquaint me with the *métro* (underground transport) system. (I bless his thoughtfulness as ever after I could go everywhere by *métro*. It is superbly laid out, and to this day there have been few changes from when I first learned the system. It is for me one of the greatest subways in the world.)

I returned to my room to prepare for my first meeting with Monsieur Staats. I stuffed my practice clothes and several pairs of toe shoes into my ballet bag, and donned my best wool suit and heels, and my pink coat.

To my great delight, Madame Garnier had decided that we would go to the studio by bus, which enabled me to see more of the city. I was so thrilled as we passed famous monuments as the conductor called out their stops: Trocaderom Tour Eiffel, Place Vendôme. *This* was the Paris I had dreamed of! As had so many people before me who had felt it to be their spiritual home, I felt as if I had embarked upon my first love affair, with this city of such glorious architecture. And the colors! Spring was everywhere, and its effects permeated the city wherever one glanced—the flowers, the sky, the sunlight. One couldn't fail to be overwhelmed by the beauty, and I felt tears sliding down my cheeks.

When our stop came, I had been so consumed by my journey that I hadn't had time to feel nervous. However, as we mounted the stairs at 16 Rue de Saulnier, my heart began to beat wildly. We entered the foyer that led to the studio, where we were greeted at the door by Monsieur Staats, who showed me where to change for my audition. I didn't know at the time that the small room I had been assigned, of the three dressing rooms shared by students, was used exclusively by visiting ballerinas and his special protégées.

The studio itself was right out of a Degas print. Of course, there were barres all around the room; there was a very high ceiling, and one wall was totally glassed with windows that rose so high that they could only be opened and shut using a long pole. As I was to learn, that stick could also be used for other purposes.

Before I got changed, Monsieur Staats, who had medical knowledge of bones and joints, asked if he could examine me inside my dressing room. Standing in my slip, I felt extremely shy as he measured my arms, legs, even the length from my ankles to the beginning of my calf muscles. All this measuring seemed very mysterious to me then, but now I wish that all teachers were as knowledgeable as he had been, when they prepare to expose a young person to serious training for a professional career. Of course, he also tested my turnout—which, luckily, I had from the hip and not just from the knees and feet. He then announced that after each daily class, I would go upstairs to Monsieur André Guichot for stretching and to gain more relaxation in my muscles for extensions, and only then I was left alone to put on my practice clothes and pull my hair back.

Monsieur Staats gave me a full barre workout and then brought me to the center of the room, where he had me demonstrate an adagio with a great deal of balances and stylistic nuances. He followed this with pirouettes and turns in every manner and direction imaginable. At last we came to jumps, my personal forte that usually astounded my observers. To my horror, he stopped me and rattled something very quickly in French to Madame Garnier. Then he turned to me and addressed me in English. Although in the classes that would follow he would speak to me only in French, I discovered here that he could express himself well in English—too well. He slowly said that I had climbed a ladder in order to reach the incredible technique I had attained at such an early age. In his opinion, I possessed a rare inner talent and style that, with hard work, *might* enable me to become a ballerina and not just a member of the corps de ballet. He felt that, in the beginning, I would need to train with less effort upon my muscles as he believed that my previous training had placed too much emphasis on weight-bearing exercises, without adequate stretching and development of the ability to relax. In my present technique, my thighs were taking all the effort, and so I had built muscles there that I oughtn't to have had. Meanwhile, he compared my upper body to that of a polio patient! My naturally thin arms were not in balance with the muscle development of my lower body. No amount of starving would reduce that extra unnecessary muscle. Only correct retraining and courage would help me. Furthermore, I would take only one class a day, when I had been accustomed to taking three classes a day plus a men's class. He explained to me that, in the beginning, I would need to jump less high, work less with the muscles of my legs, and learn to use my entire body to bear the tremendous burden that technique places on a young body. He was angry that I had been allowed to come so far with so little attention paid to such issues as relaxation and suppleness.

He added that he was giving his harshest opinion because he saw in me something unique. His analysis of my body and decision about my training astounded me. I was devastated. I fought with myself not to let tears run down my face. Was this what I had come to Paris for, to take only one class per day, and not three or four? According to Monsieur Staats, there was so very much to be undone in order for me to obtain and have a long, healthy dancing life! Would I have the courage to do less in order to be able to do more?

Monsieur Staats tried to soften the blow: "When you come across a jewel, you guard it, polish it, and never overexpose it to anything that would take away the possibility of having the jewel reach its full potential. To shine and give off its brilliance, one must nurture it with great care."

He embraced me and said, "Trust me, dear mademoiselle, we shall see. Now, tomorrow is Sunday. Walk and see Paris. Monday, buy shoes with rubber soles, for the cobblestones on many streets make it necessary for you to have practical shoes. From Monday on, you will attempt to speak in French only. You will be one of my chosen few for serious work. *Je vous embrassez, ma petite.* Now, perhaps an ice cream would raise your spirits as you sit in a nice café with Madame Garnier. Monday, we start to work."

I dressed and bid *adieu* to Monsieur Staats as Madame Garnier settled my financial matters with him. As soon as we left, I burst into tears. I felt like such a failure. But Madame Garnier explained to me that *le maître* was very excited to have me and that it was only because he saw something inherently artistic in me that he was so intent to undo what he felt had been incorrect nurturing of my natural gifts. She was in ecstasy as she explained how famous he was in Paris and how, at seventy-two, he took only the select few to work this way under his guidance, which almost guaranteed such students not only incredible training but an incredible reputation. My tears ceased, but it remained a hard comedown to accept that I would need to learn an entirely new way just in order to reach the same point and advance beyond it. For one so young, it was hard to accept, let alone truly understand. I was to take Monsieur Staats's word on blind faith and determination.

For now, we took his more soothing recommendation to assuage my disappointment with ice cream. Off we went to the Champs-Elysées, to the elegant Café Rond Point, for a delicious splurge. Monday would soon be here, but first at least I could enjoy the rest of Saturday and Sunday.

On Sunday, I was awakened by a knock, and then the door to my room flew open even before I could reply. In strode a rather short man in a white jacket, who bore my *petit déjeuner*: coffee, a croissant, and rolls. We wished me *bonjour* and introduced himself as Émile then proceeded to busy himself—arranging my pillows, placing my breakfast tray on my lap, opening the full-length double doors of my room to bring the garden into full view.

"You have the best room, mademoiselle," said Émile.

"Yes," I said. "But where is the bath?"

A sink stood in the corner of the room, but no other plumbing fixture was in sight. I had already discovered that there was a room housing only a toilet a few doors down the hall. (And oh, to think of what passed there for toilet paper: cut-up pieces of newspaper! Little did I wish to have yesterday's news rubbed off on my derriere, and I was to buy Kleenex—a very expensive import—to save my dignity!)

Émile explained, "Chère mademoiselle, when you want a bath, let me know and I will prepare it for you. You are charged extra for baths, you know."

I was aghast. I was accustomed to bathing once daily, if not twice. Bathing, a luxury! My dismay was offset by my impression of how excited Emile was to have me there; all the details of yesterday's visit to Monsieur Staats had been related to the staff, I'm sure. I was to discover that Émile was possessed of a great warmth and loyalty and would be there to help me sew on my toe shoe ribbons, cry with me on bad days, and rejoice with me as I developed more and more the bearing and body of a ballerina.

I had time before lunch to take an investigative walking tour of the immediate area surrounding the *pension*. Being that some of the streets of Paris are arranged in a star pattern, rarely do they run parallel or perpendicular to each other. It is very easy to follow one's nose down a street and, turning corners, become hopelessly lost. You can go literally miles out of your way trying to find your starting point. I didn't know that yet; my priority was to soak up all the sensations of my new neighborhood. I was conscious of the very air of Paris as it entered my body, giving an energy to my walk that seemed to lift my spirit with every step.

And then I saw it: a sign said "Boulangerie et Pâtisserie." The purpose of that shop was obvious even though I didn't know the meaning of those words. The window held trays of the most exquisite pastries laid out in gleaming rows. I gazed at them longingly. The sight was truly a dream, and even from where I stood on the pavement outside, their aroma made my mouth water. I walked in. The shop was crowded and busy. There was suddenly a great silence from all the customers in blacks and browns and navy blues: everyone stared at this strange little creature in a pink coat!

When I approached the counter to reexamine the trays and buy something, I was struck yet again by the fact that I didn't know any French with which to give my order. I embarrassingly pointed to whatever pastry first caught my eye and held up two fingers. Somehow I gleaned that I needed to go to the *caisse* (cashier) to pay as I was given a piece of paper with numbers on it. I was then gently moved in the right direction and opened my purse for the *caisse* to remove the correct coins for my purchase, which she did, diligently. People were still staring but not in a mean way. Even so, I left as fast as I could. *Dear God, what have I done?* I thought. *No one understands one word I say. I could drop dead right now, and how could anyone know I came from San Francisco? I could get sick and die and no one back home would ever know!* I rushed back to the safety of the Pension Muette in time for the lunch gong. The meal wasn't the same as our everyday fare but was special because it was a Sunday; I didn't know until much later when I had learned more about French cuisine just how glorious our Sunday lunches had been.

As promised, the afternoon would be spent learning the *métro* system with my new English friend, who mercifully spoke my own language. Richard showed me a little book, which he said was to be my bible in Paris—indeed it was, and remains so to this day. He showed me how I could look up any street alphabetically and could then find which arrondissement the street was in, the *métro* station from which to commence my journey, and the name of the station where I should disembark. Taking me into a *métro* station, he explained how I could buy a *carnet* (booklet) of tickets instead of always stopping to buy one at a time and thoughtfully suggested that I travel first class during the most crowded hours and go the more economical second class at other times (a brilliant strategy for those tired legs coming home after class!).

Inside the station, he showed me a magical board that instantly supplied all the information one needed to know to go anywhere in the system. Here, one pressed a button for your destination, such as the Opéra. The board then lit up which line one needed to take plus at what station and the direction (generally, the name of its line's end station) of any other train one might need to change for. This was important as sometimes the walks between *métro* lines were enormous, through long corridors, and one could only pray as one went along that one was following the correct arrows leading to a train going the right way.

Another trick that Richard showed me was how to make my way fully into the train's car before the doors closed. Luckily, my thinness and swiftness served me well at that game.

On board, I discovered that there were seats reserved for veterans (a courtesy that remains to this day). Slowly, the two World Wars were showing me their faces in the most unexpected places.

Richard took me to the Opéra, to Sacré Cœur, to Pigalle and the Champs-Élysées, and past the Tour Eiffel. Clutching my new "bible" and map of Paris, I exhaustedly headed back to the *pension*.

In addition to teaching me all about the *métro*, he introduced me to the weekly booklet *Semaine De Paris* (Paris Week), which listed everything from museum schedules to concert, opera, ballet, and movie listings. He also told me about another valuable resource, the *International Herald Tribune*, a wonderful English-language newspaper! But now that I realized the importance of communication (not the least of which was the necessity of speaking that tongue in Monsieur Staats's class!), I was determined to learn French by as many means I could: from my

—

phrasebook, a French-English dictionary, and *French Without Toil.* (That last book was a joke. It should have been called *Toil Without French.*)

As I anticipated Monday, I felt excited instead of discouraged. I would be starting a long climb. Maybe Leo Staats would help to bring out what I felt bursting inside of me when I danced. Maybe I could make people forget their troubles and bring them magic even if it was brief and ephemeral. (One day, I would know just how fleeting that magic would be, but at the time, I could only look forward to the beginning of a great adventure.)

I learned at the *pension* that I was *"un petit rat,"* as dancers on the lowest level of the ladder were and still are affectionately known in France. However, in Paris I felt honored to have attained even that lowly position within the extraordinary world of ballet.

Paris had long been a mecca for writers, painters, and other creative people from all over the world. Aside from the Paris Opéra (where Russian emigré Leo Staats had been a director and his compatriot Serge Lifar was the current director), the city was home to one of the most prestigious privately owned ballet companies, Le Grand Ballet du Marquis de Cuevas. Every famous dancer in the world was said to have passed through this troupe; and the Marquis de Cuevas himself had an unusual international background—Spanish father, Danish mother—and by the time he created his dance company, American citizenship and had married a Rockefeller (he had the title and she had the money.) Their repertory was intriguingly split between the old Russian School and the new style promoted by Russian emigré George Balanchine. Even back in San Francisco, I had known that de Cuevas's dancers performed works dating back to the time of Diaghilev and that, in fact, some of the sets from the old Ballet Russe de Monte Carlo were still being used for their productions. The choreography for these was lovingly preserved and coached accordingly with regard to style as well as the steps. Yet rumor had it that many of the older dancers had been fired recently so that a young gifted protégé of Balanchine, John Taras, could create a new image for the de Cuevas company, training a corps de ballet to be capable of performing not only the old classics but also such works as Balanchine's *Serenade, Concerto Baroco,* and *Night Shadows.* To perform so sharply hybrid a repertoire, one needed a clean technique, without flourishes, immaculate schooling, good feet, and, above all, the musicality and speed with which to absorb all that choreography. I was determined to become a part of this troupe.

—

As you will recall, I had known John Taras in San Francisco, when he choreographed a ballet I had danced in at the age of fourteen. At that time, he had said, "If you ever grow up and I am somewhere doing something, I'll give you a job." Little did he dream when he said that, that I would take him at his word and that he would become my great mentor. He was, for me, so gifted and talented; I adored him with a childlike adulation that was sacred.

As the Cuevas company was presently away on tour, I would have this period to train (or as I thought, with a wince, to *re*train), to become worthy of my goal. And then, as Monsieur Staats had said, "We will see."

8

The Lessons

I awoke long before Émile was to arrive with my *petit déjeuner*. I tried on at least three different leotards, desperate to discern which might make the best impression. Obviously, the leotard was not what would make me dance better; still, I always tried to dress for class as neatly as I could. I loved chiffon skirts and matching colored ballet sweaters that were imported from England. Unable to come to a decision, I stopped making my selection in favor of doing my hair, which I did very quickly, pulling it back into a style then favored by classical dancers for class: I made a chignon and then covered it with a very fine mesh black hairnet. (In the true classical chignon, one's hair is drawn over the ears and is knotted low on the nape of the neck. It was George Balanchine who began the style for placing dancers' hair higher than the classical chignon as he thought the latter position old-fashioned. I found Balanchine's preference horrendous, one especially unflattering to tall girls or those with a large head.)

My toe shoes were scattered all over the floor, and I combed through them to find the ones that were the most comfortable. Toe shoes were odd creatures that sometimes molded to my feet with great comfort or could be just plain mean, bothering me somewhere; and they never fit consistently. Only a rare few were old friends, and I guarded them with my life.

Then the door opened, and there was Émile, eyes aglitter as he saw me standing on my toes, testing their value. I must have been a strange sight, still in my nightgown with my hair arranged. I felt—and looked—like a sleepwalker. Emile sensed my nervousness and coaxed me to eat all I could to give me strength and to decide on an outfit suitable for class. I could not believe how nervous I was; after all, I had taken class every day of my life for years. However, now I was in Paris, where the caliber was so much higher and more competitive than anything I had known.

At last I was ready to leave and donned my pink coat and my new rubber walking shoes. This time, on my way to such an important destination, I did not look out the windows of my bus as I was already concentrating on what lay ahead of me. I was to learn later that being able to immerse myself in such concentration before class was already preparing me for the mind-set needed for performance.

As I mounted the stairs at the studio, I could hear the chatter of young voices. Monsieur Staats greeted me with a *bonjour* and directed me to a dressing room already occupied by another dancer who, after introducing herself in French, started to speak in school-manner English. Suddenly the maestro's voice boomed out: "Speak only in French, please!"

Luckily, ballet is always taught using French terminology, so it is not a problem to take a class anywhere in the world. Of course in Paris, everything else said in class was in French too. Understanding Monsieur Staats's corrections was my most difficult task of my first class. But I worked very hard that day, and Monsieur Staats informed me after class that I was to work privately with him, twice a week, on variations from the classics. Overjoyed, I was a very happy *petit rat*.

When I was leaving the studio, another pupil—a Filipina woman older than myself—asked me to join her for coffee. I felt really grown-up, picturing myself sitting with her at a Parisian café! I didn't hesitate to accept her invitation. She informed me that she was in Paris to increase her technique and develop a larger dance vocabulary as she was a teacher at a school in Manila. I was delighted to have her as a new friend as she seemed to know who all the best teachers were and where they were teaching. She told me about one in particular, Lubov Egorova, a genuine Russian princess and pupil of Cecchetti, who had been considered one of the three best ballerinas of her time. Madame Egorova had danced with the Maryinsky and Diaghilev companies earlier in the century and had been teaching for several decades; my new friend said she was a great teacher, that her classes were held twice a day, and that all the professional dancers attended them.

I was elated by this information but knew that for a few months at least, I should work only with Monsieur Staats. It was to be a wise decision as later I would encounter many teachers who were very good and yet who each told me something different. I wasn't ready to digest that; I needed to concentrate on moving more effortlessly and on attaining the flexibility and stretch to give me a length of line.

—

Staats's classes were based upon the French School, which in reality was Russian. His instruction had a French flavor, enhanced by a very strong technique: a very relaxed upper body, with *port de bras* used with every step or sequence of steps. For him, the head, arms, legs, body, and even the eyes had to all work together. One never learned the footwork and then the armwork in his class—one was given the entire combination and expected to reproduce it as given. This came easily to me. What was hard for me to attain then was his desired softness of the arms, which ran counter to the teachings of the Balanchine School. There was so much to learn; I felt a bit overwhelmed. But I was determined to soak up all I could.

Very often, ballerinas from the Opéra—young and old alike—would attend Monsieur Staats's class. One incident that I recall occurred when one of these women stood by Monsieur Staats to watch as I did a combination. Monsieur Staats seemed pleased with what I had done and turned to speak with her. They spoke so rapidly that I could not understand a single word; however, I gathered that what the ballerina was saying was not flattering to me, and that Monsieur Staats was arduously countering her comments. I later learned to ignore this kind of thing. Even the best performers may be critiqued pro and con, and one can only grow if one receives honest criticism. Insincere praise is ultimately unhelpful.

These were important classes for me, where I learned to refine my interpretation of all the famous classical variations: their *style,* not just their steps—how to feel them from the inside out, not the outside in. For example, during my first private lessons from Monsieur Staats, he decided we would work on the first act variation from *Giselle.* He couldn't have chosen anything more difficult. As I stood there warmed up and ready to begin, he said, "I will teach you the first steps as Zambelli danced it." Carlotta Zambelli had been a ballerina of the Paris Opéra during the time when Monsieur Staats was dancing there; she had been a precise technician, with an elegance rarely found in the native French dancers of that period. My teacher believed that I had somewhat the same style as Zambelli and demonstrated her style in minutest detail—the placement of the head and arms, and so on—for me to reproduce. He took a full hour to explain to me what he wanted to see and also explained the variation's context within the story of *Giselle.* He had me imagine where the peasants and Albrecht were standing or moving while Giselle danced, and how the ballerina needed to project her loving feelings about him *to* him and her friends as well as to the audience. In that way, the audience would be involved in her experience rather than simply danced at.

Now we were ready for me to try the sequence. I mounted on my pointes and began the first six counts of *ballonés* (bounces) when I heard,

"Stop!" With great patience, Monsieur Staats placed my head and arms where they should be and directed where my eyes should be looking. He continued to correct me as I danced, reminding me, "Here you throw a kiss to Albrecht, your hand touching your lips . . . and then . . . a beautiful gesture to Albrecht." We rehearsed the variation at least ten times. I looked down at my shoe to see blood soaking right through, from a blister developed from all that hopping. Monsieur Staats, seeing this, said, "Enough, *enfant*, tomorrow we work again." We had worked two and a half hours. I was then sent upstairs to be stretched and pulled and relaxed by Monsieur Guichot, a teacher of gymnastics who worked with the dancers to increase their stretches and extensions. I was truly bloodied but unbowed—content, as this kind of lesson was exactly what I had dreamed of.

Monsieur Staats was so very knowledgeable of style and technique and could still dazzlingly demonstrate steps himself, even at seventy-two. He once became angry in class and left his chair to execute five perfect pirouettes, including their preparation as it should be done. With a grunt, he returned to his seat and said, "Now try!" He was perpetually at war with Serge Lifar, another dancer/choreographer working for the Paris Opéra as he felt Lifar was not doing as many ballets as his rival for the Opéra. But he never said anything unkind. He had a sense of humor that I only recognized after several wild scenes in class.

The first was when we started to do turns, and one girl's hair became undone, flying all over her face. Monsieur Staats ran into his office and came tearing back, scissors in hand. Confronting this poor student, he gave chase with the full intention of catching her and cutting off her hair! All through this display, he and the girl exchanged a furious barrage of French that so terrified me that I backed against the barre. Finally, she bolted into the dressing room and barred the door, upon which he nonchalantly returned to us and continued class. Five minutes later, the young lady rejoined us as neat as could be, hair tightly pulled back. I thought I glimpsed a contented smile on Monsieur Staats's face. That was one lesson we all learned!

The second incident was while we were doing a circle of turns. This exercise was done with four girls or boys at a time, each starting from a different corner of the room. The purpose was to reach the next corner within eight bars of music and to continue in a circle, always maintaining the same distance between dancers, for a total of thirty-two bars of music. We had only just commenced the exercise when suddenly Monsieur Staats jumped from his seat and, grasping the long pole that was used to open the studio's high windows, placed himself at the center of the circle.

He began to pirouette very quickly, extending the pole horizontally, and God help any of us if we did not make a perfect circle! I well remembered this lesson when in performance I usually needed to produce at least one kind of a circle each night, under every imaginable condition, including raked stages.

Privately, Monsieur Staats continued to work with me on the classical variations from *Sylvia*, *Faust*, and, of course, *Swan Lake*—the White Swan (Odette) and the Black Swan (Odile), which I had already danced. Sometimes he brought a partner for me so that we could also learn some of the most famous *pas de deux*. This kind of immersion-coaching for a student of my age was, and still is, unheard of in America. One has to understand that those postwar years were very idealistic times in Europe. As long as such ballet masters could make enough money to live on, they would do all they could to create a new generation of dancers. That was all they cared about. There was no such thing as an adults-only ballet class; furthermore, Monsieur Staats only accepted pupils who had demonstrated the possibility of becoming professional. Under his tutelage, it was being drilled into me that one must, when the time comes, give back to one's art by carrying the torch to the next generation. Ballet is one art that cannot be learned from a book or video. Even in our technologically advanced times, videos might be sent to ballet companies so that their dancers can try to learn the steps of an unfamiliar work, but still someone who has danced in or otherwise knows the ballet needs to come to fine-tune the actual performance of it. In our private lessons, Monsieur Staats shared with me an invaluable treasury of his own experiences with the great classics and their long-retired early-twentieth-century stellar performers.

After two months of instruction with him, I felt it was time to venture out of the nest. I wanted to work with Madame Egorova, so highly praised had she been by that teacher from Manila. Her studio, at 15 Rue de Rochefoucauld, was small but sufficient so long as there were no more than twenty students in a class. My first impression was love at first sight. The class was so well put together, designed to build muscles with each exercise given in the correct order. We were not allowed to look in the mirrors in her class; it was used only for correction. Madame Egorova was the youngest of my teachers so far, at about seventy-two.

At the center of the room, she always made two groups of girls and one of boys, positioning each person as she wished in a very personal ranking system. Obviously, if *étoiles* of the Opéra were present—Lycette Darsonval, say, or Nina Vyroubova, who were both highly regarded première danseuses—they would be the first to be selected for the first line of group one. When I initially came to class, to my amazement Madame

Egorova beckoned me, "*Venez, ma petite*" ("Come, my little one"), and placed me in the first group, in the second line. I felt a bond between us from my first moment at the barre, where she corrected me continually, pressing my shoulders down, lifting my leg higher, stretching my back further than I thought I could go, and patting me, which gave me a sense of accomplishment. And I needed that encouragement. It was very daunting to be in the first group, where everyone else could see me.

In her thick shoes, she showed us all the movements, announcing each element of terminology as she physically marked it out and then asking one of her favorites to demonstrate it. There was one point in class when we would do, four girls at a time, a *grand tour*. This was a difficult combination that combined turns in various positions, with quick changes from one to the other. I didn't realize that everyone who was a regular waited for this moment, leaning sardonically against the barre as they judged the newcomers whom they didn't expect to get through it on the first try. Not knowing this, somehow I managed, and the class applauded. It was a combination I had never done before, and my execution was by no means perfect, but I didn't stop or fall. I noted that some of the students didn't even attempt this combination; for those, Madame Egorova would create a simpler sequence of steps to build their strength toward one day doing the full sequence.

After our turns were done, she gave us a long adagio. It was at this moment, in my first class, that I danced with my soul. Again, she did not treat this as merely a set of steps but engaged our feelings about what we were doing, saying such things as, "Think of arabesque"; "Pull it out from your heart"; "Continue"; "Don't stop"; "More"; and then run off the stage! She gave me that wonderful ingredient called inspiration. I was to learn that in each class, an adagio sequence always followed turns. While each adagio was different, for a week of classes it would contain the same concept of a step, each day exploring it in another way. This taught us a vast classical vocabulary of how even the same basic steps might be executed differently.

It was hard to imagine that this incredible lady had been one of the three principal ballerinas of the Maryinsky in the time of the tsar. Her circumstances in Paris were hardly deluxe, especially for a princess. Sometimes in the middle of class, Prince Troubetzkoy would come in and ask her if he should buy tomatoes or some other mundane question. He was Madame Egorova's husband, who, like her, had seen better times. He did no work, except to collect, occasionally, a pupil's tuition. I think he also did all their cooking.

—

Madame Egorova had left Russia in 1917, during a period when many people of royal or aristocratic classes had fled for their lives. Even as a sexagenarian, she held herself in a proud posture. There was something about her that one couldn't learn from a male teacher, especially as regarded *pointe* work. She had a gift too for bringing out nuances that would develop our individual technique to project charm, expression, and love. Yes, love—if she felt that a student did not love to dance, she would ignore the person during class and then tell him or her kindly to not attend the morning professional class.

She worked privately, twice a week, with Nina Vyroubova and was looking to take on another younger private pupil. To my great joy, it was me. How could I fail not to be well-trained! I had to juggle my classes around to be able to meet with her, but of course I made time for her.

In my first private lesson with her, she held my face in her hands and said, "I must break your self-consciousness because of your muscular legs. Many Russian ballerinas have your build, but you are young, and it will change. Do not come to class in silk tights, until summer. Now it is cold, and you could jeopardize your legs. It is important to raise your eyes and know everyone has something that is not perfect, but not many have the passion you show me when you dance." What tremendous courage she gave me! She understood me, which freed me. She fully supported my intensity; in fact, one day when I went to pay her after a class, she refused it, saying, "Mangez une steak, you look too thin, and you need it for such hard work." And this was a woman who taught maybe four classes a day to survive, working by a wood stove heater with gloves on her hands during the winter. She had such compassion.

I made immense progress under her tutelage and from the general atmosphere of her classes. I shall never forget the time when, in regular class after I had performed a variation, Nina Vryoubova offered a correction. I adored her as not only was she a beautiful ballerina but also a beautiful human being. Like our teacher, she also thought I would do my best with a helping word, which she would generously provide.

There was only one danger associated with studying with Madame Egorova. I had to pass a bakery on my way to and from her studio. What torture! The aroma of croissants or *pain au chocolat* fresh from the oven, so hot that the *chocolat* would still be melting as you put it into your mouth. One day, I succumbed, darting into the bakery to purchase one of those tempting goodies, which I had to consume quickly and surreptitiously as the studio was very near and I did not want to be spotted eating sweets. With great relief and self-satisfaction, I arrived for class believing I'd beat the devil, or so I'd thought. But as class began, Madame Egorova remarked, "How was your *pain au chocolat?*" To my shame, I only then discovered that the evidence had remained on my cheek! But she was amused as I was not alone in this clandestine ritual.

It was so inspiring to watch the *étoiles* who dropped by to take class. Very often, we saw Serge Lifar, Roland Petit, and the latter's wife, Zizi Jeanmaire. We all had our favorites; meanwhile, the stars themselves enjoyed the chance to work among the younger talent just on the horizon.

During this period, I also took some classes with Olga Preobrazhenska, who had been the tsar's favorite ballerina; in her twenty-five years in the St. Petersburg Imperial Ballet, she had danced more than seven hundred times! Now, she was teaching at Salle Wacker, where studios could be rented and where many illustrious teachers gave instruction. She was seventy-nine years old when I worked with her, and it was only through working with her that I came to the unfortunate realization that although she was unique and I loved her dearly, I had come to her too late. Sometimes she would say, "Arms up," and then say, "Why are your arms there?" forgetting what she had shown or said. I would try to do what she wanted, but age was slowing her mind, and it made me sad, frustrated, and nervous to take a class with her. She had been a wonderful turner in her time, and we clashed over her desire that I turn as a single unit with a very straight back, bent forward slightly to concentrate my weight over my center. For me, it was a disaster: it felt wrongly placed for my body—I had a very Russian back, strong and supple—and this style only stiffened me up and slowed me down. It was difficult to tell whether she was even correctly telling me what she wanted done. Finally, I had to conclude that one could be either an Egorova or a Preobrazhenska pupil but not both. I regretted telling her the white lie that my schedule was too full to continue with her regularly. I truly wished that I could have known her and been taught by her when she had been in better command of her faculties.

Another teacher was Boris Kniaseff, a Russian emigré who had become famous for his *barre à terre* exercises, done lying on the floor. He had strange idiosyncrasies. We would start class ice cold at the barre, without any warm-up, and after maybe two exercises, he would command that we do something strenuous, like a pirouette. This was impossible because our muscles were not properly prepared. His advanced classes—if one survived that far!—included exercises he had devised himself, which began with us lying on the floor doing barrelike motions then rising to a standing position and finally returning to the floor. These were very difficult, and sometimes I would end up in tears, only to be told that everyone felt that way at their first encounter with this regimen. Amazingly, Monsieur Kniaseff's distinctive methods of training strengthened the muscles of those who lacked them and also corrected the bodies of those who had developed muscle in the wrong place. Working on the floor increased our strength by making us use our stomach and back muscles to support us instead of relying on our thighs to carry the burden of our body weight. Once I had mastered the exercises, they proved invaluable, then and later. At Salle Wacker, I teacher-hopped with many other Russian-born masters, such as Victor Gsvosky, and also took class with the renowned French-Armenian teacher Madame Roussane (*née* Rousanne Sarkissian).

Each instructor offered different styles and different corrections. Monsieur Staats succeeded in softening the strong attack of my legs yet without any loss of my strength; Madame Egorova allowed me to lead with my heart, to develop the charm and sparkle that is an essential for certain variations. Interestingly, these teachers never gave me the same variations to work on: Monsieur Staats was most familiar with roles that related to the Paris Opéra, while Madame Egorova with the great Russian classics.

My world became the distance between my *pension* and the studios; I began skipping meals, coming back to my *pension* exhausted and literally drained as taking time for meals would have cut into my classes' schedule. But I was riding on the wave of the great gifts that these teachers were giving to me, working toward the next goal that I envisioned for myself. To achieve it would be no easy matter.

9

La Fille Mal Gardée

After four or five months of living at Pension Muette, I realized that being in the chic sixteenth arrondissement was too far removed from the area of Paris where my classes were and also where the Opéra was. My travel time was long, and one night, when I departed the metro station nearest the pension, a well-dressed older man followed me. I kept my stride even, but when I heard his steps quickening, I held my key in my hand and ran like hell! This disturbing incident brought home that I was living in the wrong place to be coming home late at night.

If I left the *pension*, I would obviously lose the protection of the women in whom my father had placed his trust and would have to ask my father to trust my judgment over that of his friend. In my letter to him, I wrote that I had found a very nice hotel called the Normandy, located at 7 Rue Échelle. It was an expensive establishment, but all the better hotels in Paris had top floors with small inexpensive rooms (originally maids' rooms); for my purposes, such a room would be adequate, and it would allow me to escape the *pension*. A particular advantage of its location was that that it was within close walking distance of the Paris Opéra. But I needed to act quickly if I wanted to move there as vacancies were few and highly coveted.

I told him that I had heard that a San Francisco dancer-friend, a woman older than myself, was thinking of coming to Paris and that she could stay with me: instant chaperone! In that single letter, I gathered all the ammunition that I could to plead for a release, and it worked. I was lucky that my father supported my decision; all he needed to do was teletype his permission for me to leave the *pension*. The bills were settled, and a bereft Emile promised to keep in touch and to follow my progress.

I was quite sad to leave him as aside from his sympathetic nature, he'd actually learned to darn the tips of my toe shoes, which was very difficult as the undersurface of the satin was very stiff with glue but which made the shoes last longer. To this day, dancers usually darn their shoes even before wearing them for the first time. Darned pointes feel better—they are less slippery upon the floor than smooth satin—and they also soften the thudding of the shoes on the floor when they are new. Darning is a truly thankless task that takes time and patience, and one doesn't trust just anyone to touch one's toe shoes. The *sensible* (in the French sense, perceptually sensitive) Emile was a great exception: he was an expert darner, and it thrilled him to be able to do this. He saved me endless time.

I had not exactly lied to my father about obtaining a roommate as I was able to convince Jocelyn Vollmar to join me in Paris. She was a *première danseuse* at the San Francisco Ballet when I first joined their school and had been a friend to me throughout my progress there. I very much admired her dancing but even more her natural selflessness and sweetness—she never had a bad thing to say (frustrating at times!)! I felt so honored to know her, and I could think of no other person who would be so delicious to be with in Paris.

I happily installed myself into my high perch at the Normandy where, throwing open my shutters, I could look out upon people rushing to and from, or just strolling, along avenue de l'Opéra. The heavenly aroma of freshly baked croissants and bread, emitted by the corner bakery, would fill my room—a unique fragrance that one would never forget as long as one lived.

This was a much more commercial area of town than the *pension* had been. I now could walk along the rue Faubourg St. Honoré, window-shopping at all the elegant and expensive clothing, shoes, and jewelry. This was all beyond my pocketbook at that age, but yet it proved productive as it was to develop my appreciation of beautiful things (and, more dangerously, desire for clothing I could *never* afford!). Even when confined to my schoolgirl budget, I began to understand the value of buying one good, costlier article rather than three less expensive ones that might not last or be as well made. And I would also watch for sales. I was within walking distance of the Galeries Lafayette, a quality department store, and they became my home away from home. There, I could find designer clothing in girls' sizes that fit me, and that cost less than adult designer garments. Plus, there was always Monoprix, which was like the Woolworth's of its time. They carried everything: one could buy hairnets,

—

soaps, and all kinds of wonderful, useful merchandise. However, there was no such thing then as a true variety store. If I needed elastic for my toe shoes, I had to find a special shop that sold sewing notions. If I needed shellac, which I used on the inside of the pointes to make them last longer (the original glue stiffening them would soften in time, even with all that protective darning on the outside), I had to seek out a paint store. It was very hard in the beginning to figure out all these finer points of shopping. My colleagues in class, who had the same needs, would sometimes accompany me to the stores or explain what I should ask for and where to go.

There was little time for shopping as in Paris everything, including stores, shut for two hours for lunch—no shopping on one's lunch break!—and, though the shops often stayed open even as late as seven or eight o'clock, those evening hours never coincided with my free time.

Once in a while, I treated myself to the Café de la Paix, where I would of course sit at one of the outside tables to watch the people passing by, as if I belonged there. I could only afford to order coffee as everything was double the price of my regular haunts. But even the coffee was so special in Paris. At night at the café, an African waiter dressed in a red uniform would serve the coffee *pressé*—alas, a sophisticated method one rarely finds in restaurants anymore. *Café pressé*—which involved pushing the grounds, with a kind of plunger, through very hot water in a tall narrow pot called a *cafetière*—tasted very different from ordinary drip coffee, *café filtre*.

Now that I lived at a hotel, I also ate my breakfast out, at cafés. In the morning, everyone drank *café au lait,* which was half strong coffee and half hot milk. I hated hot milk, but even back home, my parents, having come from the Orient, enjoyed their morning coffee the French way. In Paris, I discovered it was difficult to order *café noir* for breakfast—it simply was not done. Waiters would bring me a bit of water to dilute the strength of the black coffee, but I would always find a jug of hot milk on my tray too!

At sixteen, I was very fussy about food. Sadly for me, I excluded unfamiliar delicacies simply for not knowing or daring to discover how delicious they might be—I was not at all adventurous, food-wise. That came much later in life. I was also very conscious of needing to keep to my healthy dancer's diet. In those days, every café or bistro menu featured *prix fixe* selections, complete meals, the most popular being *entrecôte* steak (what Americans would call rib steak), *pommes frites, salade verte,* plus a glass of red wine. Included in the price was *couverture*—a cover charge that paid for one's paper placemat, napkin, silverware, bread, and service. All in all, such a meal cost around a dollar fifty—or more. I started to wire home for money as even when keeping to inexpensive cafés, my cash just seemed to disappear. I learned that it became an amusing event for my father's office staff to gather around to watch the latest teletype from Paris to begin clicking in on their machine: "Dear Daddy, Please send money care of American Express. Lots of love, Janet." Indeed, I became so well known at the American Express office that the teller at the arriving funds window did not even bother to ask my name when I appeared! In all, I received about five hundred dollars a month, and though it may sound like a lot, it really needed to be stretched to cover my expenses.

Sundays, I spent at the Louvre. It was so enormous that, even after months, I had not yet seen all that was there. It was magical to see famous works in the flesh—I remember standing in front of Gainsborough's *Blue Boy*, so overcome that it was an actual painting that tears poured down my cheeks. It was glorious to explore the collections on my own; even without any instruction in the history of art, I began to recognize the different schools of painting. I loved the Impressionists, to whom I felt a natural attraction: Monet, Pissaro, van Gogh, and, of course, Degas, who perfectly captured the essence of the world of ballet. Degas's paintings taught me to study the anatomy of the body as he painted it so well for all to see.

One day, while walking in the sixteenth *arrondisement*, I suddenly came upon a garden where, to the right of the entrance, was a small plaque that read anna pavlova. I entered the garden, and there stood a statue of Pavlova. Nobody was in sight. I kept calling, "Hello!" but to no avail. The garden led to a building that seemed to be open to the public. Timidly, I approached and walked in. To my amazement, it was a small museum dedicated to Pavlova! I spent at least an hour exploring the collection, without once meeting another soul, not even a guard or concierge in sight, despite the wealth of priceless objects in the collection. I felt as if I were dreaming; the overall atmosphere of such beauty and such solitude was so fantastical that I half-expected Cocteau's armed candelabras (of the recent surrealistic film *La Belle et la Bête*, which had made a deep impression on me) to light my way. I couldn't believe I had found this place by accident. I left dazed by what I had seen and returned to my hotel so that I could record this discovery in my journal.

To this day, that museum remains a mystery. I swear, in 1950, it existed. Yet no one seems to know where it is, and I have never been able to find it again as tall buildings that were since erected has so altered the nature of those streets. The museum was a singular jewel amidst the other many incredible sights and experiences from that precious time, which I gobbled up and would stay with me the rest of my life.

I did stand out as I walked about. Very often people would stop to speak to me, trying to converse in French, of course. They seemed amazed that I was alone in Paris, being as I was so young. What had drawn them to me was not that I appeared American, but that I had the bearing and aura unique to ballet dancers and students; understanding the difficulties of a profession so beloved to France, these utter strangers immediately adored me. I had done nothing to deserve this, and it quite took me aback. This was such a change from the general attitude in America, where people thought one was odd for a teenager to give up school dances or football in favor of ballet. Back home, I felt most people couldn't even distinguish between belly dancing and ballet dancing. But now I was in a country where fine arts had been greatly esteemed for centuries before I was born, and where to be a student of dance already set me apart as someone special.

In France, ballet was performed professionally the year round. What a difference from San Francisco, where there was one opera season, a ballet season of perhaps four weeks at the most, and, of course, *The Nutcracker* around Christmas. I looked forward to a day when, in the United States, there would be more opportunities for me to come home as a professional dancer.

Meanwhile, my classes continued. I was completely absorbed in them, without any intrusions. Looking back on that time, I think my progress was thrice what it might have been had I remained in my beloved San Francisco with my family. In Paris, I spent a lonely life for one so young, but the freedom and total concentration more than made up for it. I came away from class each day with more and more to think about. Gradually, I stopped needing to focus on the technical aspects of dance; now, I needed to perfect what I had learned, to refine it to the point of appearing totally effortless. It was a struggle to attain not only an illusion of ease but also genuine relaxation of my muscles, after having strived throughout my San Francisco training, to attack my movements with a visible thrust of power. But I continued to trust in M. Staats's judgment and passionately pursued all that he asked of me.

One evening, as I was finishing a class with him, he told me to dress immediately while he called a cab. He handed me a ticket to the Opéra-Comique, said, "Until tomorrow," and kissed me on both cheeks. I had only enough time to reach the theater; in the taxi, I undid my hair so that it fell into a pigtail down my back and luckily found a black velvet ribbon in my ballet bag, which I fashioned into a bow at my nape, the best I could do toward looking dressed up on such short notice. When I arrived at my destination, I paid the driver and rushed through the entrance of that glorious, prestigious old theater that I had never been inside before. The audience was already seated. In the few moments before the lights dimmed, I sat entranced, looking about at the splendid appointments of the auditorium. I felt excitement all around me; I sensed that this was a special occasion. I had been in such a rush that I had had no time to buy a program, so I had no idea what I was to see.

Suddenly, I felt that special magic of sitting in a theater as an audience hushes, the lights dim, and the conductor makes his way to the podium to take a bow. There is even a special smell possessed by only a theater. In such a moment, all one's senses tingle in anticipation of something that will transport one's soul and flood one's senses, taking one out of oneself and yet making one more oneself, all at the same time.

The curtain opened on a scene of a fashionable Parisian café of the 1890s. Onstage there was great activity, dancers in elegant period street clothing coming and going, characters portraying waiters carrying their trays about while other characters as their customers sat at various tables, miming that they were drinking and conversing. Then, a vision of beauty appeared: a glove-seller. This dancer wore a beautiful red velvet dress, long white gloves, and a flower in her hair. She danced a charming sequence with a very handsome *danseur* dressed as an officer, in white and gold. When they finished their variation, suddenly at center stage out popped a short, slight man holding a suitcase in each hand. He came forward in such a flurry of quick and precise footwork that I couldn't believe what I was seeing. I had never seen a dancer so totally involved in a role, not only with his feet but also with his entire being. This man's presentation had an aura that held not only myself but also the entire audience spellbound on the edge of its seat. When his dance concluded, everyone around me shouted, "Bravo, massine!" Now I understood what the excitement in the house had been all about: it was the famous Leonide Massine's sixtieth birthday, and this was a gala in his honor! I didn't need a program to come to that conclusion as I had read so much about him and gazed at so many photos of him—and now here he was, as if he had stepped out of one of my ballet books! He was of course playing the Peruvian in *Gaîté Parisienne*, his own creation! It was so thrilling to see him in live performance as he was at that time semi-retired as a dancer, pursuing active career as a choreographer staging his own works all around the world. How lucky I was to have had this inspiring interlude within all my hard work, which gave me the feeling that everything I loved was right here in Paris.

I awaited the arrival of Jocelyn with great anticipation. At last, she was there—and our priority became to find another hotel room for the two of us. We explored the streets near the Opéra and finally located, just across from an expensive hotel called the Manchester on rue Périgord, the smaller and cheaper Hotel Périgord and installed ourselves there. It was far from deluxe, but our room was light and airy and served our needs. We were, of course, on the top floor, but this hotel at least had an *ascenseur* (elevator). When just the two of us boarded with our ballet bags, we just fit! It was a wrought-iron cage rather than solid-walled, and we immediately named it "the Casket." We also discovered one day that we had a voyeur living across from us, when we looked out to see him enjoying our underwear-clad bodies! It was so wonderful to have someone to giggle with over such experiences that were I there alone might have felt so much more sinister.

Jocelyn joined me in some of my classes but also went on her own to the Salle Wacker to work with other teachers. It was summer, and the Cuevas Company was still away. Unlike in the States, we discovered that many businesses and shops in Paris began to close their doors come July, when their employees went on vacation en masse. This rampant shutdown definitely affected the world of dance.

I was determined to work with Madame Mathilde Kchessinska, a Polish-born teacher who had been another favorite dancer of the tsar. In private life, she was the mistress of Grand Duke André, the tsar's nephew. In her prime, she had been a wonderful technician, the first Russian dancer to perform the thirty-two fouettés in *Swan Lake*; now, she was very old, and I didn't want to miss my chance to learn from her. Alas, many of the great teachers took the summer off. Somehow, I came up with the idea to go to Madame Kchessinska's studio and just ring her bell in hopes of finding her in. Off I marched to her studio on avenue Mozart. Who must have been more surprised—I, that she answered the door herself, or she, to find me on her doorstep? As I'd suspected would be the case, she patiently explained to me that her studio was closed for the summer. I pleaded with tears in my eyes, for her to let Jocelyn and I take at least one private lesson from her. Finally, she agreed to an appointment with us at 3:00 pm the following day.

I was elated to think that by the next evening, I would have managed to tap into the invaluable experience of all three of the tsar's favorite ballerinas! Madame Kchessinska, however, was not in the same financial straits as the others appeared to be. She lived in the best arrondissement and had a studio in her own comfortable home (quite a difference from having a home in one's studio). Jocelyn and I were thrilled that we would have the unique honor of her accepting us as students while her studio was officially closed.

The next day, we showed up at the appointed hour. Her sunny studio had a special atmosphere all its own, and our excitement mounted as we changed into our practice clothes. We started class, but then suddenly Jocelyn felt ill. Madame made her lie down and continued with me. I felt sorry for Jocelyn, who had so looked forward to this afternoon but couldn't help feeling pleased that Madame continued the class just for me.

She wore a black silk dress, and on her feet were fuzzy slippers. At first sight, it was hard to believe that she was still able to teach as she seemed so much older than Mesdames Egorova or Preobrazhenska. She gave very strong barre work, much of it involving motion at great speed. She ended this section of class with wonderful stretches that were very long and beautiful. Then we went to the center, where she demonstrated what she wanted through very slight hand gestures, always asking me if I understood. She wanted very strong technique from me but also demanded more style and expression, reminding me that all movement had to have expression, that technique was simply a set of tools to be used and interpolated into beautiful movement. I was very impressed by her and listened closely to every word. She ended the lesson by showing me how to make a *reverence* as a ballerina should.

I remember every facet of this lesson acutely, to this day. There she was, in her fluffy bedroom slippers, somehow no longer an old lady at all. While she taught me, she became enchanted, vividly reliving her experiences on the imperial stage of the Maryinsky Theater. Most memorably, she demonstrated all the finer points of making curtain calls: First, she showed me how to accept flowers; then she walked to the right, which, in a theater, would be stage right, and bowed, explaining that that was where the imperial box was; then she moved to the far left to bow again, saying that this was where the grand dukes' box was. Moving to the center, she made a great bow to her imaginary audience. Next was how to bow if I had a partner onstage with me. Last but not least, she put down the imaginary bouquet of flowers that she had held throughout the other bows. Saying, "Now, slowly come forward, then run, and with both arms upraised acknowledge the balcony then back up and do it again, and if there are still shouts of 'Bravo!' run forward and circle your arms to the whole house before you drop to one knee with one hand on your heart."

Years later when I became a ballerina, one critic wrote that my *reverences* were truly elegant and something that other dancers should watch. When I danced a season with the San Francisco Ballet, dancer/ballet master Terry Westmorland from the Royal Ballet was there and said that every girl should watch my *reverence*.

I must say that following a dramatic ballet, my *reverence* needed to be different; it would be inappropriate to do a full classical bow. However, it is a very personal gesture, and I am ever aware that I developed my own style for it through that precious afternoon's contact with Madame, who taught me that I too appreciate and love my audience.

When my lesson ended, I asked if I could come back again when I was in Paris. She kissed me and seemed very happy with me. I sent her flowers the next day, thanking her for making the exception when her studio had been closed but most of all thanking her for all that she had given me on that afternoon, just the two of us together, reliving the glories of her past. To this day I think upon her with great reverence.

At just about that same time, Le Grand Ballet du Marquis de Cuevas returned briefly to Paris before temporarily disbanding for their holidays. John Taras met with Jocelyn and me and was agreeable to taking us both into the company when they reconvened after vacation time. We were overjoyed and felt that we too could take some time off to see other places.

We decided to travel by train to Switzerland, where we ended up in a small unknown village called Gstaad. Little would I have guessed that, fifteen years later, it would become a very chic vacation spot. We were on a very strict budget, but everything was so exciting that just being there at all kept us enthralled. The sheer beauty of Gstaad was unbelievable. One time, just to better take in the view and not to ski, we rode a chair lift to the top of a mountain. When we started, it was quite warm (it was summer), but as we were to discover only once we were at the mercy of the lift, the higher the altitude, the lower the temperature! By the time we reached the top, we were nearly too frozen to enjoy ourselves. With that one exception, our time there was lovely.

We then decided to head south, to the Côte d'Azure. We homed in on Cannes and stayed there at a small hotel run by a charming Dutch gentleman. When we arrived, the harbor area was filled with American naval officers and sailors. We were delighted to have a room that overlooked the U.S. ships docked at the port.

My father was not at all pleased that I was gallivanting abroad. There were rumors of an impending war with Korea that would involve the United States. His bankers were advising him that I return to America as quickly as possible. But our concierge offered a most practical counter-argument: so long as the U.S. seventh fleet was in port, we had no worries. It was if they *left* that, one could be sure a war had begun! Thus reassured, Jocelyn and I stayed on.

—

Ever aware of the international tensions, we would go to our room's balcony as soon as we awoke to check that the fleet was still serenely gathered below us. But one morning, I opened the balcony doors and—no fleet. Jocelyn and I looked at each other in despair, knowing what would follow.

Though America was now at war, we still didn't see why we needed to leave Europe. Still, my father put his foot down and insisted that I return home immediately. I packed my bags and tearfully left Jocelyn, vowing that I would come back.

Upon arriving home, I became so distraught over having severed my European studies that I took on an air of a tragic figure, a Sarah Bernhardt performance! I felt my father was absolutely wrong to put a stop to my classes just as I was so close to realizing my dream. On top of all that, I was in anguish over the knowledge that the de Cuevas Company was going to be in New York in November, only two months' time—how could I join them if I had broken my training? I was so upset over this that I stopped eating and speaking.

I made everyone else in the family so miserable by my behavior that finally my father took pity on me. He said he would pay for me to go to New York if I still felt that way come November. Meanwhile, American Ballet Theater was in San Francisco to perform, and their ballet master Edward Caton, whom I adored, agreed that I could take the company classes. Mr. Caton even offered to pick up the tab for my trip to New York.

When I told my father that, he informed me that I was still underage and that he would remove me bodily from the plane if I attempted to go there without his approval! He reneged on his earlier promise, saying that if I were so unhappy, I should find what I could do about it closer to home. The situation seemed utterly hopeless, compounded by my feelings about the daily classes I was taking with ABT. I feared that the advances Leo Staats and Madame Egorova had made would be lost in classes that were still entrenched in the Balanchine way of teaching.

I settled on taking classes from Lew Christensen, whose teachings were of the Balanchine School, and also with my old instructor Guillermo del Oro, with whom I took a daily class in Spanish-style and character dancing in his small studio on Bush Street. Rather like the Pavlova museum in Paris, the building was hidden by a tiny garden in the middle of downtown San Francisco. The classes were soundly based on the Cecchetti School. Even for character and Spanish dance, exercises were designed to advance in a particular order to strengthen my technique and style.

As I got to know Mr. del Oro, I found it a shame that he was tucked away in such a tiny studio, only earning part of his living from teaching—he also worked part time as an engraver. He was a very gentle person, and his having to struggle for a living touched me. I felt he fully deserved a better place, a legitimate school where he could take students full time. He quite agreed; he said he'd love to have a school where he could educate dancers properly in the Cecchetti Method. I went to my father and spoke so brightly of him that my father met with him. He was so taken with Mr. del Oro that my teacher soon became like a member of the family. Somehow I also convinced my father to advance the money necessary to start a school.

The first step toward realizing my teacher's dream was finding the right building. For many years, there had been a store in town called Visallia Saddles. They sold beautiful handmade leather saddles, made in their own workroom over the shop. We heard that the store owners were thinking of moving the business entirely to Visallia and that the workroom was about to be closed down in preparation for the move. Mr. del Oro had the idea that perhaps we could obtain that upstairs space for a school.

My father and teacher arranged a rendezvous with the gentleman in charge of the building, which was actually owned by the church right next door to it. There was a very long stairway—forty steps—to the upstairs room. As we started to ascend, I sensed an atmosphere that felt very old-world European. Then we saw it. Before our eyes was a huge room filled with workmen working on saddles. The ceilings were enormously high, and there were windows all the way up on the walls along two sides of the room, serving almost as skylights. For some reason, there was a small raised area that to me looked perfect for a stage. Mr. del Oro and I simultaneously turned to look at the floor and then at each other—it was wooden, just right for a classroom. Even though filled with leather goods, horse-shaped structures that served as a saddle equivalent of dress forms, and workmen, our first impression was breathtaking: we immediately saw a dance studio of formidable size, light, air, and atmosphere!

We were delighted to learn that there was a second room that could provide a second studio and living quarters for Mr. del Oro. We told the man that we were very interested in renting the entire floor.

My father was a businessman, after all, and wanted to be sure that this would be a sound investment. He asked Mr. del Oro for a detailed plan: what did he estimate it would cost to refinish the floors for use as a dance surface, and what else would he need to buy to outfit the space as a studio: barres, mirrors, etc. (a desk for the front room would eventually be donated *gratis* from my father's office.)?

Obviously, though he saw a future in the school and personally liked Mr. del Oro very much, my father had an ulterior motive in all this. He thought that the creation of this school would be an incentive for me to stay in San Francisco—as a teacher! Mr. del Oro told my father plainly that I was too young to teach, that I needed to dance first. He was totally honest and came up with an intelligent budget for the enterprise that even included a financial clause that guaranteed his support for the first several months until the school could survive on its own! My father was totally won over and advanced the money.

Mr. del Oro did all the planning of the interior details himself, creating from that already incredible space a dream of a studio. He named it the Academy of Ballet.

I was very happy for him, but I had no intention of not going to New York for the priceless opportunity of working with many different teachers in (what I then thought) so many different styles.

10

New York

The Marquis de Cuevas Ballet was coming to New York, and Mr. Taras had remembered his promise: he sent me a cable to come for the season. He wanted me to become familiar with their repertoire. My father gave in, and ticket in hand, I boarded the plane for New York all on my own.

Imagine the excitement I felt upon my arrival—to be a part of this city, whose pulse was faster than that of any other place I had known. I checked into the Wellington Hotel, which was then for women only. It was well situated yet not too expensive. Carnegie Hall was only a few blocks away. At that time, the world of Fifty-fifth to Fifty-eight Streets was filled with other young girls: models, actresses, singers, showgirls, many carrying hatboxes that held whatever was needed for their profession. I discovered that I was not so very original with my white one. It singled me out as surely as if I'd had a sign on my back saying "Dancer."

There were about three weeks until the company's arrival; I had allowed myself time to take classes daily from the many teachers who had settled in New York from elsewhere. As in Paris, many had come from the same schooling and the Diaghilev Company. This sharing of training was as if they had descended from the same family tree. It was really unbelievable how many people were teaching then from the same background and yet each with an individual style and personality. Now when I think about this, I realize what a fantastic opportunity I had had, to take classes from all the wonderful names I had hitherto only read about. I studied at the studios of one or two different teachers every day to take advantage of this feast of talent. Mind you, the people with whom

I studied probably said mostly the same things, but each projected a different manner in his or her way of teaching, which was important to me in this phase of my professional development. Ultimately for me, having so many teachers—experiencing so many facets of the same craft—was a way to better develop my own sense of style.

I really loved the class I took with my beloved Edward Caton. He brought out students' love of dance and allowed individual temperament and style while still demanding a clean technique and technical proficiency. He loved it when a student had and really demonstrated expression, which was rare.

New York was not Paris in that the teachers here moved more quickly and with far more distinctive, even quirky, attitudes. Also, in New York, so many people took class without any desire for a career in the ballet world. And so, on the one hand, the level of intensity in class was very high, and yet to be noticed here by one's teacher was an incredible happenstance. I couldn't help but compare this with all of the energy and time that had been given to me as an individual by my teachers in Paris.

For example, when I took Anthony Tudor's class, he stopped and wiggled his finger at me, telling me to come forward. I did so rather timidly. He then asked me what school I came from. I said San Francisco Ballet (which did not seem to impress him) and then added, "Egorova." That seemed to please him, and he then told me that my style was very good, but it was not for everything. I was only eighteen years old, and how on earth could I have deciphered such a remark? I still can't, to this day! His comment was not helpful and had been spoken in a manner that terrified me. As a matter of fact, the one constant element that stands out about class with almost anyone in New York was the apparent goal to terrify the students. Could it have been the competitiveness in New York that encouraged teachers to not only challenge but also threaten dancers? It was as if we had to go through fire, and then if we survived, all was well, and we were treated better. To me, this attitude was idiotic, and I had little patience with it.

Thankfully, this was a busman's holiday for me, and not every teacher behaved that way. Two of the "outside" teachers who taught in studios not connected with schools were really marvelous to me. Celli, who was Italian, taught very different classes, technically speaking (they were hard on the legs and built muscles), and I have kept his lessons with me throughout my life of dance. He was very kind with me but strict and demanding toward the others. This is not to say he was soft on me: he liked my work and expected that I would fulfill what he asked of me.

—

One teacher who initially confused me with a correction was Margaret Craske. Only later, when I was back in Paris, did I understand what she meant when she had constantly told me not to use all my technique. She said that you could use far less as you have so much you can throw it away. Again, at that age, I didn't understand such a comment, which didn't seem to speak to what I felt I needed to hear. Later, I knew that what she had meant was that I should dance with more ease. But, at the time, it was confusing advice to be told not to use my technique; to have been told to show less effort and less attack would have been more useful to me. But her words entered my mind and stayed with me, even in the face of conflicting instruction by so many other teachers who loved to see a strong technique and made me overuse it.

Margaret Craske and I had quite another kind of misunderstanding one day, which I sensed might have worked a wee bit to my advantage. One night, I went into a vegetarian restaurant, even though I was absolutely dying for a steak. The only reason I was there was that it was so much less expensive to eat there—I couldn't afford a restaurant that served meat. Who should enter but my teacher. She was delighted to see me eating a vegetarian meal, and I felt that she had mentally ticked off an extra point in my favor. Had she only known the truth!

I loved one instructor who used her teaching studio to live in. This was Tatiana Chamié. She would still be clearing the breakfast dishes as we arrived to prepare for class. Even the smell of toast and coffee was still in the air as we entered the studio! Perhaps it was this coziness on top of her kindness, but I felt more at home there than anywhere in the city. Mr. Denham often came by to watch her class, and she very much wanted him to see me dance. Indeed, he did and made me the offer to enter the Ballet Russe de Monte Carlo in their 1951-1952 U.S. tour. Sadly, I had already given my word to Mr. Taras and had to turn down the invitation.

At last, the Marquis de Cuevas Ballet arrived in town. I met up with the several friends I knew with them and decided to share a room with one of the dancers. Jocelyn would also be staying at the same hotel, so this arrangement would be much less costly for me. As soon as we moved in, we saw cockroaches parading in our bathroom; the next day, we moved to a different hotel, into a less luxurious room but one with a bit more cleanliness to it. This was not the easiest way to exist in the city; New York hotels in that price range were just not clean and charming! A room was a place where we put our heads down at night and where we washed our tights—but where we didn't stay, unless we had to.

We made up for our shabby digs with occasional forays to wonderfully atmospheric restaurants. My favorite place was Schrafft's, an old-fashioned tea room where at any hour one could order breakfast, lunch, or dinner. That was my favorite hangout. But, also, now that the de Cuevas Company had arrived, we went to the Russian Tea Room for dinner after several performances, and the Marquis or John Taras picked up the check. This restaurant was to prove important later in life, a place where I met so many people. It was like belonging to the best club in New York. And, if you were a dancer, you were treated very well; they loved our being there.

Even while I was thrilled that the de Cuevas Company was in New York, I still found time to take classes elsewhere. I decided to try the School of American Ballet. The two Russian secretaries looked me over and said nobody from outside it took company class. At that point, Muriel Stuart came to my rescue, overriding policy to order the secretaries to permit me and one other French girl she had seen backstage to take all of the company's classes that we could manage! My first class there was with Pierre Vladimiroff; I was in pure ecstasy. It was very much like what my prior schooling had been. At one point, he asked me to come forward and demonstrate a combination he had given, one with many beats and fast footwork. The two secretaries stood waiting at the door, watching. When I finished, everyone applauded, and he said, "You can see she is from my teacher, Egorova." Here I was, in the most standoffish ballet school in New York, being treated as a soloist! I was given a bit of space after that to change my clothes in the dressing room.

There, I also took Anatole Oboukhoff's class, which was a very difficult one, demanding of one's strength. He expected to see a full out command of technique, not to mention sheer endurance. His combinations were full of difficult steps that required a particular kind of forcefulness. In short, he was a better teacher for male dancers. In my first class, he stood in front of me during the barre work and suddenly clicked his fingers in front of my face. I thought it odd, and laughed. He stopped, obviously realizing that I was not intimidated by him. After that, he had me dance with each and every group working at center. As each group was comprised of less than a dozen students at a time, I really had a workout. The next day, my muscles were so sore that I could hardly walk.

Another memorable class was with Felia Doubrovska, who was married to dancer Pierre Vladimirov; both were teachers at the School of American Ballet. It was said that she had been fabulous in her time, and I could believe it. She always entered the room wearing a chiffon skirt over her beautiful long legs. She was not young but had a childlike air and always sang out a "Bonjour!" as she arrived—she was divine! Her classes had great style, and she calmly gave instructions to improve our ways of doing things that were even quite ordinary. I think, for us girls, it was just wonderful to breathe the same air as her. This was what teaching was about. Her aura gave us the inspiration to develop our own respective auras. What a great ballerina!

In addition to taking this panorama of classes, I stayed backstage at the theater where the de Cuevas company was based: Mr. Taras had told me to become familiar with their repertoire by watching them. And so I did that, and also took the company's class every night, longing to actually be dancing with them. (Nijinska, with whom I had studied in Los Angeles, saw me backstage but didn't know why I was there. She greeted me with a great hug and said that she must speak to John Taras about me! I explained that I had already been chosen for the company! I was delighted to see her and realized then how small the ballet world really was.)

I loved being so near and yet so far! I did try to get an idea of the works that they would perform, but there were so many and the company so enormous. The dancers were all very nice to me and seemed to admire good dancing. Everyone in the company eventually mingled backstage, creating an exciting atmosphere of artists conversing in French, English, and Russian. And to think I would be a part of this incredible band of dancers! It was like a dream.

But, finally, the season drew to an end. We were all told to come to a meeting. Little did we imagine that with all the success the company had had in New York and the glamour galore that there always was about the troupe, we were on the brink of a catastrophe.

Mr. Taras was present at that meeting, as was Edward Perper. He was related to Sol Hurok, who was managing the company's appearances in America. We were told that the company could only continue on a very small amount of money, and for only one year. Although the company was considered French, what with the Marquis being married to a Rockefeller, the feeling was that our financing should come from America. However, the U.S. Department of Treasury very much considered our company a foreign concern and placed a ceiling ($25,000 per year) on what the Marquis's wife could contribute to us in American funds. We were therefore asked to take a very small salary while based in Paris to try to continue, though of course any touring would be more costly. We would also get a new manager, Ben Carlin, who would capably oversee any financial decisions. It was now up to us dancers to say whether we would work for so little pay in the coming year.

Our main concern was the future of the company; we were stricken with grief and disappointment, to think that even with this sacrifice on our part, the stage might go dark in a year's time. The undeniable shakiness of our financial situation was a shock to everyone. Agreeing to the salary cut was not too difficult on the French dancers as most of them would live at home when Paris was our chief domain. There were few Americans or dancers of other nationalities, and we too voted to continue. Whatever I would be paid, it was to my great joy that I was now a true member of the Grand Ballet de Marquis de Cuevas!

Everyone was to return home for a week's break at Christmas, after which we would convene in Paris on January 7, 1951. In spite of the company's financial problems, I looked forward to my new adventure!

11

Paris Encore

Jocelyn and I arrived in Paris as planned to join the other dancers before we were to leave for Cannes, where the company would rehearse before the start of the season at the Casino. Of course, we were anxious to let Mr. Taras know of our arrival. We were told he was holding auditions at the Salle Pleyel for the few places that were vacant. We were also informed that he had fired many of the older dancers with the intention of making a corps de ballet with a higher level of technique than had existed there before. This was rather a scandal in Paris, but he held the reins and had the audacity to accomplish such visions.

We reached the Salle Pleyel just in time to see the end of this audition. I must say I was very happy not to have to audition: the girls crowded into the room were told to finish off with thirty-two *fouettés*— what a full-fledged ballerina might be asked to demonstrate (they are best known as the show-topping sequence of whiplike pirouettes performed by the Black Swan in *Swan Lake*) but not ordinarily something expected of applicants for positions in only the corps! Especially within the already tense situation of an audition, many of the girls fell off pointe and could not make it through to the end. I am sure Mr. Taras just did it to be wicked! The girls appeared downright happy to be dismissed after that although some were asked to stay.

At the conclusion of the audition, Jocelyn and I finally had the chance to kiss him on both cheeks and say hello. The other dancers from the company then showed up to read the postings on our board, concerning our departure from Paris to Cannes. We were to leave by train the next day from Gare St-Lazare. All our orders were spelled out on the board. Jocelyn and I bid Mr. Taras good-bye and returned to our hotel.

At that moment, of course, everything seemed marvelous: just to think, at long last, I would finally have the opportunity to dance in this world-famous ballet company, which at that time was considered the best in Europe! What advantages I would gain by learning such a distinguished repertoire that included not only the classics but also Balanchine ballets as well!

It was very hard to sleep that night, but not because of sugarplums dancing in my head. I kept thinking about those thirty-two *fouettés*.

But the following day, my doubts were erased. In the morning, we assembled at the train station with our luggage and hopes and great anticipation. This was not a small company; there were at least fifty members of the corps plus the soloists and principal dancers. The manager collected our passports and gave us our car numbers. Never again have I ever experienced that feeling of pure joy as I did when about to embark on my life's journey. Inside, I thanked God for giving me my wish and was filled with excitement, thinking about the future, about the work that lay ahead of me.

As the train puffed out of Gare St-Lazare, we slowly passed through the outskirts of Paris. I stared out the window at France. In 1951, there was still a great deal of destruction from the war, signs of the bombings. It shocked me as it seemed as if the war had been over so long ago. I pondered upon all those people who had once lived in those farmhouses that were now without a roof, the people who were still struggling to get back to their lives even as I was just beginning mine. For me, this was a Europe rising from the ashes, a time of promise.

At long last, we arrived in the south of France. The change was immediate and formidable. It was much warmer than Paris, and the people there seemed more lighthearted, less serious. The scenery enchanted me, and to this day, it makes my heart skip a beat when I go to Monte Carlo or Cannes. The region is a dream setting, with its blue waters and promenade and villas dotting the hillsides. At that time, there was not one high-rise apartment building as there is now.

Finally, we pulled into the station at Cannes and, reunited with our luggage, were assigned hotels and roommates. Jocelyn was going to be at my hotel. During our journey, I had already become very attached to another wonderful dancer who had trained with the Royal Ballet in England. Her name was Ruth Helfgott, which had been changed to Ruth Galene. Her parents had left Berlin in 1938 just in time to escape Hitler's master plan. They had emigrated to Australia and settled in Sydney.

—

There, Ruth had studied and danced with Edouard Borovansky, who had his own company. By chance, the Ballet Rambert, based in London, had come on tour to Sydney; Marie Rambert saw Ruth there and asked her to join the company. Ruth did so with great happiness as she knew Europe offered the best opportunities for advancement. In London, she studied with Volkova and then went to Paris. Although Roland Petit wanted her for the Ballet de Paris, she decided instead to spend a year studying with the same Russian School of teachers that I had encountered in Paris, concentrating upon working with Madame Olga Preobrajenska and Victor Gsvosky. While in Preobrajenska's class, she met Rosella Hightower, who was also taking class there, and Rosella arranged for her to audition with John Taras for the de Cuevas Company. She had a great deal of culture and intelligence, was very well read and very musical—we would often philosophize about things and analyze matters together, and, of course, had many wonderful conversations about dance, being as our minds and hearts were so utterly absorbed with it. Plus she had a marvelous sense of humor that was to frequently come to my aid: she would suffer along with me but also laugh with me. She was a perfect companion. Jocelyn (who was higher than we were in the company, a full ballerina), Ruth, and I quickly became close, the "Three Musketeers." It was a tremendous boon for me to have these two dancers as my friends.

We were given the first night off and set out to know Cannes. In 1951, it was a small but very active city. We searched for a nice restaurant as we had not eaten all day. One looked better than the others—our noses actually led us to it. The proprietors couldn't have been nicer, and we ordered *pommes frites,* which we all adored (never would I eat French fries in America, which have no resemblance to *pommes frites!*). Very pleased with ourselves, we then found a lovely café where we took our coffee. We felt very French indeed!

The next morning, we found our hotel was within walking distance of the theater. We already had our practice clothes in hand (it was company policy for the dancers to always carry one set of practice clothes separate from our suitcases in case luggage was lost or delayed in transit).

In the next few weeks, I learned many ballets very quickly. Most of the other dancers had performed with the company and thus were already familiar with the productions; I had to push hard to ingest so much choreography. I was immediately given some demi-soloist roles, the first being one of the four little swans in *Swan Lake.* Ruth was also a cygnet; the other two were Solange Galovine and an American girl named Dolores Starr. We had to move as one even though we were four: not only feet but heads and even eyes danced in absolute precision. This Dance

112

of the Cygnets is a test for the technical strength of any company, and usually the audience loves the piece—it is something of a showstopper if it is done well. Breaking down our motions piece by piece, Mr. Taras strove for sharpness and clean technique in our feet; we discovered that keeping our heads in sync was far from easy when their movements needed to be matched with the separate original choreography of steps! We rehearsed it for what felt like a hundred times. Years later, when I taught this, I was so grateful that I had learned it thoroughly; and I was also able to coach it properly so that every head was able to do one thing even while the feet and legs did another. Alas, one rarely sees as sharp and brilliant a Dance of the Cygnets today.

I loved being in *Swan Lake* and was also thrilled to be the first member of the corps on stage. I always stood in the rear wing waiting for the overture to start: the music always inspired me, putting me inside the ballet from the very first note.

The next big classic was *Giselle*. Here too I danced in the corps and also as a demi-soloist. As I had previously danced the role of one of the friends, this ballet drew upon my memory bank. Mr. Taras, on occasion, danced Hilarion, and Jocelyn performed Myrtha in the second act. There is a moment when Myrtha rejects Hilarion and commands her Wilis to send him to his death. In doing this, each girl in turn pushes him down a diagonal path to the rear edge of the floor, where Hilarion then plunges out of sight. Many a time we took advantage of the opportunity to give him a rather hard push.

I also learned *La Sonnambula* and Balanchine's *Concerto Barocco*. I loved to dance the latter as I felt I was dancing it for myself, for the sheer pleasure of its storyless demands of technique. It involved such perfect timing and so many steps (sometimes in opposition to the flow of its music or in counterpoint to other dancers' movements) that it always gave me such satisfaction to accomplish a performance. Yet once Mr. Taras told me that I had too much expression on my face during *Concerto Barocco*! I truly could not understand this as for me the dance brought out only my joy of the movement itself; I did not feel I was putting any expression on my face, except to reveal my love for the dance itself. But he was, of course, operating under the Balanchine concept that one's body was totally an instrument of the choreographer. I still say today that my sheer physical pleasure in the choreography of even this "emotionless" piece could not help but be reflected by my entire body—I was not a zombie!

One other classic work *Les Sylphides* was in the Cannes season. Having danced in that one before, I was at ease with it. Again, Mr. Taras excelled in teaching us every movement correctly, having been a pupil of its originator, Fokine. He made me learn every solo in that ballet so that I would be prepared to replace any soloist. This training was worth its weight in gold. What a contrast to today, when dancers learn this work from videos and are then rehearsed under the supervision of other dancers with little experience of its true heritage. I doubt if I could ever have learned the intricacies of the ballet in such a manner.

As the season in Cannes proceeded, I was learning literally a new work per day. Mr. Taras put me in everything. I didn't face any jealousy; everyone else was always very nice and caring, ever encouraging me: the lovely Helene Sadowvska, with whom I remain in touch; Nora de Wall, a Dutch girl whom I adored. One day, when we were in the dressing room, Nora noticed my vaccination scar, on the side of my thigh. She let out a scream and said, "I have one exactly like yours!" In America, it was very unusual for a baby to be vaccinated on the leg, and even in Europe, most babies were vaccinated on the arm. She asked me where I had received a duplicate of her scar. I remember thinking that she would not even know where Surabaya—my birthplace—was. But, believe it or not, she too had been living in the Dutch East Indies when she received her vaccination from the very same Dutch doctor a few years before I acquired my scar! Somehow this coincidence made us great comrades, and thereafter, Nora was often a help whenever I was unhappy. She was a gifted girl and smart—scar or no scar, I was very fond of her.

The season was in full swing when Paris experienced its grueling cold January and February. People would come to the south of France to do what the French do grandly: enjoy the warm weather, buy beautiful clothes, dine well, and enjoy themselves at the casinos. Going to the ballet was also a tradition of winter. And there was so much for us dancers to see and learn from these seasonal visitors and their favorite southern destinations.

On one of our free days, I decided to treat myself to the hands of a coiffeur. I had ordinarily had a horror of beauty shops as my hair was very curly, especially when wet. With great courage, I took myself to an expensive and reputedly good salon and explained as best I could that I had problem hair. The hairdresser assured me that even in France some people had curly hair, and that it would not be a problem. I sat in the chair feeling extremely worldly. After my wash, he sat me up—this is the point when I would look like a wet curly-haired dog, and even in that salon, my appearance then was no different. At that moment, a great commotion erupted as the Marquis de Cuevas himself walked in for a hair wash and manicure! I tried to sink down in my seat but could not escape the horror of his notice. But he was a gentleman: he simply kissed me on both cheeks with a polite *bonjour,* totally ignoring my discomfort. Aside from my mortification over my hair, it was also a very new experience for me to see men in the same hair salon as women, both sexes equally sharing such visual vulnerability. How advanced the French were in such things! In the end, I was indeed treated very well by my hairdresser, my hair straight and pulled back with a ribbon by the time he had finished with me. I could hardly wait to tell Ruth and Jocelyn of my adventure. When I reenacted the incident, we all cried with laughter.

Life continued with rehearsals, performances, and making the most of every minute of our free time. In that last respect, we didn't behave much differently than the tourists—we were interested in everything Cannes had to offer. It was during this season that our company's manager, Edward Perper, left, to be replaced by a couple from New York: Judy and Ben Carlin. Mr. Carlin was evidently a businessman who, despite knowing little about ballet, was yet enraptured with dance; he was willing and able to keep the company afloat on very little money for that one year when the Marquis could not fund the troupe very much. The Carlins had their work cut out for them, given the size and reputation of the company. Somehow Jocelyn and I began seeing a lot of them—for us, they were Mom and Pop Carlin, our parents away from home. Once they were in daily contact with the dancers, the Carlins began learning about ballet and following various performers' progress, to the degree that they could soon distinguish between the good ones and those less talented. Most of the dancers were hard workers, on top of which we had the challenge that the company had to survive this difficult year if it was to continue. We took our reputation for high quality work very seriously.

Mr. Taras was very strict with us. At the end of every performance, a special notice was put up on the board, indicating "amends" (fines). The money to be deducted from our pay was quite beside the point; it was horrifying to see one's name and for what fault one was being fined posted for all to read. It could have been anything from the end of a toe shoe ribbon sticking out from its knot or a hair out of place to missing a step. Mr. Taras saw everything.

Once when we were doing the first entrance of *Swan Lake,* a true nightmare occurred onstage. As I have written, I was the first girl to enter—twenty-three girls following close behind. We would do a serpentine until all twenty-four of us were in place in lines of four. That placed the four cygnets of the Dance of the Cygnets in the front row; I, being the first, was upstage at the far right. The entrance music needed to be counted in beats by all as everyone then needed to turn and raise their arms at the precise same moment that the soloists did. Lo and behold, twenty-three swans turned to the left, and yours truly turned to the right. When the musical count for our second turn came, and now I was accidentally facing them, to my horror I saw forty-six eyes bulging at my mistake! Of course I quickly assumed the correct position and prayed that John Taras hadn't seen this. Thank God Ruth saw how nervous I was and talked me through the rest of the ensemble under her breath: "Tranquil, Janet, tranquil," trying to calm my grief-stricken face. I managed to continue without further mishap. To this day I think this was one of the most unforgettable mistakes I ever made. When the ballet was over, I anxiously ran to the "amends" board—nothing. No name or fault. I heaved a great sigh of relief, thinking the incident had gone unnoticed. I should have known better as the next day, posted on the rehearsal board, was the notice, "Second Act *Swan Lake*—24 swans' entrance only." There it was—Mr. Taras was sarcastic but not without humor. At the rehearsal, he announced in a loud voice, "Sassoon, another mistake like that and you are fired." I must add that he would never have fired me, but he seemed to like cultivating that kind of Noel Cowardesque quick-tongued sarcastic humor. I seemed to love this kind of personality from a very young age.

Other postings were more pleasant: rehearsal announcements for unfamiliar works. To my delight, my name was posted for a rehearsal of William Dollar's ballet *Constantia*. There was a lot of dancing in this piece, and the music—Chopin's Piano Concerto in F Minor—was divine to dance to. The adagio was performed by Rosella Hightower and George Zoritch. When I would stand in the wings watching that movement, it would move me to tears, though not for long as the final movement was for the entire company. This work was a gem and a delicious ballet for me to participate in; I cannot understand why it has apparently never been performed in America.

Marc Chagall would come to watch class or rehearsal sometimes, and I thought him a nice old man. He would always ruffle my hair with a hearty "Bonjour, petite" (I loved the words but hated having my hair disturbed!). Another occasional visitor was Picasso, who sometimes stood deep in conversation with the Marquis. At that time I thought nothing remarkable about a Chagall or Picasso mingling with us; I only wish now that I had been older at the time to have known better who these men were and to have taken that opportunity to ask them questions about their art. At the time, I simply enjoyed that they were sweet with me, that they called me their "petite fille" and kissed me on both cheeks or patted my head or both. Everything seemed to be going so well for me during those lovely Cannes days.

In addition to my friendship with Jocelyn and Ruth, another dancer I became close to at that time was a girl from New York, Harriet Toby (her surname had been Katzman, but in France it was changed to Toby). She was older than me, but because she recognized my admiration of her, she always let me into her dressing room to chat. She became like an older sister to me. Offstage, her mother never left her side—an absolute ballet mama! Harriet was beautiful, olive skinned, with marvelous legs that had just the right amount of muscle. She had technique and expression both and was headed for stardom. She danced in *Le Moulin Enchanté* (The Enchanted Mill). One day I found her alone and in tears in her dressing room. Everyone else had already left the theater, but I stayed behind to try to find out what was wrong. She sobbed that Mr. Taras had told her that he thought her breasts were larger in her costume than what he cared for in that role! Here again, a dancer was subjected to a subjective caprice. I asked her to show me the bodice. It was shiny satin! As young as I was, I remembered learning from Russell Hartley, when he made the tutus for *The Nutcracker,* to never use satin. It catches the lights and has a tendency to make the dancer's body look fuller. Amazing what learning my craft from the bottom up had taught me! I turned to Harriet and said, "Give me scissors. We will use the wrong side of the fabric." With her help, I refashioned the bodice over the next four hours. When we had finished, she put it on—and the difference was remarkable. She now had a perfect body, with nothing that even Mr. Taras's eye could find fault with. She gave me a hug, and we both knew that from then on she could and would demand that her bodices be made under her personal scrutiny. She was so grateful that I had given her so much of my free time and knowledge while I, in turn, felt a surge of joy. None of us had everything. A perfect body for one person could be totally different for another. At that time, Balanchine was creating a whole new species of dancers, with a preference for tall, very long-limbed girls. Yet in Europe, in the 1950s, this was not the typical or desired body of a dancer. In Europe, artistry and expression was preferred over a statuesque build. As Harriet and I went out for coffee, I rejoiced that she could now dance with the company without developing a needless complex about her body. And her next performance of *Le Moulin Enchanté* was truly magnificent. I watched the *pas de deux* from the wings, fighting back tears. Harriet danced like a dream. I was so happy for her and for the ever more strengthened bonds of our friendship. Then God felt my happiness (as the Chinese would have said, "Don't let him know"), and disaster struck.

After several months there in perfect health, I woke up one night at around 4 am with welts all over me. My lips were swollen to twice their size. I felt miserable. There was no way I could keep this mysterious disability a secret. The Carlins took me to the doctor, who immediately announced, "C'est le foie" (It's the liver). Every disease at that epoch in France was attributed to "Mal de foie"! But obviously, I had had an extreme allergic reaction to something. The problem became more serious as it would disappear only to reappear—usually at 4 am! I could not continue to suffer like this, so the company phoned the best dermatologist they could find, Doctor Professor Michner at the University Hospital in Zurich. I was duly shipped off to Zurich. We all cried as we said good-bye; the dancers all wished me courage. Courage, indeed—I, needed, more than that to go off on my own for expert diagnosis of a disfiguring ailment while still a teenager, on top of the strain of having been pushed to the limit while memorizing so many roles and having to take in a totally foreign lifestyle. The French language was still at this point something of a barrier, and dealing with French food remained a major adjustment. I never told my parents about my collective difficulties because I was sure that my father would have rejoiced over the most current events and demanded my immediate return. All I admitted to him was that I was experiencing some kind of allergy and that the company had given me a break so that I could recover in Switzerland, where I would receive the best care. This was not to be the first lie that I had fed my parents.

Jocelyn, Ruth, and the Carlins all accompanied me to the train station. It was a highly emotional scene. As we embraced, Jocelyn, being her usual positive self, assured me that I would be back in no time and that all would be fine, that it was only a small setback. Ruth echoed this, adding that I would be missed and how much I was loved. The Carlins—Mom and Pop—promised to call and keep me posted on events back in Cannes, reminding me that the company would be picking up the tab for my medical bills and accommodations in Switzerland. The Carlins had arranged for me to go to a *pension* very near the university and its hospital. All too soon, the train was about to leave, and I boarded it, leaving behind all the joy I had felt upon my disembarking not so long ago.

As the train pulled out from the station, I hung out the window until all the faces I loved disappeared from sight. Again I stared out at my beloved south of France but without being able to take any pleasure in the view. I felt very alone and frightened, not knowing what to expect. Also, I was physically exhausted; I had not been sleeping as the welts always seemed to come forth in the wee hours.

I was riding in a second-class compartment that was comfortable and not filled. When lunch was announced, off I went to the dining car.

Despite my inner turmoil, I remembered what a treat it was to dine on a French train, and this meal did not disappoint me, its inexpensive price even including a small carafe of wine. As I enjoyed my lunch, eating slowly to help the time pass, my pain and despair lessened somewhat, and I became calmer and more mellow. As I regained my courage, I thought, *Okay, let's get this over with. I will be fine and I won't miss much anyway, as the company is returning to Paris for rehearsals before its season there. I'll be back before I know it.* The wine was a great help in my construction of this false bravado!

Back in my compartment, I had many books to read. I was and am an avid reader, particularly for the classics and mythology. While in Europe, I read all I could about the places I saw as well as biographies and autobiographies. Of course I read as many dance books as I could lay my hands on. Although the books I had brought along were intended to keep me occupied during my stay in Switzerland, I began to read after lunch, barely thrilling to the moment that we crossed the border (which I was aware of, as the police came through the train to check everyone's passport).

The comportment of the Swiss police already gave me a taste that life would be different in this country while outside the scenery also immediately seemed somehow different. My destination would prove quite a contrast to Cannes as I would be staying in the German side of Switzerland, where the language was Swiss Deutsch (although everyone was able to speak English, French, Italian, and German). As the beautiful snow-covered mountains came into view, I began to take more of an interest in the scenery and began to look more positively upon my stay as being an adventure. I must say that it was also my nature to accept what I could not change and to make the most of a situation.

At long last, the approach to Zurich was announced, and passengers began gathering up their belongings in anticipation of disembarking. When the train halted, a porter took my bags out through the window and placed them on a cart in the station and lugged them to the main entrance. I looked around frantically; I was supposed to have been met by the professor's nurse, Frau Elsa, and I had no idea what she would look like. But it did not take long for her to locate me amidst the other passengers, even though she had never seen me before: I looked like a dancer!

To my relief she spoke English and told me that we would go first to the *pension,* from which we would then walk to the hospital where Doctor Professor Michner was awaiting my arrival. I felt in safe hands with Frau Elsa as she bundled me into a cab, and also the *pension* turned out to be very charming and homey.

Switzerland was so much colder than the south of France. I have always been very sensitive to the cold, I am convinced from having been born in the tropics; I am happiest in a hot, humid climate. Plus dancers have no extra body fat to insulate them. As we walked from the *pension* to the hospital, Frau Elsa could not help but hear my teeth chatter and suggested that I invest in some warmer underclothes, perhaps the next day.

Doctor Professor Michner turned out to be very cultured; he loved ballet. He was very sympathetic to my situation and suggested that I check into the hospital for observation. He took some preliminary tests, and then Frau Elsa and I returned to the *pension* to pick out only what I might need for several days at the hospital. Instead of finding hospitalization daunting, I found myself feeling relieved that I was to be kept there as my nocturnal allergic symptoms had been worsening. During my first night in the hospital, I had the support of the wonderful sisters as nurses. That night, my reaction was terrible: I awoke with welts so large that I could barely open my eyes. This was a very serious attack as, had it been only slightly lower, it could have closed my throat. Doctor Professor Michner was called, and despite the hour, he examined me and gave me an injection. Within an hour, the swelling had reduced enough for me to enjoy my first good, sound sleep in days.

The following day, I was tested for possible allergies. The welts had been a mystery to me because I had never before suffered from allergies. But in the hospital, I learned that I tested positive for virtually everything! The doctor explained that this situation was temporary and that I would be placed upon a strict regime to reduce my exposure to foods I was reacting to. Also I was placed on pills that were effective against uticaria (hives), which was what I had. I asked how I had become so allergic, and he said it could have been triggered by anything. I suspected that the culprit might have been a jar of honey I had enjoyed in Cannes as a spread on my breakfast *petit pain*. I had stored it on a windowsill to keep it cool. When I told this to Doctor Professor Michner, he said this was precisely the sort of thing that could have set off a general reaction, compounded with my having been so run down from rehearsals and performances.

Everybody at the hospital was so sweet, but I must admit that my treatment was extreme and unpleasant. The procedure consisted of injecting me with a substance to induce a high fever, stimulating my immune system to knock the allergy out of my body. As the treatment was about to begin, the nurses assured me that they would always be by my bedside. I remember the next days only vaguely: I would drift in and out of sleep, awakening drenched with sweat. The Sisters of Mercy were indeed ever there to bathe and dry me. On the third day, the fever was allowed to reduce, and I began to feel more like myself again, to everyone's relief.

Because we would not know the results of this producer upon my allergies immediately, I was permitted then to return to my *pension*, from which I would go daily to the hospital for an examination by the doctor. I was given pills to be taken in the event of a reaction. The goal now was to get whatever remained of the allergy under control so that I could return to work. The doctor reiterated that the uticaria would eventually disappear altogether as mysteriously as it had appeared.

Life at the *pension* was an experience! At my first dinner there, I was introduced to the other guests by Herr Wein, the proprietor. Most seemed quite old, except for those who were studying particulars of diseases or medicine at the university hospital (not as students per se but as established professionals keeping up with the latest developments in their field). But two of the guests were young men who were studying at the university: one was a Dutch boy, Bob Krom, whose father owned a chain of department stores throughout Holland; the other, Richard, was from Oxfordshire and also from a good family. After that first dinner had concluded, Bob, Richard, and I retired to the sitting room with our coffee; everyone else returned to their respective rooms. The boys and I felt at ease at once when speaking with one another, and they soon became my cavaliers and partners in mischief!

One evening, we found it too quiet at the *pension* and engaged in a roaring good pillow fight, throwing every pillow we could lay our hands on. Herr Wein, although amused and I think happy to see such energy and youthful play on the premises, put an end to the fun as the other guests were sleeping. He brought us juice to quench our thirst from such vigorous activity as we sprawled, exhausted and giggling, in the sitting room. My health and spirits were obviously improving!

Meanwhile, my visits to the hospital continued daily. Although some foods needed to remain eliminated, I was finding that others were now safe again to eat. Again, Doctor Professor Michner said that this was a temporary adjustment to tide me through the situation. Being able to control my allergy through my diet indeed helped to give me a sense of hope, and the fever treatment had indeed worked to reduce my overall level of reactivity.

A Swiss holiday was coming up, and Frau Elsa had the idea to take me to see Davos and Arosa, and I enthusiastically accepted, eager to see a ski resort during ski season. This trip was a great treat for me, and the short break from my daily visits to the hospital actually seemed to improve my health.

On our return to Zurich, the doctor was satisfied with my progress and told me that I could return to work. I was not at the point where I could completely control my allergy through diet and with the pills that he gave me.

I was sad to leave my new friends and said that I would keep in touch with them, but any regrets were overwhelmed by my happiness to rejoin the de Cuevas Company in Paris and to resume my life.

12

Le Théâtre Empire and Touring

I had telephoned Mr. Carlin with the news of my release. I flew to rejoin the company in Paris, and he met me at the airport. While driving me directly to the Théâtre Empire where the troupe had just begun a long run, he assured me that I had been very much missed. He had kept the precise date of my return a secret from all, except from Mr. Taras.

When we arrived at the theater, the performance had not yet begun. Leading me backstage, Mr. Carlin knocked on each dressing room door, which elicited shrieks of welcome. I had never felt so welcomed home as when rejoining my friends in this company. Mr. Taras, too, appeared relieved to have me back and asked if I could be put in several of the season's ballets as soon as possible. Of course—I just needed to settle in for a few days.

Jocelyn and Ruth, joyful to see me looking so well, had reserved a room for me at the Cecilia Hotel, a few blocks from the theater. After the performance, we joined the Carlins for a bite to eat at a restaurant called Chez Mercier, across from the theater on Avenue Wagram. It was "our place" as our company turned up there at all hours. One night, during the run, the Carlins invited me to join them at Chez Mercier, and I so enjoyed the steak that I ordered. Afterward, Mr. Carlin asked me how I had liked the horsemeat. I was so shocked that not only did my jaw drop with surprise but also I needed to hastily excuse myself so that I could run into the ladies' room, where I left the horse in the sink! Poor *cheval*. I enjoy performing *pas de chevals* (a classical ballet step that imitates the pawing of a hoof), but *eating* a horse was going too far!

I loved being back in Paris as when time permitted I was able to see Monsieur Staats and Madame Egorova, in addition to taking class and attending rehearsals. I remember obtaining tickets for Monsieur Staats to attend our *Swan Lake*; I made a point of asking him to come backstage after the performance. How very proud I felt when this great teacher greeted me with "Très bien fait" (well done) as he came behind the scenes. Staats in hand, I then knocked on Rosella Hightower's door (having previously asked her whether I could bring him to see her). She could not have been more gracious as she dismissed me and invited him in to have a private moment with this great and very genuine man who had been a prominent dancer at the Paris Opéra in his time. I was very pleased with myself for having orchestrated this encounter.

During our stay at the Théâtre Empire, the Marquis came as often as he could to watch us onstage. Often at the end of a performance, when we were in our dressing rooms, we would hear over the backstage loudspeaker, "Tout le monde sur scene, s'il vous plait" (Everyone onstage, please). This announcement could mean two things: one (which we dreaded) that Mr. Taras wanted to make corrections; or two, that the Marquis wished to see his *enfants* (children), each one lining up to make a quick "Bon soir" (good evening) and be greeted, in turn, with a kiss on both cheeks. The latter was always such a lovely ending to a performance. (The Marquis knew how to make us feel cherished; at the end of one of our seasons, he even arranged for rose petals to rain down upon us as we took our final bows! Spontaneously as we looked up to see what was falling, we raised our arms and ran forward rapturously to meet it, to the audience's delight.)

At the time, it was believed in Europe that a dancer had to belong to this company, for the prestige, before he or she would ever have a "name" in the ballet profession. As viewed from the outside, there was some intangible, incredible glamour attached to the Grand Ballet du Marquis de Cuevas. But, as a member of the company, I wasn't so much concerned with our external reputation as appreciative of how much the Marquis himself adored and nurtured us.

Although we were well aware of our glamorous image, of course. For instance, at a fashionable party given in Venice by the designer Jacques Fath, Fath made a grand entrance with two enormous Greyhounds, but the Marquis topped him by arriving with two ballerinas! And within the company's home base of Paris, we were quite spoiled—one had only to say, "Je suis avec Le Grand Ballet du Marquis de Cuevas" for those magical words to open many doors!

Behind the scenes, though, life could be a struggle for those of us who could not rely on the support of families living in Paris. Money was very tight. Once Jocelyn and I became very hungry after class and ventured to a Russian street stand that sold meat broiled on skewers, accompanied by black bread. The cost was maybe fifty cents. As we held our skewers aloft, gobbling down the meat, something struck us at the precise same moment: we had a *fou rire*, laughing so hard that we had to sit down on the curb of the pavement yet unable to articulate to each other what was so funny. In my mind was *If my father could only see me now, gnawing on a piece of black bread as if I were starving.* Our hilarity was contagious—as we sat there, holding our stomachs from the pain of laughing, with tears of mirth streaming down our faces, passersby began to laugh as well. Would that they knew that these two hungry girls were members of the prestigious de Cuevas ballet!

On another occasion, Jocelyn and I felt exhausted from having worked so hard to fit in as many classes as we could and decided that treating ourselves to a massage would do us a world of good. Dancers are ever in need of a good massage as it helps the muscles to untangle, so to speak, and so we asked one of the dancers of the Paris Opéra to tell us which massage establishment she used. The dancer phoned ahead to arrange a time for both of us, gave us the address, and off we went.

We rang the bell, and when the door opened, to our great surprise there stood the most beautiful-looking man. Gulping, we gave our names, and he stated that he was indeed expecting the two of us. For a moment, I couldn't look at Jocelyn's face as I knew what she was thinking—and vice versa. Finally, I said to Jocelyn, "You go first," and she responded, "Oh no, I'll wait and you can go on in." Somehow, I managed to sit down quickly, book in hand, with an air that nothing would budge me. Jocelyn coolly went off with Mr. Gorgeous, and in reality, it truly didn't matter who went first, as it was just as awful to be waiting as if I were to be slaughtered. I never knew an hour's time could be so intimidating. Finally, there was nothing to do but make the best of it. In an anteroom, Jocelyn dressed as I undressed, neither of us daring to look at each other for fear of bursting out laughing. I modestly wrapped a sheet around me and marched out to the massage table, where Mr. Gorgeous draped another sheet over me— and gave me a great massage.

When my session ended, we paid him, and he asked when we would come again. We knew our schedule and made appointments for the following week. Jocelyn and I thanked him then left in silence, not daring to say one word to each other while within his earshot. It was not until we reached the street corner that we finally looked at each other—and roared with laughter. We had gone there expecting a masseuse, not a masseur; neither of us had ever been massaged by a man—and to think for our first time, we would have one so handsome! We laughed so hard that we could not even voice our identical thought: *If only my family could see me now!* What a scandal it would have been, in the early 1950s, and our being so young!

We decided a glass of champagne at the Café de la Paix would be just right for our present mood. There we sat, feeling very French, drinking champagne and eating green olives. But it certainly wasn't the champagne that went to our heads that day!

Somehow the week passed, and as we were preparing to return to Mr. Gorgeous, I noticed that Jocelyn was certainly taking her time dressing. To my amusement, she put on her best lingerie—while I had found my black lace pants. Again, we howled with laughter. After braving out this second round of massages, we again capped the experience by retiring to the Café de la Paix, where with great laughter we relished our thoughts of Mr. Gorgeous while feasting on champagne and green olives.

It was so wonderful to be with Jocelyn. This was when we started with my saying, "Onward, McDuff," and her replying, "Okay, Dingy." These became our secret names for each other, and to this day we continue to address each other in writing as McDuff and Dingy.

Although our lives were very well organized, I experienced great pangs of homesickness during this period. I had fought so hard to accomplish what I was doing that I couldn't admit this to them openly, but I am sure that my parents read between the lines of my letters. I wrote to them almost every other day, telling them the funny things that had happened but also assuring them that I was still reading the books that had been recommended to my father that I study in lieu of having a college education. He had given me a list of one hundred such books before I'd left home. It was not always easy to find the books on the list, but Paris had a W. H. Smith on the rue de Rivoli, which carried English-language books.

Ruth and I also enjoyed going book hunting at the rue de Bac, where all the great rare bookstores were. One that especially interested me was run by an older woman who wore her lovely white hair in a chignon. She sold rare French dance books and had almost anything about dance that had been published in English as well. She has a formidable knowledge of ballet and made a point of knowing dancers, following our progress and picking out the talented ones, to whom she showed great kindness, voicing compliments and encouragement. One never left the shop without a book tucked into one's bag. Years later, I returned to her shop, and she remembered me perfectly; however, more recently, after a long absence from my beloved Paris, my husband and I went to the rue de Bac and found it had changed enormously. We were told that this shopkeeper had died. With her went the breed of special handmaiden that had spurred us on with such interest and insight in our art.

After two months, we came to the end of our Paris season. It was now summer, when we would participate in various festivals throughout Europe. Being so prestigious a company, we would stay in each city at least a week, sometimes up to a month.

In Orange, we were to dance in a vast arena that had been built by the Romans. To give an idea of how enormous the stage was, let me describe its effect upon the Dance of the Cygnets in *Swan Lake*: The entrance of the four dancers usually consisted of our simply walking onstage from the wings, with our hands crossed and arms interlinked, for five counts and then stopping, at which point the music began. Not so here—we rehearsed it with *ten* counts and were still barely in sight! Finally we increased our steps to a total count of sixteen—and that was before we even started to dance. We panted through the ensemble as we tried to conquer space.

It was very difficult to stay centered on so large a stage and also to keep lines exact as dancers spread out. The cool outdoor air only added to our problems; performances, of course, took place in the evenings, and keeping our muscles warm was a challenge. Resuming motion after standing still was difficult.

Since it was summer, my olive skin tanned easily during the day without my even needing to sunbathe. I was happy to be in such a warm climate, but to my chagrin I received an amend for makeup: Mr. Taras decided that I needed to whiten my face, arms, neck—all that was not costumed. Rosella came to my rescue, and we slapped on makeup everywhere. But after every performance of *Swan Lake*, I received an amend for having looked too dark! Mr. Taras was being very wicked indeed, but Mr. Carlin never took it out of my check.

Following Orange was Valence, again performing out of doors. During the daytime, it was sweltering. When we had a call for a 10:00 am class onstage, I had the idea to play a joke on Mr. Taras. With the help of Wardrobe, I wore body tights from neck to toes, long white gloves from *Sleeping Beauty* and a veil from something else—in effect, I was completely encased in fabric. I was ready in class ahead of the arrival of Mr. Taras, and the entire company was in on my scheming to put an end to those amends. We started with *pliés* and with that did many *ports de bras*. Mr. Taras was quick to catch on and announced, "Let's do the ports de bras in triple tempo." During these exertions, my veil fell off, and everything I wore became soaked through with sweat—particularly the long, borrowed gloves. But then Mr. Taras said, "I like what you are wearing—keep it all on." By this time the whole company was in hysterics; finally I could bear it no longer, left the stage, removed the excess garments, and then returned to class, glaring at Mr. Taras. He and the troupe enjoyed this episode immensely, but in the end the joke had been on me.

We continued touring, dancing nightly. Our days now revolved around class in the morning then a rehearsal and then back to the theater in the evening for a short warm-up class and then the performance. I made a point of arriving at the theater hours earlier because it took time to set up my dressing room: makeup, good luck charm, etc. Then I would need to make my selections from a lineup of toe shoes. I might try on as many as ten pairs for this (a neurosis shared by most dancers): one pair needed to be very soft for *Les Sylphides,* I needed a stronger pair for *Swan Lake,* and so forth. I would need to check that my tights were clean, that no jewels were loose on my costumes (a small hard ornament rolling around on the stage could cause a disaster) and that any necessary hairpieces were there. We were required to wear our hair in the classical style for *Swan Lake, Les Sylphides,* and *Giselle* (this style is divine if you have a thin face and a long neck; for others, it makes them look like a washerwoman!). I could change the style for certain ballets; for *Sleeping Beauty* and *Concerto Barocco,* I wore my hair in a chignon but left my ears exposed. But such changes were not left up to each dancer's whim; everyone in the corps and all soloists were told at dress rehearsals which styles were expected of us, and to assert one's independence risked being given an amend.

Another thing Mr. Taras detested were toe ribbons sticking out from their knot. Even if we appeared in three ballets a night, with sometimes as many as six shoe changes, we took care to sew our ribbon ends in. Also, it worked wonders to wet them down and then dunk our bows into rosin (a tacky derivative of pitch, more commonly used on the soles of our shoes to keep us from slipping onstage). I didn't know it then, but all these conscious preshow rituals were things I eventually did automatically as I progressed to becoming a ballerina.

On tour, we went wherever the elite French spent each season: from January to February, the Côte d'Azur; March and April, Paris; June and July, summer festivals; August, Biarritz; September and October, Paris; November, Deauville; December, London or Paris.

I can't remember now whether we went to Le Mans before or after Valence. All I remember is that it was an embarrassment. We were all scattered among different hotels as in Le Mans no one hotel could handle such a large group. We had one day off, which we all spent sleeping in, washing our hair, and so on. Wouldn't you know it that Ruth and I had

—

just gotten up and decided to start the day with a leisurely walk. As we approached the center of town, we caught sight of army vehicles carrying soldiers—in our direction. Suddenly, Ben Carlin seemed to appear from out of nowhere and asked us frantically if we knew where Rosella was or Marjorie and her husband George Skibine, or George Zoritch. When we said no, he began to drag us away, saying, "You'll do—just stand there and represent the company." We were horrified. As we approached the town square, there marching ahead of us was a magnificently uniformed group of soldiers. They were a unit from the French African Colonies. I had never seen anything like it—and they were marching in our honor! It was really sad that the principal dancers from de Cuevas were not there, that at that moment these two young girls had to stand for the entire company. Ruth and I nodded and said in our best French how honored we were to be so welcomed, making it up as we went along. Finally the ordeal was over, and the Carlins were so pleased that they treated us to drinks at a café. We had a great giggle once the incident was through. To this day, if I see photographs of those gorgeous uniforms and extraordinary-looking soldiers—right out of Kipling!—I am transported back to that excruciating and glorious moment in Le Mans!

Touring gave us the opportunity to see and hear other artists, such as symphony orchestras, on their own respective tours. One day when we were in Cannes, Rosella told me that Sascha Guitry, a famous French actor, was doing a one-man show at the casino; she insisted that I go to see him perform in spite of my less-than-perfect French. She said it wouldn't matter, that he was an incredible performer. I went, and to my amazement, this man held his international audience spellbound. He had a lectern in front of him, which held props. In one moment, he would be speaking like a man then in the next he would duck down and reemerge wearing an ape's head and then continue going back and forth between the two personas. Obviously he was philosophizing alternately as a man and then as a beast. The French love philosophy, and the act clearly struck a chord with those in the audience who could fully understand his words. I had always thought deeply about such things, and despite my difficulty in following what he was actually saying, I apprehended that I was indeed watching a great artist.

We now started dancing outside of France. Our first big stop was Geneva. The impresario there had arranged for us something that he thought would be sensational: the stage was outdoors, and the audience was seated away from it, across the narrow part of a lake. The orchestra was placed beside us. This staging indeed had an effect: one enormous catch was that we couldn't keep warm!

Prior to stepping onstage for *Les Sylphides*, we huddled in wool leg warmers and bundled ourselves in shawls, dreading the moment when we would have to shed our wrappings. The entrance of the corps went all right, and then they needed to stand still while two soloists performed. I happened to be one of the soloists. My muscles had already cooled during the first *bourrées* (tiny, fast steps taken with the legs together), and as a consequence, my legs could not move quickly enough to keep pace with the other soloist. As we were to mirror each other's movements, the problem was immediately noticeable. Somehow we got through the first part and departed from the stage, replacing our warm garments as soon as we were out of the sight of the audience.

Our dressers were Swiss, and each time we were offstage, they handed us what we thought were cups of some kind of tea. We were so grateful for the hot drink that we gulped it down. Then off came the sweaters for our next entrance. During this next section, I tried to go between two lines of the corps, an action that demanded I turn my back on the audience and then turn to face them. To my horror, the two lines looked like they were tottering, almost rolling downstage. What was transpiring before my eyes? Thank God I had another exit while Marjorie Tallchief went onstage for the big *pas de deux*. Again in the wings, I was offered tea—and looked out to see Marjorie wearing fire-engine-red leg warmers as she did the first lift with George Zoritch, a position that placed her head toward the floor with her legs fully in view at the top of the lift! The other dancers and I began to laugh, and even without that comic relief, we were all oddly lightheaded. I think it was here that I was to do the jumping solo, which takes great strength even in optimum conditions. I had good body memory and danced the solo as if nothing was wrong, but I felt curiously airy as I performed it—and for good reason. Once the ballet had concluded, we learned that what we had all assumed was tea had been grog: tea laced with brandy! No wonder we had all been dancing so strangely!

Our classes, conducted by Mr. Taras, continued daily even while we were on tour. Barres were lined up right on the stage, or one used anything else one could find of the right height to hold onto. These were not warm-ups but full class on most days, complete with corrections. Mind you, we had no mirrors most of the time, so we had to rely on the corrections given to us to know how we were doing. Sometimes the dancers gave each other corrections, which were accepted gratefully in the helpful spirit with which they were meant.

—

In August, we went to Biarritz. This was always a month's stay, at least. Often we found a small hotel near the ocean. My first night there, I had left the verandah doors of my room open, only to hear waves crashing on the rocks just below—and the ocean rose so high that the verandah flooded and the water began to approach my room! I learned my lesson that night and only left windows open!

We had a few days off in Biarritz while the Marquis and the company's principal dancers attended a grand party. I had the idea to use that time to visit San Sebastian in Spain, which by car was not far away. Nancy and Paul Maure went along, with Nancy's parents, who were visiting. We drove into the Basque countryside. Suddenly, we saw a Basque man with a pick digging a grave. We stopped as I always loved old cemeteries—their stones tell you a story of their times. There was a portal where he was digging, with a little inscription in Spanish. I wrote it down so that I could have it translated and also took a photo of the doorway. In English, the inscription read, "Today it is me, tomorrow it will be thee." How very Spanish.

We also happened upon a small movie theater that of all things was screening Spanish dance films! To my great delight, I was able to watch a very old film featuring the great Spanish dancer Vicente Escudero and Argentinita. How amazing to come upon by chance something that I could otherwise never have hoped to see!

Soon, we were back at work again, in a beautiful old theater. Our schedule was full, yet it was less hectic here, and we had a chance to enjoy the sun. Also, Ruth and I discovered the best ice cream ever. French ice cream in 1952 was not creamy, but one shop in the old town made its own rich, divine version that we felt we could not get enough of. We were in heaven and purchased two cones apiece, which we blissfully licked, holding one in each hand as we walked down the street. Suddenly from out of nowhere came Mr. Taras. I stopped dead in my tracks as he said, "Stuffing your faces!" But Ruth kept her cool and in her very English accent said, while holding out a cone, "Have a lick, won't you?" I took my cue from her to stay calm as she simply walked on. But I was appalled that we had both been caught in the act.

Following our sojourn at Biarritz, we returned to Paris, where we were to rehearse for our Deauville season. We were to perform a company revival of George Balanchine's *La Sonnambula* (also known as *Night Shadows*), which he had first set for the Ballet Russe de Monte Carlo in 1946 and then staged for the Marquis de Cuevas in London in 1948. I was in the corps and was pleased to be included as I loved the ballet, which I felt was one of the most unforgettable of any choreographed by Balanchine. It was very dramatic: A poet finds himself at an evening *fête* given by a baron and is attracted to the coquette, the mistress of the host. When the other guests dance off to supper, he sees a mysterious, spectral sleepwalker—the wife of the host—and they dance a strange *pas de deux* together, in which she is unaware of his presence. They are seen by the coquette, who, in her jealousy, betrays them to the baron, who becomes furious and stabs the poet. Still asleep, the sleepwalker reappears and, without waking, lifts the poet into her arms and carries him out of sight into the baronial manor. As she goes up the stairs within the house, the audience sees a light at each landing followed by the silhouette of the two dancers' heads. Only as they reach the top floor does the curtain finally come down slowly. It is a deliciously spooky finale. There is a trick to performing the ending effectively as the woman portraying the sleepwalker appears to actually carry the male dancer as she *bourrées* upstage and into the house when, in fact, the man does not place all his weight upon her.

After Paris, we had two weeks off, and I flew home to San Francisco. We had a great reunion, and it was heavenly to be back in my own room again. I had not appreciated what a luxury it was to be at home. Meanwhile, many in the company had opted to spend that time in Cannes. One day, I was horrified to read newspaper headlines that an Air France airliner had crashed after takeoff—with no survivors but for one person who had lived only briefly and then died. Harriet Toby had been one of the victims of the crash. I went into a state of shock, and all I wanted to do then was to be with my—and her—friends in the company. I returned to Paris and immediately contacted a friend of hers who was not a dancer but who had been very close to her and her mother. He told me that she had been going just for the weekend to do an interview for the magazine *Elle*. Our pianist had almost boarded that same flight but had canceled at the last minute as had Marjorie Tallchief and George Skibine. Everyone at the time was deeply affected by the accident. The first performance of the company after the disaster had the curtain opening slowly to reveal only a huge basket of flowers onstage.

The airline said that birds had flown into the engines. The woman who had briefly survived had been able to speak and described how the people on board had panicked during the last moments, knowing the plane was about to crash. I had nightmares for months afterward, thinking about my lovely and gifted friend perishing so young and in such ghastly circumstances. I still wonder what her life and career would have been had she not taken that ill-fated flight.

—

13

Bordeaux and Deauville

I had a day or two before all the company dancers slowly reentered Paris. Meanwhile, Jocelyn and I were taking classes from our favorite teachers. It was with joy that I returned to Mme. Egorova as she now made a bit of a fuss over any dancer from the Paris Opéra or Roland Petit's* company and also the Champs Élysées Ballet that was just beginning there. Our being in the Marquis de Cuevas's company gave us a good deal of prestige amidst such dancers. In spite of this, we really worked hard in class.

The war had caused the French companies to disband, but now in Paris, there were four ballet companies. It was a very exciting time to be there as we all felt ourselves to be part of the beginning of a new era in dance.

I learned from Jocelyn that while I had been in Switzerland, Massine had begun to choreograph a new full-length ballet for the Bordeaux festival. He had seen our company and cast the roles. They had already had one week of rehearsals. Luckily for me, Rosella and John Taras had spoken to Massine about me, and he had assigned some parts to me during my absence. I even had a solo!

Our time was very busy prior to Bordeaux as we had some performances in Paris. This season, John Taras gave some of us the chance to do more important roles. I danced the *Concerto Barocco,* and in *Giselle* I was one of the friends. We also performed *Sleeping Beauty,* where again solo roles fell into our hands.

Ruth and I decided to visit the marquis as we had heard that he was not well. Off we went to the Quai Voltaire, where he lived in a handsome building that was pure Paris: courtyard, large doors, concierge. It had a terrific view of the Louvre across the Seine. We entered the courtyard and asked the concierge to phone up to say we would like to be admitted. That being done, we boarded a very old beautiful elevator that took us to the next floor. It was very exciting as we had never been to such a grand flat. Ringing the bell, we were met by a maid, who showed us into the sitting room and then withdrew. After a moment, she reappeared and asked us to follow her. Ruth and I each held a bouquet of flowers, which had been quite dear, considering our salaries.

We were actually shown into the marquis's bedroom. I will never forget my first glimpse of this extraordinary man in a large four-poster bed, wearing a white ruffled nightshirt. His little white dogs completed the scene, surrounding him on his bed. It was truly a scene out of another century!

The marquis accepted our flowers and seemed genuinely pleased that we had come. He patted the bed, and like children, we sat near him. He was very upset because a newspaper had written about how badly he looked. We were, of course, quick to assure him that he had never looked so well. I had the feeling that this was all a dream, and that I was an actor playing a part. However, this was rather a charming interlude and has remained a memory that I treasure.

We left Paris and arrived in Bordeaux to commence rehearsals. The money for the festival came from the city of Bordeaux, which was the center of the wine country. This was to be a very important series of performances for us: it was to be a big festival, and we were to be its greatest sensation. First of all, we had Massine; second, there was Dupont, who made the *régie* (production); third, our costumes were to be made by Karinska; and last but not least, Massine's ballet had music by the great French composer Henri Sauguet, a native of Bordeaux. We were joined by a chorus of fifty, plus fifty little children from the opera school. The ballet took its name from its score, *Symphonie Allégorique*. We renamed it "Symphony Allergic" because of all which transpired during this very unusual time!

I arrived at the theater after checking into the hotel. When I approached the stage, I couldn't believe my eyes. Under only the stage light, a slim-bodied, not-very-tall man seemed to be doing a class workout. I kept very quiet and stayed inside one of the wings to watch this sleek figure, hairnet on his head, do the quatre-pirouette combination. Again, it was déjà-vu—it could only be the master himself, Massine! Even today, I know every detail of what I had seen as if it were yesterday. To have happened upon in the already heady atmosphere of an empty theater with only one stage light, this great man of ballet performing his own work gave me shivers. For a few moments, I alone watched this great dancer, then sixty-five years old, demonstrate the amazing discipline that would come into action the next few days.

As people began coming in, he stopped and put his towel around his shoulders. He took a seat, stage center, and waited for us to be warmed up enough to start rehearsal.

I was learning my solo from a dancer who had learned it expressly to show me my part. Not one thing did Massine miss. The other dancer and I were working off in a corner of the stage, but he interrupted. Massine called me by name and said, "I will show her."

I immediately went to where he was seated, offering him my hand with a quick curtsy. He seemed pleased to see me. As for my feelings— at last, here was someone who had adored Tamara Toumanova and who loved olive skin and exotic features. For good reason, anything Spanish was a positive passion.

He rose to stand in front of me then began doing steps. I followed quickly as he moved swiftly through my entire variation. It was very different learning it directly from him. He used his whole body at once, as was appropriate, as I was to be a *grillon*, a cricket—a fun part. I think he was pleased with my interpretation of it.

In this ballet, I also did other parts with another girl or two girls; in all, I appeared in six parts, each of them important. That meant six changes of Karinska's costumes and color-coordinated toe shoes!

The company worked one week with Massine. Then, the second week, all hell broke loose with the arrival of our conductor, Henri Sauguet, Dupont, and Karinska, plus the symphony, everyone of them complaining, at any given moment, it was the musicians or Sanguet or Dupont and Karinska. Finally Massine shouted (in French, of course), "Out!" The orchestra was dumbfounded. The great maestro Sauguet left plus the entire army of costumers!

Massine called for order. He picked up the baton and conducted the orchestra himself, correcting us as we went along. And that included conducting the adult chorus plus another of fifty children! The rehearsal was a success. We all breathed a sigh of relief as it came together.

However, our lack of communication with Karinska and her workers continued. Dress rehearsal was a joke. We could not time anything properly, with so many costumes missing. Finally, in the third week of rehearsals, we were all handed out shoes, which had been dyed to match our costumes. They were French toe shoes, which meant *hard*. I received my sixth pair and thought, *Never will this work*. The other dancers felt similarly about their shoes. By now, we were on the verge of hysterics: all you need are highly skilled French people with different ideas, all in one room for a new ballet! All were important, and each wanted his or her own way or individual time. But by now, there wasn't enough time for a full-dress rehearsal, which this ballet needed desperately. We were exhausted by the end of our shamble of a rehearsal. We left the theater, dreading the fact that we would be opening the very next night without sufficient preparation.

I took my shoes with me and returned to my hotel where, late at night, I began to wet the insides and walk around in them. But I was too tired to last; I went to bed dreaming about the six total costume changes that Karinska had insisted I would have to make the next day—including changing my tights (it was devilish, trying to quickly remove tights as they stuck to one from the sweat of dancing)! I slept badly, wondering how I would ever accomplish all this, quite apart from dancing my actual roles!

I awoke at 6:00 am after a restless night and immediately put on one pair of toe shoes. There I was, at six in the morning, in my nightgown, trying to break in shoes!

Jocelyn had the room next to mine, with a connecting door. I opened her door slowly—and what a sight met my eyes: There was Jocelyn in *her* nightclothes, hanging on to her bed frame and doing relevés! She looked very funny, but then I wasn't looking great myself. We both saw each other having the same thoughts and burst into laughter. This, however, was no laughing matter. Jocelyn, always positive, said, "We'll just have to do it." But how?

On the day of the performance, the company held its final dress rehearsal, which seemed like the real performance as so many people were in the audience at the invitation of the man who was in charge of the festival.

In my dressing room, there were the six costumes with my name on them, six pairs of tights, six pairs of shoes that were in no way broken in. Indeed, I had almost succeeded in breaking down my feet! I really had a stomachache, looking at all this.

The music started. My appearance was in a bunny costume, for a dance with two other girls. Unaccustomed to its correct fit, I ran onstage with a fluffy puff on my front, nearly bare where I was supposed to have had a nice fluffy bottom—the costume was back to front! To make matters worse, we all three had little white gloves to stand in for paws. As I hurried onstage, one of mine dropped into a crack in the floor, all the way down to land one floor below the stage. I tried to hide my hand, but making like a bunny required me to disclose that one little paw was uncovered.

My quick costume change for my next part had to be made behind a special curtained-off area backstage. I had placed my things there neatly but didn't have sufficient time to peel off my damp bunny tights. To my horror, I heard my cricket music being played—to the sight of no cricket onstage. Jocelyn whizzed past me, on her way to her own next part, and suddenly I found myself screaming, "Dresser! Dresser!" until someone backstage said, "Janet, speak in French." My mind went blank, and it was all I could do to dance in French until my *habileuse* arrived.

If this was a rehearsal, what would the performance be like? Mr. Massine called us all onstage at the end and dismissed the entire French team, except Karinska. It was obvious that she had overdone the costumes; as beautiful as they looked, we couldn't dance in them. Massine settled the problem of tights: pink would do for all the girls who had no time to change. Also, he did away with the color-coordinated shoes for those who had quick changes. Suddenly, he seemed to calm us all down, with the simplification of these problems. He knew our struggles were real as he himself had faced the difficulties of quick changes on many an occasion.

A last, it looked as if the ballet would appear onstage. And so it was; however, for all our trials, "Symphony Allergic" would always be remembered but would never be danced again after that festival.

Massine was very sweet with me, and said, "One day, you will dance one of my ballets. You have the fire and looks of what I love." I was dancing on clouds, and his prophecy was not far from becoming a reality.

Back to Paris we went, to prepare for the next leg of our tour. Rehearsals commenced as usual, with the additional anticipation of having a long stay in Deauville. Paul Maure, one of our lovely dancers who had been very good to us, as was his wife, Nancy, suggested that a number of us rent a house together in or near Deauville, an easy train ride away from Paris. On a free day, it would be possible to ride out there, house hunt, and be back by evening. Paul suggested that Trouville might be less expensive, and it was just across a bridge from Deauville. We thought it was a great idea. Ruth and I were elected to scout out the rental properties.

The weather was rainy; Jocelyn had lent me her rubber boots. Ruth and I set off from the train station, and every other step, I would trip! Jocelyn's boots were simply misbehaving. I would be walking normally then suddenly the rubber would stick and I would look almost drunk. Ruth was dissolved in hilarity as she watched me lurching about. We found a rental agency; before we entered, I removed the offending boots—at least I would be dignified.

To our dismay, everything was already rented; even small hotels in the area were too expensive for us. And so we returned to Paris, wet and without having secured a place of our own. However, this problem was not overlooked by the company. They had acquired what they called a villa by the sea—a tall, towering building that was within walking distance of the theater and shopping. Even Trouville was within walking distance.

It was decided that Rosella and Jean Robier (her husband, and the controller of our toe shoes) would take the tower. Above the tower, in the belfry, would be Jose Ferran (a great dancer and person) and another member of the company.

We drew straws for the downstairs, which was a huge room with four beds—two on one side and two on the other—with its own bathroom. Jocelyn, Ruth, Dolores Starr, and I got that room. We were all close friends, so we were happy to be the lucky ones. We were set—or so we thought.

This was our winter season. Deauville is supposedly not as cold as Paris, but it is by the sea. Our so-called villa turned out to look like something out of a Frankenstein movie, an isolated building with weeds all about. As in any seaside resort, there was a promenade and shuttered swimming cabins along the beach.

As I now look back, the interior could have come from a Visconti scene. Things were quite expensive there, so to save money we cooked our dinners in our room, over a little alcohol burner: steaks, salad, ratatouille. But this was not without disaster; once, some of the fluid spilled onto the table, and it began to catch fire. I grabbed my ratatouille while somebody else swatted the flames with a wet towel. Rosella's group ran down the ridiculous stairway, attracted by the smells of food—and burnt wood! We invited them to join us, provided they brought their own plates and silverware (amazing, what you can do when you have to). We had lit candles, and our haunted villa really came to life that evening.

Skibine was doing a lovely ballet for Marjorie, *Annabelle Lee,* inspired by the poem by Edgar Allen Poe. There were only three girls at the beginning, representing the sea, and then came the pas de deux. The ending was quite dramatic as the three girls enfolded Marjorie's body as if she were taken by the sea. I truly adored the piece, and I was to understudy.

There was to be a small party for the company, given by the Aga Khan and his beautiful wife, the Begum. Everyone was very excited as she

—

had some entertainment planned for us. Those of us who had rehearsal, including the understudies, were required to attend the party after the rehearsal, necessitating a late arrival. On our arrival, the Begum greeted and escorted us to the buffet table. She was truly elegant, beautifully dressed and so attentive to so many of us. She was a true lady I have never ceased to remember. On that evening, we forgot our worries as we watched some delightful Indian dancers that the Begum had arranged as part of the entertainment. For me, it was the calm before the storm.

During our stay in Deauville, John Taras had decided to talk to each dancer one at a time as we were due to have our contracts renewed and our positions reviewed as well. Every day, he would call in about six dancers, one at a time. On my day, I became absolutely frantic as each girl came out crying. These were beautiful dancers and colleagues who had struggled to get this far and had danced their hearts out. What faults was he finding? It was truly strange as I felt so close to this man I had known since I was fourteen. I admired and loved him and could not imagine what he might be saying to create such sadness, though to his credit he did not fire a single dancer. Obviously, I was about to find out what lay behind that door.

My turn came, and I sat down facing Johnny as usual, without a clue of what was to come. He began with positive comments: I had a brilliant technique for my age and was now ready to be a ballerina, not a soloist or a member of the corps. I gave a sigh of relief. But he continued: As long as my legs appeared muscular, he felt that I must do something "drastic" to try and correct this so I could soar to the top of my profession. He did say that it was his honest opinion, that he genuinely felt this would hold me back. He was emphatic that I was old enough to face the problem square on.

I was speechless, shocked to hear those words. Obviously, my contract was being renewed, but were my legs going to hold me back from the ballerina roles he said I was ready for?

I left the room and strode on the beach. Walking on the sand as the waves lapped helped me to think although tears were streaming down my face. It had come from out of the blue; I couldn't cope with this by myself. Jocelyn and Ruth saw me coming toward them, and it took just one look at my face for them to know something was not right. I blurted out what Johnny had said. Both of them were quite shocked. I, being the youngest, depended on their support. I felt so desperate and lost.

They quieted me down and convinced me that, since he had no desire to fire me, I should continue to dance in the company while beginning to consider other opportunities. They were both very positive, but the weather in Deauville was dismal, and that kept my heart low. Every free moment, I would pace under gray skies along the sea, trying to think of what my next step should be.

Even while I was in such turmoil, there were still some lighter moments. Deauville was a popular spot for celebrities. One day, Jocelyn and I saw Orson Welles with Rita Hayworth. Also, there was a very strange man who was always backstage, eyeing us. Once, he asked if I would go out with him for dinner; I did not care for him and said no. Later, one of the girls asked me, "Don't you know to whom you were speaking?" I told her that I'd thought him rather bold and certainly not someone for me. She laughed and said that I had just turned down Aly Khan! But I honestly couldn't have cared less; I found it strange that the other girls felt attracted to him. I was indeed naïve but wise enough to know to keep myself aloof from strangers.

Our next stop was London, where John Taras had assigned me to many ballets. At that time, it was one of the big four cities in ballet: Paris, London, New York, and Berlin. This was not the time to quit the company. But it took a great deal of courage to continue after what Johnny had said. And despite his criticism on that fateful day, I not only danced well but became better than ever. This is not so unheard of. Sometimes, having a problem can destroy you or make you stronger. And so, following a brief rehearsal time in Paris, I found myself happily looking forward to London. English would be spoken there—that alone was something that would cheer me up. In France, having to speak French all the time could sometimes be quite draining as it was still a great effort for me; I was at that stage of understanding more than I could speak. I felt ashamed of my improper grammar.

Also, London was familiar to me in that we still had family ties there and my father spoke of the city often. His school chum in Rangoon, who had left to finish studies in England, had become a great character actor at the Old Vic and had toured with Helen Hayes. His name was Abraham Sofaer. Being known in England at that time was not the same then as being in film; after Abe came to Hollywood to act in the movie *Quo Vadis*, he became very well known in character roles in films and television. He eventually moved his family to Los Angeles; I didn't get to meet them until much later. But just knowing he was in London made the prospect of going there feel a little like home.

While packing my things, I somehow felt that in London would lie the answer to my problem. I sensed that, during the London season, I would make a decision that would allow me to move on.

—

14

Cambridge Theatre, WC2

We arrived in London during an extraordinary time as the city was still struggling to get back on its feet from World War II. It was amazing to us that in the rest of Europe that had actually been occupied by the Nazis, there was butter, cream, meat, chocolate, and eggs, but in 1952, the British were still using ration stamps! There was something about the spirit of the people there that one couldn't help but admire. Nobody complained; as a matter of fact, they carried on with great strength and wonderful humor. I found them most remarkable.

We settled ourselves in the Strand Palace Hotel—a grand name, and it was quite respectable, but it was hardly the Ritz. But our hotel was within walking distance to almost everywhere: a boon, as London is not an easy place to get to know. As usual, I quickly became familiar with what we now call the West End theater district, Piccadilly and the Strand, at that time. Amidst such an absence of other pleasures, the one thing that Londoners did have was the theater. The theaters were filled; people queued up for tickets.

We were booked at the Cambridge Theatre and were sold out at every performance, including matinees. We did full-length ballets—the traditional storybook ones—as those were what people wanted to see: *Giselle*, *Swan Lake*, *La Sylphide*, *Sleeping Beauty*, and so on, rather than the shorter and more modern ballets from our repertoire.

One night, during the second act of *Giselle,* one of the stagehands opened the back doors and then closed them to allow the fog in as our stage fog, providing the perfect atmosphere for the entrance of the Wilis without the use of steam machinery to create that effect! But the fog there

—
141

was not a laughing matter; it could be so bad outside that people could not see a hand in front of them. We actually had someone walk our bus back to our hotel after that performance; that's how dense it was!

Most days, we never really left the theater as they added matinees to fill the demand, and those gave us little free time to do anything during the day. Luckily, St. Martin's Lane was nearby, where one could go to Freed's, a famous shop for dancewear and toe shoes. Madame Freed tried desperately to fit her shoes on my feet. Sadly, my heels were too narrow, and no matter hard she tried, they never worked for me. And then there was Charing Cross Road, a mecca of antiquarian bookdealers. One in particular, called Under the Sign of the Harlequin, was Cyril Beaumont's own incredible store, filled with everything imaginable about dance.

He was a wonderful dance writer himself, and many writers came to him seeking information or to find the books they needed. I came upon him in a very strange way. Of course, I had heard of him as he was held in high esteem in the dance world. I had just finished a matinee performance and was a bit tired and down, feeling rather uninspired. I thought a walk might help and soon found myself on Charing Cross Road—where I saw Cyril Beaumont's name on his shop. I couldn't believe it. I entered, wide eyed, and as he greeted me he very courteously offered his hand, which I shook as I introduced myself. He did not need to introduce himself! He was so stately; if he were in a room filled with people, I think my eye would have been drawn to him. But he made me feel quite at home. He asked where I was dancing, and I told him that I had just finished a matinee and needed to return to theater for the evening performance. He said, "Oh, well then, if you have the energy to climb that ladder, on the top shelf is a box you can bring down." Up I went, curious as I could be. And there was a box that I carried very carefully down the ladder. With twinkling eyes, he told me to open the box, and I did—and there were the most beautiful decorated combs I had ever seen. He told me, "Go ahead, pick them up"; naturally, I was longing to. I put one on each side of my chignon and admired myself in them. Then he said, "Those combs belonged to Taglioni!" I immediately put them back into the box. He looked at me with great compassion and said, "I think you will perform very well tonight."

Through the years, I made many more visits to Mr. Beaumont's shop until it closed in 1965. But never will I forget the day when he had encouraged a young girl who went back to the theater and danced her heart out because she had touched the combs of Taglioni. A small gesture that carried the man's great passion for an art he truly understood and loved. I feel forever honored to have had that long-ago encounter, ever carrying with me a small bit of the past I had been privileged to touch.

The company danced well and was well received. London, Paris, and New York were the hardest places for good reviews at that time. We worked at a taxing pace: some days, we had two full-length ballets, matinee and evening. That's a lot of dancing. Most of the time, the theater brought tea and biscuits to our dressing rooms as we didn't even have time to leave between shows.

Giselle was memorable for more than its naturalistic mist. We had finished the matinee, and everyone said, "Janet, you are looking like the theater—go out for a bit." This time, my wanderings beyond the theater found me at Leicester Square, where I spotted what looked like a nice place to get a bite. I went in and saw that they had scrambled eggs on the menu. At that time, to find eggs or meat or chicken was like finding gold! Of course I ordered them and felt deeply content as I paid my bill and returned to the theater. But by act two of *Giselle,* I was turning green! I had never been so sick in my life. A poor dresser held a basin into which I heaved every time I came offstage, and not always in my proper exits either. It was a nightmare, this Willi who kept disappearing to heave in the wings! Of course, the culprit had been the scrambled eggs. After the ballet, when I said where I had eaten and *what* I had eaten, the dressers and crew said, "Oh, never touch the stuff." What I had ingested had been powdered eggs, which clearly had not liked me nor I (at least as they exited) them.

The London season really flew by even though we were there an entire month. All too soon, it was time for me to say my good-byes to those I loved, with whom I had gone through the emotional situations unique to the world of theater. Now I would have to face the real world, with no friends to truly empathize with me when I was sad—nobody to laugh with or be with but, most of all, not to take class and perform with. This had been my life, and now suddenly I would be without the things that made me feel alive. I needed to take hold of myself and remain positive and hoped that what I would be doing next would be for my best interests. I had made up my mind about what Mr. Taras had said, and I was determined to proceed with a strong heart and spirit.

15

London Odyssey

During our stay in London, I had made up my mind to see what I could accomplish toward reducing the calf muscles in my legs. By this time, Mr. Taras's remarks about their overdevelopment had convinced me that I must do something if I were to reach the top.

I had heard that Margot Fonteyn had gone to Sir Archibald Mcindo, a prominent plastic surgeon. That was where I would start. He was a very kind man and received me most graciously. He was fascinated by my story and understood my quest for perfection but said that he could not help me. However, he knew who might be able to and made a phone call on the spot to Osmond Clarke, a famous orthopedic surgeon, as I had so little time—this was my one free day off from the company. Mr. Clarke said that he could see me immediately; Sir Archibald literally took me in hand and whisked me to the hospital where Mr. Clarke awaited us.

I again explained my dilemma. Mr. Clarke examined my legs and exclaimed, "You have the perfect legs for dancing!" But I detailed how I would not be able to advance in the present climate of the ballet world: the preferred mode of the Balanchine dancer was long and thin. Since I had a slender torso and slim arms and was of slight build, my legs appeared disproportionate to the rest of me, obviously from having been overtrained.

I then went into my proposition: I asked Mr. Clarke, "If you were to put my legs in plaster—as you would do for a broken leg—would this reduce my muscles?" I remembered how, when a former San Francisco Ballet dancer Scott Douglas had broken his leg and had been in a cast, when the cast came off, the leg was emaciated, totally stripped of its former buildup of muscle. My theory was, if I could reproduce that effect

—

and then retrain the proper way, rebuilding my muscles slowly, my legs would become and remain slimmer.

Both of these very famous doctors were amazed by my request, by my passion to do anything I could for my art. Osmond Clarke spoke first. He said that he had never put healthy legs into casts—yes, in theory, doing so would reduce my muscles, but then he couldn't say what might happen next. He said that some people could actually become quite strong from moving their legs about while encased in plaster, that for the procedure to succeed I would need to remain still for weeks. He thought that two months in the hospital—without moving—would do it. Both doctors felt that if I were willing to undergo such radical treatment, they would support my decision.

I quickly agreed to the arrangements: I would finish the London season and then check myself into Saint George's Hospital the day after the last performance. Again, Mr. Clarke asked me to think very carefully about what the procedure would demand of me in terms of pain and courage. I replied that, if I didn't try, I would never know, and if I failed, then I would at least do so knowing that I had done all I humanly could. When I bid them good-bye, Sir Archibald wished me luck and said that he would come by to visit when I was in the hospital.

When I returned to my hotel on the Strand, it suddenly hit me: that I really did not know at all what might be the end result of this treatment. I tried to tell myself to take it one step at a time. But as soon as I met Jocelyn and Ruth, staying at the same hotel, I burst into tears and blurted out everything. They were stunned as though I had already told them what Mr. Taras had said, I had never discussed with them even the notion of undergoing a medical procedure to reduce my legs. As I look back on this episode, I think I had kept both my inner turmoil and plan a secret, precisely because I did not want to know everyone's opinion. John Taras had said what he thought to me, it was enough that I carried that in my heart. I was also concerned that I might not have the courage to follow through if too many people gave me their opinion not to go ahead with this. I had not told Jocelyn or Ruth until now because I did not want to place this burden of both the secret and the keeping of it upon them.

Jocelyn now asked me if I was certain that this doctor was the very best. She understood my desperation and was very comforting, even while I knew that in her heart she did not agree with my decision; she knew me well enough to know I simply had to see through this horrendous experiment.

When I told the Carlins in advance of the season's end in London, they were very upset and angry, calling my action drastic, which is exactly what Mr. Taras had said to me. I only learned later that Mr. Carlin told John Taras, "If anything happens to that girl, it will be your fault." I am sure this didn't cause any anxiety on Mr. Taras's side. He had expressed what he felt, and that was that. Mr. Taras's opinion was so respected by all in the world of dance that I was sure that whatever he had told me had to have been for the best; because I was so young, I was willing to do all I could to improve my image.

The last night of the London season was very sad for me. As far as the company was concerned, I was only taking a leave of absence. I then packed my theater bag in the dressing room—this held my makeup, shoes, practice clothes, etc.—and handed it in as usual before we went off to the closing-night party. Then I returned to my hotel to pack up my bag of personal things. I began to feel quite frightened now, not the least of which consisted of wondering what to tell my parents! I couldn't tell them the truth, but they had to be told something to conceal my whereabouts.

Jocelyn and Ruth sat down with me to think of something. Finally, I came up with a believable story: that I had injured myself and would be staying on in a London hospital until I was perfectly healed. In my letter, I was deliberately vague about how long that might take, assured them that I was in good hands, and took care to stress that the injury was mild but that I needed to rebuild my strength. Otherwise they would have come to London on the next plane!

Nobody knew the truth, except Ruth, Jocelyn, the Carlins, and Mr. Taras. After everyone left for the evening, I began to feel very frightened and alone. I went down to the hotel's restaurant to have my last tea before my hospitalization. The waitress, who had served us every day of the run, asked me where my friends were. That was all I needed: I dissolved into tears and disclosed that I was going into the hospital. She asked me if I knew anyone in London, and I said no. With incredible kindness—and how very English of her!—she asked if she could visit me. And I answered yes.

My entire hospital experience was like a bad dream. It began nightmarishly, to be sure: just as I was about to go into surgery, somebody said, "She is not of age to sign." I was literally ready to be put to sleep when this person noticed that I was underage for legal consent (which was twenty-one years of age). The last thing I wanted them to do was phone my parents for permission! Frantically, I gave them the Carlins' telephone in Paris; with great luck, they were there and accepted full responsibility for me.

—

All continued as planned: I drifted off to sleep and was encased in plaster from my hip joint down to my partially covered foot! I awoke to find myself nearly immobile.

Those two months at the hospital passed slowly. I kept busy reading everything I could. Luckily, Mr. Clarke had a wonderful library and brought me almost everything ever published of Cronin (author of such books as *The Citadel*), whom he admired. (I doubt if Cronin was on my father's list of one hundred books, but I gobbled him up anyway.)

The lovely lady from the hotel restaurant came to visit often. Once, she even brought me an egg! As I'd discovered the hard way, a real egg was a very precious commodity of postwar London of 1952; and her generosity so touched me.

Overall, the courtesy and care extended to me by the hospital staff was extraordinary. When the casts were removed toward the end of my stay, even they were shocked as I gasped in horror: my legs were *gone*. I must say that I had never visualized what the immediate outcome of my extreme treatment would be, and the reality was a huge jolt. I had to literally relearn how to walk! The therapist worked with me daily, teaching me to rethink even the simplest motions as I struggled on crutches.

It was at this point that my friend from the restaurant arranged with the hospital to take me out to dinner. They had all saved their ration coupons during this period to be able to buy me a steak! The English had been through so much during the war and for long after were deprived of sweets and basic foods; no other people in the world would have endured with such good mien nor been so sharing of what little they had! Appreciative of their sacrifice, I ate the steak with great gusto—and it was real English beef, not horse flesh—but on the way back to the hospital, I began to feel awful. After I was deposited back into the hands of my nurse and we had said good night, within moments, I could not stop throwing up. The explanation was obvious: hospital food then consisted of porridge and other starches, without any meat. Even eating normally after such a regimen had to be done gradually. In addition to reducing the dimensions of my legs, I had lost weight while confined to my bed in the hospital; I was physically and emotionally drained and so looked forward to moving ahead.

Finally, the time arrived for my departure. I was to return home to San Francisco, still on crutches, to begin retraining. I called home ahead of time to speak to my brother, trusting him to break the details of my appearance to my parents so that they would not be too shocked. I give my parents great credit for not reproaching me—they called the family doctor in to examine me the very day after my arrival! I think the least said here about that, the better!

As upsetting as this was to everyone, my feelings were respected, and everybody did whatever they could to bring my life back to normal. To be back home with my family, to feel loved and cared for, was so very important to me at this turning point in my recovery—and I was fighting all the way to get back to my life.

My next step after I could walk normally was to start classes again. Here, I was very lucky to have Guillermo Del Oro on my side. He, too, was flabbergasted and outraged about what had occurred; however, now we could only look forward, not back. On a day when there were no classes at his studio, he asked me in to work privately with him. The first time I walked to the barre, I felt like a baby lamb tottering to stand on its legs. I burst into tears as I had never dreamed that this would be the aftermath of my ordeal. Mr. Del Oro calmly walked with me around the perimeters of the room, saying softly, "First we walk, then we run, then we start to dance." This comforted me even while the thought of being fit to participate in a *Swan Lake* or *Giselle* seemed an eternity away. We continued to work behind closed doors.

Every day, as time passed, I became stronger. This time, I trained with great care not to overdo it. Madame Egorova's classes became my guideline as she had given me the ability to work on my own in the correct order to gain strength and also to stretch my muscles to give me length and extension. My legs began to work with ease—and, as I had so fervently hoped, their muscles rebuilt without bulk. Everyone I met attributed this to my being so thin; I said nothing about what I had been through in London. I was delighted when, at long last, Mr. Del Oro said that I could join the advanced class of dancers to work out every day.

Meanwhile, the de Cuevas Company had gone to Istanbul and had toured Algeria and Morocco. Postcards arrived daily but although I missed them, and my life with them, I was too busy to remain sad. This unforgettable interlude had proved to me that I had the strength to rise above all odds and still be me.

—

16

Missing the Boat

At last, I felt strong and fit and very eager to start working again. I knew the company would be back in Paris preparing for their Paris season and summer repertoire. A perfect time to return. Spring was my favorite season there as all the world cannot help but love Paris as it awakens and bursts forth in all its beauty. My mother and her best friend, Mrs. Henry Robinson, decided they would come back with me on the ship and that my father would join us two weeks later. That way, I could tutor both ladies on the boat as to where to go and so on as I would be rehearsing while they would do what tourists do until my father's arrival. That being settled, we became busy with our preparations.

We left San Francisco and stayed at New York's St. Regis Hotel, which was small and known for not being known (that's the way, in those days, they wanted to be; it was quite snobbish since everyone knowing about them hardly made them exclusive). My brother had a friend who was kind enough to see us off at the pier at 8:00 am. We arrived at the first-class entrance of the *Île-de-France*, where the officer who was checking passengers' passports said to me, "Do you realize your passport will expire in mid-ocean?" This well-seasoned traveler was dumbfounded—how could I have overlooked this? He assured me that if I went to the New York state department, they could stamp my passport and I would make the 11:00 am departure. I left the ladies with our escort, Hy Levy, telling him that on no account should they not depart and dramatically hailed a cab. The faces of Mother and her friend were impossible for me to look at. As I sped away, I shouted, "Don't worry—I'll make it!" With that bit of bravado, I left. Obviously, this awkward legal

–

development was not something I had anticipated would mar my mother's first European voyage.

My taxi became snarled in the narrow streets of New York's garment district, a nightmare of rolling racks of garments. We inched our way to the state department, where I was second in line outside their doors on the twenty-fourth floor. They did not open until 9:30 am; as the line behind me grew and grew, I was so anxious that by then I was truly in tears. When the doors finally opened, people shouted good luck to me. There were ten windows; I, being a fatalist, randomly chose one without any thought to the clerk's possible disposition. Its sour-faced lady looked at my passport and said, "Three days required."

I cried out, "No! I will pay extra. I need it now. My ship sails in one and a half hours!"

She then informed me that, since I was not U.S.-born, she could not just stamp it but needed clearance from Washington.

I said, "Fine! Get it!"

Suddenly, a colleague told her that a man from the pier was on the phone and wished to speak with me. She refused to hand me the phone.

I asked her, "Please, get the telephone number, and I will call him back."

There he was, so close and yet so far. The clerk told me to go down to the main lobby, where there were public telephones, during which time my passport might be stamped. Down I fled, all twenty-four stories.

The caller was Hy Levy, my brother's friend. I told him to calm the ladies but to take my luggage off the ship if the timing looked bad. I'd come as soon as possible. A very nice man in the lobby of the building noted my dilemma and asked if he should hold a cab for me. I said, "Yes, please," and back upstairs I went. Everyone let me through. The lady at the window told me the extra charges I had to pay for being a naturalized citizen; I paid and ran out the door to the applause of the others in line.

Downstairs, I told the cab driver that he had a ten-dollar tip if he could get me to the pier on time. I closed my eyes and thought of France, as the saying goes.

When at last I arrived at the pier, I heard the loudspeaker announcing, "Passenger has arrived! Passenger has arrived!" However, the ship was no longer in the dock!

I shouted at poor Hy, who had innocently come to see off his friend's sister and instead I had worn him out completely. Of course, he had had no power to hold the ship until my return. By this time the *Île-de-France* was already at the three-mile zone.

—

A lovely gentleman from Cunard said his company had told my mother not to worry, that I would leave that night on the *Queen Elizabeth*. They had removed my luggage from the *Île-de-France*, and so I had everything, except two long evening dresses that were in my mother's old and beautiful steamer trunk. The man also informed me that the Cunard Line would have taken me out to meet the ship at the three-mile zone had I been their passenger, but evidently the French Line had experienced too many late passengers on other voyages and had refused to cooperate in my instance.

I was suddenly exhausted; my situation seemed so unreal. There was nothing to do but return to the St. Regis Hotel to wait out the day until the *Queen Elizabeth* would sail. Dragging along my brother's friend to assist me in this final duty, I presented myself at the reception desk. You can imagine their surprise to see me back! Luckily, a room was available.

Next on my agenda was to call home, in San Francisco. My brother answered, which was a great relief; I felt he could soften the blow to the rest of my family. I rattled off the whole morning's experience, including that his friend was still with me. Then I heard him say, "Dad, guess what? Janet missed the boat." I could hear in the background my father's anxious questions—"Are they all right? What happened? Where is Mother?"— and suddenly I couldn't speak. I was doubled over with laughter and couldn't stop. I had to hand the phone to Hy. The whole affair seemed so outrageous and impossible that I was in sheer hysterics (I also think my nerves just gave way to laughter as a release). When I was able to finally take the phone, I informed my father that Cunard had booked another ship for me and that I would leave at midnight.

Daddy arranged a ship-to-shore three-way phone call with San Francisco and Mother on the *Île-de-France* so we could all speak with one another. I learned that not only had Mother and Mrs. Robinson left New York in tears, but also that when they entered their cabin, where they were met with a huge bouquet of long-stemmed red roses that I had pre-ordered for them, the sight had set them off all over again. Indeed, I had thought of everything to try to make their voyage special—everything but my passport's untimely expiration date!

At the hotel, the hours passed quickly, and—lucky me—I alone boarded the most beautiful, fabulous ship I had ever seen, the stately and majestic *Queen Elizabeth*. My first sight of her was breathtaking—she was enormous in length. I was received with such courtesy; the head of the Cunard Line came down personally to put me on the ship, as he had promised. I was traveling first class as Mother had purchased a first-class ticket for me on the *Île-de-France*. I boarded the *Queen Elizabeth* to discover that everything had been done to accommodate me: there were flowers in my cabin, which was huge and an outside one with a luxurious bath; and also fruit and chocolates, again courtesy of the Cunard Line. All in all, this certainly seemed to make up for missing the other boat— yummy! I was in my element! It was after midnight and had been quite a day, and I was ready to jump into my nicely turned-down bed—but not before I sampled a delicious chocolate! As the ship started to move, I drifted with the waves off to a new adventure.

I awoke early and was washing my face when I heard a knock. I quickly jumped back into bed as I answered, "Yes?" At the door was the steward, with a cup of tea. It was so lovely to be spoiled! I decided to take full advantage of this luxury and told him that I would not be going down to the dining room for breakfast and would like it in my cabin. I ordered what I wished, and off he went. After enjoying a private breakfast in my cabin, I dressed casually and ventured to the open deck. The deck steward already had my own deck chair and red-and-black plaid blanket waiting for me. Such niceties that existed in the days of leisurely travel are gone forever in today's world; I feel so fortunate to have just caught the end of that.

Sitting next to me was a Chinese lady in a dark suit and with jet-black hair pulled back into a bun. She was truly beautiful in a very special way. Only later did I realize that her bearing and the natural elegance when she moved were much a part of it. We liked each other immediately and decided to take our lunch at the same table in the dining room. My voyage looked promising; already I had a most interesting companion. She introduced herself as Mai Ti-sen. I recognized by her surname that she belonged to a great dynasty, the Sens. She was not very forthcoming at the beginning, but in spite of this and our age difference, I was content to accept her friendship on her terms. After lunch, during which she heard that my evening wear was sailing on another ship in my mother's trunk, she invited me into her cabin and said that perhaps I could find some gowns to borrow.

I entered a cabin that was twice the size of mine. There were packages everywhere; she said she had had things delivered directly to the ship. She was so unassuming that soon we were both opening packages, I sighing with delight at their luxurious yet unostentatious contents. Obviously, it was as much fun for her to see how much I appreciated a simple black silk bag from Cartier, with a delicate ruby and diamond clasp. Everything was exquisite, not vulgar. One would have needed a very good eye to see the detail and subtle beauty that made her selections special. I thought to myself, *When I get older, that's how I would like to be.* I had no idea at that time that this divine lady would be such a great influence in my life.

Mai found, among her things, a lovely black lace gown that she thought would suit me. Like me, she was very small and thin, and it fit me. She urged me to wear it, saying that I had enough other dresses to tide me over the voyage as even on the *Queen Elizabeth* passengers did not don formal wear every evening. I was enchanted by her generosity—I adored just *being* with my new friend, and to be permitted to wear one of her gorgeous dresses was deeply thrilling.

The plot thickens: when the passenger list arrived on my breakfast tray the next morning, to my surprise I saw that the Marquis de Cuevas was on board. What a coincidence! I also met some other people who asked me to join them as they had a young lady in their party, just a little older than me. They were Dick Reed, who was then president of American Express, and his wife and the firm's vice president, Pete Bradford. They were always joined by all the young bankers from Barclay's who were on the ship, and I guess young women were a rarity in first class. Happily for me, I danced my feet off each night as the Reeds retired and left the young people to dance; at midnight, we had supper in the Club restaurant.

I liked one of the bankers named Tom Lodge, who was typically English, with perfect manners and was extremely well spoken. I learned that he had really wanted to be a writer but had ended up a banker. He was much older, but I truly did not enjoy people my own age. From the age of about seven, I already knew what I wanted to do with my life and had actively pursued it, which was and still is rather unusual; most people do not take so firm a command of their life's path until college or later. Here I was, at seventeen, a member of a world-famous ballet company, having already danced most of my life. Between my pursuit of a career and my European travels, I felt so much more mature than the average teenager.

Everyone was very curious about the marquis as he was keeping to his cabin; he was not too well. Finally, one day, he appeared on deck, bundled in woolen scarves. I went to greet him and received a fatherly "Bonjour, petite," with kisses on both cheeks. He then said in English, "Come, my child, walk with me," as he tucked my arm into his. As we chatted about his health and other matters, of course, every eye turned. Pete gave me a big wink, but everyone who did not know of my professional association was sure that the marquis was flirting with a *jeune fille.* He was truly like a father to everyone in the ballet company, but it was so nice to have him to myself on board ship and so amusing to be the object of gossip! I must say that the marquis had what is now called "star quality"; just his appearance made people look at him. Not because he was bizarre, quite the contrary.

He had a wonderful profile, and somehow he stood out as really special. I felt very proud as we promenaded around the deck. When he had had enough of a walk, he kissed me good-bye and expressed the hope that we could walk a bit each day. I was quite content. As we made our daily promenades, I became known as the marquis's ballerina! (Even though, in the ballet world, I did not deserve the title of *ballerina* just yet.)

One day, everyone became excited as we were to be passing the *Île-de-France* in mid ocean. The passengers who knew my story were very encouraging, pressing me to stand on the upper deck for the best view. Obviously, I could not see anything but the ship itself. But even the sight of that was somehow very moving, and, of course, I began to cry—and yet in truth I was having the best time ever on the *Queen Elizabeth*. I just hoped that my mother and Mrs. Robinson were also enjoying themselves instead of dwelling on my absence. We did make a ship-to-ship call eventually, which required special arrangement, and they seemed fine and happy. I certainly was, despite being sorry we were not together.

Then the sea changed, and the ship began to roll. I was reminded of my first trip. No way would I allow myself to be so sick again. Pete Bradford decided that if I drank nothing but champagne, I would lick seasickness. The night before the ocean became really rough, we drank grasshoppers, a mild concoction of crème de menthe and cream. Ugh—to this day, I can't go near crème de menthe, and I am sure this is why I felt so sick. The grasshoppers were really jumping. I thought Mr. Bradford's method would kill me or cure me; I was so queasy from those grasshoppers that I lost everything! But by the next evening, I was back on my feet, dancing the night away.

By then, the sea was calm, and Tom and I went for a walk on the upper deck. It was very beautiful and romantic as Tom turned to me and kissed me. I think every young girl dreams of her first kiss as being special, and mine certainly was there in the middle of the Atlantic Ocean. We held each other closely, and at last, I knew what it was like to feel one's heart pounding as one was being kissed for the first time. It was the beginning of my first real romance. I went back to my cabin walking on air, not believing how all this was happening to me just because I missed the boat!

The next day, I had a long conversation with Mai. I gathered that she was married to the elder Sen, who when she was in Paris or New York always hired watch guards to accompany her for protection. She gave me her telephone number in Paris but asked me to give it to no one. Pete Bradford wanted us to meet for lunch once we were in Paris, which she agreed to do. But then she would be traveling. She gave me another number at which I could reach her when she returned to New York. Her life was still such a mystery to me.

Two nights remained to the voyage. Everyone was issued invitations for cocktails or dinners. On the next-to-last evening, I was invited to sit at the captain's table, where I felt very much like a young woman. Gone was my ordinary peach organdy dinner dress; in its place I wore my lovely black chiffon dress with an off-the-shoulder pink silk neckline. It was very flattering and elegant. I had my hair pulled back, with small curls clinging to my neck. After dinner, we joined the Reeds for coffee and one final night of dancing until dawn.

The next day, I awoke early as I did not want to miss one minute of this special day. I ate breakfast then started to pack. I was already thinking ahead. It had been a great trip, but soon I would be back in class and working. I had but two weeks before rehearsals began. Luckily, in spite of all my shipboard dining, I was thin!

It was an unusually lovely day in early summer; we had not had the sun often during the voyage, but it came out for us then. On deck, Mai and I shared our hopes that we would not lose touch with each other. I so adored her even though I knew so little about her life. During the voyage, all I was able to establish was that she was married to an elderly and enormously wealthy man and that she spent some of her time in China. I didn't believe she was happy; I think our trip was probably the happiest she'd been in a long time: unwatched, no duties, no rules, no husband. I felt sad for her as well as for myself as I had a feeling that after Paris, I would never see this lady again, that she would never know what a great influence she had been in my life. My solace was that at least we had a firm lunch date in Paris. Also, Tom said he had to be in Paris in ten days, which was wonderful news for me as I would not yet be rehearsing.

On our last evening at sea, long dresses and black ties were not worn; instead, one just dressed elegantly. It was on this night that the captain told me I would actually arrive at Le Havre a full day ahead of my mother on the Île-de-France. That pleased me because it meant that I would be there to meet her and her friend at the pier.

We didn't spend a late night on deck that evening, instead saying our good-byes after dinner and then returning to our respective cabins to finish packing. I prepared my little envelopes that contained tips for the various services given me (I hate handing money to someone but was already prepared, having gone to Chinatown in San Francisco to buy the little red envelopes used for monetary gifts on the Chinese New Year for good luck; to this day, I still give tips in these little red envelopes). Once I had sorted out my shipboard obligations, I crawled into bed. It would be a hectic morning.

17

The Needle in the Haystack

Morning arrived, and we disembarked at Le Havre. I already knew the system and headed toward the first-class train cars that would take me into Paris and Gare St-Lazare. I then took a taxi to the Continental Hotel near the place Vendôme and faubourg St-Honoré.

I chose this hotel for my mother, Mrs. Robinson, and myself as, at the time, it was still very Old World, with a grand dining room and impeccable service. I loved the rooms, with their red velvet drapes, white walls with very rococo gold, and all that a first-class hotel in those days should have. On the whole, I felt my selection was a good one. I unpacked somewhat but was eager to go out exploring.

The area was perfect for the ladies. In both directions along faubourg St. Honoré, they could look to their heart's content. The Louvre was within walking distance, the Champs-Élysées—everything. I spoke to the concierge about arranging a private tour for them to familiarize them with the neighborhood, filled their rooms with tulips and other spring flowers, and made other arrangements I hoped would please them. Time flew by. I had my dinner, thinking about how soon tomorrow would be here, when I'd be reunited with my mother and her friend.

I awoke early to freshly baked croissants, yummy butter and jam, and delicious strong coffee. Sadly, it was pouring rain, but I thought it was wonderful. For them to see Paris in the rain was even better as that had its own magic.

I had made a deal with the doorman to call one of the old cabs of Paris for me to take to the train station (taxis were starting to change to ordinary cars, and that would never do for this occasion). I choreographed everything, with God's help, for this arrival! Flowers in hand, I explained in my limited French to my very French cab driver what had transpired, and he became very civil, as if delighted to become a part of my plan. I rushed into the station as the train was just arriving. Perfect timing. There were not many people on the platform, so my task would be easy. I commanded a porter who stood waiting with his cart in hand. Now, if a familiar face would appear out of a train window!

Lots of windows opened at the same time, and every head known to man popped out. But there was that little head of my mother—she looked different from everybody else, and I ran toward the window shrieking, "Mother!" and we both started to cry. We had only been apart seven days, but we were crying with the sheer joy of being reunited. She and her friend disembarked, and we exchanged hugs while the porter rounded up their luggage. So far, so good.

When we boarded my awaiting taxi, Mrs. Robinson's first remark was that we could have afforded a real car! I pretended I didn't hear her. As we approached the place de la Concorde, I quickly said to Mother, "That's Cleopatra's Needle." My mother, trying her best to see anything out the window in that pouring rain, replied, "Huh. It's like looking for a needle in a haystack!"

I was struck as if by lightning. How could they speak this way about the place de la Concorde, the taxi, the rain? It was all *Paris*. Didn't they get it? To me, everything there was a perfect entrance for them, but poor Paris did not appear to them as it did to a seventeen-year-old who already loved this city. I decided there and then that they could be on their own as they went about as tourists instead of seeing the real Paris as I knew it.

Over dinner, they were a good audience as I told them all of my adventure on board the *Queen Elizabeth*. I left out my great romance, of course. I would tell Mother about that when we were alone. It was really very nice for me to have Mother there as we had always been close.

The next day, as I prepared to go to class, to my surprise Mother insisted on going with me as she had heard so much about Egorova. That was fine with her friend, who would spend the morning roaming around with plenty to do. I was so excited to see my beloved Egorova again. I had called ahead, so she was expecting me. Classes had not officially started yet; it was still the company's holiday time. I approached the familiar door on avenue Rochefoucauld, seated Mother in the studio, and went to change. Five minutes later, I came out just as Madame entered the room. I gave her a big hug and then introduced her to my mother. She was sweet to Mother but was clearly upset by what had occurred in London. She knew just what I had done, and why, what John Taras had said. Egorova was so angry that I could not answer as she berated me. "Why? Why? You are young, beautiful, strong technique like Russians, strong back, big jump, body of Russian ballerina, expression, and you dance from your heart. You are not Balanchine. For that, you were in wrong place, wrong ballet master, wrong decision. It is crazy what he told you. My dear child, you suffered too much. With different schooling, your body would change with time. Extension change, upper body change, porte de bras change—you must go from this idea of Balanchine. It is not for everyone, and especially not for Europe or public. You will be only like the next girl instead of ballerina with classical possibilities and dramatic ability. Technique is not a problem for you, already so young. Artistic possibility and ease and effortless motion must now be your training." She was in tears as she told me this. I was sobbing by then, and Madame just rocked me, holding me, as Mother sat there also in tears, understanding only too well this daughter of hers and the heartbreak I had been through. She knew I needed her support, following Egorova's outburst. After that first day, Mother never missed coming to watch Egorova work with me to see my strength and my soul magically return.

During the adagios she was setting for me, Egorova would close her eyes as she spoke, using her hands to show the movement. As she explained the physical actions, it was by watching her face that I understood the feeling of what it was that she wanted. There were times when I felt totally released from technique when only that feeling motivated my body to move. Was this what she meant should empassion my dancing, not perfection of technique? During these moments, I so loved what I was doing that I even forgot Mother was there.

Until this private time in Egorova's studio, my mother had not seen me dance since I'd danced with San Francisco Ballet. This was three years later, after I had performed professionally and been coached by great teachers. Now, Mother announced to me that I was the best dancer she had ever seen. This, coming from my mother, was very touching as she had never said anything like that to me. Time would tell as my classes with the de Cuevas Ballet began.

When class and rehearsals began with the company, Mother came to the class that John Taras taught. I reintroduced him to Mother, whom he had met in San Francisco years earlier. He seemed happy to see me, but his only comment to me was simply, "You are looking well." I shrugged it off and went on, as what could anyone say?

When I looked at the rehearsals schedule, I saw I was listed for two new ballets—I felt I was off to a good start. I was happy to see everyone, and the Carlins were overjoyed to have me back, but something had changed. It was *me* that was different. I thought I could stand up to anything now because I knew what I was worth to the company.

Mother and Mrs. Robinson went to Switzerland for a week, and that left me free to work and think. My friend Tom arrived from London, and that was an extremely happy occasion. We made a date for dinner as I still had all-day rehearsals. When Tom arrived at the Continental, I felt quite grand being fetched from this elegant hotel. It was a lovely, balmy night, and I had on just the right little dress that seemed to meet with approval from the hotel staff that always kept an eye on me. It's hard to explain that if you were a member of Le Grand Ballet de Marquis de Cuevas, you belonged to Paris. We dancers were pampered, just because. Tom's eyes lit up as he took my hand and kissed it. Very un-English! I loved it! At that moment, the world was perfect. I was in Paris, I was making my living as a dancer, and I had a boyfriend.

We went to a small bistro and talked for hours. When we finally realized how late it was and apologized to the owner, he insisted we could stay as long as we wanted to. We, of course, left with rounds of handshakes and *mercis*. The owner expressed the hope that mademoiselle would return again. I did, very often, and to this day, Chez George is still one of my favorite places. Tom and I walked back along the Seine, where again he took me in his arms and kissed me. This time, I kissed him back.

It was very late when we returned to the hotel—and the large doors were locked shut! I was horrified that I had to ring a bell. The side door opened, and their night watchman let me in—but not before Tom had kissed me once again as he would be leaving for London the next day. The watchman seemed perfectly content with our kissing. As Tom said good-bye and promised to keep in touch, I again thought to myself how very un-English he seemed in Paris! I never would have guessed it!

One day, I returned from rehearsals to find a telegram from my father, saying he would arrive a few days earlier than expected. What fun that would be! I saw no reason to bring Mother and her friend back early from their trip. I made sure his room would be ready and that all the hotel arrangements would be in order for Mother to join Daddy and for Mrs. Robinson to have her own room when they returned from Switzerland. Of course I stayed where I was.

When my father arrived, all the world seemed right. It was then that I began to understand what had seemed not quite right. I needed to make a serious career decision and could not do so without the counsel of my parents and perhaps one or two ballet professionals I trusted and respected. But meanwhile, I meant to show my father the Paris I knew. The tourist stuff, I thought he could do with the ladies.

He was so happy and excited to be there with me. Daddy was so inquisitive about everything. He loved people and people loved him. He had no fear of anything. If he did not speak the language, he picked up a word or two and charmed his way through the rest. Oddly enough, everyone understood him. (In his younger days, he had learned many other languages; perhaps he also simply had an overall facility to communicate!)

For our first night, I wanted to take him to Le Table du Roi, a very expensive restaurant with one hundred violins. I'd heard of the place but would never have been able to have afforded it myself. With the help of a tip, the concierge of our hotel arranged everything. That night was truly unforgettable. The restaurant was divine; we were literally surrounded by a hundred musicians. They had one trick: every once in a while, they balanced a glass of champagne on a violin as they chose a victim from the audience to drink it down while they fiddled away! It was just in fun, and everyone seemed to be enjoying themselves when suddenly, they stood in front of me! I felt like saying, "Wait, I'm not old enough to drink!" But in France, that would have sounded ridiculous. My father thought it perfectly all right, so I went ahead with it. Everyone laughed, except me, as I gulped down an entire glass of champagne without stopping. I finished to a round of applause. I would have been arrested in America, and the bartender would have had his license revoked. Oh, Paris, you wicked city!

Daddy was having a wonderful time, and he loved that I could manage (just manage!) in French. I could see he was proud of his daughter who had flown the coop and learned a great deal. I looked like a young European, not American at all. But my looks, clothing, and manners had already been totally European as my parents had raised me; Paris had only put the final touches on.

The next night, we went to the Caprice, which, again, I had heard of but never been to. This, too, was someplace extraordinary. It was all homosexuals but not as we had seen in America. I, in San Francisco, had gone often to Finocchio's where one saw performers in drag, probably the best in America. But the Caprice was in a different league. First of all, they really appeared to be women. Second, they appeared to be very beautiful women. And third, they were talented: they put on a show that was highly imaginative, and after a while, you forgot or disbelieved that they were not really women. This was by no means a campy drag act; I was told that these men strove to credibly resemble genuine women in both their physical appearance and their movements. However they achieved it, they were simply gorgeous! My father loved the Caprice as it was so

—

different and amusing; I felt I was really giving him an education (the club no longer exists, but I'm sure that in Paris they have newer ones that are just as good)! Daddy surprised me with his own cap to the evening; as we began our return to our hotel, he suggested that we take an old-fashioned horse-and-buggy ride back to the Continental. This was a first for me! It was the perfect ending to the time we shared prior to the ladies' return. The next morning, my mother and Mrs. Robinson arrived, and we had a grand reunion over breakfast.

As I had class and rehearsals, I left the three of them to the museums. We continued to do something together each night, thanks to the concierge, who arranged for tickets to the ballet performing at the opera house and tours of the antique and silver vaults, Versailles, the Eiffel Tower, Sacre-Coeur, and so on.

After a few days, Mother asked how things were going for me. I said, "All right for now." She surprised me by saying that, having discussed the situation with my father, they both felt that I should leave the company now. At that moment, Mr. Taras was immersed in the Balanchine school, and I clearly did not fit in with that. They felt that such a strong Balanchine influence created an atmosphere in which it was unhealthy for me to remain. In my heart, I knew they were right but felt that leaving the company would be a very big change for me.

The next day, after class, Mr. Taras vanished into conference with my parents. I proceeded to my rehearsal but sensed instinctively that I would not go on to perform that ballet. Later, when I dressed to leave, my parents reappeared with Mr. Taras. I couldn't look up at first, but at last my father said to me, "Janet, we have decided to withdraw you from the company."

I looked at Mr. Taras, and he said, "Well, your parents seem to think you should leave after all you did, and I understand that. You know you are always welcome here." I gave him a quick kiss and fled. My parents followed, with a great sigh of relief.

My father looked at my sad face and said, "We shall now see a bit of Europe. And you, dear child, will go with us for a holiday."

18

Voyageurs

It made me very happy that my father had opened his heart to the vibrancy of the Paris that I too loved, despite speaking so little of its language. As the time approached for us to leave Paris, he asked me to save one afternoon for him before we got too busy. He was very secretive about his plans for that afternoon.

When the day arrived, he said he wished to visit the great couturiers' houses. I was enchanted by this idea as I had always wanted to see them but had not known how to do so without the escort of someone older than me. We started at Dior, where I bought the perfume Miss Dior, which I wear to this day. Then we went to Chanel and, last but not least, to Jacques Fath. Here they showed us a dress that was a dream! It was a pale tea-color strapless silk organza evening dress with a hem that was lower in the back than in the front. There were organdy flowers appliquéd all over the skirt. It was unique. My father said to try it on. I left with the lady, and she pinned it in a bit, assuring me that apart from a little alteration, it was "made for mademoiselle"! I couldn't agree with her more. I walked out of the dressing room to model it for my father. Everyone oohed and aahed, and Father's eyes lit up. He seemed very proud to see his little girl turn into so well possessed a young lady. He said, "That's it, we'll take it!" I quickly gave him a big hug, well possessed or not. At this, everyone was all smiles—and there was no mention of money! There was no price tag on the dress, and I certainly hoped that my father knew this was not just any dress. They assured us as we prepared to leave that the alterations would be made and that they would deliver the dress to our hotel; my father, having taken care of the monetary matters, thought that was fine. Everyone was really happy that this was my first real long evening gown, and that our selection seemed to be such a special occasion for us—where else but in Paris could this special purchase have taken place? My first evening gown, and by Jacques Fath!

I returned to Chanel, where I bought a pair of silk shoes to match the dress. As was typical of their service, Chanel would even write my name in gold inside them! They would also be delivered to the hotel. I still have those shoes today and would never part with them; they too have memories of having danced the night away!

We were to leave Paris for Switzerland, arriving in Geneva by train in first-class accommodations. What a treat for me as on my own I always went second class. All this excitement obviously allowed me to make the break with the company a bit easier. I was so determined to make our trip a happy one for my parents in return for all they had done for me. They were so proud of me; the decision to leave had been made, and I was not going to spoil our time together by pining for or over my future with the company. I also had the positive feeling that this had opened the door for something good to happen. I have always found that if you let go of something, it allows other things to enter your life.

For a while, it was difficult not to be dancing—no class, no rehearsals, no performances. I was rather mixed up inside as having begun my studies so young, I had never lived without dance being a part of my life. Even while recovering from illness or while laid up in London, I'd always anticipated going back to it as soon as I could. Now, I could eat what I wanted, sleep when and however long I wanted, surprisingly neither an easy task after all the years of self-discipline and work. I knew I had to be very strong with myself; there was plenty of time to face the future. This was a very special chance for me to spend time with two people whom I loved very much. I adored my parents, and they were great company—my mother and I loved the same things, and we could almost read each other's mind at times; Daddy was so very inquisitive, curious, delighted at all he saw and whoever he met. He had that great gift of opening himself to and accepting people as they were, and they loved him for it. He was never a snob or a show off; he never made others feel little. That is what made him a gentleman.

In Geneva, my father had some business to attend to in which Mother and I would not join him. We were now staying at the Bauer Lac Hotel, which in those days was one of the best hotels in the world. There, everyone dressed for dinner, and I must say I loved the elegance that one felt in those surroundings. Knowing that the morning after our tour of couturiers my father was going off very early on a business trip, I decided to do a bit of mischief! Before retiring, everyone had set their shoes in front of their door, which was the custom in hotels at that time. In the morning, one would find one's shoes beautifully polished, outside the door. Well, I decided that things were too quiet around there and changed everybody's shoes to different doors. So that my father would not be late to his appointment, I added one shoe to his genuine pair, to make three, knowing that despite this curiosity to the hotel staff, he would find his shoes perfectly shined at 6:00 am and simply leave the lonely one in front of the door. I slept very well that night, having done my damage gleefully, only wishing somebody like Ruth from the company had been with me.

The next morning, I met Mother in the dining room for breakfast. I kissed her good morning and gave my order to my favorite young waiter, who was learning the ropes. My mother asked me if I had heard all the rumpus in the hallways and the bell ringing. I was barely able to face her as I said, "What noise?" She then proceeded to tell me that that had brought a huge tray of shoes to each door. Now I truly could not look at her as I knew she would see right through me. I just said, "Oh, really?" My eyes were then so large that surely she guessed who had been behind the affair, but there in the dining room she could hardly scold me in front of everyone. We would have been thrown out of the Bauer, for sure. All she could reply was, "What would your father say!"

Our nice young waiter returned with our coffee. I had been speaking to him in French. We spoke a little, and I said, "What a beautiful language French is, like music, n'est-ce pas? Whereas German was so brutal." He looked at me with those beautiful blue eyes and for the next two minutes recited Goethe in perfect German, beautifully pronounced. When he finished, he said in French, "C'est jolie, mademoiselle, n'est-ce pas?" and walked out of my life. He taught me a lesson I have never forgotten. I think I grew up that morning.

Our journey continued by car. We had a driver and took pleasure in stopping for lunch at small restaurants located in public gardens as this was summer. I began to worry about my weight—I had never eaten three meals a day, except at birth! My old dance regimen was very spartan compared with my present one. Both my parents were not big eaters; they ate very little breakfast, had only a small lunch, and for them, dinner was always the main event. But they also enjoyed afternoon tea. This was a must for my mother, the one British habit she could not break. I loved four o'clock tea but previously had not had the time to take it.

Father announced that we would spend three days in Rhinefelden, where one drank the waters to become healthy and rejuvenated. In other words, it was a spa for rich Americans, English, and any other nationality that could afford such expensive water! I had never been to a spa before or to anyplace quite like this. There was nobody under the age of forty as they were all there to regain their youth! Massage was given, which was great for me; and I certainly did *not* drink much of the waters, which for the others was the big thing to do. I had drunk enough on my first day there to feel like a volleyball. Somehow I managed to last two days; I knew that if I said I wanted to leave, it would not happen. But the gods smiled down on me.

On the evening of the second day, my father and I were in the garden, dressed formally for dinner, and we sat on the swings to pass the time spent waiting for Mother. My father started with, "Do you like it here?" Direct hit, but I said, "Well, it's not very exciting. I don't feel much younger—too many old people around." With that, I let out a roar of laughter and said that I thought there were much happier places to be. He replied decisively, "Tomorrow, we leave!"

Mother was overjoyed by the news as she confided her own horror story that had only just occurred that afternoon: someone had nonchalantly said to her, "You see, this side is Swiss, but across the Rhine is Germany. During the war, people tried swimming here from across the water. Jews trying to get into Switzerland. So many shot in the water." With that, my mother's eyes had filled with tears as here we were, alive and free. She could not bear to stay at the spa one moment longer than was necessary. Before we left, my father went to the shoreline and recited the Kaddish, the prayer for the dead, while my mother and I stood there with our heads bowed.

Our next stop was Düsseldorf, where my father left us for one night to go off on business. While my father was away, my mother and I spent the day sightseeing; she spoke Dutch, in which she was markedly more fluent than I was. Sadly, another most unfortunate incident occurred.

As we were window-shopping, a man stepped in front of us and spat. Recognizing us as being tourists and obviously not quite all there himself, he began screaming, "Americans!" For my mother, that was it. I have never seen my quiet, gentle, soft-spoken mother go into action as she did that day. She turned to me with a grim expression I had never seen on her face and quietly said, "We will return to the hotel." Once in the lobby, she said, "We are leaving—now." I tried to explain to her that this could have happened anywhere in Europe, but she felt differently: we were in Germany, and we were Jews. Nothing I could say could convince her to await my father's return. Perhaps this incident frightened her because she had never had to look anti-Semitism or hatred straight in the face. The spitting man had seethed with both. And so our arrangements were changed for us to proceed to our next stop, which was Holland.

Father joined us in Amsterdam. What a delightful city, and what joyous people! Both my parents could speak the language, and I am sure they felt a wonderful release in being able to fully communicate. We stayed at the Amstel Hotel, with a wonderful view of the canal. There were many Javanese restaurants, and we all looked forward to a good Nasi Goreng (Indonesian-style fried rice).

My old friend Bob, whom I'd met in Zurich, lived in Amsterdam. I called to let him know I was in town, and he took me to dinner at a well-known restaurant on the outskirts of the city, with a name that translated to something like Devil's Den. I'm afraid it turned out to be a very angelic evening on my part, in spite of Bob's having become quite the sophisticate back home in his own country. But we had a good time, and I enjoyed his wonderful joie de vivre.

My parents and I made Amsterdam our home base, from which we made various side trips—for example, to the region where Gouda cheese was made. It was really charming there, the ladies all wearing their provincial dress; I felt as if I were looking at a Dutch painting.

Being in the Netherlands really pulled the trip together for my parents. For all her other travels, my mother had never been to Europe; she seemed to feel most at home in Holland. For my father, it was a different situation; as a young man, he had visited numerous places in Europe but never with a wife and daughter along. I know for them both, having the opportunity to speak Dutch again brought back many memories of the Dutch East Indies, where my parents had spent the early years of their married life. They had enjoyed a good life under the Dutch even though they were British subjects. I'm sure being able to eat some of the dishes they remembered gave them great pleasure, even though, of course, the scenery was quite different from that of the Indies. Everyone we met in Holland was quite astonished to find out where my parents had learned to speak Dutch (frankly, Dutch was not the most beautiful language to my ear, but after my experience with the waiter in Switzerland, I was not about to voice that opinion!). When we had our fill of steeping in the atmosphere of the Netherlands, our thoughts turned to our final destination: London.

Unfortunately, we had not allotted enough time to this leg of the trip for my parents to see all the friends and relatives they would have liked to, but perhaps this was for the best. There was always the question "What if?" Ever since I was old enough to think it, I'd asked it silently. My father, though, had rejected England before he'd married: he loved to visit it but never for one second would he have lived there. He loved America and especially San Francisco, as did my mother. In contrast, the rest of his side of the family had become very Anglophile.

As we boarded the plane that would take us to London, I was really looking forward to this conclusion to our marvelous travels in a city that felt like home to me. First, my departure from the company had been eased emotionally by the strong support of my parents and by their gift of this luxurious travel experience that I knew I would remember my entire life. Also, I had had a time-out period, during which I came to understand what people who were not dancers did while on holiday. I was exposed to other forms of culture beyond that of the ballet world. For instance, this was the period when girls were swooning over Frank Sinatra, but I had been so immersed in dance and classical music that I barely knew who he was! Conversely, to most people, ballet was an entertainment while to me it was almost a religious act once I had become a professional.

In London, we checked into the renowned Savoy Hotel. We were given a suite, which meant that my parents' bedroom and mine were on either side of our own sitting room. We even had our own butler. I loved the man's attentive service as he was very sweet with me; my father also enjoyed it immensely; but my mother was a bit uneasy until she got used to him. I think she would have preferred a female in such an intimate setting.

Each morning, we would gather in the sitting room for breakfast and to plan the day's activities. Royal Ballet was then called Sadler's Wells Ballet, and they were not in season during our time in London. We booked two nights of theater instead.

This left me very little time to see my friend Tom. I phoned him to let him know I'd arrived, and he invited me to a full evening of theater then supper then dancing at the Savoy, which meant respectively we'd be wearing an evening gown and a black tie. It all sounded so grown-up and delicious! I excitedly gave my Jacques Fath gown to our wonderful butler to remove the creases from its having been packed, confiding to him the agenda of the approaching evening. He handled it as if it were a princess's ball gown, saying, "Don't worry, miss, everything will be perfect."

In the meantime, my father and I went to Saville Row, where he had ordered several suits that were now ready to be picked up; I enjoyed accompanying him as I have always found shopping for men far more interesting in London than for women. London was and still is a paradise for men's attire; they cut suits with such precision that a one made to order in England would last a lifetime. It never goes out of style because it is of such a classic cut, and of the best fabric. My father had ordered two suits with vests—for San Francisco—plus a navy blue blazer and casual trousers for the boat trip back, and I selected for him one very English bowler hat, which I have kept to this day in memory of our time together that summer. He had great fun, and my father seemed pleased to have me along. Oddly, I sensed that this time would never come again, that it had been borrowed time, that soon I would be returning to my world of dance.

On the appointed day for my date with Tom, I had butterflies in my stomach, and my parents were as nervous as I was. London is a walker's city, but I was determined not to tire myself out during the morning and afternoon as I had every intention of dancing the night away. That day, Mother and I went to Simpson's, then one of the city's great department stores. There, we found some gifts to take back with us, and then we returned to the hotel. I couldn't wait to jump into the tub for a long soak.

The butler greeted me with shining eyes as he told me my dress was waiting for me in my room. He had taken the liberty of ordering a few open-faced chicken sandwiches and tea for me as he feared it would be quite late before I had supper. I thought that was a lovely idea; I arranged to have my tea after I had bathed and enjoyed a long bubble bath. I didn't dress in my gown immediately, donning a robe instead so that I could put on my makeup and fix my hair into a nice chignon. Satisfied that I could do no more, I entered our sitting room to discover the butler awaiting my arrival. Although I was not very hungry, he insisted that I eat the sandwiches, actually standing by me as I ate to be sure I had put something in my stomach! Then my mother and I went into my room so I could finish dressing while my father remained in the sitting room to read the newspapers.

This time, the gown fit perfectly; my mother helped to arrange it in place. She was beaming as she stood back to look at her daughter. I trusted her taste as she was never overdressed nor wore a great deal of jewelry despite my father's fondness for giving her beautiful pieces. She would always say, "If you have on five pieces of jewelry, you should take off two." That night, I wore a beautiful strand of pearls, earrings, and a gold bracelet that was a very old family piece of 24-karat gold. It was most unusual and very beautiful. I also had a silk purse from Paris, my Dior shoes, and a stole of silk organza that matched the dress. I made my grand entrance into the sitting room, feeling very elegant indeed.

My father looked up approvingly as our butler said, "Miss, you look very beautiful, if I may say so." Of course, I do believe my audience was rather prejudiced!

My parents escorted me to the lobby, where they would be introduced at last to Tom. He looked dashing and very English, though obviously our age difference was noticed immediately by my parents. Tom assured them that we would be back at the hotel for supper and dancing after the theater. Looking relaxed, they wished us a wonderful time. I had the feeling by this time that the entire staff, from butler to front desk, knew that this was my first-ever formal evening.

Imagine kissing your parents good night in the lobby of the Savoy! But I couldn't just shake hands with them. At last, Tom and I were off to the theater. But funny, I recall every detail of that evening *except* what we saw! This is astounding to me as I so adore London theater, where one hears spoken words at their best. In fact, I have no memory of what I thought or did those entire two hours! My recollections pick up with our return to the hotel, where a table had been reserved for us. The evening proceeded just as I'd imagined it: we had champagne and ordered and danced and talked.

Tom told me more about himself. He had wanted to write plays but had gone into banking to make a better living than he would a playwright. He had a talent for words, and I am sure he could have been a good writer given the chance and time. It made me feel so lucky to look back and think of how I had seen my first ballet at five and knew even then that nothing would ever stop me from becoming a ballerina. Now I was nineteen years old, and I had already danced for more than half my life.

I also realized that I knew nothing about being with men! Because of the nature of my family, I had been exposed to many other things, but not to dating. I also found young men boring: I had nothing in common with people my own age outside of my profession, where I always saw them more as colleagues or pals than as potential boyfriends. I liked older men because they were far more evolved and secure, and I could learn from them.

Somehow the time arrived when we had to say good night—and good-bye. Neither of us wanted the evening to end. As Tom held my hand, we promised to write to each other. I thanked him for the most wonderful time I had ever had. But things were a little different in England: in Paris, it had been all right for him to kiss me, but no way would that be repeated even after so romantic an evening in London— because a British gentleman didn't kiss a lady in the lobby of the Savoy! I couldn't believe how important that social rule was! I was very disappointed as we merely looked into each other's eyes as I boarded the elevator. I wished at that moment that we were in Paris, at the gate of the Continental Hotel, where he had held me in his arms. But the humor of the situation was inescapable, and I could hardly wait to tell my mother.

As I put the key in the door to our suite, I saw lights on in the sitting room. My father was up, reading. I slipped into my room where I kicked off my shoes and removed the gown, putting on a comfortable robe. I then returned to the sitting room, where my father was now peeling fruit, as he always used to do after dinner to serve to us. I said, "Great—I'm starving." He looked so shocked as he said, "But you've just had dinner!" I realized then that I hadn't really eaten anything. At this point, Mother decided she couldn't sleep either and joined us in the sitting room, where she saw her elegant daughter stuffing herself with fruit and biscuits and chocolates! Perfect, n'est-ce pas? I then related the entire evening to them, including what a letdown it was not to have been kissed just because this was London. I think they were shocked initially, but then they laughed so hard! I was furious, which only made them laugh the more.

As a doctor would say, our trip home on the *Queen Elizabeth* was uneventful. Which means everything went well, and we had a very good crossing. This time, we all sat at the captain's table, which was not lively for me. Otherwise, we did all the usual things one does on a ship, and I found myself quite at home on the vessel itself. Everyone onstaff remembers a returning passenger, and so I had so many "How nice to have you aboard again, Ms. Sassoon" that my parents became alarmed. I had to assure them that I had done nothing to earn such recognition, except to be courteous to everybody. They seemed to accept that explanation, but I know they must have been wondering if I would want to dance all night or go to the Clubhouse for midnight supper. Well, I would just have to disappoint them.

My father loved betting on how many nautical miles we had traveled and sat every day in the ship's library with his abacus, trying to figure it out. He was incredible with numbers and loved the challenge. Happily, he came the closest and won! This pleased us terribly. And so we were content on board even while I knew my parents were eager to reach home. Actually, I too yearned to be settled for a little while as for years my life had been such a round of rehearsals, theaters, and living out of hotel rooms. I had no complaints about that life, but I still wanted to go home. We three were very complicated on this point: we simply adored traveling but while traveling felt the urge to make a nest somewhere—and then, once in the nest, we ached to escape it. I had had the additional pressure of

—

having worked so hard from such a young age; in time, a dancer's life does become broader, but I had not yet reached that point with the company when I had left it. I had before me my next big step, professionally speaking, and most likely that would involve my going back to New York. But for us, New York was not home. We still had that primal need to renew and refocus ourselves in San Francisco.

On my last night on board the ship, everyone said their farewells early and prepared to retire. I wished my parents good night and went to my cabin to put on my coat, bundling up. I had decided to go back on deck to say my own farewells to the grand ship itself, and all I had experienced with her. As I strode about the deck looking at the waves shining on the water, the view was breathtaking. Nobody was there but me, and I also felt very lonely. So much had happened: it hit me full force that I had voluntarily left the most prestigious ballet company in the world. I thought of all the classics I had danced, of the people I had met. I didn't know when our paths might ever cross again. What a long way I had come. Where was that young girl who, frightened to death, had boarded another ship only a few years earlier, dreaming of dancing—dancing *anything*—with the famous de Cuevas company? Now, my dreams had changed. I desired to perform true ballerina roles. It was time to pursue that new dream. As I looked at the sea, I said farewell to all that I had experienced, the good and the bad. I was ready to land back on American soil—and on my feet.

Janet Sassoon—Age 14

Anne Rodgers (center), Celina Cummings (left), Janet Sassoon.

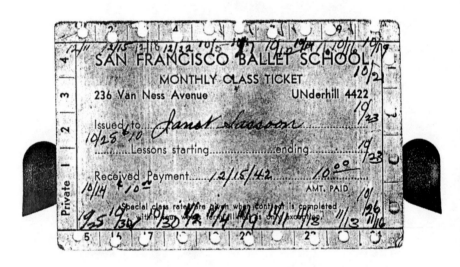

First lesson starting ballet at SF Ballet School

Ruth Galene and Janet in Paris

Janet and Jocelyn Vollmar. Leaving
San Francisco Airport for Paris.

Janet in front of theater

DANCEMAN'S HOLIDAY: The little lady in the babushka using the piano as a barre is Madame Lubov Egorova (Princess Trubetskoy), whose first ballerina appearance was in *Raymonda* in 1912 at St. Petersburg's Maryinsky Theatre. Madame Egorova, now 82, has been teaching in Paris since 1923. Her pupils include some of the most illustrious stars in contemporary ballet.

Madame Egorova's studio was one of those recently visited by dance shoe manufacturer James Selva, of Selva and Sons. He's shown seated at the fireplace. On holiday in Europe, instead of "getting away from it all" Selva and his wife visited many prominent European ballet teachers and schools. Among these were the Royal Ballet School in London, and the schools of Madame Nora and Solange Schwartz in Paris, Rosella Hightower in Cannes, and Claude Newman and Grant Muradoff in Rome. While at Madame Egorova's studio, Selva saw old friends Marina Svetlova and Marjorie Tallchief, who had stopped by for class.

Andre Biro

Madam Lubov Egorova
Janet's Teacher

Le Grand Marquis de Cuevas Company

Company in Cannes with Janet

Two dancers and
Janet at Deauville, France

Janet and
Jocelyn at Cannes, France

Jocelyn and Janet leaving San Francisco for Paris

Janet Sassoon and Alan Howard

Janet Sassoon & Alan Howard

Studying score of Ballet Giselle

Janet Sassoon and Alan Howard

Back Stage—Warming Up

Janet Sassoon and Alan Howard

Pepe Urbani and Janet Sassoon in Berlin Festival

Adriano Vitale

Romeo & Juliet with Roderick Drew

Romeo & Juliet

Juliet

Portrait Don Quixote

Portrait of Janet

Portrait of Janet

Janet

Janet

Portrait of Janet from Buenos Aires

Buenos Aires

Ballet Das Tor

Cassandra in Cain and Abel

Signale

Signale

Sleeping Beauty, Janet

Gert Reinholm & Janet, Signale

Gert Reinholm   Janet—Signale

Harold Horn   Janet—Signale

Janet Sassoon   Gert Reinholm, Signale

Signale

Signale

Signale

Signale

Janet Sassoon   Signale

Marquis de Cuevas with company

Janet's Russian Teachers

Graves outside of Paris—Nureyev

Janet in Studio

Janet teaching

Students practicing how to put on stage make-up

Janet teaching

Janet teaching

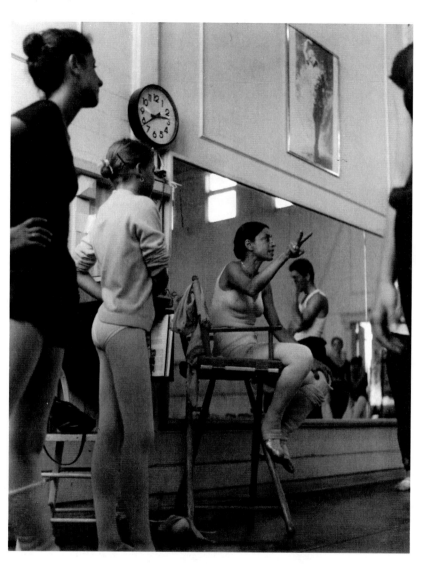

Janet addressing dancers

Janet demonstrating an exercise

Janet teaching

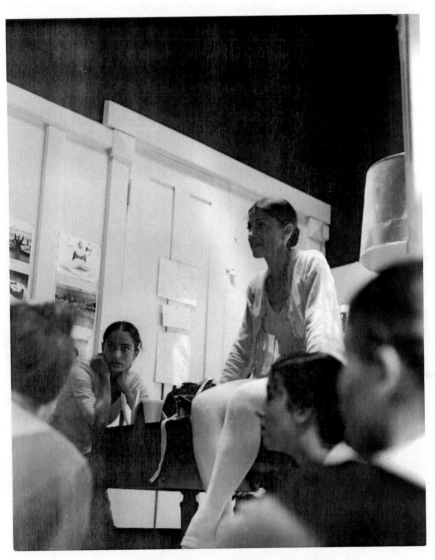

An informal moment with students

Janet with a visiting first dancer

Janet with students

Janet with students

Janet in the studio of the Rosin box

Janet, "Pas de Quatre"

Studying score of Ballet Giselle

Janet

Janet with Gisella Caccialanza Christensen just months before she died

Janet at Tamara Toumanova's grave in Los Angeles 1997 paying my respects.

TAMARA TOUMANOVA'S GRAVE LOS ANGELES 1997

Janet Sassoon

Val Caniparoli, internationally recognized S. F. Ballet Choreographer

Anna Reznik Ballerina Cincinatti Ballet with Janet Sassoon
before a performance. Last-minute instructions

Anna Reznik and Janet (having coached) Cincinatti Ballet before a performance

Janet coaching
First dancers
Anna Reznik, partner, Cincinatti Ballet
Alexei Kremnev

Tatjana Gsovsky, choreographer and Janet Sassoon, Prima Ballerina

Janet's first meeting with Gert Reinholm, Tatjana Gsovsky and
German Consul General in San Francisco

Janet Sassoon with Impresario Spencer Barefoot

Backstage with dancers from the performance of "dancers world"

Fiona Fuerstner, Jocelyn Vollmar and Janet Sassoon

Flower Drum Song

Janet's Portrait

19

Marriage and a Meeting

My return home became a whirlwind. The Academy of Ballet, the school that my father had financed, went through several hands. First, Carolyn Parks, a teacher and former dancer, was in charge. She, in turn, gave it to Alan Howard. Obviously, I wanted nothing to do with it as I was in my twenties and I felt my dancing still lay ahead of me. I could not have had a career as a ballerina while running a school. Poor Father lost the reason why he had supported it in the first place—he'd hoped I'd settle down to teach in San Francisco and be content. Still, part of his wish came true as my stay in San Francisco became longer than I'd intended. I started classes with Alan Howard, who, in addition to now being the head of the Academy of Ballet, also had a small company called Pacific Ballet.

At this time, I met a German dancer named Herbert Fiedler and his friend Glen Schneider, who were very kind and loving toward me (as might be imagined, my presence was not received with delight by many of the other dancers, which was understandable). Herbert was really a rare and sincere person that by pure chance one met and became attached to.

He had been in Berlin and talked to me about Berlin Ballet and Tatjana Gsovsky. He had worked for her as a master of all trades. He felt her ballets were for me and that I was a type she would like. Now began letters back and forth to Berlin.

In the meantime, besides classes, I also had a bit of a social life. For the first time, I went out with men for dinner and dancing. I was always petrified. Imagine, facing an audience of two thousand people was nothing compared to going out to dinner with one man.

—

So much was happening at once that I had no time to move slowly. At the age of twenty-one, I met what I truly felt was the love of my life. A friend of my brother's who worked for my father asked my girlfriend to join his friend and me for dinner. She was not only a dancer but a also real beauty who had escaped Hitler's Germany as a baby and ended up in Shanghai. I adored and admired her and loved her mother and what was left of her family. They'd survived! Her escort, Jerry, had escaped from Buchenwald—almost an impossibility. He was smart and later left my father's employ to do very well on his own. His friend turned out to be a young man who nevertheless was older than me by some years. He had been sent out of Berlin by his parents after much pleading by his uncles, who had established themselves in London. His uncles had begged their sister to leave Berlin, but like many Jews, she and her husband owned factories and thought they would never be touched. Finally, Peter and his brother, ages seven and nine respectively, were put on the last transport to England, one of the Kinder transport, with signs around their necks that simply said "Jude." Each uncle took one of the boys and raised them as their own. When Peter was of age to join the British army, he changed his name from Hamburg to Hall. His brother joined the RAF.

Peter and I started to see each other, and soon it turned into a great romance. I was totally in love, as any young girl should be. My parents felt particularly compassionate toward Peter as he had no parents. They gave him their hearts. Peter asked for my hand in marriage. My father took him into his office and evidently asked him whether he could afford to marry me. He then told Peter I had expensive tastes! I was mortified when this story was repeated to me months later. But we were a good match, so it seemed. Peter was gentle, elegant, soft spoken, and very much in love. He was also very romantic, which obviously was exactly what I then thought was true love. It was not too long before we announced our engagement, which in those days appeared in the newspaper with our photos, and so on. I never stopped class through all this. I just became very thin. I have always thought that being in love makes you very thin.

I wanted a small wedding, but an elegant and unforgettable affair. We settled on seventy-five people, with a candlelit ceremony at Beth Israel Temple (on Geary), which no longer exists. The reception was to be a black-tie sit-down dinner at the Room of the Dons at the Mark Hopkins Hotel atop Nob Hill.

Mother and I went to I. Magnin's, which at that time (1956) was the most complete department store one could wish for. In the center showcase, as we entered the store, was a dress that was a dream: white organdy pleats with a blue sash around the waist. I held my breath as I could imagine the price. We went to the second floor, where I tried on the lovely dress, just made for a bride-to-be. This had to be *the* dress. It was no use to try on anything else. Mother agreed, and we moved on to purchasing my trousseau, entirely at Magnin's. Beautiful lingerie was next, and we chose a white silk and lace gown and peignoir made in France. Then there was a beautiful Dior gray suit for my honeymoon. We also selected my wedding dress, white silk with Alençon lace. I wore a small crown made of silk and lace, with a veil.

Was all this truly happening? It was hard to believe as I still took my class every morning. Sometimes, I had the feeling that there were two of me: one still disciplined and anxious for my career, and the other in a totally different world. It became quite frightening as we began to choose silver patterns and plates. Suddenly I became quite worried as I had spoken to Peter before and made it clear that I would continue to dance for several years before I would settle down with children and a normal life. I had to make sure that he truly understood what my dancing meant to me and that if he thought it would interfere with what he expected, then we should not marry. Peter always laughed at my concerns and told me he understood completely and that it was his total wish for me to continue to dance for the next few years, that he would do all he could to make this possible. He said he understood I might be away from home as now was the time and I was at the age for me to dance. I could not lose these years. Once I had made a name for myself, I would take the time to have a child and perhaps another kind of life. Still, I couldn't believe I could have my cake and eat it too! However, true to his word, we were married on July 18, 1956.

No sooner than did I return from my honeymoon than I went right back to class—and Herbert Fielder told me that Tatjana Gsovsky would be in San Francisco with a small company, which was to dance in Berkeley as part of a USA tour. This was great news for me—at last, we would meet!

I received an invitation to a reception given in San Francisco by the consul general of Germany in honor of Madame Gsovsky and her dancers. I was very excited to at last have the opportunity to meet this distinguished lady and also the premier danseur of Germany, Gert Reinholm. Herbert was very excited because he had given her my résumé long before.

My first impression was overwhelming. I was pathologically shy, and she was so great a personality without even trying. Her face was fabulously expressive and different; she didn't look like anybody I had ever seen before. But most of all, I felt immediate respect and a response to her as a person. We spoke in French (she spoke French, German, and Russian, but no English). As Herbert had guessed she would, she seemed to like my dark looks. This was amazing as her entire company was blond or had light or red hair, all very pretty girls. Gert Reinholm looked exceptionally interesting too: besides being very good-looking, he had the perfect height and physique for a premier danseur. He too had a wonderful face. I felt sad that we could not really converse much as he spoke only German! However, Madame Gsovsky kept me by her side throughout the entire party.

I had seen the company dance at Zellerbach, and I'd loved the choreography. I felt I could learn so much from her—the choreographer—and that what I had seen was more difficult than anyone else was producing at that time. It was strong, dramatic, technical, and yet classically based. It was in a totally different direction from Balanchine's work. The dancing was stylized to fit Madame Gvovsky's vision of what she wished to portray, a very new way of dancing. In what I had seen, Gert Reinholm was obviously the main strength of the company.

At the party, Madame Gsovsky spoke to me about dancing in her company and asked if I could meet her in Maryland, where we would have more time to arrange things. That would be their next stop in the tour, and of course I said I would come. I left her with a good feeling as she seemed very happy with me. I also felt that, technically, I had already danced far beyond the level of what I had seen from her dancers in the company. She needed a dramatic ballerina for her work, and I hoped it would be me!

I followed up by meeting Madame Gsovsky at the hotel she had instructed me to go to in Maryland. As soon as I checked in, I called her room. She was glad to hear from me and told me to put on my practice clothes, that she would be there shortly. I was appalled—she couldn't mean that I was to try out for her by dancing in a hotel room! On a carpet! This was out of the question. However, I did what she asked of me and changed. Shortly, there came a knock on the door, and there stood Tatjana and Gert. She looked at me and asked Gert to stand behind me. I then did a few points with my feet but practicably suggested that I do a class with the company. She said that she would never audition a ballerina of my reputation (i.e., she already knew, apparently, from others in the profession, all she needed to know of me) or put me in such a position; what was important for her was to see how Gert and I looked together. She knew I had a very strong technique and said she thought it was important to bring this into the company. She liked what she saw, and it was obvious that in me she had found her dramatic ballerina. She said she would have a contract drawn up for me and that now I should change and we would go to dinner. I thanked her and hurried to put on a nice dress. I was very surprised as this was such a strange beginning, to start in a hotel room in Maryland.

Once home again, it seemed as if my waiting period was plagued with so many political happenings that I really began to believe that dancing with Berlin Ballet was not to be. The first of several incidents was that I was totally prepared to leave, having had a good-bye lunch with a friend, when I was suddenly interrupted by someone I knew who said, "Janet, have you heard the news?" Of course we had no idea what this person meant, and then came the blow of "Berlin is closed!" It was in the headlines of all the afternoon's papers. I turned as pale as a ghost and jumped up to see if I could find out exactly what was going on. I discovered this was the aftermath of the Russian attempt to force the foreign powers out of Berlin.

This meant my trip had to wait as only the military could enter or leave Berlin (by air). All civilian travel was canceled and forbidden. My disappointment was horrendous. I was packed and ready to go, but Berlin now seemed inaccessible to me. Telegrams flew back and forth, and I learned that to them it was thought to be only a delay. As unbelievable as the situation seemed to me, I was to learn that such crises as this were considered normal when it came to Berlin.

After several weeks went by, everything was replanned. I held my breath as I finally arrived at the airport (I, too, could enter the city only by air). I was so frantic about the odd situation; I had little time left over to think about leaving behind those I loved. Suddenly the time came to board, and I kissed my parents and Peter good-bye, pleading, "Write, please!" All the things one says while holding back tears as all of a sudden the thought of leaving home hit me. Until that moment, I was so intent on dancing in Berlin that there had been no time to think about the actual leave-taking, even though so much thought had gone into the going-there in the first place! I think at that revelatory moment I just ran out of gas. I got on the plane exhausted with emotion.

A new, long voyage had begun. It would be one of many trips that would fly me over the North Pole, refuel in Greenland, and then move on toward Europe. It all seemed like magic that I and my tutus were finally on board.

20

Tempelhof, Berlin

At long last, I was at the end of my very long voyage: flying from San Francisco over the Pole to Frankfurt and now from Frankfurt to Berlin. This was different than all my other travels. From every sentiment, I was entering unknown territory. Professionally speaking, it was a great opportunity to work at the right time in the right place. Berlin was then the epicenter of German culture, and I would be entering the company as a dancer of the first rank—a ballerina. How many talents had failed simply for lack of this kind of recognition.

Yet, on a personal level, that this city—this country—was where my future lay was ironic. I did not depart without criticism from some of the most elite Jews of San Francisco, including my own family. Imagine, in 1958, a young woman going to Germany, still filled with the horror stories of people who had been loved and lost in Auschwitz! On top of these feelings, my husband had fled Berlin during the war and lost his parents to the Nazis.

Obviously I had had to make a difficult decision. My choice was based on cold reality: You have so many years to dance while your body is able to reach its technical possibilities, along with your inner capacity to develop artistically. I only knew that as an artist, this was where I would be able to grow and mature. I was given that chance, and I had to take it. America could not offer me such an opportunity at that time. As I faced the last hour of my trip from Frankfurt, I felt as excited as any young dancer would be at the prospect of working with the German danseur Gert Reinholm and with the most distinguished choreographer Tatjana Gsovsky.

Finally, I arrived at Berlin Tempelhof Airport. I gathered my hand baggage and my tutu holder (a case specially made for me by Eloise Arnold; in those days, Mrs. Arnold made all the costumes for San Francisco ballet; her granddaughter Bene Arnold, a fellow dancer with SFB, was also a dear friend of mine), which the porter had put with the first-class coats! I was quite a sight as I stepped off the plane trying to be graceful while dragging my tutu bag along. Suddenly, a press flashbulb flashed, and Gert came forth to offer me a bouquet. I immediately discovered that he spoke only German—no French, no English. He had brought along a company member, Herbert Dolpp, as interpreter. Somehow we managed, and even with the language problem, I was aware that Gert was a superstar in Germany. He was charming but aloof. He intrigued me rather than being off-putting. I thought, *I can learn from him.* Little did I know how much, how deeply my life would intertwine with his. We were so very formal at that first meeting.

When I arrived at my hotel, fancifully named Hotel Fruhling am Zoo (Springtime at the Zoo!), more journalists were lying in wait to again besiege us with their cameras. I went up to my room, which had a small balcony overlooking the Kurfurstendam, which was then the main fashionable street of West Berlin. The photographers insisted upon tagging along for a photo session in my hotel room, to depict me putting on my toe shoes (in my Dior suit!). I gathered that this was how the press operated there, so I did it.

I was dumbfounded by the paparazzi-style greeting but was soon to learn the power of the German press and the value of their interest in anything that had to do with the ballet company. What appeared in the paper the next day was outrageous and funny. What made them decide I was a princess from "One Hundred Thousand Nights"? The headline read, persian princess arrives to dance in berlin. True, my mother was born in Baghdad, but her mother had fled with her last-born to Singapore because of plague. I guess they assumed I was from Baghdad from that and the Persian on my grandfather's side, but as far as being a princess went—onstage, there are many ballets in which one could dance the role of a princess, but certainly my life wasn't anywhere near being that of royalty, except for the constant work while always needing to show a good face! So be it. I was soon to learn I would play more roles in the press than onstage in Germany and elsewhere—that as a dancer, I had three faces: my own, what I presented as a performer, and what was seen by the public. At any time, I wore at least two out of three. It would not always be easy.

When at last I was alone with Gert, he informed me that we had to meet Tatjana and Herr Enklemann for still more photos, this time with the company. They needed shots of me dressed and posed for the ballets in which I would be dancing. Mind you, my trip from San Francisco had been long and tiring, without sleep. It was now very late at night for me. Amazing what strength one can conjure up, to keep going without time for rest or even comfort. How could I have refused? Despite the chaos of confronting the press, checking me in, and so on, Gert Reinholm seemed to have the power and authority of Cecil B. De Mille. I followed his directions without question. We jumped into Gert's car and headed back out, down the "Ku dam" (German slang for Kurfurstendam), to head toward the studio of Herr Enklemann.

On our arrival, Frau Enklemann greeted us both, with a kiss for Gert and a handshake for me. Then the photographer appeared, a very distinguished gentleman with a mass of white hair. He was very genuine and looked into one's eyes as he spoke. He was renowned for his dance and theater photos, and I felt honored to be photographed by the best. It was the beginning of a great friendship for me. Then Madame Gsovsky arrived with her arms full of costumes. She addressed me in French as she did not know English but could speak French, Spanish, German, and Russian. Tatjana lost no time, pinning me into a costume and giving Gert (also hastily costumed) and me a position to take for the camera. I was lost as I could not produce on cue a face or body expression from nowhere, not without knowing the story of the ballet whose pose I was striking. I asked Tatjana to please give me a clue so I could conjure up what I needed to convey. We began with what turned out to be far from a "pretty face" ballet—at the end of *Signale*, Gert was to strangle me! So the shoot proceeded as follows: Tatjana would dress me in a costume and just say a few words, such as *Flee from him*. Oddly enough, when I finally danced the ballet, I would continue to speak such word cues to help my body feel totally involved. And so at Herr Enklemann's, we worked on into the night, until finally Tatjana said, "We must take this child to eat something." That was when I suddenly realized that I had been going nonstop for twenty-four hours. For the last few hours, I had been on autopilot, pinned into costumes that didn't fit me, and adjusting my body into poses foreign to me amid conversation in three languages, and now I was hungry and very, very tired.

My first German meal was at Berlin Kindle, a huge restaurant near my hotel where, although the food was German, it had the air of a French bistro. One could order anything there—and did. To my horror, other diners were eating enormous amounts of foods I had never seen anywhere before. Everyone seemed quite stout.

In this most undancerly atmosphere, Tatjana explained to me that I was to have a rehearsal with a boy in the company to learn the only role I would be dancing with him and four other boys. It was to be in a jazz style although I would be in toe shoes. But I had been hired as a classical ballerina! I voiced my thoughts right then and there. She assured me that this ballet would be my greatest success as she felt that, as a dramatic ballerina, I would be assured by acceptance by her audience. She also kept her word that I would do a classical pas de deux of my own choosing to retain and demonstrate my classical schooling, whenever a program permitted its inclusion. We concluded our dinner, and I was deposited at my hotel.

Rehearsals were at several locations. The first was Tatjana's studio on Fassanenstrasse, just walking distance from my hotel. There was also a small office run by Ursula Zigurs, a part-time secretary. Tatjana lived nearby with her daughter Lena and their dachshund. Lena gave classes at the school and spoke fluent English. I liked her immediately and felt the feeling was mutual. I would often take her morning class. Rehearsal was scheduled here with Ralph Smock and me for the first part of *Signale* that required the leading character I was portraying to enter and dance with four men plus the leading man. I would basically be doing some jazz movements and a Charleston-like step *en pointe*. In the ballet, it is part of a dream sequence, but this rehearsal was a nightmare! Dancers coming from America, I suppose, were thought in Berlin to have all trained in jazz! I found it so difficult to let my body go and really felt I had been miscast. Madame Gsovsky came in after four hours of work. Ralph, dismissing the rehearsal staff, said I was doing fine. After he left, I burst into tears and announced, sobbing, that I was all wrong for this part. Madame told me that she would be gone for three days, setting a ballet in Frankfurt, and assured me that I would be fine by her return. Before her departure, my late afternoon rehearsal would be with her and Gert for the last and most difficult part of the pas de deux.

The pas de deux was quite hard, but the beginning went very well as at times, in between an enormous amount of choreography, was a great deal of acting through my body, without words. Tatjana (I could not call her this to her face) did not show me steps but gave me what ideas she wished portrayed. For example, she said I should play a woman disenchanted with her man and that as I was to feel indifferent toward him, to just walk in at the beginning. Then there was definite choreography for a pause as I met his eyes and he questioned where I had been—he had imagined I had been with other men (this would have been shown before the pas de deux, in the dream sequence). At this point, I was to bend back as he slapped

—

my face! The actual sound was to come from offstage (a loud slap in the wings) with only a mimed slap onstage although Gert got carried away and I began to turn my face away faster and faster. We continued to work like this: definite choreography of lifts and jumps laced with dramatic movements of pure, improvised acting. For the latter, she let both of us find our way as we worked together, and how I came on initially was something left to me to experiment with. If what we did was not to her liking, she would say such things as "Try again—in this moment you are in shock. Why does he question you? You love each other." A new idea came to me movement-wise as Gert caressed me, and I imagined him loving me. Suddenly, I pushed him away, as if to say, "Leave me—don't touch me!" until his rage built to my final strangulation and the disaster of a train crash (the train portrayed by dancers being the people on the train). Gert's character was to be so enraged at that point that he forgot the train signals, which is why the ballet was called what it was.

Tatjana worked this way on all her ballets for Gert and me. She did not do this with the others in the company. As a matter of fact, I had been invited to attend a performance at the opera house (Berlin's old one), a ballet night in which Gert was dancing with a very nice ballerina—blond, large in the sense of having a big bone structure but quite beautiful. When I mentioned to Tatjana that I thought his partner was quite good, she answered, "I choreograph where everything goes on every walk or movement. Every gesture, I put in." I didn't understand at that moment why she said that. It wasn't until much later that she said to me, "I work with you and Gert in dramatic ballets very differently than I do with others. You both give me, by yourselves, what I want without my telling you to do this or that. You cannot work this way with every dancer. With the two of you, I give you the idea and it comes from you inside out rather than your mentally thinking of how to do it." This is the artistic melding between dancers and their choreographer.

Tatjana allowed us artistic growth. Because of this, no two performances were ever the same in the dramatic sense. It was under her auspices that I grew as a dramatic ballerina.

Tatjana asked one of the girls of the company who spoke French to accompany me for fittings at the opera house. Little did I guess that this girl, who was a few years younger than me, would become a lifelong friend, first as a fellow ballerina and then as a director. We adored each other; she was wide eyed, eager to learn from me, and obviously had very little luxury because of the war. Her name was Constansa Herzfeld but later that changed to Constansa Vernon. She was dancing at that

—

time with the opera as well as with our company, as Tatjana believed she had talent. I eventually met her father, who was a scholar and writer of books pertaining to music. He was very well known, and his books were translated into four languages. Her mother was, like all mothers, living for her and her brother, who played with the Berlin Philharmonic Orchestra. Constansa, whom I called Connie, went everywhere with me whenever we had free time.

Madame also introduced me to an American in the U.S. Army, whom she thought would be of some use to me. This friendship likewise turned out to be lifelong and loving to this day. His name was Simon Karlinsky, who had been born in Manchuria and who had arranged some music for Tatjana. He was fluent in Russian as well as in French, German, and, of course, English. His job in the army was to aid in the release of American soldiers who were in the Russian zone of the city. He also made weekly visits to East Berlin's Spandau prison, wherein were many of those indicted for Nazi activities. Simon had studied music and loved ballet and was so intelligent and fun to be with. And, as Tatjana had surmised, he was indeed useful—he even allowed me to use his APO address to have my toe shoes sent to Berlin (by this means, they arrived quickly, and with no customs taxes)! Instead of going to the army's PX, which Tatjana had thought I would utilize, I was taken by Simon to marvelous dinners at the Maison de France, the only private restaurant in Berlin while my toe shoes elegantly appeared in batches of ten pairs every two weeks in an army camp! Stranger than fiction?

With Simon, I attended the world premiere of *König Hirsch* (The Stag King), a new opera by composer Heinrich Henze. Boris Blacher—a famous German composer of twelve-tone music in the style of Schönberg and one that composed music for Tatjana's ballets—was a friend of Simon's, and he came along with us. It was my first time at a world premiere in Berlin—an even quite grand and important in the music world. Critics from every European capital were there plus the audience was elegantly dressed and prepared for a special night.

When the opera concluded, the artists appeared for their curtain calls to tremendous applause. Then the curtains opened to reveal the full stage, and Henze was brought on. To my horror, there was whistling at his appearance, which in Europe was the equivalent of booing, and a voice screamed from the balcony, "Wagner is better!" I was appalled by what was going on. Again, the artists came forward to renewed applause then the composer again, this time with the people in the orchestra section of the opera house applauding as they faced a balcony that began anew to boo.

A war was erupting between the two schools of thought, the new and the old. Simon saw my face as I thought, *This is to be my audience*, and laughed and said, "Don't worry about it."

As Boris Blacher predicted (correctly; Henze's photograph appeared on the cover of *Time* the next month), the opera would be deemed a great success. He and Simon both explained to me that, in Berlin, the audiences were very vocal but fair; it was acceptable for them to express themselves as I had seen demonstrated. I had this to look forward to but not right away as Tatjana's company would first tour before having a premiere in Berlin.

21

Berliner Kind– Brandenbergerstrasse 47

Company rehearsals continued in another location off the Kurfurstendam. Part of the building was in ill repair from the bombings of the war, though the part that we used as a large studio that was perfectly fit. Still, it seemed very strange to me to be going to work in a partially bombed-out building. I would take a taxi from the corner at my hotel and struggle to say in German my destination, *Brandenbergerstrasser seiben und frishtig*. The driver always took me to the correct address. Until one day, Gert walked in with a newspaper, and there was my photo with a charming article about the little ballerina who asked each day to be brought to number seven and breakfast. *Forty* in German is difficult to pronounce—it is spelled *vierzig* and pronounced "feer-sik"; I was saying *frühstück*. A good laugh was had by all, especially Tatjana and Gert. My work with Gert was coming along, but our lack of a common language was hampering us; coming up in a flash second with what we could both understand to have the same meaning was very difficult. Soon, we were concocting a German-English of our own to fill in the gaps.

My other partner was an Italian, Pepe Urbani, from Milan. He was tall, beautifully trained, and a wonderful partner for the classical roles. He partnered me in *Hamlet,* where I was the queen who danced in two pas de deux, one with Pepe (the new king) and one with Gert (Hamlet). I also had a solo in this and appeared throughout the ballet. Pepe and I spoke French, so there was no language problem between us.

We prepared two programs for the tour. The opening ballet was to present the two ballerinas plus the soloists and corps. It was a tutu ballet and allowed us to dance in a fairly classical manner as we felt out our audience and the stage. Then came either a pas de deux *Orphée,* danced by the other ballerina, or the *Don Quixote* pas de deux danced by me; then a longer ballet, either *Signale* or *Hamlet.* This meant we principals danced three ballets every night. We never changed roles—in that company, a role choreographed on a dancer was his or hers. This way, we developed and perfected our roles all the time. We were able to renew an idea each time we danced it. Obviously, the steps never changed. Sometimes we had a hard moment that was always there waiting, but other times it improved on repetition.

Work went on every day, and finally I danced *Signale* to Tatjana's liking, including the jazz part followed by a fabulous pas de deux with a partner who was built like a Russian dancer, very muscular and masculine. This pas de deux was sensuous, beginning with a barre between us and then using the barre itself for me to flip myself into his arms. The pas de deux continued in this very physical manner, with overhead lifts, throw lifts, floor rolls, and other difficult steps. These rehearsals all went well with the dancer Harold Horn. He was experienced and very willing to help in the lifts. The ballet remained a big challenge for me as it was choreographed in a different style that built up to a most violent, dramatic ending. *Signale* required a great deal of technique that could not be shown as one had to act out one's character beyond just demonstrating technique. The technique just had to be there, to get one through it. I would return to the hotel every night with new aches and pained muscles. Obviously, for those lifts, I was using muscles I had never used before. This was a healthy pain that all dancers experience when learning new choreography that requires different motions from what one ordinarily does.

Meanwhile, my fittings at the opera house continued. On my way one day, I passed a bombed building with a wreath on what had been a stairway that was now closed off by barbed wire. To my horror, I saw what was left of a Star of David and the word *synagogue.* I stopped dead in my tracks. Up until this very second, I had lived only in my world of dance. Suddenly I saw in front of me what had become of my people. I went on to have my fitting and afterward was to go to Tatjana for my crowns and other headpieces, which she had made herself. I was glad that I could go to her that day with my heavy heart. I knocked on her private door, and she said, "Oui, Janet, entrez." I did, sobbing out to her what I had just seen. She listened and then waited for me to calm down, handing me a tissue.

She then proceeded to tell me the real story of what had happened the day the synagogue was destroyed.

The Jews of that area were being hunted down, and therefore many ran to the synagogue, thinking they would find protection and sanctuary in the temple. Instead, the SS came and, with flame-throwers, killed them en masse, also destroying the building as Tatjana and others who lived nearby came out of their homes but could only stand and watch. As Tatjana started back home, she saw a Jewish child standing in the street gaping at the disaster. Tatjana put the child under her coat and walked quickly away to her own place on Fassanenstrasse. Now she had a problem of getting the child to his people. This took a few days, and she really put herself in danger, being Russian, not German. Somehow, she told me, a ballerina at the opera house found out and threatened to report it. By then, luckily, the child was gone. I could not believe that a ballerina could do such a thing. This story helped me understand Tatjana so much better as she was not uncomplicated. I think that night was the first time she let me get really close to her.

And here she was, not only a choreographer but making masks, sewing jewels onto the bodice of my tutu, and making headpieces! I had given the costume department one of my own tutus to copy as they did not know the art of construction (using piano wire) that its maker did. This style of tutu allowed the skirt to stand out yet be flexible against the body of a partner. The art of the tutu is really a subject worthy of study as there are so many ways to go about making one, especially today. Anyway, time flew by, and we were finally ready to leave Berlin to go on tour.

22

On Tour

The company left by bus for Baden Baden, but Gert, Tatjana, and I—plus one boy—had to depart Berlin by air because we could not go through the East Zone. Therefore, the plan was that we would meet up with the rest of the company at a given place.

This would be my very first performance with the entire company that, to date, I had not even seen! The other ballerina on tour with us was Natasha Trofimova, a Russian who had danced mainly in Germany. She was very good, certainly better—technically speaking—than I had seen so far. Her personality was a bit strange; she kept to herself and wore the same pants and sweater every day although she brought along a huge suitcase of personal belongings. (Usually sets and props went way ahead of us, but we never knew for sure when the trucks would get there. We each had one suitcase of theater things that went with in company truck—containing makeup, robe, shoes, and so on. However, we were obliged to carry with us at all times practice clothes for class and shoes that if the trucks were late so we could still have class and even rehearse if necessary.)

Upon arrival at our first theater in the tour, Natasha and I shared a dressing room. She was very helpful, and I had no problem with her solitary attitude as I certainly did not need a lot of talk while preparing for performance. I put on my practice clothes, did my warm-up, and went onstage. As I was the first one onstage, our theater manager told me a little about the house. He said it was very old and really beautiful and asked if I would like to see it. Of course I was eager to do so. When he opened the gold outer curtain, I gasped. It was exactly like a grand opera house but in miniature, with red velvet seats and carpets. It was a dream of a theater. I was thrilled that I would be performing there.

Soon, other dancers appeared, and class was given onstage. I already had my makeup on, which I always did before a preperformance class or a warm-up, then it was back to my dressing room for what I now label "neurotic time." Ten pairs of shoes, one too soft so off it came, another didn't feel right, and so on until by some miracle one pair felt just right for the first ballet, where I had a lot of jumps. I needed a pair that was already soft but with hard points for the turns I had to do with my partner. Then they had to be tied around my ankles, for which there were two systems of keeping the ribbons in. The best was sewing, but sometimes, time was so short that one had to make do with wetting them and then rubbing them with rosin and tucking them in (rosin is what dancers use on their floors and the soles of their shoes to prevent slipping, before the advent of Marley flooring that is used today). Tatjana had a very tight covering made for her tours, which went over whatever was the theaters' regular stage floor. It truly saved us from injury and gave us the security of having the same floor every night, no matter what holes were underneath.

Now, our dresser appeared—Frau Valoon, whom we lovingly called Valoonschen, who dressed only the principals. On went the tutus and crowns; we had to be hooked into the former, holding our breath. Last came a powdering of our shoulders and arms and perfume. Whatever few minutes remained were spent onstage to test a final pirouette with Pepe, Tatjana at my side, smiling at my transformation. She looked happy and calm.

We all took our places, and with the opening notes of Schumann, I began to move. I loved my jumps, which received applause. That was unexpected and inspired me to relax and have a wonderful time for the rest of the ballet. In just that short time, I had the feeling of the stage and the response of this audience. I came offstage after this knowing that *Signale* was in a very different style, not at all in the same genre as this tutu piece.

Now, I had to make my preparations to appear in *Signale,* which had three costume changes involving hats, shoes, and what-have-you. For this, my hair would be loose. The ladies who worked with nothing but hair at the opera house had made me a beautiful hairpiece that I could attach to my own, and that looked like my own.

When I heard the five-minute call for *Signale,* out I went, on my way to the stage checking a makeshift dressing space that I would need to use for my quick changes to make sure everything was there. Valoonschen was there to take my shawl, and Tatjana took hold of my hands, which were ice cold. My body was ready on the outside, but inside I was pure fear. I knew I would have to use every bit of my concentration to get through the piece as we had never had time to go through the entire ballet at one go. I was so petrified, Tatjana literally pushed me onstage to begin the first section, cueing me with the words, "You do the dance with Pepe." It went quickly. I returned to the wings to change costumes and shoes, Tatjana again holding my hands as I nervously did a few relevés, and she prepared me by saying, "Pas de deux with the barre." I slithered on during a blackout of the stage, and then suddenly the music and the spotlight came on. By now, I was more in the character, and the lights enhanced the sensuous movements of the choreography. I found myself dancing more strongly, requiring more force from my technique. I knew better than to give in to it because this is what can cause a dancer harm. This pas de deux was so difficult and subtle that I needed to go easier at the beginning to reserve my strength. Then came the difficult lifts. I held my body rigidly in one piece, which makes it easier for your partner to lift you overhead. Then he threw me to turn me, catching my way down as I was to roll on the floor. The first time onstage, I held myself in every necessary position so that my partner could do his movements more easily. Finally, there was another blackout, and the corps came on as I headed back to the wings for another costume change. I had one big pas de deux to go. Gert was already onstage, frantically dancing as he imagined his wife had been unfaithful to him. I watched, and then Tatjana said, "Now," and I walked in, swinging my purse, ignoring everything until Gert slowly came toward me and I leaned back in his arm for the slap on the face. However, I saw a different face on Gert than he had worn in rehearsals. I continued with the pas de deux, and everything went all right, but this time, I felt him so strongly during some passages that on some things I really was fighting with him. We had a repetitive step from one corner, in which I had to do three pirouettes and then finish with a bent knee. I felt an unexpected forcefulness from Gert as he turned my pirouettes. I could actually do the three alone, unsupported, so I did not need the extra force, which nearly made me come off *pointe*. The pas de deux proceeded, and believe me, I really began to feel I was fighting for my life! Our one last circle of jumps before he strangled me was a fight to the finish. I audibly pleaded, "Fini fini," as he just missed bouncing my head on the floor before dragging me offstage, where the company boys helped me up as Gert returned to the stage for the signal and train crash.

Curtain down. Gert and I walked in very slowly, in a bow much different than what I would do for a classical ballet. Off we went, and we heard stamping from the house, which made me think the ballet had been a disaster. Gert pushed me out, saying, "Good." My first audience, and I had been well received. The whole company then came onstage, there were flowers for me, and I gave one to Gert. The audience would not stop; there were curtain calls for the full company, the conductor, and then Tatjana, at long last. It was a happy beginning.

For me, though, there were a lot of corrections to be made. I went to my dressing room, and Tatjana came to me there. This was the start of a long tradition between us. Nobody was allowed in before or while Tatjana was there, and I always asked her for corrections. She said then that we would work on some parts that were not smooth but that, all in all, she thought it dramatically the best she had ever seen. She added that, at the end, she hadn't known if I was alive or dead! The murder scene was truly hard for her to watch as it was so strong. I complained, looking at my costume where all the handprints of my partner, as well as makeup, were everywhere. No part of me was spared nor sacred! We both laughed as my costume was taken off for cleaning.

We were invited to dinner by the head of the theater, so I quickly dressed and joined Gert and Tatjana. Everyone was in a good mood. My one remark to Gert was, in our fractured language, "You had very much force onstage, especially when you kill me. I think you like to kill me." He laughed and said, "You are very strong also with me." I asked him if we could rehearse the series of pirouettes, and he replied, "Yes, yes." I could now understand Gert's enormous success. He was not trained totally classically because of a late start. But he was well schooled and knew himself and what he could do and not do. Tatjana choreographed for him based on his strengths. He projected a large personality onstage. He also looked divine; one could say he looked to perfection. He was also a fabulous partner (that first night notwithstanding!). I have to say he almost forced you to dance to a higher standard than you thought you could. But he was already at his peak while I was still learning how to handle so many different roles.

Tatjana left the next day, and we continued our tour, traveling in a Mercedes Benz bus that was quite comfortable. We principals were assigned two seats apiece so we could ride with our legs up.

The company's girls and boys were really nice. To my surprise, they spoke English, or tried to. The girls were young, about seventeen to nineteen, and I was still in my twenties. Overall, it was a young company and very special. We all wanted to be there, and we all wanted to dance plus we felt honored to have Tatjana Gsovsky choreographing for us and Gert Reinholm, the most well-known leading male dancer in Germany, dancing with us.

We received a great deal of attention from the press. Tatjana was experimenting, using dancers from the opera—such as Gert, who normally danced only during the ballet seasons at the larger house—and choreographing for them in a smaller company. We had minimal scenery, designed for example by Jean-Pierre Ponnelle for *Signale*. The sets were easy to hang and greatly imaginative, with a minimum number of props.

The tour took us to many small German towns as well as large cities. I was amazed that there were state-run opera houses in most places. We performed in many of these and were always sold out. In larger cities, we stayed three days, at least, which gave us time for laundry, hair washing, and shopping. We were often invited after performances to a reception, and for these, everyone would read on the board "Please dress." Gert would make a point of telling Natasha, but nothing new ever appeared out of that mysterious suitcase! We soon organized our lives while touring to take into account that we sometimes arrived late.

When we did not use an orchestra, we had high-fidelity tapes and large speakers. Their operation fell to the conductor and pianist. Our lighting was quite complicated for *Hamlet* and *Signale*, and our own stage manager always traveled ahead of the company to work these out. So much went into these performances that we dancers never saw. I might add that backstage equipment was far ahead of what was in the theaters in the United States at that time as many of these theaters were old and others had been modernized during rebuilding or newly built. I did not like dancing in the ultramodern theaters; for them, I actually had to change my way of dancing. For example, the new theaters had deep orchestra pits. These were great if you had a conductor and orchestra but not if you looked out to see only a yawning black space there. I had to learn to spot the floor with my eyes only, without lowering my head or tilting my face downward.

The lighting was controlled from a light board backstage. Spots came from the top of the stage, which really threw me at first as sometimes I could not see the floor. If I had to do a series of turns in a circle, I had to learn to spot the floor, only lowering my head to look downward. It was not easy to feel my way, and no one else could teach me these things; I had to work them out for myself. This is what experience teaches you; a dancer gets better at dealing with some of these unique problems with time. From the point of view of the audience, it all looks so easy. This is one reason why ballet is an art.

After months of touring, we finally returned to Berlin. The corps girls especially, as much as they loved touring, cried with joy when they were reunited with their families. Pepe, who had just gotten married in Italy before he joined the company, was joined by his wife in Berlin, so he too was very happy. By then I had formed other friendships, but still it was mainly Gert and Tatjana—plus Herbert Dolpp and a great comedian in the company, Jurgen Freindt—who really kept me in good spirits. Jurgen was also an amateur photographer.

We had just enough time off—two days—for me to call Simon, get the ten pairs of toe shoes waiting for me at his APO address, and have a wonderful dinner with him, telling him all the adventures of our tour. He, in turn, told me what was going on in the world, and especially in the East zone. I asked him what the possibility were of my going to the East zone to take class at the opera as there was a very good ballet master there. Simon told me that, in my case, he could do nothing to help me if the border guards stopped me for any reason as I was a civilian. Moreover, one excuse they might use to detain me was that I was not an American by birth, and my passport stated this clearly. I was a naturalized citizen, holding American and British dual citizenship. Although I never considered myself British and to me it was a technicality, he said it was enough that they might try to hold me. I gave up the idea for the time being.

We were to start rehearsals the next day for *Snow White and the Seven Dwarfs* that would be given for Christmas, with Tatjana narrating some of the story. I was delighted as it was pure classical ballet. I was the queen and was not too wicked, except for one part.

Our rehearsals were a period of fun and also rest for us. These performances were held in a small theater in Berlin, called the Eric Remarque Theater. It was the perfect theater for children and for a Christmas ballet that, for me, brought back memories of all the *Nutcrackers* I had danced in. Our little orchestra was cut down to a string quartet for this, and they played from a box in the auditorium. We held afternoon as well as evening performances and, as always, played to a full house.

It was all very chummy and cozy. Tatjana spent a great deal of time in my dressing room, and we chatted away. One time, Connie came in and asked for something from my makeup case, which I handed to her without a thought; after she left, Tatjana showed her displeasure, saying, "I pay all my dancers, therefore she needn't use my ballerina's makeup." I have to say this shocked me as what it came to was the star system, which I personally had done away with in my relationships with fellow dancers. Tatjana didn't realize that what made her company so special was how everyone treated one another with the greatest respect, down to the last person in the corps. I said to her that the loan was nothing and not important, but Tatjana kept her own mind about it. But apart from slight ruffles like that, this was a very happy period for me.

23

West German Tour

We continued the tour, and we were to dance in Essen. Again, there was a beautiful old opera house with its own ballet company directed by Kurt Jooss. He was world renowned for *The Green Table*, a ballet that won the Archives International de la Danse choreographic prize in Paris in 1932. He had established the Kurt Jooss Ballet that had toured the United States in 1933 to 1934. Establishing the company at Dartington Hall and later in Cambridge, Jooss had spent the war years in England before returning to Essen in 1949. He was white haired and looked very dignified.

The theater listed a full program, so not only did we dance several times at the regular evening hours but we also had later performances that started at 11:00 pm, following an opera. We were totally sold out, and even had early matinees on the following day at 11:00 am. I would enter the theater with my black coffee, pull down every shade in the dressing room, and pretend it was night. One reason was that although technically I could dance at any time of day, my body and mentality both were attuned artistically and emotionally for nighttime performances. I can offer no explanation because I think this feeling is individual for each artist. However, Gert also shared my feelings.

Mr. Jooss invited Gert and me and some other company members to a special rehearsal of *The Green Table* on our free day. Although it was choreographed in 1932, the ballet was remarkably unique and potent. The use of the diplomats at the table left a great impression on me as did the manner in which the Death figure treated the women, partisan, young girl, and mother. We were all very honored to see this performed by his own dancers as I am sure no matter what company it was later mounted on, it could never have the same essence achieved at his personal direction. This was a really lovely man who genuinely admired Gert and my performance in *Signale*; his comments relating to my dancing made me feel very special.

The tour continued as we headed to Hamburg in our Mercedes bus. As we rode, Irene Skorik darned her toe shoes, I sewed on ribbons, Frau Wallonschen repaired a costume, other company members ate, some slept. There was always laughter, and rather than feeling tedious, our little drives felt like short holidays.

We loved to stop at a roadside rest on the Autobahn; these were incredible places where one could take a shower, have one's shoes shined, eat very good (not fast) food, and, of course, go to the bathroom. In providing these comforts, Germany was so far ahead of the rest of the world. This was, for me, outrageous; I couldn't believe Germany's Autobahn was so ahead of us. But, of course, the Marshall Plan permitted then this luxury.

Most of our bus trips were brief, perhaps five hours; on many occasions, we managed to get to our destination in time for the evening performance by leaving early in the morning, checking into our hotel, and then going straight to the theater for our 6:00 pm call. Tatjana's tour schedule broke my habit of being at the theater four hours before every performance. She felt this was just energy wasted, that two hours were sufficient to apply makeup, warm up, and be ready to perform; at most, three hours. As I became more experienced, my makeup took practically no time, at most twenty minutes before an hour's warm-up, and that left half an hour for hysterical shoe time before I had ten minutes for nerves in the wings or onstage.

The theater in Hamburg was true to the notes I had read on the bus: a beautiful theater, wonderful audience, super hotel, good food. We stayed several days in that city, dancing programs 1 and 2. That meant I danced at least six ballets. It also meant that we were reviewed: the critics' reviews in such cities were very important for the company because we were subsidized by the Bonn government, and the columns documented our successes.

Which meant that Tatjana—along with the company at large, and especially the leading dancers—were very nervous. Partly because of my poor command of German, I didn't realize the importance of the Hamburg reviews and was not yet clued in to how the company was financed. And so I set out to as I usually did—hopefully well, perhaps better. And perhaps this was just as well; I would not want to have known someone important was out front.

When we arrived at the theater, I found my name on a dressing-room door, my theater case already inside. I could arrange my dressing room properly—practice clothes, makeup, good-luck charms, all my habits of preparation—in less than fifteen minutes. After donning my robe, I then proceeded to the ritual of making up. The moment I began, when my hand touched the foundation jar, for me that was like saying a prayer. I became very composed; my meditation would continue as I applied my makeup. I did not speak to anyone while accomplishing this task and appreciated it so much when I had the exclusive use of a dressing room. Even Frau Wallon never disturbed me at this hour. Next, in practice clothes, I went onstage to either join the company's warm-up barre or do my own barre, depending on what I was dancing. Following the barre, the dancers would clear the stage, and if I was performing a grand pas de deux that evening, I was allowed to have the stage with my partner alone until the stagehands required it. Pepe and I checked the tempo with the maestro, and I checked the wings for entrances and exits. In Hamburg, on program 1, I danced in every ballet but not in a separate pas de deux. Program 2 required that I dance every ballet plus a grand pas de deux, in this instance from *Don Quixote*.

A grand pas de deux means you make your entrance dancing with your partner then perform a slow movement, then he dances alone while you pray, offstage, that he gets lots of applause so you have extra time to breathe and stretch your muscles. Then you dance a solo while he prays the same for himself. Then he comes back, dances alone for a few seconds; you return and do the same, and then the two of you dance your heart out. The music is structured: entrance, adagio, male solo aggressive, female solo with bravura, and coda. The pas de deux shows off your respective and combined strength, technique, and personality, underscored always by the musical tempo and appropriate instruments.

One has to realize that in Germany at this time, except for guest artists, doing pas de deux from classical repertoire was not an accepted practice. They are designed to be a tour de force within a story context; however, lifted out, they are still spectacular to see and enjoy. I learned the *Don Quixote* variation from Tamara Toumanova when I was fourteen years old. Toumanova herself had danced the role at the same age with Anatole Oboukhoff, who had received his handwritten piano score with an inscription from Léon Minkus, the ballet's composer.

Program 1 ended with *Signale* and program 2 with *Hamlet*. In *Signale*, standing in the wings with Tatjana, hands like ice before the last pas de deux with Gert, I was struck with terror. When I heard the music for my entrance, there was nothing to do but enter. I walked in, swinging my purse with a great deal of cheek, struck a pose, and looked at him as if to say, "What's wrong with you?" Slowly, I took notice of Gert's eyes as he walked toward me; my fear was not just acting as I placed my weight on my back foot. I don't know just what happened on that particular night, but what followed was not what had been choreographed. I dropped my purse and clutched my thighs, which I had never done before. The next action was the slap on the face, and I really had to move quickly to avoid being actually hit; luckily, coming from offstage, the sound of the slap was loud and strong. Then I somehow continued, attempting to appear indifferent, until I reached the couch.

I reached down, and as he approached me, I gave him a kick to push him away. He caught my left foot, used it to pull me up, and turned me around; my left toes rested on the couch as he lifted me by the armpits to carry me to center stage. This prepared us for the ensuing pas de deux. We started to dance, and I could feel the power of Gert's technique and of his partnering, which was so strong that I felt I had to hold myself with all my strength just to stay on my pointes in a series of triple pirouettes done diagonally from one corner. Having done triple pirouettes without a partner, these were not a problem for me, and so I hardly needed to be pushed around, as he was doing; with this degree of force, I could have done ten rather than three! However, the music did not allow for that, and so I was fighting to stay on point and *stop* at three! After that sequence, I tried to escape (and, believe me, if I could have I would have). As I attempted to flee for my life, there was a brief change to his caressing me, and I remember momentarily responding lovingly, but then our characters both returned to their reality, and I did a circle of extraordinary jumps with Gert again holding me beneath my armpits until we reached center stage. He turned to me and pretended to choke me, holding my head to the floor, strangling me as I gasped, "Fini, fini." He then dragged my body offstage. The ballet concluded as the train comprised of dancers crashed to the floor while Gert tried to signal—alas, too late.

After one of the boys helped me up off the floor, I was a mess. Our curtain calls were well rehearsed: we walked slowly and dramatically forward, joined by our conductor, and always received flowers from the intendant of the theater. Then the stage curtain was closed, and the two soloists went out. Then Gert and I went out to applause I had never imagined one could have. It touched me deeply at the time but oddly did not remain in my mind afterward. It was how we had danced that night that always remained in my brain and in my heart.

Tatjana came into my dressing room and told me that she had had to look away as Gert finished me, when I appeared to be truly fighting for my life, and suddenly her ballet became terrifying to her. Both of us started to laugh as I said to her it was true, I had never danced so badly as when I was fighting Gert all the way just trying to stay on point! I said he must have taken a strong black coffee before the ballet. She said no, that he had known important people from the Bonn Senate were in the audience, and that it was very necessary that we had such a success in *Signale* as they decided what money went to the company. So it was really Gert who had been fighting for his and our lives!

One more tour was completed, and we all survived it, with a few free days to do laundry. Obviously, the dancers who lived in Berlin were glad when it was over so they could go home. In three days, our rehearsals would resume.

I spent those three days with Constansa Vernon, who was already a soloist in the ballet at the Städtisch Oper. We would go for a massage and paraffin bath. Then, thinking we had lost one kilo, we would promptly proceed to the first Chinese restaurant to open in Berlin at that time, on the Kurfurstendam. I—knowing and loving Chinese food, having grown up on eating rice at least four times a week—needed to eat rice twice weekly as my inner clock stopped with potatoes (being born in the Orient, the food I ate at home was Sephardic or Iraqi-Jewish food, which was always served with rice; it seemed lighter and healthier than potatoes although some of our cooking had potatoes in it). I introduced Connie to this cuisine; she went into the restaurant as if entering another world. I did the ordering, purposely selecting simple things. When the food arrived, Connie was wide eyed, astounded by the display. She then asked, "Where is the silverware?"

I said, "Right there!"

And she picked up her two sticks as if she were about to conduct a symphony orchestra. And that was when I gave her her first lesson in using chopsticks. Alas, the food was not very good as so many foods at that time could not be transported into West Berlin. However, I must say the chefs tried to use whatever was available, such as cauliflower. I could not help laughing as I watched Connie struggle with her chopsticks and drop so much food back into her bowl as she loved to eat, but so little reached her lips! But she took it in good spirit as we would always laugh together. She was then my closest friend, and we never lost that special closeness even though we sometimes had to go in different directions.

We had one great adventure in Berlin. One of the dancers whom I relied on and was a good friend of mine and Gert's was Herbert Dolpp. Herbert was very well educated; his parents owned a chain of clothing stores. In Berlin, he was living with a well-known producer and was usually very busy, but he was our perfect escort to the fun spots. Often, Gert would tell Herbert to take me somewhere when he was too busy to, and then he'd meet us wherever we were. To my delight, Herbert told me we were going to Resi, an elegant bar and restaurant, so, "Dress up." I loved to dress up and had little opportunity so far to do so. Dress I did. When Herbert came to pick me up at the hotel, I was hardly recognizable compared with how I looked in my rehearsal clothes, and he was very chic as well. I complimented him on his good taste.

We headed in Herbert's car along the Kurfurstendam and then turned off somewhere that left me lost. And suddenly we were there. The car was driven away by the restaurant's valet. As we entered Resi, I couldn't believe what I saw: lots of tables with huge numbers sticking up on poles visible to everyone in the room, and a telephone at each table. We were seated, and Herbert was beginning to explain the system to me just as the telephone rang. Believe it or not, it was for Herbert! A friend at another table had seen him enter and wanted to know who I was. I felt a little better when I heard, "Nein, sehr schoen aber spricht nicht deutsch." That line I knew. We ordered our drinks and I kept asking Herbert to translate something shocking for me to say in German. He didn't know how to say "Come up and see me sometime." I offered for translation every come-on line in every movie I'd seen, such as "All you have to do is put your lips together and blow." Herbert was rolling with laughter, and so was I, when the phone rang again. This time I picked it up and then panicked. Whatever it was that the man said to me, I answered in my best Swedish-accented English, "I want to be alone." It was the first thing that popped into my head. From that hilarious beginning, the evening proved to be a success, and we left knowing that tomorrow would be our first rehearsal for a new ballet, on a strict schedule with little room for fooling around:

Class	10:00-11:15 (B salle)
Rehearsal	11:30-1:30 (then 2:00-6:00 for nonleads, B salle)
Sassoon	1:30-3:00 (A salle)
Urbani-Sassoon	3:00-6:00 (A salle)
Reinholm-Sassoon	6:00 (A salle)
Sassoon-Urbani-Hobart	6:00 report to sixth-floor costume

24

Cain and Abel

I was very excited to see our new rehearsal schedule as we were going to be doing a world premiere. It had music composed specially for it by Peter Sandloff, with décor by Jean-Pierre Ponnelle. Tatjana would choreograph directly on me in the ballet *Cain und Abel*. It would be her interpretation of the biblical story of two brothers, which updated them to working in a hotel where Cain has been relegated to working in the basement after a brawl. In the basement, he meets with a young laundress who loves him, but becomes jealous when he sees her present Abel, an elevator boy, with a flower. In a fit of jealousy, he pushes Abel down the hotel's elevator shaft; only once his brother is dead does he realize what he has done, and leaves with Abel's body in his arms, to spend the rest of his life alone, in repentance. Gert would be Cain, and a wonderful American boy, Jeffry Hobart, would be Abel.

Tatjana prepared me for my first rehearsal by saying, "At last you get to dance happily. In this solo, you are alone on the stage, and you dream of love and you are free." We commenced with a sequence of steps. We had a pianist, as it was new music, but the steps were not easy. Tatjana liked my work, and we did two or three sequences, not in their final order. After an hour, she asked the pianist to play the first thirty-two measures then asked me to do sequence 3 followed by sequence 1. I had to mark the steps in my head first, standing still as I walked through in my mind what I needed to do, and then I was ready to try them straight through with the music. By some miracle, it worked. Tatjana then asked me to try only certain steps that were difficult to execute on point but extremely challenging as sometimes they seemed physically impossible. We would throw some away, and sometimes she would say "Good" at others; still other times she would close her eyes as her own body moved. At such times, she would not have to speak; I knew now to try to follow her movements. I would watch her feet but also see what her upper body was doing, her head and arms. Finally, she said, "I think I have it here, but you don't know what I'm saying." For me, dancing Tatjana's ballets were always a dialogue. You did not dance to show patterns or just technique or abstract movement without a story or meaning behind it. Everything went toward conscious actions to which the participants had to be committed. She continued to explain: that I was simple and young and loved for the first time, but also complex. The laundress would sense that there was some danger in her liaison but proceed with Cain anyway. At last, I got it all. And that was only one variation! We still had a long way to go. Tatjana said, "Rest, meine kind" (my child). Our language was normally French, but occasionally she would slip back into a few German words.

We had a good feeling from our first session as we had accomplished a great deal. And she had already started me thinking about my character. This is so important at the beginning of rehearsing a new part: you cannot just learn steps and only after that imbue them with the role you are playing.

Gert arrived and, as always, was in a good mood. While he changed, we went through my solo. Gert came in to watch and seemed very surprised that the steps seemed so easy for me, that I was already using expression while I was dancing them. Just in that short time, already thinking about my role had begun affecting how I was executing my steps. Tatjana again told me to rest as she related to Gert and me what we were going to do. There was to be a great deal of pantomime for Gert and me in this one scene. This was so exciting for me as I always felt it was such a privilege to be a part of this creative process.

Our work went slowly as we had to adjust to changes from one language to another—in this case, three! However, when you are so centered upon what you are doing together, you are really working in all of them, using all your senses. You don't just mimic the choreographer's steps but also seek the ideas behind her manner, what this motion or that touch means. I also think a dancer being choreographed upon sometimes gives the choreographer fuel for the creative fire. Sometimes you start a sequence, and it isn't coming out as it had been shown to you. And yet you will hear, "Good, I like that. Keep that in."

I could never write how magical these rehearsals were. Tatjana trusted me to work by instinct. Her directions were precise, and yet the process was loose as how we interpreted her instructions shaped the results.

—

In this scene, Gert was in the cellar of the hotel, putting coal into the huge furnaces used to heat the building. Tatjana explained that while I work in the laundry in the basement, I see him and feel sorry for him, so I bring him water to drink out of my hands. I needed to walk like a very young girl. I thought about it and tried out several ideas until I walked heel first, very slowly, with my cupped hands in front of me. Gert was sitting down with his head lowered, but slowly he raised his head and we looked into each other's eyes and truly, immediately, I knew that was it! Gert felt it too, and Tatjana said, "Bravo!" Just a walk. Imagine what goes into maybe one minute onstage. But that walk set the scene and atmosphere for what was to follow. Tatjana would set a step or a jump going into a lift. Amusingly, I would always start before she had finished explaining it—I had no fear. It was actually very dangerous, and sometimes, the movements were so complex that Gert and I would have to figure out once we were in the midst of what we were doing how to do what she wanted. She knew our difficulties. Sometimes she would step in, be the man, and hold me, which was so nerve-wracking—she weighed barely one hundred pounds. Here is where our concentration was needed the most. In the most difficult lifts, we had to stand and wait until Tatjana clarified how we were to achieve what she envisioned.

It has always amazed me that a good choreographer can not only see a step or lift but also know how to get it to work. Mind you, sometimes it doesn't look right, and you have to try many ways before finding the best way to go into a difficult action gracefully and then move on from it. In a lift, both partners work hard. The boy does the lifting, but the girl must know how to attack the lift, how to keep her energies centered in one place and toward her intended direction so she can be lifted more easily into the air than if her body were fighting it. An arm or a leg or even her head, moved the wrong way, could shift her weight dangerously. Timing is also in play, and this has to be perfect.

We continued to work on the pas de deux until we finally finished it. The next day was a full rehearsal call for *Cain and Abel,* a morning all right after class—not my best hour. We went at it all day, including the corps. That week was to me unbelievably busy and yet was not unusual for that company. Every day, I had a costume fitting alongside another rehearsal.

Time was precious as we needed to be ready for the premiere at Titania Palast for the Berliner Festwochen, which was in September. The theater was very large, seating two thousand people; during the festival, it held evening performances plus two matinees during its single week. This was a festival for the people, with lower ticket prices than when we danced at the opera house. Therefore, every performance was sold out.

In 1957, Berlin Ballet was the big attraction at the Festwochen. We were preparing two premieres, which meant that everybody was working full out. Besides *Cain and Abel*, Tatjana choreographed for the festival *Die Kameliendame*, based on Dumas's *La dame aux camélias*, with a score by Henri Sauget; it was designed by *Cain and Abel*'s Ponnelle. In Berlin, the part of Camille would be danced exclusively by Yvette Chauviré. This was indeed a great chance not only for the public but also for the company and dancer, as it meant having one of the world's most famous ballerinas connected with our company. She would not have considered dancing with a troupe that was not of high standard. For me, personally, it was a great privilege as when I had been in the de Cuevas group, I had tried to see her dance whenever I could. Observing her now with Berlin Ballet would be a new learning experience: now, I would be right there with her in the same studio! It was all very exciting.

Gert and Tatjana introduced me to Yvette, and I immediately liked her as a person. I could speak with her only in my bad French, but that was good enough. For some reason, my interest in her worked both ways. As I was not in her ballet, I was able to watch some of her rehearsals for it when I could find the time. Also, Gert was to be her Armand, and that meant he would be partnering both of us during the festival. We began going to dinner together as her hotel was only five minutes away from mine. She was so sweet with me. Yvette was marvelously feminine and fun to be with. She had had a fabulous career, and I think dancing with us was wonderful for her because here she was, surrounded by people who really honored and appreciated her. Being in the Paris Opéra but having reached a certain age meant that her roles there had become less frequent; new ballets were being choreographed on younger dancers.

Apart from our evenings off, our time was consumed with running back and forth from rehearsals to costume fittings and, finally, orchestra rehearsals. At last, we were installed in the theater in which we would be performing. Yvette, Gert, and I each had our own dressing room.

To my surprise, the day of the dress rehearsal, Jean-Pierre Ponnelle knocked on my dressing room door with Tatjana in tow, and together they broke it to me that they had decided to make me black for my role as the laundress. I stared dumbfounded at both of them, trying to fathom why and how this was to change my facial expressions and interpretation. I looked at Tatjana, pleading with my eyes, begging her to leave me alone, at least for the premiere. I must say, had it been any other ballerina, this would have been a scandal; however, I trusted Tatjana, who spoke to me quietly and said that it would change nothing about my performance—if anything, it would be sensational (if Paris could feature Orson Welles and

—

Eartha Kitt in *Voice of the Turtle* and be a rage, why not?). But this was 1957, and we were about to do a rather sensual pas de deux plus a pas de trios involving a black female character and two white males.

Jean-Pierre insisted on doing my makeup himself as I made mad faces at him at every chance I got (he was a very special person with whom I kept in touch for many years, right up to his death). Jean-Pierre made my lips outrageously large and sassy. He put gold glitter on my cheeks to highlight them. When he was finished, I thought I looked like a tart. But he and Tatjana loved the result. Good thing this was a dress rehearsal as it took five minutes for us to end our fit of hysteria.

Again, the critics were in attendance plus my darling friend from New York, Carl Sawyer, would be there. Carl was a manager who knew theater from top to bottom. He produced on Broadway and managed Richard Burton in *Camelot* plus handled the careers of many other performers, including Marcel Marceau; he was married to actress Barbara Bel Geddes at that time. Knowing he would be in the audience made me happy—finally, someone I knew would be out front!

We started with *Die Kameliendame*, and there was great excitement in the house for its presence of Yvette Chauviré. I stood waiting to watch the ballet from the wings. She approved of my makeup as she prepared to go on. I was astounded to find her awaiting her entrance with as much nervousness as I would feel before going onstage. She seemed to have more energy and strength rather than less, as a result of her heightened nervousness; it brought her level of concentration into focus. We didn't need to speak; we understood each other. I took her hand for one second and held it very strongly. She then went onstage, and I must say she was very beautiful to watch performing. Technique was not the prime factor; her upper body was so alive and conveyed what she needed to say, so much so that I did not look at her feet. The most magnificent moment was when Armand threw at Camille's feet the money he had won at gambling, not knowing that his father had persuaded her to leave him. Yvette's acting was incredible, and one understood why she was considered the most glorious ballerina in the Paris Opéra.

The ballet finished with great success, and then technical errors were brought to the attention of the stage crew while Gert discussed certain tempos with the conductor. This was done informally in spite of the fact that the orchestra seats were totally filled with an audience consisting of the press and invited guests.

After a break, Gert changed and was ready for *Cain and Abel*. It's a role that I had to make more important than it was as, especially as compared with Yvette's Camille, the character I was portraying that didn't possess a great deal of depth. I didn't struggle in this role, but I could hardly wait to get out of it. When I walked onstage before the curtain rose and the other members of the company came out to warm up, I could hear one gasp after another at this ballerina who was unrecognizable to them— my makeup had transformed me into a flirty young black laundress. I just opened my eyes wider and sauntered provocatively about the stage. Paradoxically, the black makeup helped me to define the role.

The ballet began very well, the dancers awaiting my entrance with bated breath. I had no idea what the reaction from the house might be; there was nothing to do but enter as I was supposed to. I looked straight at the audience so that they all got a good look at my face, especially my large, saucy lips. I had my pas de trios with Cain and Abel, then Abel left after I had flirted with him a little. I also left the stage, and there was dancing by the corps de ballet before a scene in which Cain sat dejectedly alone in the basement because there was to be a big party for the employees of the hotel—for which his elevator-operator brother had been given a wonderful new uniform—whereas he had to stay downstairs, out of sight, stoking the furnace with coal. I made my next entrance and slowly walked toward him, a young girl questioning his sadness, and I opened my hands as if to give him water to drink. Soon, he took my face in his hands, and we began a beautiful pas de deux that grew quite passionate. Then the participants in the hotel's party were shown celebrating, and I joined them, very happy with my new love in my heart, and danced a solo with a rose in my hand (that solo was always a subject of great amusement between Tatjana and me because it was the first time I was not sexy, killed, raped, or dead, just alive and dancing at the end of a ballet; Tatjana said, "Anyone can dance in a tutu and be pretty, but you are dramatic, and not everyone can die the way you can and still dance in a tutu"). The ballet came to a dreadful end with the death of Abel, pushed down the elevator shaft, and then the epilogue of Cain faced with his solitude and guilt. As for the laundry maid—she has departed with the other partygoers, knowing nothing of the death and despair in her wake.

We finished *Cain and Abel* to tremendous applause, and then, with the curtain opened, we stepped onstage to make corrections while my black makeup dripped down onto my white blouse. I then proceeded to my dressing room, where I met my friend Carl and gave him a big hug, leaving a big black mark on his cheek.

I had begun to remove my makeup when I was given an order to attend a press conference as soon as possible with Gert and Tatjana. Since the makeup would take so much time to remove, they were going to begin without me.

I turned to Carl, burst into tears, and said, "I can't go, and I won't go. This makeup is impossible. I need to take a shower, and I refuse to go to this press conference until I look half-decent." I just couldn't stop crying, I was so angry. Carl listened very calmly and said, "Get on with it. You're in the theater, Janet, and you're to do what is expected of you. And that is to get on with your undressing and dressing and to go to that press conference. If you are the prima ballerina, your place is to be there at that press conference." Never having heard Carl speak like this, I obeyed. He knew what he was talking about; I could see he meant business, and I got on with it.

25

A New Ballet

The company was given some time off, but sadly, it was not long enough for me to go home. I was only too happy to work again plus we were to have a new ballet that Tatjana would choreograph on me. Everyone was always glad when new ballets were added to our repertoire as it gave everyone the possibility of dancing different roles. And we now had a new soloist from Sweden, Ulla Paulson, a lovely lyrical dancer. The new ballet was called *Das Tor* (The Gate), to a score by Heinz Hartig. It was based on the legend of Helen of Troy in the *Iliad* although as with *Cain and Abel* Tatjana had taken considerable liberties with her staging. I was to be Cassandra, and Ulla was cast as Helen. Pepe Urbani was to portray Paris. Again, our designs were by Jean-Pierre Ponnelle.

Tatjana worked with me alone for my main solo. She started by showing me sequences of very difficult steps without any music. She crisscrossed among three languages in discussing my movements with me—sometimes she spoke in French, sometimes in English (e.g., "My mother is good, but my father is not good"), sometimes in German. Somehow it all came together even though the steps were all but impossible to count out as they were to be danced to a twelve-tone score. We just continued as if it had no music. She would demonstrate steps when I needed to watch to see what she wanted; she already envisioned what she had in mind, and I had to see it too to create the same image in the flesh. At this point, I had no idea what the music would be; however, during this first rehearsal, the composer came in to say he would work with me musically. The reason why this particular variation was so important was that Cassandra foretells the future by the famous line

"Beware of Greeks bearing gifts." This is at the very heart of the ballet and pulls the story together. I understood what I had to do; now I needed to think, listen, and put myself inside the technique and come out as Cassandra. It certainly wasn't something that would happen with everyone standing around me at that moment. I needed to digest Cassandra's character, Tatjana's choreography, and Hartig's music.

I begged Tatjana to please give me two hours alone with the pianist and to then come back with the composer. But Maestro Hartig and she explained that, on a piano, there was no way for me to hear the counts one has in tonic classical music; sometimes, the score consisted of such orchestral effects as booms, squeaks, and so on. I said, "We shall see," and though they were sure it would not work, off they went.

At last, the pianist and I were alone. He played the score through for me as I stood behind him, reading the music. That was my first great luck—I had reached a high level as a pianist before I stopped playing to pursue my career in dance; music was always a great part of my life, and I could read a score with precision. We played it again. And then we did just the last thirty-two bars, and it all fitted into place for me.

With the music, Tatjana's choreography started to make sense to me dramatically. Those steps of lifting the heel of my standing leg while the other leg stuttered with the point of its toe shoe indicated my prophesying a catastrophe. Now, there was expression to the movements—Cassandra's musical ravings began to make the steps speak. Even without the orchestral special effects, I could hear every note.

Tatjana and Hartig returned, and I sat them down. We commenced. When I finished dancing the solo, they were astounded. I congratulated the composer on his music. Tatjana was ecstatic and said, "Yes! That is Cassandra!"

This was only the beginning. When you start learning a role, usually there is very little time to be spent mulling it over. I found, by taking the time now for this musical preparation, I could feel immediately where the steps were going and the essence of what the choreography was trying to say, which would save me time from now on. For me, in any ballet, the music was the most important factor. The steps, if well choreographed, fit the music. When something—certain steps, for instance—doesn't feel comfortable or doesn't seem to flow together, it usually means that they are not really well suited to the music. Obviously, that realization usually does not come until you have rehearsed them for a long time, when whatever problem you are having with the movement seems insurmountable apart from anything to do with your physical abilities. Even in very modern or

—

neoclassical ballets, the music and the movements need to correlate with each other.

This doesn't mean you are always comfortable. That is another matter. Sometimes it is necessary to be uncomfortable, or you get stuck and don't progress in your ability to execute something your choreographer has in mind. Tatjana was extraordinary as she set ballets to the most difficult music. Every movement was there for a reason. She demanded expression from her dancers from the very beginning of rehearsals.

I was dismissed until that afternoon, when we would start the pas de trois. This was now my worry time. Yet I must admit that as anxious as I always felt when learning a new role, it was also extremely exciting for me. I went to rest at my hotel and then treated myself to a nice *Kaffee ohne Schlag und Kuchen* (coffee *without* whipped cream or cake).

For the afternoon rehearsal, the corps de ballet had assembled to rehearse what they would do with the soloists. This is when the leading characters had to piece together into a ballet what we had learned separately that morning. Amazingly, it worked! I had studied an entire sequence not totally understanding what it meant within the larger piece—now I knew that the Trojan horse enters and Cassandra stops it. As with the train in *Signale*, the horse was comprised of dancers. I stopped to look at the girls and boys in this remarkable form, one serving as the head, several as the body and legs. Pure genius, from Tatjana's imagination! It was to be even more so once the corps were in costume and masks. But even with their wearing only unmatched rehearsal clothes, it was awesome.

The ballet was beginning to grow. We had a middle, and now it was shaping up. What had been a puzzle was now fitting together with an order. The corps worked hard, and I must say the spirit running through us all was truly unusual. I had danced in several companies by then, but the Berlin Ballet was a group of dancers who loved Tatjana Gsovsky and her choreography and appreciated working on her ballets all the time.

Ulla, Pepe, and I now held our rehearsals together trilingually. At times, especially when I was tired, I have no idea what language I spoke! We now had Irene Skorik with us, who was French. She had studied with Victor Gsovsky in Paris, as well as with Preobrajenska, and had danced in Les Ballets du Champs-Élysées before my time in Paris. However, I knew of her and looked forward to another French-speaking ballerina.

We would now be doing two difficult programs at the festival. *Das Tor* was to premiere there.

The day of the first dress rehearsal, nerves were rattling everywhere. Costumes were being whisked from dressing rooms to be replaced by others. These people who work behind the scenes are really the heroes. Frau Wallonschen worked exclusively for Gert, Irene, and me. She was like a tiger protecting her cubs, making sure we had everything. There were three other dressers who were also fabulous. They did their job lovingly, and it was wonderful to be in such a *gemütlich* atmosphere in this place where we spent so much of our days.

I heard the orchestra warming up as I checked all my good-luck pieces that were pinned inside the bodice of my costume. Suddenly, I could not remember a single step of my solo—panic! Tatjana was in the wings. My hands were ice cold; she took them in hers and smiled. I said, "I can't remember." She said in French, "It will happen, ma petite oiseau," as she called me—her little bird. Then suddenly I was onstage. The horse arrived, Ponnelle's masks magnificent. Cocteau could not have done them better. Even I was frightened as I tried to stop the equine dancers from advancing. As for the music, I certainly didn't or couldn't have counted. But I didn't need to; I just danced. I exited and returned after a blackout then performed my prophesy. It was a most difficult solo, on point. It required me to hammer my steps into the stage, so strongly that at one point I really felt as if my feet had become nails entering the floor. It was very hard to do. When I finished, there was a definite stir from the front of the house, and I could feel the excitement.

This was a true premiere—new music, new story, new décor and costumes. Finally the first dress rehearsal was over, and it had gone very well. Because it was a premiere, Pepe and I were allowed to return to the stage as the curtain opened to speak to the maestro about the tempos. We adjusted very little. We then thanked the orchestra for working so hard. They, in turn, applauded us. Tatjana made some comments herself. Then it was on to the next piece—I needed to go back to my dressing room to change for *Hamlet,* while the orchestra took a break.

Gert came to me and said *Das Tor* was wonderful; he had sat in front to watch it. He said it was astounding, how strong it was and dramatic. The technique I had been called upon to use was not something normally seen in Germany. I noticed that every time he did not dance with me, he raved about my work onstage, especially my schooling, technique, and discipline as well as my artistry. Yet when we danced together, he would say things like, "You didn't do well." This became a very in joke between us when we were on tour; while we boarded the bus the day after a performance, Gert would be the last to enter the vehicle, his face buried

in the newspaper as he read aloud the review: "Sassoon danced brilliantly."
I would stare at him and burst out laughing. Luckily I couldn't read
German, so I never knew what any of the critics really thought. Gert had
arranged for a profession clip service to send us all the reviews that we'd
received on tour throughout Germany. I kept them for years, unread, in a
box at home, until I needed quotes for my résumé.

26

Festwochen Final Dress Rehearsal

Symphonic Etudes (entire company)
Orphée pas de deux (Reinholm and Skorik)
Das Tor (Sassoon, Paulson, and Urbani)
Nutcracker pas de deux (Helga Sommerkamp, Urbani)
Hamlet (Skorik, Reinholm, Sassoon, Jurgen Feindt)

As usual, our final dress rehearsal had every important critic and local VIP in the audience. I could never understand this mentality. Thankfully, in time for it, Tatjana had finally managed to get a very smooth carpet for the stage, one that was very flat. At last, we did not sink into holes in the floor or hit a gold ring marker; we never knew what might be lurking under out feet to trip us up or cause extra wear of our shoes. This was before the Marley dance floors of today. I bless this *tapis* (carpet), as it was called.

In the first ballet, every ballerina had a solo and something to do with a partner. There were three of us, and Tatjana choreographed around our respective good, natural technical feats to show us off in this piece. I loved it as I had Pepe for my partner, as I did for anything classical. He was a very good partner—outstanding as a dancer, supportive, and a joy to work with. Our classical training was very much the same, mine in the Cecchetti method. Besides being a wonderful partner, Pepe was a close, dear friend. He was married just before he joined the company and had a beautiful wife in Italy.

I shared a dressing room with Irene Skorik, who was cool as a cucumber. On the other hand, my regular neurotic behavior over shoes went out of hand although I had been nice and calm before the ten-minute call rang out. I couldn't control my feelings, but if they affected Irene, she never showed it (very French!). I finally settled with a pair that I thought might work, dashed to get them on, rosined the ribbons, and also wet them before I tucked in the ends so they wouldn't show. Then I went onstage and did some preliminary pirouettes with Pepe. I noted all my entrances from and exits to the wings so I wouldn't have any surprises. Tatjana gave me a good pat and said nothing, but her eyes said it all. Then "Take your places" was called, the overture began, and the curtain opened slowly. There we girls stood in sky blue tutus with jeweled bodices, the boys in white tights and romantic white shirts with puffy sleeves and vests made from the same fabric as our tutus. We must have looked pretty good as the guests clapped a welcome. I loved this ballet because it was a warm-up for me. I could get a feel for the audience, and they for me. I also enjoyed dancing it because it contained everything I danced by nature— high jumps and small, fast beats that require good elevation and pointed feet. My chief enjoyment was to be this free onstage.

Orphée was, as always, very beautiful, choreographed in such a way that was very intense. It was complicated to achieve its required technique while telling its story, which was based on the original Greek legend of Orpheus and Eurydice. Orpheus seeks out his late wife in the Underworld and is permitted by the gods to bring her back to Earth, provided he does not look back until he has crossed the River Styx. Eurydice, unaware of this condition, beseeches him to show her his love. Orpheus finally gives in, only to lose his beloved again.

The genius of the choreography was that the whole pas de deux was constructed without having one step place the dancers face-to-face. Instead, the movements wound the dancers around each other, with great extensions and long line. This took tremendous dramatic as well as technical ability to achieve. In this regard, Tatjana was somewhere between Balanchine and Macmillan and yet absolutely unique.

Then it was time to dress for *Hamlet*. As I entered my dressing room, there was Irene with a blond wig! It was awful! Tatjana kept saying, "Absolutely no!" but Irene went on with this crazy idea that Ophelia had to be blond. Time was passing, and I just continued to change, to prepare for my first entrance as the queen. My toe-shoe hysterics were put off as Irene's wig was so mesmerizing that I forgot to change my shoes from the last piece! Luckily, I did not need strong shoes for the first scene I would be in. The worst was yet to come.

—

While we were onstage, Gert came on and took one look and stopped the rehearsal, announcing loudly, "What on earth has Irene got on her head?" and demanding that she remove the wig. We stopped for a ten-minute break to allow Irene to go backstage to redo her head in more ways than one! I knew if I looked at Gert it would be finished, that both of us would be dissolved in laughter. There were critics and important people in the audience, and this was the wrong moment for a dancer to insist on her own ideas about costuming! Here again is where I understood how important it was for me to trust Tatjana totally as I was young and still growing into being a prima ballerina. I had the enormous luck of youth in being pliable and searching for what was right for me. I knew I was in good hands and that this was not a place to try to assert my own ideas.

Irene returned sans wig, and we ran through *Hamlet* without any further interruptions. Everyone was happy with its rehearsal. Tatjana came onstage and made some small corrections, and then dismissed us.

Our season started the next day with the Berliner Festwochen. New York City Ballet was also going to be in the festival on alternate days. I remember seeing Tanaquil LeClerq warming up, and I thought to myself how overly thin she was. We all love to be thin, but I was a bit frightened, thinking *What if she gets sick?* However, once she began to dance, all one saw was a beautiful, long-legged creature moving in her unique way. She was very nice to me when we bumped into each other on occasion.

When Berlin Ballet finished the festival run, we would then do our usual German tour. I think we were all anxious and ready to show our ballets to other cities. So ended our Berlin performances. We had danced for four weeks, six days a week plus two matinees. It was time to move on.

27

On the Road Again

During the mid to late fifties, Germany was divided—East belonging to the Soviet Union and West controlled by the Allies. Berlin was in the middle, which meant that to go in or out of Berlin, if you were Russian or originally from the East, they could stop you. Tatjana, Gert, and I would fly out of Berlin and meet the company at a given place to avoid complications.

Once we were clear of the city, we again traveled with the rest of the company in our Mercedes bus. It had a glass ceiling, lots of overhead space for our personal belongings, plus principals in the company were allotted two seats apiece so they could stretch out.

Everything was very organized. We each had a tour plan, with details of times, departures, hotels, and so on. At every theater we went to, on the bulletin board would be posted our rehearsal times and with whom, our class times, our warm-ups, and which dates and dancers would apply to programs 1 or 2. On arrival at hotels, everyone but the principals shared rooms; sometimes Gert and I even went to a different hotel that afforded us more luxury. Also, it was nice just to get away from seeing everyone all the time.

Shortly after we left Berlin, we were all in the bus ready to leave for the next city when Gert arrived, last as usual, reading the newspaper aloud. Only this time, he wasn't joking: it was reported that Tanaquil LeClerq had contracted polio and was in Denmark, fighting for her life. I burst into tears. We had just left her ten days ago, when she was backstage warming up. Then I remembered how thin she had looked and how one of the girls from New York City Ballet had told me that they had all gotten their polio vaccines except her because she had not had the time. Not one person on our bus could speak—we were all in shock. It didn't matter that my colleagues didn't know her; still they felt for her as dancers are connected in some strange way to one another. I could only think of one thing to say, and I stood up to face everyone. I said very sadly, "We will dance for her tonight." Everyone understood, and indeed we did.

Touring has its own atmosphere. For dancers, it is not as easy as for a symphony or theatrical group to go on tour. We use our entire bodies for our art and need to be fit. Quite aside from the perils of being seated for hours at a time on a bus, I don't know how we survived some of the theaters we went to. For example, in Schweinfurt, the curtain was controlled by electricity, managed by a stage man who was located backstage. During one of our performances there, during a storm when the electrical system unexpectedly had a mind of its own, I was dancing with the corps behind me when suddenly the curtain descended. I kept dancing, screaming at the others to keep in tempo and dance. Slowly the curtain went back up, and we were exactly with the music. Again, this happened. This time, I turned to the dancers with such a serious expression that they kept going behind me until the curtain again rose. And again, we were right on. After that, Schweinfurt became a magnificent joke for us, never to be forgotten.

I began to keep a diary then, which documented every tour. When we returned to a place where we had danced the previous year, I would check my book and give everyone a short rundown—for example, "Stage not deep, audience good, dressing rooms cold."

On tour, we were very much in our own world. We danced and live only to dance. It was the only life we had. Luckily, we were very loving toward each other though we principals were a bit isolated socially from the other members of the company. All the boys and girls were so polite and had such respect and dedication for their work and for us. I tried slowly to change that old-fashioned system; I would ask one or two of the girls to join me for coffee, and so on. I don't believe the star system works when you travel as you live year after year with basically the same people.

One incident that was an absolute nightmare for me occurred in some city where we were doing *Hamlet*. It happened near the end of the performance, when for me, as Gertrude, all the hard dancing was already over with. Hamlet and Laertes were to fight with swords; all I had to do was get up from my throne when Hamlet was slightly nicked, as if to say, "Dear boy, is it bad?" whereupon he would nod and resume the fight and kill Laertes. I was then to grab the goblet of poisoned wine meant for the king, feigning drinking from it, and, clutching my throat, die in Hamlet's arms. After that, everyone was to die one by one. Well, this performance didn't quite work out as planned. After finishing my dance, I headed to the throne where I was to sit during Hamlet and Laertes's duel. The music proceeded, but there was no Hamlet, no Laertes. I was left alone onstage with no choreography for me to dance to as the music played. I thought, *My god, do something, anything!* and I got up and ad libbed a series of great jumps as I glanced into the wings, trying to figure out what was keeping the other dancers offstage. I did turns, everything I could think of, until my music signaled it was time for Gertrude to die. Suddenly Gert arrived onstage, I grabbed the wine, staggered across the stage—and I mean staggered—and collapsed in his arms. The rest continued as choreographed, with Hamlet and Laertes picking up with their mortal swordfight, and finally everyone was dead and the curtain came down. I was livid—where *were* they?

When we took our curtain calls, Gert pushed me in front alone, to great bravos echoing in the theater. I was still outraged. At last the curtain closed, and Tatjana and all the rest of us stood together onstage. What on earth had happened? It seemed that the two girls who normally put the swords into a special place for Gert and Manfred (his Laertes) forgot, and so while I had been covering for them onstage, they had been desperately looking for suitable weapons. Why couldn't they pretend to fight then? Tatjana said they had lost their nerve. And meanwhile, there I had been so relieved after having danced in two ballets and a grand pas de deux and then in *Hamlet* my hard part was finished, thinking now I could just sit and watch the duel and then die. Well, die I did, in more ways than one, that evening.

Connie Vernon had been out injured and been seated in the audience, where she had watched the disaster unfold from the front of the house. She said she almost died when no one appeared and that when I leapt around peering into the wings, it had appeared as if I was watching an offstage duel in great despair (well, the despair was for sure). She said her mouth was open the whole time as she thought what will I do if I can't keep dancing so strongly. Actually, I was so mad that I had super strength from where I don't know.

When all was said and done, we laughed until our stomachs hurt. Everyone's imitation of me failed, and I am certain what I did that day could never be repeated. It remains one of the great tales of the Berlin Ballet.

28

Through Germany, On to Switzerland

I found touring Germany enormously interesting. The small towns were charming, and we always enjoyed local produce from the farms just at the fringes of town. The smell of bread was almost everywhere as the local bakery supplied the entire town with its goods. And what was especially interesting to me was that there did not seem to be any leftover signs of the war. Berlin was still full of bombed-out buildings, but these towns showed little or no damage!

The very day we were to arrive and perform at Celle, with a reception to follow the show, was a very holy Jewish holiday, the eve of Yom Kippur. On that evening, even a person who does not keep any other Judaic tradition tries to go to temple to hear the Kol Nidre. So I asked the concierge of the hotel if there was a temple nearby, and he said yes. He pointed it out to me and said, "Gerade aus" (straight ahead) then "Link" (left), which would bring me to the old section where the synagogue was. Dressed in my black coat with its ermine collar, looking very chic—and not telling anyone in the company where I was going or what I was planning to do—I simply walked to the old city. People stared at me as I walked, but this was not new; anywhere I went, people stared. I was just so obviously not German and did not look American either, so what was I? I continued on my way and then stopped a man and asked, in my best German, "Gibst hier eine synagogue?" He responded, "Kommen mit mir" (come with me), and proceeded to turn down a narrow street while I thought, *Am I crazy going with this man? I am well dressed—he could kill me or knock me out and take my purse, and no one knows where I am!* On the other hand, I believed in my heart that while I was searching for

God's temple, surely nothing could happen to me, which gave me some comfort although intellectually my argument with myself remained fixed on my first idea. Finally, we stopped at a small door, and he said, "Ja, hier." He pointed for me to go up the stairs. I said, "Danke," and tried to give him some money, which he refused, I then started to climb the stairs and, to my joy, saw a mezuzah on the door, which I touched and kissed. The door opened upon what looked like a normal apartment, where a normal-looking man waited for me to speak. I began to ask in German whether this ordinary place was a synagogue when he interrupted me and said, "Speak English." He asked me to sit down and called to the rabbi, who was in the other room through which doorway I could see candles were burning. I knew then that I was safe and in the right place.

In came a man who asked if I was a Judische Frau (Jewish woman). I said yes, but for some reason, he asked me again. Finally, I said, "This is the holiest of nights, and I have very little time, and I need to be in temple to show my respects." He told me that small ceremonies and meetings were conducted in the place that we were, but for something as important as Yom Kippur, the congregation usually went to Frankfurt, very close by. He said they would be honored if I would join them. I told him how much that would mean to me but that my schedule would not allow me the time. He then said, sadly, that before the war there had been six hundred Jews in Celle. "And now we are only six, with no children." I put my head down as I could feel tears in my eyes. I heard myself saying the Kaddish (the Jewish prayer for the dead) to the very end as nothing else could have been as appropriate.

We then parted, and he sent someone with me to see me back quickly and safely to the hotel. I barely just made it; Tatjana was waiting for me. We were to dance for the British armed forces that night. While we rode on the bus to the theater, I found myself wondering about my German colleagues—did their parents tell them the truth about the war or still think of Germans as being the master race? And did my generation living there even ask or care? Tatjana picked up on my mood and asked why I was so sad. I told her about my evening's experience. She held my hand and said quietly, "Your fellow dancers were not even born during the war, or those that were could barely walk or talk" (the average age in our company was very young). I could remember how, in America, children as young as five or six were aware of a war going on as we all did things for our soldiers or the Red Cross. I recalled also our having had air raid alarm tests. My father was an air raid warden (he did not qualify for active duty on account of holding a British passport), and we took it quite seriously.

As a child, we had added to our prayers at night, "God bless Mummy and Daddy, etc., *and all our soldiers overseas.*"

I knew Tatjana was right, but it was so hard for me spiritually to be in Germany, especially on this night of all nights. However, as soon as we arrived at the theater, in entering it, I entered my own synagogue or church because here was where I felt that, by giving of myself, I was doing what was right; it made me happy to know that if I touched one life out there, I was doing what God had given to me to do.

The stage was very small, but the audience loved us. I danced with all my heart at this performance, and it showed. We were gratefully received, with flowers and all.

Tatjana left us as she was needed at the Oper. The tour was going well; everyone was working very hard. We had so much dancing to do that no one complained. As a matter of fact, Gert and I decided that in one of the small towns we visited, we would let one girl from the corps de ballet, who became a demi-soloist the next season, do my variations in the first ballet. Things had become too easy for us, and we decided to give someone else more of a challenge. We put the casting on the board, and the girl nearly fainted, asking me what was wrong with me that I would not be dancing. Very professionally, I told her that we thought it would be a good idea for some of the girls to do the variations for the experience and to gain some sense of the enormous responsibility solo work carries. I reminded her that "When you dance as a ballerina with twenty people behind you, you don't just think of yourself—you need to make the effort to dance best of all, because if you don't, they don't look good either, to the public or to the critics. You set and carry that responsibility."

I felt that she understood this; still, that night, she did well yet was barely able to get through the one variation. She learned that night about saving her strength, not to knock herself out at the start of, and then to have no endurance to finish a solo. Of course, pacing comes with time and experience. So she did learn something, not the least that dancers like Gert and myself, where we were only after a great deal of dancing.

I truly believe that, in most careers, one must go through this process. The corps actually dances the most in any company. They are the heroes. They change costumes, wigs, hair, shoes, sometimes six or eight times a night. They dance the whole night, often in rows, moving as a body in precision step, never daring to move an arm or leg in a way that would spoil the line of the whole. Sometimes they have to stand in exactly the same position without moving. They go through all the pain of blisters, swollen ankles, and cramps, but they have to dance identically every night in spite of everything. All the while, they are getting tough and learning their craft; once they know their craft, many of the problems disappear, and even staying still or in alignment with one another becomes as if second nature. The lucky ones stand out in spite of their uniform demands, and it is those dancers who advance to solo work. The others become exemplary corps members, as necessary to the productions as the soloists.

Touring brings with it a new set of rules. It is harder to perform when you are always changing hotels, eating differently from how you do at home; washing the same tights out every night and living out of a suitcase; having to get up too early in the morning to catch a bus, train, or plane; arriving in some city you don't know and have little time ever get to know; and then starting the process all over again in a new theater and dressing room and stage. Out comes the makeup, shoes, costumes; and then you have to check that you have all the crowns, roses, and other items you need for that night's program. When I think now, how this is all simply expected of you at such an early age! You grow up in this world of constant change and yet constant repetition, and you have to love every minute of it, or else you don't belong there doing it. For dancers, life is all a dance, all a constant demand for concentration, and for most of us doing it, we would not change a thing about it—except the pay! But these tours through Germany were hard, as our itinerary shows.

We were once in Dillingen-Saar, where they couldn't decide if it was French or German to the degree that, there, one could use either francs of Deutschemarks. We arrived quite late and therefore went straight to the theater. We only received the keys to our hotel rooms very late, after the performance, and of course tried to walk as quietly as we could down the hallways. As I was not quite feeling well, Gert had asked Herbert, one of the boys, to help me get settled in my room. Herbert left me there to get something to eat. After he'd gone, someone banged on my door. I opened it, and to my horror, there stood a fat German businessman in his night attire, screaming at me that we were making too much noise. With that, he pushed me, and luckily I landed on the bed or else I could really have been hurt. Satisfied with that shove, he banged the door shut and left me speechless. I was feeling too ill to care. Herbert came back and was shocked by what had just transpired. Finally, we said good night, Herbert left, and I retired to my bed.

Suddenly, I had a pain in my lower abdomen. It was so bad that I was just able to get to the sink when I began to vomit. I seemed to be foaming at the mouth! I thought I was dying. Finally I crawled to the door, knowing that the horrible man who had accosted me was in a room very nearby. But I couldn't call for help even if I'd wanted to make noise—I didn't know where anyone else's room was. Luckily, two of the girls, Dritta and Gitta, were in the hall. They saw me and I fell into their arms. Still afraid to make any noise, I had them help me back to bed, and they said they would get Gert. When he took one look at me, all curled up, he knew I was really sick! He went downstairs and asked for a doctor. The man at the front desk said there was no doctor. Gert then requested an ambulance—and the man said there wasn't any ambulance. By that time, Gert was furious and told the man that this girl is a ballerina from America, and if she dies, he will make a scandal in the newspaper because he is the head of the company and very well known. Finally, the man admitted that there was a Catholic hospital three blocks away—we could walk. At this, the two girls and Gert got me into my coat and literally dragged me to the hospital. At the time, I felt as if I were in some nightmare!

When I got there, a nun opened the door. Gert spoke with her, and I kept hearing the word *blinddarm*; not knowing any medical German, I hadn't a clue that they meant "appendix." I was taken to a very small room with a cross over the bed. I made Gert swear that he would not leave me there. I felt as if I were in no-man's land. He promised to come back early in the morning, by which time a doctor would have looked at me. When he kissed me good-bye, I must have looked desperate.

They did give me something for the pain, after a doctor examined me. I was determined to be well by morning. What I didn't know was that when Gert left the hospital, he turned to the girls and said, "She will be fine tomorrow." He knew very well my mentality, and also I must say that the pain had not been appendicitis at all but an early warning of what later proved to be an ovarian cyst wrapped around my appendix, which years later was finally removed. The next day, when Gert came to the hospital, I was never so happy to see anyone. And by morning, all indeed was well, and I left swiftly.

Gert laughed so much, saying I'd been in a *Sterbe zimmer* (death room), and the story became outrageous as he imitated me all curled up and then how horrified I had looked at the tiny spartan hospital room with the cross on the wall. I think for at least twenty years, we would remember my being dragged through the snow to what I'd been certain was my deathbed. With time, Gert's imitation improved and got even funnier than I think the story in of itself actually was. Another Berlin Ballet tale. When I look back at this time, I think, how did we ever survive? It is most important in life to have a sense of humor, and with

Gert, I shared a special one that was truly unique and only happens once in a lifetime.

We proceeded to Koln, where we were joined by Tatjana, which was always a treat and put us in good spirits—we danced better, I think, when she was in the theater.

Our performance was in the Stadtbühne (State Stage), which meant that the stage was large, in a house with a good feeling. We knew this from a previous tour. Many ballet people were there, and we gave a good performance.

The next day, we left for Heidelberg. I found it charming. And, finally, we had three days in one place! For the girls, this was time to be used for washing hair and clothes and so on, not sightseeing.

We were dancing at that city's Stadttheater. Tatjana gave a full class at 10:00 am. After class, I got to rehearse the *Don Quixote* pas de deux as I felt classically perhaps my body was not placed well. We used the company's studio; therefore, we had a mirror and proper barre. It was heaven to have such a space to correct my body as normally our class was held onstage without mirrors. Pepe and I started the pas de deux, and Tatjana watched the first part. She stopped us and said, "You are both so strong; do it again with less force, as you have technique to throw away" (at last I understood that statement Margaret Craske had made to me in New York when I took a class from her at age sixteen). We did it again and continued to the slow and beautiful adagio movement, which starts abruptly after the first allegro section. Obviously, this was better, because now came the hardest moment for the ballerina, in the Oboukhoff version: here, I offered my hand to Pepe and made a fifth position (feet together) *en pointe* and then stood in attitude (one leg raised, bent at the knee) on one foot for a count of four measures. Pepe, on a good day, would actually start to walk away from me. Sometimes, the audience would start to applaud this, but the good balletomanes would shush them so as to not break my concentration. I would then do it again, and if it was a very good night—with a conductor who would watch me for when to continue—I wouldn't totter. I'd just stay. By this time, the entire audience would be rapt in total attention and excitement over display of mastery of technique. When I now rehearsed it with Pepe, Tatjana loved it and said, "Bravo! Don't dance so much—you have to dance tonight." But I said to her, "Please watch the variation."

The girl's variation takes real skill as you need to use a fan. The fan alone, Toumanouva took the time to show me: when to hold it behind your back, when to flip it on a jump, when to close and disguise it, and then when to open it. Not easy at all. The hardest part is at the end, when the ballerina does a long series of *pas de chevals* (horse steps), never coming off her pointes and with the fan opening, closing, flirting all the while. The variation finishes with a *pas de chat* (cat step).

I looked at Tatjana, and she was beaming. She did not often see pure classical ballet, especially of the Russian schooling of her past. Pepe and I wanted to continue as it was my theory that if you rehearse once on the day you will dance, it will go well in the actual performance because you lose your nervousness. Tatjana could only say yes, so we danced the coda to the finish, and Tatjana applauded. We did our *reverence* with a grand *salut* to her. We were drenched with sweat, so Tatjana said, "Go and wash and change," and kissed me on both cheeks.

That night, we danced program 1, which switched to my pas de deux being on the program. I was pleased as I had the really important places to dance in the selections. I don't think this was by chance. Tatjana set the programs with Gert. When they were together, they displayed great respect and professionalism toward each other. We did the first ballet, showing the audience our classical side. There was a short pause, and the *Don Quixote* pas de deux followed. I changed shoes to a pair I had ready and had only to place a rose in my hair. Frau Wallon had my fan and shawl; my good-luck piece was pinned to the bodice of my tutu. I said my prayer, always asking God to help me dance, giving love and pleasure to others. There was Pepe, always in "good mood" readiness. The wings were often full of dancers as this pas de deux was special for them as well, but we truly ignored this. Heads down, fifth position, signal ready, the music starts, the curtain opens slowly, and applause. Then three chords, and the arms move with the head. A slight pause, and we begin. This night, I started well, and Pepe did a slight throw lift (at the top of the lift, tossing me upward, even higher—rather sensational); and in the three pirouettes that followed each lift, I correspondingly bent sideways and up, echoing the vertical movements.

Now we were approaching the adagio. I tried to slow down and elongate my movements, especially before the lifts, but not for the lifts, when I had to be in one piece, using my stomach and back muscles so that Pepe could lift me as if effortlessly. Finally, we did our last walk around and then with a chord, *boom* came an arabesque. Now came the first balance in attitude, concentrate please, and I stayed perfectly straight. I didn't want to come down; I was happy to stay. On the second balance, Pepe walked away because he knew I was okay then we finished the rest of the adagio. Then came the variations, Pepe's first, wonderful *tours en l'air* on a diagonal. He came back out for applause. I said, "Go again." Frau Wallon handed me my fan and I heard my music start, and out I went, doing my best to keep my dancing at an even higher level than when we started. My variation went well. The coda is really a marathon of turns. Pepe went first and did then *à la seconde* (leg raised and open to the side), every third one a double. I came in from the corner, doing a very hard step, a series of *relevé arabesques* followed by a circle of piqué turns around the stage, before joining Pepe for the end.

The pas de deux was a success. Out came my flowers—and I always gave strict instructions for any flowers presented to me to have one pulled out so that I did not have to stand onstage tugging to free one to give to my partner. I presented Pepe with a flower, he gallantly kissed my hand, and we went forward. After that, the curtain closed, and we reappeared in front of it. To our surprise, the applause continued, and suddenly some young people ran forward, throwing flowers at us. Pepe picked them up and gave them all to me, and I thought, *Enough is enough.* I was already thinking ahead to the next ballet.

Finally, we were free to leave the stage. I kissed Pepe; he said, "It went well." We did all right but still had to keep to a certain level. That is the reality for every prima ballerina and premier danseur: sometimes, hopefully, you surpass that level, but you must never lose your vigilance and fall below it.

Gert caught me in the hallway as I was going to my dressing room and said simply that he had watched from the wings and thought it was marvelous. I said it was okay but that we could do even better.

Tatjana was in my dressing room, as Frau Wallonschen started to remove my tutu. She said all the balances were extraordinary. Frau Wallon wiped away my sweat as she dressed me in my *Hamlet* costume. I began to redo my hair as it was intermission and I had the time to do so. Tatjana continued to speak; she said, "Also, on the pirouettes, keep the shoulders down." She gave good criticism, and I listened to every word. It was so hard not to have a coach or someone out front watching and telling you these simple stupid things that can literally change the caliber of your performance no matter how good you are! I knew she was pleased, and I felt so much love for her. I also never took all this for granted; Tatjana and Gert were pushing me to get my own talent working.

At the five-minute call for *Hamlet,* I was ready, except for shoe hysterics: three pair still to try on. Then I left for the stage with Tatjana as Frau Wallonschen and everyone who had stood by watching the pas de deux, smiling at me. I could see Gert was very much in his strong mood. Well, so was I!

What I danced with him in *Hamlet*, however, called for appearing loving and caring, not strong. The dancer who played the king, Harold Horn, was the wonderful, strong partner I had in *Signale*. *Hamlet* presented no a great problems for me as long as everyone else did what they were supposed to. Everything went well, and then we had to pack up and move out as our next stop was Tübingen, where we were to repeat program 1.

But then the schedule changed. Following Offenburg, we were to leave Germany for Zurich, Switzerland.

We were all very excited. Tatjana. Gert, and I flew to a small town in Switzerland to meet the company traveling there by train. Everything was planned out like a James Bond movie! We had a brief layover until the train would arrive. Tatjana at the lead, fur coat trailing behind her, we entered the best hotel in town, where she announced, "I am Tatjana Gsovsky, and I want one room for three hours." For some reason, Gert looked at me, and we went into hysterical laughter. The woman at the desk repeated, "One room for three hours?" Tatjana asked what was wrong with that. The man at the desk then said, "I have no room for three hours." At that, Tatjana turned around haughtily like the Queen of the Wilis in *Giselle* and left—and, once out of earshot of the desk clerks, ordered us to stop laughing, which only made us redouble over. At the next hotel she tried, she left us outside while she went in alone to try to explain who she was and why she was in great need of a room for so brief a time, that her principal dancers merely needed to rest after their travels while she would sit in the lobby. This time, everything was understood, and we were beckoned inside. It didn't seem fair to us that Tatjana should sit in the lobby while we rested on beds; however, Gert knew nothing would change her mind. The hours passed quickly, and then it was time to meet the company.

For some reason, we wanted to avoid another principal dancer, so Gert and I went into a compartment with Dritta and Gitta, the girls from the corps who had aided me the night I was ill. We ate some bread and cheese then snuggled down to rest. Gitta suddenly warned that we were about to be caught hiding out with them; Gert and I covered our faces with the blanket, and the danger passed. We cautiously stuck our noses out from the covers, and Gitta and Dritta thought we looked so funny that they couldn't stop laughing. We all joined together in yet another great chapter of our lives in Berliner Ballet.

Zurich was the last place we would dance before ending our tour. We would be there into December, and I dreamed of warm weather. Because of the cold, class was given just before every performance, if possible in the studio of the theater, so we would be warmed up sufficiently to perform. We also started earlier because we worked our bodies differently in that climate. Our class was always done with great care and consideration to such matters as temperature, and also the length of our journeys, during our tour. In my lifetime, I have found teachers who do the same class daily with no thought of climate, mood, or anything. One cannot and should not prepare a class and stick to it without observing the people at that given time and place. Even within a school in a fixed location and regular hours, other factors affecting the dancers need to be weighed for a class to be a success for all participating in it.

In Zurich, we would do programs 1 and 2 at the Schauspielhaus. The Swiss are very conservative, so we didn't know how we would be received. However, the theater was nice and a good size for our company. Our cases had arrived long before us, and also our conductor had gone on ahead to prepare the orchestra to provide us with live music. We had time for a rehearsal with orchestra on our very first day.

I loved these times the most (I think sometimes rehearsals were for me and gave me joy whereas performances were for what I gave to others). All our rehearsals started on the dot—Swiss time means *on* time—and during the first playing of the music, we were not allowed to interrupt or dance. Soloists could mark their steps, but this first run-through was a general orchestra rehearsal for the instrumentalists. The next rehearsal was dancers and orchestra. The Liszt went well for Gert and Skorik. *Hamlet* was remarkable as the music was so difficult. At the conclusion of that, we soloists went to the edge of the stage and applauded the orchestra. We then had a break before the Don Quixote pas de deux.

When we resumed, Pepe and I were in our places, me in my practice tutu, not the real costume (whenever one rehearses a tutu ballet, one needs to wear at least that as its positioning tells your partner so many things). Obviously, we had an audience already as the entire company got to see this! Pepe said, "Merde," which to dancers means "good luck," and then we started our usual curtain up, three chords, and so on. We were already having a wonderful time as the orchestra gave us a special kind of energy. Then came the adagio balances—not brilliant but good. I still had time to fine tune those; instead of working more on them, we proceeded all the way through. From the front came a bravo or two. But both of us had things to say to the conductor. At the beginning, I needed for him to breathe yet not slow down the music. I hummed it, and he understood, and the orchestra tried it this way as Pepe and I danced it again—perfect. Then, at the end, Pepe asked him to not rush the music while I balanced so as not to distort the final note while I held the pose. At last, we were satisfied and thanked the orchestra; they tapped their bows on their music stands, in the manner I was to learn that instrumentalists use to applaud. That was so nice and new to me.

As we came offstage, Gert was the first to comment and said we were marvelous—so good, and with technique that was beautiful to see. Tatjana then came into my dressing room, and I asked her immediately if my shoulders had been down. She was pleased that I'd remembered and said, "Much better." She added that she loved the coda and had never seen a ballerina do the *relevé* with the arabesque turn, with such strong feet and yet the body so seemingly at ease. I told her that the trick was to stay totally yet loosely suspended *en pointe* all in one piece as otherwise it could not be done. It was precisely for this reason that she brought into her company dancers who had had classical schooling and training and who had danced elsewhere successfully. It was a challenge to her dancers to see what they needed to be reaching for.

Our rehearsals went very well and were a great inspiration to all of us. I thought back to my other sad times in Zurich and my happy days with my parents. Now, almost ten years later, here I was dancing with a formidable company. What a long road I had traveled to finally reach this far. Time had just seemed to fly by.

The following day, Gert and I went shopping—until we realized everything was so expensive. Still, we enjoyed ourselves before returning to the theater.

That night, there was a lot of excitement in the house as it was to be a gala affair for Zurich. The excitement reached the performers, an upbeat and expectant mood that was very helpful, at least to me. We were to do program 2, which meant I was in three ballets out of four. I concentrated on warming up, which I always did on my own. I loved those moments—everyone busy, stagehands avoiding the dancers as they focused on their final tasks, strains of music floating around, and, most of all, everyone preparing for performance. All the work, traveling, hotels, leading you to here, to this particular moment when you are about to do what you have trained for practically all your life, and that is to dance. How lucky I was to have all this, I thought.

That night, I also made a great decision because two nights earlier, I had forgotten to remove my good-luck piece from one costume to put in my next and yet had danced perfectly without it. This night, no good-luck pieces would be driving me crazy—they were not dancing; I was. My one remaining superstitious act would be to touch a card from John Taras, who had sent it with a bouquet to me in San Francisco when I was fourteen years old. And that night went like a charm—without the other charms pinned to my tutus.

After Zurich, our tour was officially over until March. After April, we would go to South America. Gert would not come everywhere with us on that tour as he needed to appear in Berlin. So the decision was made for me to rehearse with another partner for certain roles. Pepe would switch to some of the Gert roles, and for others, I would be partnered by Ranier Weise, a very good dancer who was able to do classical partnering. I decided we needed to have more than the *Don Quixote* as a classical pas de deux, so during the spring tour in Germany, we would test the changes to the program.

March was quickly upon us, and we were back home in Berlin, rehearsing again. This time around, *Signale* was perhaps technically cleaner, but I think that nervous excitement of "What will happen next? Will he kill her?" was missing. It lacked the spontaneity that would make it exciting. I made a great discovery for myself as a dramatic prima ballerina, which was now my official title in Europe: you pull something out from your insides each time you perform, and *if* you have a Gert Reinholm, he responds and does the same. A partner like that pushes me to the utmost of my feelings, which in turn changes my response. The actual steps don't change; we don't think about them. But something changes about how we communicate with each other and the audience when that happens. I think this is why *Signale* was such a success of all the ballets Gert and I had done everywhere together.

I began teaching Rudi (Rainer), as everyone called him, the *Raymonda* pas de deux. In this, he was perfect. He responded to the style and looked the part, likewise in *Don Q.* We dedicated some time to rehearsing *Raymonda,* using the original choreography from the Ballet Russe de Monte Carlo.

Tatjana walked in as we were trying a lift, and she just sat and watched. We started from the beginning, into the adagio, male solo, my solo, and then the coda, which I loved—I screamed out "Faster!" on the *passés.* We were both out of breath and couldn't say anything as we finished. Tatjana actually had tears in her eyes and said to me, "You have become a lyrical ballerina also." I said, "But this takes acting, and I love dancing it." She was thrilled.

I thanked Rudi, he kissed my hand, and then Tatjana and I were alone together. I asked her to watch my solo for corrections. I did it again, and she corrected the beginning *bourées* to move more. Then Gert arrived, and she said to do it from the beginning if I had the force. I whipped through the *bourées*, starting and ending with a clap of the hands, and Gert said, "Marvelous. Janet, you make big progress." I laughed and said teasingly, "You don't dance this with me." This produced a big laugh from him, with a *Gott ist Will!*—Gert's favorite expression.

I changed quickly as we were going to dinner (I had brought a nice dress but hated not to shower; the old buildings that had been bombed did not have showers, and I was grateful that they had a toilet there!). Tatjana was in a festive mood and named a restaurant that I knew to be special and expensive.

When we were out together, our conversations ranged across many topics. Never could you ask her, though, where she actually came from. But we discussed Victor Gsovsky, whom she still admired and I think loved in a certain way. She even bore him a child. But Ljena was of no help to Tatjana. I never really went into that in speaking with her as it would have been neither helpful nor good on my part.

During those two months, we kept changing partners to test how the South American tour would go. Pepe wanted to add and choreograph his *Suite Italiana*, to music by Giuliano Pomeranz, and Tatjana put in *Don Juan*, set to music by Werner Egk, which she always said would be mine; however, Andrée Marliere, a new soloist, danced it when I left the company for two weeks.

I spoke to Tatjana, and she thought this was the perfect time for me to go home and then to meet the company in Recife, Brazil. I had ten frantic days to go home, revive my wardrobe, and talk my head off! I also gave some interviews to our local newspaper. I wanted my parents to see me dance in this company, so we made plans for them to meet me when we reached Caracas, Venezuela. My father had a very nice business friend down there. Daddy cabled him of my arrival.

I no sooner got home than it was time to leave. But I was also excited to be going to yet another continent. It was summertime there; I would be warm. And coincidentally, the San Francisco Ballet was making the same tour, and I looked forward to meeting up with old colleagues in my new locale.

29

Bom Dia, Brazil

There I was in San Francisco, with the legal aspects of the tour still to be sorted out. First, the letters poured in about salary; then came a contract, which I immediately signed and sent back. Tatjana spoke to me about dancing a grand pas de deux; we had Helga Sommerkamp to do *Swan Lake* act 2 (this is all she did, and that was understood by me). Tatjana wished to show me off in roles that were new so no comparisons could be made with whatever world-famous dancers had performed in the South American venues before. I agreed with her completely. That being settled, I received news of my airline tickets and our program schedule. I looked at a globe of the world and felt that coming from California, I was so much closer to Brazil than were my colleagues from Berlin. Ha!

The flight arrangements, which required my going almost backward through time zones, were daunting:

UAL #108	June 3 San Francisco	8:20 am
	New York	7:20 am
PAA #273	June 3 New York	11:15 pm
	June 4 Belém, Brazil	8:00 pm
	June 5 Belém	12:15 am
PAB #251	June 5 Recife, Brazil	11:00 am

I took one look and said, "I can't believe this." Luckily, we had no performance until the seventh, at Recife.

After many hugs and kisses, I set off on the horrendous journey. Everything was according to Hoyle until Belém—where they announced that my flight was canceled. I said, "I must get to Recife. Please help me!" It turned out that there was another plane, used for a run that they called the "milkman" flight. It had about ten stops along its route, servicing the local people, but would arrive at Recife eventually. Anything, at this point, would have to do.

The plane I was to board was called a DC-3. It had two seats on each side and was so small that, as I got on, the plane tipped! I was so exhausted and disoriented from the previous flights that nothing mattered anymore. The pilots were really sweet and kept asking if I was okay as we went up and down, up and down, picking up not only people but also a man who held live chickens in his lap! At one stop, the pilots asked if I was hungry. By that point, I would have eaten my flightmate's chicken if it were roasted. The pilots brought aboard sandwiches and also beverages that they kept up front specially for me, and things went much better from there on.

At long last I arrived at Recife, where I was met by a tall good-looking man who handed me flowers. Hungry again, I felt like saying I could eat them. I looked like something the cat dragged in, three days on a plane! My legs felt like rubber.

The man introduced himself as Mr. Hoffman, the manager sent by the impresario, Mr. Bernard Iriberri, to oversee our tour. He'd known about the canceled flight; I could never understand why San Francisco had not. He then gave me the good news first: we would go to the hotel and I would have dinner and a good rest, but then came the bad news: I would have to be up and ready the next morning to meet the plane the rest of the company was arriving on, to appear as if I were coming off it with them for the photo shoots and press! It was so ludicrous that I burst out laughing. At least my makeup would be fresh for the pictures! And, hopefully, one night's sleep would help also (I sometimes think we dancers obeyed all orders as if we were in the army). If ever I wanted to behave like a spoiled star, here was my chance. Obviously, the thought was delicious, but I was much too self-disciplined. Instead, I wished Mr. Hoffman good night, fell into the shower, and went to bed.

The next morning, I ordered breakfast (one thing I cannot bear to do is eat breakfast in a communal dining room), and already I saw things in a different light. Mr. Hoffman arrived on the dot (very German!) of 11:00 am to bring me back to the airport. The Pan Am flight was just landing

—

from Rome. Everything went like clockwork until some of the girls saw me, and our embraces went on for some five minutes until order could be restored. I was so happy to see my colleagues and realized at the moment how much they all meant to me. In contrast, home was so filled with family that I never had time to think about myself.

Mr. Hoffman arranged us, and photos were taken; the ballerinas were all given flowers; and it was over very quickly. Gert and Tatjana were not yet with us, but our ballet mistress was. Pepe and I felt responsible for the company as we were really the next in line.

Everyone told me they had had a lovely flight, from Berlin to Rome and then on to Recife. I decided to tell them nothing of my travails. They were so excited, with champagne and gifts and so on; why spoil it? And so we all went to the hotel, the Grande Hotel, to settle in. Recife was very small, very tropical in climate. Now that I had rested, it was thrilling to be there. For one thing, for once, nobody around us stared at me! Instead, they all stared at all these fair-haired damsels as white as the sand. Already, Brazil felt like everything I thought it would be.

When we arrived at the theater, it was immediately obvious that we would need to find people who could speak (Portuguese-derived) Brazilian for us—whatever Spanish anyone knew was useless. The technical staff were all very busy, and no one wanted to say a word. We managed to find our so-called dressing rooms, which were partially outdoors, as was the theater itself. The heat was difficult to adjust to on such short notice—we were drenched in sweat even before we did anything! After class, Pepe and I decided we needed to speak to the dancers ourselves as we'd both had experience in this kind of weather, or so I thought.

I suggested that if any of the boys did lifts, they should rub their hands in rosin first (we still carried a rosin box in spite of our carpeted floor). To the girls, I said to powder their entire exposed body. Everyone was to be cautious with regard to lifts—or really, any body movements—to prevent slipping. Pepe then showed the boys how to really help the girls in a turn. After that, we did finger turns but realized that we were the only ones whose programs required those. We ended by advising everyone to concentrate as the hot locale presented a whole new set of potential problems with which they would all have to cope as best they can. Little did I know that as soon as we dismissed them, I would run into one of those very difficulties.

Back in my dressing room, I lifted my powder puff and shrieked, running out of the room. All the stagehands arrived in seconds as I described a big lizard that had leapt out of the puff. They laughed and laughed, but I have two phobias—snakes and birds. Anything that crawls or flies is enough to send me into shock. Well, the scaly visitor was gone, I was assured by every stagehand, so I had to believe it was all right again.

We opened with Schumann, during which I put on a new pair of shoes to get them ready for *Signale*. The stagehands and audience alike were won over by the first ballet despite the problems the dancers were already experiencing from the heat. The girls were crying because the glue that was stiffening their shoes was melting; they could hardly stand on point. I circulated among them as much as I could when I was not onstage dancing to tell them to do the best they could and to look happy because the audience was in pure heaven. Unfortunately, I had the most of anyone but Pepe to dance as we were doing program 1. Somehow we got through it, and everyone was pleased.

When we took our bows, I noticed young people sitting way on top of the wall surrounding the seats. Others were sitting on the floor in front of the stage. It was so touching that all our ills seemed worth it.

Backstage, the notice was already up for our first call the next day, at 10:00 am, when we would have our class and then a rehearsal. That morning, everyone was already happier as we were on familiar ground, in our usual routines. After class, we aired the damp shoe problem. This was not something that normally occurred in theaters that were indoors and air-conditioned. However, to conserve shoes during my days with the Marquis de Cuevas company, we would varnish the toes, swishing the substance around to permeate the satin, and then let the shoes dry. But I also pointed out that working in softer shoes would strengthen the girls' feet as they would have to rely more on their own muscles rather than on the shoes to hold them up. The boys, of course, had no such problems with their footgear.

After class, everyone was dismissed, except Rudi, as *Signale* needed some rehearsal. Pepe was replacing Gert in Cain, so he rehearsed with me after Rudi. When we finished, Mr. Hoffman introduced me to a wonderful young woman who would be there to handle any difficulty for us. Her name was Dina, and she spoke every language necessary. We immediately liked her; she came across as a person you could talk to and who could be able to solve problems. To our relief, she would be with us for our entire time in Brazil.

After our performances in Recife, we went by bus to Bahia—a tropical paradise, with beautiful beaches—the perfect place for a honeymoon. There, we performed in a regular theater where we were entirely indoors. We found a notice on the board that the French consul general had invited us to a buffet supper following the show. He was a tremendous

—

balletomane, and very good looking. It was lovely for me to be able to practice my bad French again.

The next day, we left behind all that exquisite scenery for the bustling city of Rio de Janeiro. I had just seen the movie *Black Orpheus,* whose cast had included a Jack Cole dancer I knew from San Francisco, Valerie Camille.

This time we went by plane, and we dancers took great advantage, or at least tried to (during our tour, we sometimes ran into the same flight crews; poor souls, who had to deal with us again—for instance, Jurgen, our comedian, would stand behind one and play stewardess while we all laughed). I asked the pilot if I could sit up front, in the copilot's seat, when we were coming in to land. He said okay, and I have to say it was breathtaking. Sugar Loaf was right there, surpassing everything, sparkling like a jewel in the sunlight. That experience—seeing what a pilot would see when entering Rio (Rio!) has stayed with me all my life. I almost kissed him, I was so excited.

When we landed, the usual announcement about local time and so forth concluded with "And we would like to wish the dancers on board with us good luck and good dancing." This brought an uproar of clapping.

In Rio, we stayed at the Novo Munde (New World) Hotel. We had one free day, and we wanted to see everything! First, we went walking with Dina along the Copacabana—very expensive hotels and shops. Then we took a cab to where *Black Orpheus* was filmed, had the taxi let us out at the bottom, and walked along the same path all the way to the top. It was exactly like being in the movie: all the small wooden houses with laundry hanging out, the ladies cooking what emitted good smells, the palm leaves, the children running around, the chickens and other animals. One had to wonder how the local people fared in the rain. It made one very grateful for what one had.

In addition to our call board in the theater, here we had one in every hotel we stayed at, so we knew where we had to be and when. The next day began with class at 10:00 am at the theater. As they had their own ballet company, we used their studio for our class. Rio de Janeiro, São Paulo, and Buenos Aires all had excellent ballet companies—and critics. It would almost be like dancing in New York.

I missed Tatjana and Gert. I felt especially unhappy not to have Gert; he was by now a part of me, and now that part was missing. To perform such an exacting dramatic ballet as *Signale* with a totally different partner, I had to search for a new way emotionally. Rudi was totally unlike Gert, and it was me who had to draw out of him something he had never used before. The love section was fine, but the death sequence was not; it needed more anger, aggression, and fury from him as he killed the thing he loved. I decided to rehearse with him after class; it was all right with the theater as no other rehearsals in the studio space had been scheduled. I asked Pepe to watch. He knew the problem. I was going to speak aloud through the entire death pas de deux, whatever came into my mind, as I did always silently to myself. I wandered in swinging my purse, and I said, "La-di-dah, what a bore." As Rudi came toward me, I said, "You again," then registered shock. "What is going on?" (slap). "You are ridiculous!" I sat on the bench, hat off, discarded my gloves, and said a little fearfully, "What is wrong?" until he was close enough for me to kick him. Then a turned pose—no speaking here—then we started on the hard dancing that was in the choreography, which spoke for itself. Until one moment when he touched me tenderly and I almost fell for it but then said, "Leave me." Then I tried to escape as he blocked me, again the choreography expressing everything that was necessary. Finally, two grand jetés and turns in a circle. I said, "No, no" until I felt Rudi on his knee and me slung over it, with him almost choking me as I said, "Fine, fine" as he dragged me off. Pepe said, "That's good!" I got up with Rudi's help and said, "That's *too* good!"

The performance that night went well; the best received was *Signale*. I was very pleased for Rudi as he did so well and understood that this was a big chance for him as a dancer. The applause and bravos seemed never to stop. I kept thinking, *Thank you, Tatjana and Gert.* There was no doubt that we secured the success of the company.

Performances continued in that city, with Programs 2 and 3. Our time in Rio seemed to fly by. Sometimes, when a group of young boys knew who we were when we walked down the street, they would follow us and dance for their own amusement (and ours). There was always music in the air coming from somewhere. People all seemed to move to a certain rhythm. I loved what I heard and saw, and later began to collect albums of Brazilian music.

On our last night, the boys in the company decided to go to the beach. We girls were a bit shy of entering the water, but once we did, we had a great time. Helga, Dritta, and I began to get out of the water on our own when we saw four men walking toward us. I kept thinking, *Don't panic, the boys are near.* We turned to see three of our muscular, wonderful boys walking out of the sea looking like gods compared to these men, who left in a hurry. It was such a funny scene, and we laughed so much. What an unforgettable exit from Rio.

The next day, we left for São Paulo. Helga, it appeared, had cut her foot and couldn't dance. The doctor looked at it and said she'd be out at least a week. We eliminated the pas de deux, replacing it with one of the girls in the Schumann piece to do her variation from that. Helga was actually the easiest of all the soloists to replace.

I was in the dressing room at the theater in São Paulo when Dina came in to say, "Janet, the impresario insists on a classical pas de deux." I suggested we bring Pepe in on this. Then it came out: could we do *Don Quixote* the following night? I said, "We haven't danced it in two months. We did not bring the costumes. No music. No fan. No, we cannot." Besides, we had left it out on purpose: Alicia Alonzo was in her forties by then, and I in my twenties. No, thank you, to be compared to one of the greatest ballerinas in the world! That is why Tatjana had not scheduled such ballets for this tour in the first place!

Dina calmed me down as by now I was close to tears. She said I could wear the tutu from *Dame of the Camellias,* which was black and red; the wardrobe department could create puffed sleeves for my skinny arms. She would find a fan or borrow one from the resident company. They had already asked the Rio de Janeiro ballet troupe to send the orchestral scores, which would arrive that evening; as the orchestra in São Paulo had already just played for Alonzo, they would not need to rehearse just to be given their tempos.

The next day, we performed a matinee; there was no time for rehearsal with the orchestra anyway, but between the matinee and the evening, we would have time to confer with the conductor about the tempos for *Don Q.* I then took my last shot at it: "I must have a red rose for my hair." My voice was very small; I knew I had lost the battle. Pepe stood behind me and said, "Janet, we will do it. I promise you, I will help you." And I could only say, "Please, can we rehearse after the performance tonight and then tomorrow between matinee and evening?"

"Yes, but you have two other ballets to dance on program 2, and they are big ballets," he reminded me. I was desperate and was very quiet that night. Program 1 was a success, but I thought, *Just you wait until tomorrow, when I'll fall flat on my face.*

That night, I could hardly get to sleep, but I had never been unrehearsed and so unprepared for it mentally. I tried to reassure myself: I did have total body memory of this and my other pieces. I just had to hear the music, and the steps would come. Some people have a more intellectual memory and need to take notes of their choreography. Even so, dancing a classical pas de deux that everyone knows, and without adequate rehearsal, is another cup of tea.

Morning finally arrived, and I set off for the theater. I suddenly missed Frau Wallon, whom the company could not afford to take. I would have to depend on the theater dresser instead. I went to the wardrobe department to try on the tutu, which needed to be taken up a bit and be given some extra hooks. The dresser also had me try on one of the puffed sleeves as she couldn't believe how small it was. It was fine, not so tight as to cut off my circulation. That being accomplished, I asked if there was a fan—nobody knew. At that point, I went to my dressing room to make up, which for me is always a tranquilizer. Somebody knocked just to say good morning and ask if I was all right. I called back, "Thank you, see you onstage," and then *Liar* to my mirror. Finally, I just told myself, *I am going to dance what I love dancing. I have already become known for my Don Q. Just dance it. I will do it as my body knows it. It's in my body. It will come out as I imagine it. Think now of what has to be done. Set an example for the younger members of the company.*

I took my place at the barre that had been set up onstage for class, and the other dancers drifted in. Pepe was giving class, which was something that always worked for me as we had somewhat the same schooling. Often, we would do our barre work together. He gave a wonderful class. It is such a different world to do class onstage than in a studio. There are no mirrors, so your body has to be in perfect balance purely from within. Pepe excused me from allegro work and jumps as I had so much ahead of me. I did a quick reverence to him and left the stage, thanking our pianist.

I returned to my dressing room, put on my makeup for the matinee performance, and thought about what I had to do that afternoon. I really couldn't cut back on any piece in the program to reserve my strength. The Schumann was not difficult, but *Signale* was a knockout, and after that came *Hamlet*!

As usual, *Signale* was an absolute success, which was encouraging. As soon as the matinee was over, Pepe and I retired to our dressing rooms to change back into practice clothes. The conductor was waiting for us along with our pianist, and we started the pas de deux from the beginning. We needed to make the usual tempo correction of elongating the phrase—or, as I put it, breathing—the moment we got to the top note of the first measure. The conductor got it right away. The rest was okay. We were just marking our steps at first so as to save ourselves and just refresh our memories. Next, we tried it out onstage without a stop from beginning to end.

Wardrobe had my costume fitted and ready, and Pepe wore the black tunic that he used for Hamlet, with now some beading added to it. It still felt unreal that we would be performing this ballet in São Paulo.

—

Performances started early, because people ate late. Our curtain time was seven o'clock, so we just waited in the theater after rehearsal. Someone got me a pot of coffee and some biscuits, but the biscuits just stuck in my throat. I ate some Chococola for energy. *Oh Gert, Tatjana, please come to me,* I prayed. I was told the house was sold out, standing room as well. Great news; the more the merrier!

Everyone spent the hour before seven doing warm-ups, and then I heard the five-minute call for us to begin program 2. We started with *Das Tor,* which was hard dancing for me; Pepe was also in this ballet. For this piece, I needed to wear my hair down, so I would have to put it up quickly afterward for Don Quixote. There was an intermission, not just a pause, thank God.

I raced to my dressing room, prepared my shoes first, and then arranged my hair with a rose on the side. The dresser was very nice, but not Wallon. I gave her the fan and told her, "Don't move from this place in the wings!" I armed her as well with a towel and my shawl. Dina was there, so I trusted her to take over from this point as far as communications went backstage. Then the call came: "Frau Sassoon, Herr Urbani, bitte!"

Standing in the wings, I looked at Pepe, and he kissed the top of my head. I said, "What the hell, here goes my career." Head down, I quickly asked God to help us both.

The curtain opens. Applause. Three chords as we move our arms into position; we facing outward, returning the gaze of the audience. And off we go—I remember to do this lightly, easily, to save strength. Last chord—I am in arabesque. Pepe offers his hand, and I take it, looking him straight in the eye. Suddenly I heard him whisper, "Bella, bella." I take my time for the first balance and stay. I repeat this with not a single falter. This is one of those special balances that happen so rarely, when I could have stayed forever. We finish the adagio and receive great applause, but we do not go back out to take bows as now come the variations, Pepe's first. The music continues. I say, "Merde, Pepe," and he makes his entrance. I think he is brilliant in his double air turns. While he dances, I wipe my hands dry on the towel and take my fan. Now it is time for my entrance. This is the hardest part. I catch somebody's eye in the audience and really flirt with the fan, right through to the last jump. Off I go, fanning myself. I take one bow to gain some time before the next part, but we can't do more than that lest we break the mood and interrupt the music. While Pepe begins his steps, I stand in the wings trying to catch my breath. Then I reenter, do my relevé balances, holding every one, though actually missing the first step of the repeat—no time to fix that, so I just stay there and start my piqué ménage from there then try a single,

single then double turn that repeats four times before we come together to end in my final pose. We get to take bow together, and I hear people stamping their feet as they applaud. That sound shocks me as I think they are doing it to show displeasure. But Pepe says, "Janet, that's good! If you hear a whistle, that means it was bad." When they open the curtain again, even the stagehands are clapping. And everybody in the company had been standing in the wings! Flowers are presented to me, and as I hand one to Pepe, he bends down on his knee to kiss my hand. I am so touched I could cry.

There was no doubt that we were successful; maybe they had thought we were young, but we had conquered them with our good technique and presentation. We would know eventually how well we did; meanwhile, I was convinced that it had been mostly luck and that were we expected to repeat the pas de deux, we would not have been able to do it as well. Sometimes, under fire, you are better than usual, or else you fail.

The program concluded, and everyone took wonderful curtain calls, especially the four principals, including Pepe and me. What a day this had been! I returned to my dressing room to change and put my dirty clothes and toe shoes into my bag.

It was a second shock that no one waited after the show to have dinner with me. I walked alone to the stage door, carrying my flowers and bag, stood alone as I checked the board for the next day's schedule. Outside, a group of young people had gathered to cheer me. I wasn't far from my hotel, and before I knew it, the boys had me on their shoulders, carrying me there as a group. I was overwhelmed. I thanked them all for their kindness and appreciation but told them that now I needed to rest. When I reached the hotel, I asked the receptionist to send tea, cheese, and bread to my room, too exhausted to deal with going out to dinner by myself.

I had so many flowers! I dumped them into the bathtub then began to rinse out my tights in the sink. As I did so, I talked to myself in the mirror, in tears: "Well, my dear, this is your life. You had the greatest success of your life tonight, and now here you are—alone, washing tights and cleaning your shoes. This is what your success will bring you most of the time. Gert and Tatjana would never have let you go home alone, but think upon this life, and remember very well what comes with success." Then I took a good look at my face in the mirror and started to laugh. Suddenly, the flowers in the tub and me washing the tights seemed like something out of a maudlin B-movie!

One more performance in São Paulo, and then we were off to Port Allegro. Nothing extraordinary took place then; and by then Helga was back on her feet, which was a relief to us. I took heart that Gert would shortly meet us in either Montevideo or Buenos Aires; he had a great following in the latter city as he and Tatjana had spent a long time with its ballet company, which was supposed to be fabulous. I looked forward to being there. Every once in a while in Paris or elsewhere, I would run into a dancer who had been trained in the school run by the theater in Buenos Aires, and they always had outstanding technique and stage presence. They were Russian-trained, beautiful dancers.

While in Montevideo, which reminded me of San Francisco, I had some time to myself finally and bought a very smart woolen suit there. By now, we had been touring for almost a month and were a happy crew.

30

Argentina, Chile, and Beyond

Buenos Aires was a place I had read so much about. It was a very international city that people wrote about, filmed, and either loved or hated. Since politics was not our mission, it was art that we carried there, which can reach people everywhere and speak without words. How often have artists from all over the world brought people together with music, dance, or theater? All of these thoughts ran through my head as I was flying en route to Argentina.

It was the home of Dina and Mr. Hoffman, and I am sure they were glad to be back for a while. On the plane, lunch was served with the aid of Jurgen and Benno, who were very funny. I couldn't believe we were getting away with such behavior on a commercial flight with regular passengers! In fact, we had a special section set aside just for us; I don't blame them, as it protected the others on board! When the pilot announced that we were nearing Buenos Aires, and for all the passengers *including our dancers* to please stay in their seats, I burst out laughing as we had had this pilot before and he already knew what we could be like. From that moment on, we were on our best behavior, as God had just spoken over the microphone. Still, I had a good laugh sitting with Dina.

Mr. Hoffman and Dina helped us clear customs. Here, as happened sometimes elsewhere in the decades after the Second World War, I was held back, perhaps because I am a naturalized rather than native-born American citizen, which was really none of the customs agents' business; after all, I carried an American passport and should have had every right any American-born traveler has. But in those years, it could be a problem. This time, eventually the agent allowed me to pass through.

—

Here, we would stay at the City Hall Hotel. Our ride to our accommodations always told a story, usually of poverty, small children running around, women working and doing heavy jobs—or else doing nothing! It's the children I can't bear to see, the ones with distended stomachs, meaning they have total malnourishment and will usually die. Argentina was no different until we entered the city itself, and I loved what I saw there. There was a touch of elegance about it in contrast to what we had passed through.

Gert was waiting for us at the hotel and was greeted by all the dancers as I held back. Then we hugged, and in our Gert-Janet language, he said, "My darling, you make *Don Q.* in Brazil, mein Gott I hear everything." I felt tears in my eyes as I continued to hug him and say, "Thank God you are here." He turned and went to the deck of the hotel, where there were beautiful flowers, and handed them to me, saying, "Wait here, and we go and eat with Mr. Iriberri." I spotted Dina and Mr. Hoffman and introduced them now to Gert, excusing myself.

I changed quickly into a new silk dress and twisted my hair into a chignon then returned to the lobby, where Gert was now standing with the most elegant white-haired older gentleman. In a second, I could see he was refined and very sophisticated. As I approached, Gert quickly said, "Here is our ballerina, Janet Sassoon." The man kissed my hand. Mr. Iriberri, the impresario, was a gentleman of the old world! Except for the fact that they held similar positions in the world of theater and art, there was no resemblance at all between him and the famous Mr. Hurok, his North American counterpart!

Mr. Iriberri suggested we depart for lunch as his car and driver were waiting for us outside. This was a free day for us, and so we took advantage of the pleasure of his company and this opportunity to see a little of Buenos Aires. Meanwhile, all my things would be moved to a better hotel, the Sussex, where Gert was staying.

That afternoon still resides in my memory to this very day. We enjoyed a lovely lunch with Mr. Iriberri, and I told him all about the tour so far, how well we had been received and so on. He said he had been informed of this and knew what had transpired in São Paulo. I tried to change the subject, but he went on to say, "What a tremendous outcome from an almost disaster." I simply replied that we had done what Tatjana would have expected us to do, trying not to choke on those words.

We asked about the Teatro Colón, which was famous the world over. He said that the ballet there was trying to raise the dancers again to form a company. I asked, "Why? You have a great company." Gert's face fell, as he already knew the answer. Evidently, the entire company had been on tour, traveling by air, and the plane had crashed—leaving no survivors. "It will be ten years to bring up the next company," Mr. Iriberri said sadly. I was absolutely stunned and tried to hold back my tears as I tried even to imagine an entire company of fifty people, all young and strong, all dying in a single tragic accident. This possibility had never occurred to me; at that age, one feels indestructible. To think too deeply about it was too painful. Somehow, we got off the subject.

That afternoon, we spoke of many things other than ballet. I was interested in the culture of this capital city. The population obviously fell into two extreme categories: the very rich and old families and the very poor. We would be touring the provinces, so we would see the great divide for ourselves. But in the meantime, Gert and I returned to our fine accommodations at his hotel, where we had coffee by ourselves in the establishment's parlor and I told him all the news. He had news too: he would not be staying with us for the entire rest of the tour as he needed to go back to Berlin from time to time, where they were experiencing a big problem with *Signale*. A producer wanted to film it as a short film to show in theaters. This would be fabulous for Tatjana. The problem was that the dates we were expected to be in Bogotá, the original city intended for the shooting, wasn't good for the film's producer, so we would have to make time in our schedule to return just for the filming when we were not otherwise performing there. Also, Gert was to dance in it, not Pepe. So we had some hurdles ahead. I told Gert I was happy to have him back as I didn't feel right doing certain ballets with another partner if they were choreographed for us.

The next day, there was a rehearsal for Gert and myself. As we arrived for class in one of the theater's studios, Gert was greeted by almost everyone there. For him, it was a happy return in spite of his just having lost so many colleagues. He called me over to introduce me to the ballet mistress—naturally a Russian! We instantly felt a connection, as so often has happened in my professional life. I suggested that it would be nice if she gave us a class. She was delighted, and as for me, I was happy to finally have a class that went back to my own schooling.

We all took our places at the barre. Gert said in advance that he would only take part of the class (I don't think I had ever seen him actually take an entire class). I was immediately in my element as everything we did at the barre was in the right order for my muscles. For once, I was working up a sweat with a good attack. I could feel Madame's eyes on me, and in passing, she would put her hand on my shoulder to keep reminding me to pull them down, then she would say, "Good." We then progressed to center, and she asked the leading dancers to be in the front row then made two lines, girls in one and boys in the other. Then she divided the soloists similarly. This is actually automatically done the world over. Sometimes, as a guest visiting a company, I would stand back until asked to join the first line, out of courtesy to the troupe's ballerinas. Again at center, as class progressed, my schooling—Russian and Cecchetti (and Cecchetti had been in Russia, so who's to say how the techniques truly differed)—was used totally. I feel in my heart a dancer is either well trained or badly trained. It is in the style of how one presents a step that makes the greatest difference and separates so-called schooling from the real thing. Plus there is one other difference altogether: Balanchine, who was Russian-schooled, decided upon a different method of the arms, which enormously affects the presentation and expression. I could dance Balanchine's ballets, but I was not a Balanchine dancer; I had left America at an early stage in my career precisely to avoid the American stamp he was putting on his dancers and those who emulated his technique. Now, here in Buenos Aires, I was pinching myself, loving every minute of being at the Teatro Colón, taking a Russian-style class. We continued right through to the last *grands battiments,* did our reverence, and then all spontaneously applauded Madame for her wonderful class. Just as it ended, someone called, "Ten minutes," then "*Signale*—entrances Reinholm, Sassoon."

I reached for a towel as I was dripping wet, yet I was filled with joy as a class can do that to you. Madame congratulated me on my work and said, "Obviously you had a great teacher." I responded, "Egorova, mainly, and Preobrajenskaya." She said, "It shows—very strong and clean technique with big jump. I like." Gert walked over, laughing. He said, "You work very hard."

At that point, I left quickly to change for our rehearsal. We already had our schedules explaining what the cast changes would be with and without Gert. His absences would really affect only the principals. During the times when he would be with us, I think the others would be relieved to be doing their old roles again.

That evening was a tremendous success for us. During our final bow for *Signale,* it was I who stepped back, raised my arm toward Gert, and left the stage so that he stood alone. He had not been forgotten after ten years' absence from that city. The curtain came down, and still the applause continued. Gert refused to go back out alone and made *me* go out alone. To my surprise, the audience clapped just as hard. Then, in spite of this being a modern ballet, Gert and I made a last, long reverence, I down to the knee, the most deeply felt salute a ballerina will make to an audience.

Our success continued in every program we danced in that city. The people there loved dance, and we provided them with new ballets, with fabulously inventive choreography from Germany and the rest of Europe, where Maurice Béjart, Hans van Manen, and Forsythe were then all creating new works based solidly in the skills of classical ballet and yet using those traditions in different ways.

Tatjana had been the first, but she never had dancers skilled enough to meet her demands until she invited guest artists to infiltrate her traveling band of wonderful, young dancers that she had herself trained from her school. She also used the best from Berlin's Stadische Oper when she needed additional dancers since she was its director.

We enjoyed Buenos Aires and would now spend some time touring the provinces. I noticed that, amid the company, I was using German more and more. It was Gert who pointed it out one day. Oddly enough, that was what came out of me when I was not in a German-speaking country but in a South American one where, when I asked, "Do you speak English? French?" It would often turn out that the person spoke German. I think it was less intimidating for me to speak it there. Within the company itself, everything was in German.

When we toured the provinces, Gert changed the program to put me in *Don Quixote*. In this case, though, he had my tutu for it sent from Berlin, along with the other items I needed. During this leg of the tour, the audiences, in their primitive theaters, really appreciated the glamorousness of this ballet. I so loved dancing for them as their excitement was palpable immediately.

And I do not exaggerate in calling out venues primitive. In one theater, as I was preparing for this role, Pepe came into my dressing room and said that in the middle of his last solo in another ballet, a bat flew right over his head. That's all I needed to hear. "What bat?" I asked. He only shrugged in reply. I did my barre in my dressing room but refused to go onstage until they actually dragged me there. I lowered my head and prayed that the bat would not like me or the music. During the ballet, every moment that I could steal a look upward, I did. My balances were the best ever, I think, because I was too petrified to move! How we got to the coda, I'll never know. At last the ordeal was finished, and I ran off that stage. Our manager brought me back for curtain calls. I stayed very close to Pepe and made a grand gesture to the upper gallery (actually looking, still, for the bat). Finally I returned to the safe haven of my dressing room. When I came out again, I said to the head stagehand, "The bat has to go." His answer? "That bat has been here twenty-five years." In other words, it was there to stay! Gert had a very hearty laugh over it all, and I so hoped that the bat would descend during *Hamlet* right during his duel scene so that they would have to fight with the bat in the middle of it!

This tour was certainly full of human disasters. That night, we were to fly to Chile. We were staying at a small hotel where we could eat and rest and where there was a swimming pool. The ground crew at the airport said it was impossible to take off until daylight. Everything had been packed up, and all we had were our leotards. So we all ended up in the pool! I must say we behaved pretty well, though, as all the other guests at the hotel were sleeping. Then we all got dressed in our street clothes again as dawn approached. The airport was not far away. The next surprise was that people were setting lighted torches along the runway to illuminate it! Nobody was laughing anymore when we saw that. I certainly prayed for "the dawn's early light" as we watched the plane that was to carry us come into view above its torch-lit landing strip! I have never witnessed such a perfect landing. We all cheered as the pilots descended from the plane.

When daylight finally came, we really began to feel the tropical climate coming slowly to life. Sadly, so were my fellow dancers. Weary as we were, our comedians were already thinking up their next move. We were served breakfast as soon as we were on the plane. But then the pilot made an announcement, welcoming the dancers aboard and warning that the plane might dance a bit—therefore, no one was to leave their seat. I was sitting next to Gert, and we were laughing, when suddenly the plane began to lurch up and down. Gert's hand was on mine, and we were sure this was to be the end of us. I looked out the window to see snow-capped mountains, and my first thought then was that if we crashed I would freeze in the tropical clothing I had on! And this was just the beginning. The turbulence returned several times as I wondered how we managed to stay above the mountain peaks. I looked over at Benno; he was the color of chalk, clutching his seat with both hands. I think this was the first time we ever flew anywhere where the passengers rode in complete silence. I think everyone on board was praying despite the reassurance of familiar rattling sounds from the galleys. After a good half hour of this, the captain took the microphone again to say we would not have a peaceful flight—and that we had now passed over the Andes.

That was an experience I would never forget, especially in the wake of having learned the terrible fate of that other touring company of dancers. Only after we had disembarked did the captain say to me, "It is sometimes quite dangerous for smaller planes to get up high enough to miss the peaks." I felt like kissing the ground.

We would spend one week in Chile, performing in Santiago, Concepción, and Valparaíso. Our stay in that country was not a happy one for me emotionally because of two things. The first was, late at night after performing I would see small children begging for money. I was giving all my money to them until Dina stopped me and said, "Offer food instead and see what happens." They refused the food; they were collecting the money for their fathers or mothers to use for other purposes. That was very disheartening.

The performances themselves went well in Santiago. There was a large German population there, and between them and the local ballet lovers, they absolutely filled the house. The same happened in Concepción and Valparaíso.

We were frequently invited to receptions. However, at one of them, as I was holding a glass of wine in one hand and speaking with the consul general, I was shocked to hear him comment, in passing, that he had been "Hitler's right hand" in the elite SS! I froze and said in perfect English, "I am American and a Jew." I quickly found Gert and told him to take me away from that place immediately. I could not believe that that man could brag about this. Gert was just as angry and left the affair without one word. I told our manager, Mr. Hoffman, that if something derogatory was said, I would continue to leave anyplace where we attended an official gathering. He understood me and my anger at such bad taste.

Alas, this unhappy evening was also Gert's farewell as he had to go back to Berlin. I couldn't bear to say good-bye.

Peru was next on our list of engagements. We had some free time in Lima and took full advantage of it.

Our first night there, a very elegant bachelor invited everyone to a cocktail party. He was very suave, good looking, and well versed. I kept pushing Helga and Bianca to him, but they were not making an effort, and of course, I was married at the time. I sensed he was intelligent and well brought up, and it didn't hurt that he was rich as well. He wanted to have a European girl as he did not find the local women very interesting. The next day, he invited Helga and me to lunch at his club. Before we met him, I lectured her on how interesting life could be. She had no boyfriend; most dancers do not have time for such things. But this was perfect, I thought. The club was elegant, the waiters serving us with white gloves. Conversation flowed easily—but not between the right persons. I gave up playing matchmaker and enjoyed every minute of it.

I must say this was not the first time the attention went to the girls on tour. The one thing my parents had showed me was how to behave with guests: to be polite and draw them out and not talk about yourself. Good manners were a must in our home, and I always observed this courtesy between my parents as well. I also had the opportunity to meet people from all parts of the world as my father's business was importing and exporting. I had never realized how useful this upbringing would be to counteract my innate shyness. And now in my own career, I was always meeting people from different parts of the world, but now in the role of guest.

From Peru we continued on to Ecuador to dance in Guayaquil and Quito. Travel was, again, by air. There, we had a closely packed schedule.

I had spoken to my parents by telephone, and they promised they would come to Caracas to see me dance, when we got to Venezuela. My father also had a business connection there with a lovely man, Raphael Alcantro. I was so looking forward to getting together with them.

Meanwhile, the next leg of our journey took us to Colombia, where we had not a single day in Bogotá to get used to the high altitude before having to perform. I remembered there an old story from ABT (American Ballet Theatre) from long ago, that they had actually had a dancer have a heart attack and die from performing at high altitude. I didn't know if that was true, but those are the kind of stories that circulate through the ballet vine. Well, we indeed felt a bit funny that first night, especially when we saw, in reserve in both wings at the theater, oxygen tanks and masks! That was certainly eerie to have to look at.

Pepe gave our first class, very nice and slow so that our bodies could adjust to the altitude. We were all okay; one really forgets everything while dancing. The program began that evening, and we seemed fine. Then, when I was dancing in *Das Tor*, I couldn't raise my legs very high. At that moment there was supposed to be a lift with Pepe, when he whispered, "Don't jump *pose* in arabesque—I can't lift." I went offstage after that and saw a girl taking oxygen, bent all the way over to prevent her fainting. I thought, *None of that for me—just save your strength where you can and dance where you should.* Suddenly there were two doctors, one in each wings. I wondered, *Is this a ballet company or a hospital?* Meanwhile, all these huge, muscled men in the company were dropping like crazy. At last, the first part of the program was over, the curtain came down, and at intermission the call went out, "Please change, and everyone onstage." Pepe and I were already onstage, working out how to cut the high lifts out of *Don Quixote*. In the makeshift company meeting, a doctor gave instructions to everyone on how to cope—to try not to gulp in air but to breathe as evenly, though one's nose, as possible. This was almost an impossibility for a dancer to accomplish in performance.

Then "Clear the stage!" was called. Pepe asked the conductor to watch our tempos. I prayed that I would not cramp over as that girl had done. As usual, Pepe gave me a kiss and a small kick. I said, "Merde." He said, "Double merde," and here we were again. I kept thinking, *Don't do the first lifts, just arabesques.* Everything else remained the same, except that instead of running for the last chord's arabesque, I took it by walking there. I was quite enjoying myself, not feeling at all out of breath, cool, calm, and collected as I prepared to start the balances. I gave Pepe my hand and took my first balance—not super good; the second was much better. Ah, good. Now the fish lift. I'd forgotten to cut it while we'd rehearsed, so I just did it, and Pepe seemed okay with it. Next came a shoulder lift, which we replaced with a pirouette; likewise a second one. Then we finished, I remembering to walk and not run. We made it, and to great applause not only from the house but also from backstage. Now Pepe had to think of how to jump less in his variation as I caught my breath before mine, refusing the oxygen. Thinking quickly how I could lessen my harder steps, I realized almost nothing could be done to change them other than to substitute a long arabesque for the first *pas de chat*. But onstage, my legs didn't do that; they did automatically what they always did (here is where it shows if you have muscle memory). I realized that I could not cut out anything. I willed myself to finish the variation and then took three slow bows to allow Pepe to catch *his* breath before we would swing into the coda. For this section of the pas de deux, we had already agreed to discard the jumps in favor of arabesques and pirouettes. We were not out of trouble yet. I watched Pepe do his *à la second* turns (in which the nonsupporting leg is held out straight to the side) perfectly and thought, *Fine. I, too, can do my* relevés *and then turns in a circle.* We both did this, using every bit of determination, good sense, and experience we had of how to save ourselves without letting it be seen. The house was ecstatic over whatever we did. Taking the curtain calls was another matter. We both crashed but finally came out to receive our very appreciative audience. I was even afraid to bow by this time because I was sure I would not be able to get up again! Somehow, this night felt very special as it was such a challenge, and yet the audience never had a clue of what was going on backstage. We gave them all we had inside of us and brought them something magical that helped them forget their worries and problems. I could only say to Pepe, "Ça va, toi" ("How are you?" or, literally, "How goes it?"), and he answered, "Ça va" ("It goes"). By now, we were both bent over backstage trying to breathe. The program finished with *Hamlet,* and somehow everyone survived!

We went to our manager afterward and said that this night was a lesson in why no one should ever arrive and dance on the same night in a place with such high altitude. He said he was sorry but that the tour had been arranged without anyone's considering this.

From Bogotá, we proceeded to Medellin and then to Barranquilla, Colombia. Gert called and said that the decision had been made not to film *Signale* in Bogotá after all, to my great relief.

My father had called; he said he and my mother had a terrible case of the flu and possibly might have to cancel their plans to meet me in Caracas. I was devastated and said I hoped at least he would feel well enough to join me there. The company and I continued our tour, flying again on small planes. Even though my parents might not come and Gert had returned to Berlin, I felt very happy to be going to Caracas. My plane was met there by a very nice-looking man who turned out to be Raphael Alcantra, my father's business associate. He seemed glad to meet me and insisted on my going in his car to my hotel. I liked him very much as aside from the fact that he was extremely polite, he bore the cheering news that my father was about to arrive in a few days.

In Caracas, I was staying at the best hotel in the city as were the other members of the company. On the board, it was posted that we were to attend a cocktail party reception that evening at seven o'clock. I thought I would be free for dinner by nine o'clock, and that seemed agreeable. Our dancers really looked quite beautiful when they were dressed up, and the girls loved to do so. Even the boys looked elegant in with jacket and tie, some in white jackets, as Berliners always took care with their appearance, plus as a group we were ambassadors of West Berlin. We arrived by bus at a stately home. I think every German consul in South America lived in great comfort. Evenings like this one were always something of an effort for me because my German was not good enough to discuss anything of importance. However, in the midst of all the champagne and chatter, a gentleman asked, "Where are you from?" and I answered in English, "San Francisco." Excitedly, he said, "I saw it." I replied, "Oh, how marvelous—did you like it?" He responded, "I was on a prisoner-of-war ship." A long silence. At least he was honest, but still I found it very difficult to come face-to-face with any Nazi supporter from that terrible time. I excused myself and departed gracefully.

I had the feeling that if one wanted to find all the SS men who had been in Germany during World War II, all one had to do was visit anywhere in South America. I was then in my twenties, too young to fully understand what had happened in Europe during the war yet old enough to have been told by my parents, as a child, to be aware of other children abroad who needed food and clothing. In my family, we had all had some duty to perform for the war effort; I had collected more money for the Red Cross than anyone in my class. Now, again and again throughout the tour, I was coming face-to-face with the Nazi elite, all of them wealthy and walking about freely. I only wished that evening that Gert was with me as he was always so supportive and always felt horror when we came across such people bragging about what they had done. This time, though, I didn't have long to think about it because I was soon back at my hotel to meet Raphael for dinner at nine o'clock.

What a full day it had been, and I still had dinner to get through. And our schedule for the next day indicated I had to be at class at 10:00 am, so I could not stay up late this night. I enjoyed a beautiful dinner and loved being spoiled but bade Raphael an early good night. I would see him again after the performance the next day. When I got to my room, the telephone rang—it was my father. He said Mother was still not well enough to travel but that he would be there the day after. Raphael's office was going to receive a teletype from his office, giving the details. I was sad about Mother but so happy that Daddy would actually be there.

The next day, I felt ready and energetic. At the theater, I discovered I had my own dressing room—I didn't mind sharing once in a while but I loved being able to spread out and make my own space. But already I missed Gert so much. His force alone was really something to admire, not just in dance but in life also. It is why I loved him. We laughed so much together, even at ourselves. I remember once we walked down a street in Germany, somewhere on tour, and we hunched over and tottered, pretending we were two old people. Gert reminded me of this incident six months before he died; we laughed again at how now we could play the roles for real.

When I prepared for my first class in Caracas, I reminded myself that this was not the time for thinking about and missing him. Gert would expect me to be strong and keep up my own spirit and to dance well, which helped to hold the company together. This, too, is probably one of the most important things you must be responsible for when you are a prima ballerina in the literal sense. you can't be a prima ballerina, in the egotistical sense: those who dance with you are also your responsibility. You cannot think only of your own performance, it is yours and theirs that will be a success, depending on your inspiration and encouragement and care for the other dancers. Contrary to the belief that you have your nose in the air, it is more likely that you have your feet on the ground and your eye on everything. If you dance badly, the entire company is viewed negatively; if, on the other hand, you lead and they follow, the company is a success. This kind of thinking when you are young is what will bring you great rewards when you were older. It starts in the studio with the great dancers as your teachers. Egorova told me I must one day pass it along, as did most of the dancers who had performed for the czar. Only now, in my time, I had to dance nightly, which is something my teachers never did! How times had changed! In fact, on tour, I not only danced nightly but sometimes also in three different ballets or pas de deux on the same night! But I loved this because it gave me a chance to perfect my art. Each time I danced, I could experience the role differently emotionally. That is why ongoing live theater can never be replaced by film or television or a single live performance. This ephemeral quality is what makes dance such an art.

Class was to be held onstage, where the barres were already set up. There were always a few people watching from the auditorium—friends and so on. I had invited Raphael but didn't know if he was there or not. Pepe arrived quite cheerful and gave me a kiss on both cheeks. This time, I gave class. I always gave Egorova's barre, which progresses through the muscles. The last thing: girls stretched at the barre, boys on the floor. Center class, I did in two groups, the girls in pointe shoes always. Sweat began to flow. Adagio came next. I must say, this is always the most meaningful part of class for me as an adagio should contain almost all of the elements one needs to be a great dancer. Besides holding the legs steady, the emotions must flow with every phrase, and the sequences must change fluidly from one to the next. The face must be relaxed yet breathe with the top of the movement and the emotions of the music. My adagios are never easy; that, I got from Egorova, who lived her adagios! Everything was in her face, and she expected that from you. Not everyone can do this, it is rare. "Girls first," I called. "More—more—yes—yes—good—higher—breathe," then I made corrections and moved on to the next group. Then the men—it was much harder for them, with more balances, more effort, higher legs. We then followed with turns—everybody loves turns—little jumps (allegro), then lastly the big jumps. I ended with sixteen *grands battements,* eight front, eight back, without pause; three *entrechats trois* et *quatres* (little jumps with leg beats), for thirty-two measures; then reverence.

Everyone clapped, something I always cut short as I find this unnecessary. We then broke for ten minutes. I dried myself off as that was a hard class for me to demonstrate, actually do myself, and also correct. But I felt good in my body. That is so important for a dancer after a class. I looked out into the house to try to see if Raphael was there and saw him approaching the stairs that are always put out for rehearsals, at the edge of the stage, to make everyone's comings and goings that much easier. He was very excited to be there, able to watch what happened even before we would start to dance. I excused myself then as I needed to change for our rehearsal. Happily, he would stay awhile to be able to watch us rehearse.

First, we went through the Schumann variations and really cleaned up each variation, which had become a bit sloppy. Classical variations show all faults! There is no hiding or cheating—you either do them with clean technique or forget it! It was mainly the corps that needed to be rehearsed, but I felt that we should all do our variations, whoever was not dancing sitting out front to provide corrections. It was a very good rehearsal.

Then the call came for lunch break. We were to return at 2:00 pm. Mr. Hoffman came to my dressing room with a telegram—my father would be arriving that evening. I asked him if he could arrange with Mr. Alcantra to have a car meet him to bring him to the theater as it would probably be just after intermission when he arrived. He could then go directly to a box seat and be escorted backstage afterward. Mr. Hoffman promised even a police escort! I was so excited that I had a good cry, better now without makeup! My mother always understood me and my great passion for my work whereas my father, who had opposed my career, would now see me in a new light, dancing with a European company, outside America, as their prima ballerina, having conquered my dream with hard work and determination. Just as he was successful in his own business, he would see for himself why I had sacrificed the life he had wanted for me.

At last it was time for makeup and solitude in my dressing room. However, by then, the entire company knew that my father was to arrive that night. Every five minutes, there was a knock, someone stuck a head inside the door with a kind "Merde, Janet" or "We are so happy for you." Several of the girls brought me a small lovely bouquet. My dresser found a vase and put them on my already crowded table, along with my two good-luck charms. One was a stuffed sleeping cat that was always in Gert's car until I took it because I would always teasingly call him *meine schlaf Katze*—my sleeping cat. Gert was always taking catnaps; once I even saw him closing his eyes while he was driving! The other was an old Russian icon that opened up, which Tatjana had given me. It felt like opening night to me, and in a way it was.

Now that my makeup was applied, it was time for a warm-up, not a lengthy one. I found myself a spot on the side of the stage and began. Pepe joined me, and soon we were doing a very slow, easy warm-up together. After Pepe did some pirouettes with me and I tried my turns in a circle, I was satisfied and left the stage. I went back to my dressing room to change into my costume for the Schumann. I tried not to look at the clock because I knew my father would be rushed to the theater in good hands.

The first ballet on the program went well, with warm feedback from the audience that we could feel onstage. We all seemed inspired, and that was a good start. Everything went as it should; the last ballet was *Hamlet*, which was not the most difficult of my ballets. As usual, the company received a great ovation, and we had Caracas in our hearts. We would do three other performances for this appreciative city and felt happy with our first night's curtain calls. As I came offstage, my arms full of flowers, my dresser put my shawl over my wet shoulders and relieved me of my bouquets. She also showed me a basket of flowers, which was huge! I asked her to have one of the stagehands carry it to my dressing room. After ten minutes of waiting in the wings, still no Father. Finally, I withdrew to my dressing room and changed into a robe.

Suddenly I heard a great commotion outside in the corridor then a knock at the door. Finally, there was my father. I jumped into his arms, and he hugged me. Naturally, I began to cry—tears of joy. He was his usual charming self, and as I asked him where he had been, he proceeded to tell me how he had met so-and-so and we were invited for lunch. As tired as he was after that long trip, he had already managed to charm everyone. I finally couldn't hold it in another moment longer. I asked, "Did you like the performance?" He said, "Wonderful! All so beautiful. But I was so tired during the last one." At least he was honest, and there was always tomorrow, when I would dance *Signale* and *Don Q*. Hopefully that would wake him up.

I asked Mr. Hoffman and Raphael to take him to the lounge and give him some coffee and said I would be ready soon. Everyone in the company was so curious to meet my father, but I did not have to worry about that as I found out later that he had invited them all for lunch and swimming at our hotel the next day after checking our schedule with Mr. Hoffman! He was off and running already! I should have known this; I would just relax and enjoy him, as usual.

When I joined him in the lounge, he had revived and was not at all ready to go to sleep. So we went out—Raphael, Daddy, Dritta, Gritta, and me. Of course, we dancers were starving as we eat little to nothing all day before a performance. Afterward, we eat like horses, and most of the time I have been compared to a racehorse, especially by members of the medical profession (I never minded the comparison as my great love was horse racing; it was part of my Sassoon blood, as some of the Sassoons in the Orient owned racehorses, and my father also enjoyed this sport immensely). After dinner, as we passed the reception desk at the hotel, the receptionist wished me "Good night, Ms. Sassoon, and now we have the pleasure of your father."

The next morning, I broke my one golden rule and came down to the dining room for breakfast with Daddy. Now, as we passed, the receptionist cooed, "Good morning, Mr. Sassoon and Ms. Sassoon." Not yet twenty-four hours, and already my father had radiated the special charm he had with men as well as women; everyone was bowing and scraping. I loved being his daughter.

When I saw the board, I was met with another surprise: the next day was free, except for a reception in the afternoon: principals attend, no exceptions! Raphael had a racehorse that was running that day, and we were invited to go with him in the owners' box! But I had a plan: I reminded Daddy that he had invited everyone for swimming and lunch. He was just beaming, in his element, and said he would arrange everything if I needed to do other things. I could leave and come back, which was exactly what I did.

By the time I had returned from my morning's shopping, they were already at the hotel, squealing and splashing in the pool. When I passed the receptionist he said, "Your father is—" and we finished the sentence together "—in the swimming pool and restaurant. I know." I couldn't resist taking a peek. Everyone was jumping into the water and diving—Berlin had taken over the pool. All the girls had gorgeous figures in bathing suits; the boys were in terrific shape also. When they spotted me, they wanted to throw me into the pool, clothes and all, but I pleaded that I had performances coming up plus I threatened I'd kill them in the next class! I went upstairs to change into a swimsuit and cover-up and went back down, but not to swim. I found my muscles relaxed too much after swimming, and therefore, I avoided doing so on any day I had a performance.

I suggested we all have a light lunch being as we had to be in the theater that night. By then everyone was calling my father Papa Sassoon, and that's what he was. He had captured everybody's heart, and they were eager to dance well for him that night. I had lots of ballets on this program, so I left early.

Again, I found myself missing Gert even though I believed whoever danced Tatjana's choreography would have a great success as it was the choreography that held the story and the power to make her ballets different, avant-garde, for their time, and she was skillful at engaging our emotions as well. We were not just an instrument for her choreography; she demanded of us our inner strengths and feelings, which emerged in a good way, never vulgar or showoff-ish but with a kind of eloquence of our body and selves.

—

As I gazed at myself in the dressing room mirror, I thought about how far I had come, what a long way from home it was emotionally as well as physically, and that my father would be in the audience. It was like a dream being fulfilled. I wasn't at all nervous, which amused me. I chitchatted with everyone as they passed me at the barre while I warmed up alone (this was necessary before having to perform in so many ballets; I had to warm up at my own pace). I always loved this time backstage, everyone doing his or her own thing. There was even something special about the smell of a theater, a scent that is instantly recognizable and always stays in your memory.

The first call came, which meant that I had to leave the stage and prepare for the Schumann variations. No shoe hysterics; I had already had those earlier that day! They had to be perfect for the jumps in this piece, strong in the toe. My dresser helped me into my tutu as I powdered my shoulders. I tucked in and wet the ribbons of my shoes so that they would not come out. Then I checked my headdress. I tapped the cat and my icon and was ready to go. I said a prayer quietly to God, thanking him for allowing me to dance so that I could make others happy or help them forget their problems. Then we all took our places, and the curtain rose to show us all in classical positions, ready to move. And so we did.

The ballet was a success with this night's audience, but I couldn't dwell on that; I had to change for *Don Quixote*. Shoes first, then my tutu—my wriggling didn't help my dresser any as I attached the rose to my hair, making sure it was well secured. My tiny arm puffs were put on then, fan in hand, I rushed back to the stage, dresser behind me, to be stationed in the wings to be ready with my fan for my variation. Pepe was waiting for me, in a very good mood, and greeted me with his "Bella, bella." There was something different about tonight, with my father in the audience. I would love this pas de deux even more and dance it with all my heart and joy so he would feel it too.

There were those familiar moments again, when the curtain opens and the audience applauds us. Then the four chords as we raised our heads and arms together. We were off and running—and everything went as well as I could possibly hope for. All the balances were rather spectacular, and Pepe was fabulous in his variations and the coda. We danced without holding back, without caution. The audience gave us a huge ovation. Pepe received my rose with such love and dignity that I dropped to my knee to him. He lifted me up, and he and the audience were clearly deeply touched. Backstage, the company members who had gathered to watch us were waiting to applaud us. They, too, had seen something that would be with them always.

Next came *Hamlet*, where my father would see me die of poisoned wine, and then our unique *Signale*, in which he would watch me be strangled to death! Our curtain calls were endless, and finally we called the entire ensemble onstage to wave good-bye to the audience. I hurried to leave the stage, but people already gathered around me to talk, until my dresser took me by the hand, saying, "She is wet, she will catch cold, she must change." I returned to my dressing room and asked Dina to please find my father and send him there to me. I didn't want to see him with so many people around.

I stayed in my dressing room, and at long last, there was a knock at the door, and in came Daddy. "How hard you work" were his first words. My answer: "I love it." He then seemed to be more himself and said, "Wonderful! You did very well." I was happy to hear that. I was told later that when everyone applauded, he did not—I knew this about my mother, but not my father. But he sat with tears in his eyes; my mother would actually cry out in joy. This was their way, never to brag about their daughter. My upbringing had been so different from those I was always around; it would never be understood by anyone how I was raised. Even though I had grown up in America, it was different from a European upbringing as well as an American one. I was comfortable with it, even more so as I grew older.

Now was the time for us to leave the theater. Some of the girls would have dinner with us. I inched my way to the stage, which I did any night I left a theater, to say, "Thank you, gentlemen" *and* good night to the crew. That always filled me with such happiness as they work so hard, and no one ever says anything nice to them, only complaints.

Raphael and Daddy tried to shield me from the stage-door madness, but I believed performers should do what they can for those who wait to see them. So I did, and finally, we were able to leave.

We ate at an outdoor restaurant where everyone seemed to know Raphael—and to know that we dancers were starving. We ordered our dinner and had lots of good red wine. My father appeared very happy, and I knew he was proud at this moment because his love for living and people were now in full force. It really didn't matter if I danced or not; it was that this put him in the middle of excitement, of living life to the fullest. I suddenly thought to myself a poem I love dearly, by A. E. Housman:

> When I was one and twenty
> I heard a wise man say,
> "Give crowns and pounds of guineas
> But not your heart away;

Give pearls away and rubies
But keep your fancy free."
But I was one and twenty,
No use to talk to me.

And that moment, there it was, all in my head: what a great time this was for me.

We returned to the hotel to the accompaniment of three musicians who followed us—my father had secretly arranged in advance for them to serenade us in the streets of Caracas. We kissed everyone good night, and I went to bed looking forward to the racetrack the next day.

Obviously, I had told no one that I was not going to the reception for which attendance by the principals was apparently mandatory. I waited until I was sure everyone had left, and then I called Mr. Hoffman's room to say I could not possibly come because I was sick to my stomach. I also claimed to have a headache, saying that I would not accept phone calls so I could rest. I would be well, I was sure, by evening. I threw that in as obviously I had no intention of missing out on enjoying a free evening. At any rate, Raphael's horse awaited me. Raphael sent a car, and I escaped to the racetrack.

I went to see the horse as soon as we arrived. It was a beautiful animal—and the jockey was as small as I was, and probably weighed just about what I did. We then rushed off to the owners' box but not before Raphael told me he had placed a hundred-dollar bet for me on his horse. He handed me the stub. Daddy asked to do that too, so Raphael sent a boy to do it. Except for Raphael's part in this, I did not know the horses or the owners or the jockeys to even know the odds. When I do play the horses, it takes considerable study to keep up with what they do where and how.

Now was the big moment. It was announced in Spanish that they were at the gate. Some of the horses appeared nervous, just as I felt, and then they were off, I was so excited that I started jumping, screaming, "Go! Come on!," hitting Daddy's shoulder. Our horse advanced from the back to be almost in the lead then he did it, passing the lead horse. I yelled and screamed and was totally out of control. We'd won! Raphael took my hand and said, "Follow me." We went down to the winning horse, where they put flowers around his head. They asked me to put a hand on his nose for a photo with Raphael and the horse and jockey. I loved it even though my short white gloves got a good snortful!

I felt so happy, but then my father told me I could not take any money from Raphael, that it wasn't proper. Raphael argued, but Daddy instead gave me his winnings to settle the argument.

We returned to the hotel, where everyone asked how I was. I said much better as the rest did one a lot of good. They also said they had never seen me so radiant! I ignored that remark for fear that I would give myself away. We had an early dinner, compared with that of South Americans, as I would have my last performance in Caracas the following day.

The next day found me at the theater when Dina knocked on my dressing room door, newspaper in hand, to show me the front page: BALLERINA BETS ON WINNING HORSE! I couldn't do anything but laugh. She asked, "Did your horse have to win?" And we got totally hysterical. I felt badly that I'd lied, but I would not have been excused from the reception so I could go to a racetrack, and that was that. Besides, I had walked out on so many of these so-called receptions because of the comments I'd had to politely endure, that I felt as if I didn't really attend them half the time anyway. Mr. Hoffman was obviously displeased, but I ignored that, as I had been more than good during this tour for the sake of PR. Enough was enough. A little laughter and fun helps to give the spirit a lift. Each night for our performances, we had to be immediately and totally disciplined, no matter whether we had a headache or cramps or our period. We had to dance at a certain level, and that was not always easy. Sore muscles, a bad knee—so much would happen daily on tour to at least one of us. We are not superhuman, and yet we went on as if everything was all right. We all deserved to be naughty, on our own time, once in a while.

By now, the whole company had seen the photo because Mr. Hoffman had pasted it on the board! And it lifted everyone's morale! It showed that their ballerina was human and had had a wonderful time doing something outrageous. I did my warm-up with a big grin on my face. Each person who passed me laughed or said, "Du hast macht gut." I must say, this company's morale had never been so high on this whole tour, and to keep it up toward the end is not an easy thing to do. I felt very proud and was very thankful toward Daddy and Raphael and the horse for helping the company. We would give our all to the audience that night as we were full of life, and to dance is to live life to the fullest.

31

Panama and Farewell

Our last leg of the tour would be Panama.

It was very hard to say good-bye to my father and Raphael. Luckily, I had to go on ahead to the airport with my fellow dancers, leaving Daddy in the hands of Raphael. The whole company on the bus opened the windows and called, "Bye-bye! Auf Wiedersehen, Papa Sassoon!," while my father beamed with delight. It had been a wonderful time for all.

Once on the plane, our comedians went into their routine, offering newspapers and magazines in various languages to the wrong people! This was a new idea and truly original. Luckily, the stewardess stopped them before they went too far. One would think we would use this time to rest, but the truth was that our energy was so bountiful compared to that of the average person that it needed to be released. I think if a way could have been found to give us dancers a good class on a plane, that would have solved the problem. When we were given our in-flight meal, the pranksters settled into their seats, and everyone closed their eyes for a while. That moment in a trip always presented difficulty for me as, unless I was ill, I could never sleep during the day. However, I was an avid reader and was never without a book or two.

I was quite excited about this part of the trip because that meant I would see the Panama Canal, which for me was one of the manmade wonders of the world. And soon we heard an announcement that if we looked out our windows, we would see the canal. It was awesome—there it was! One couldn't help thinking about how many lives were lost during its construction. Now we were so easily flying over it as we prepared to land.

As I peered out my window, I saw what looked like a tropical jungle. I knew this would be a place I would adore. I loved humid heat, hated the cold, and was very happy when I had a warm climate to work in. Most of the dancers were not used to the hot weather, and their white skin would turn red; they liked the climate yet found dancing easier where it was cooler.

After we cleared customs, we went to the Panama Hilton Hotel. As I was checking in, I was told that I had a suite with a large balcony overlooking the grounds, and not too far away was the jungle. We had an early taste of that: while we were still in the lobby, a woman came strolling through with a baby lion cub on a leash, as if it were a dog. I couldn't believe my eyes and stopped to speak with her, asking her if I could pet it. I was a bit timid as this was the first time I had ever been so close to a lion, let alone able pet one. It was like a big pussycat and very lovable. Also in the lobby, there were several interesting characters, as if out of a Hemingway novel. I did not know that I, too, could have been added to that list.

My suite turned out to be very large and deluxe! It had veranda doors opening to a huge balcony outfitted with a table, umbrella, chairs, and beautiful bougainvilleas. It looked absolutely delightful. Alas, I had little time to enjoy this as I had a rehearsal and needed to go to the theater.

I took a taxi and arrived before the others. Our crew was already there since the early morning, setting up. I wondered if an audience understands all the people involved besides the performing artists who go into making a production work: the secret elves behind the scenes who travel at night, working every day to prepare everything before we arrived, and those other offstage workers who clean our costumes, sew anything that needs mending, put the right costumes into the right dressing rooms in time for us to just put them on. These are the heroes that make the magic work. I so appreciated them and always tried to acknowledge them.

In this performance, I was to dance *Raymonda* in preparation for our next tour that I was trying to negotiate with the company. That tour would take us to Hong Kong and Japan with Paul Szilard, a New Yorker and good friend who became an impresario.

It was the first time I would dance a classical pas de deux with Rudolph Holz instead of Pepe, who was so overworked without Gert's being with us. He was my second partner for pas de deux, a very good height for me and built like most Russian male dancers: compact body and muscular legs. He looked very attractive onstage, and we went well together. I had rehearsed the piece in Berlin before this tour began, and we had short run-throughs but never really for force and actual performance.

I had danced this with Alan Howard, who had been in the Ballet Russe de Monte Carlo, so it was not new to me; with him, nothing really needed any great adjustment—I was used to dancing it with him. Most ballerinas are very lucky if they have one or two partners in a company that they continually dance with. There are many reasons for this. Bodywise, it is always better to work with someone taller than yourself when you are on point. It makes all the difference in turns where his hands are placed on your waist, for his posture to be straight rather than leaning with his behind out, which distorts his line. Also, on finger turns, it is very easy if you are not overly tall so that he can reach easily over your head to turn you with one finger. Lifting, again—the height needs to be appropriate. It goes without saying that everyone is thin, but that does not make lifts easy. Being lightweight helps, but the preparatory jump is the secret that makes a ballerina look as if she is light in the air. All these things become easier if you have a taller partner.

I now had two male classical partners and Gert, of course, for all of Tatjana's dramatic big ballets. This was the most perfect position for me to be in; if Japan came through, I would be very happy with these partners.

For tonight, we would see how the *Raymonda* pas de deux would succeed on its own. It was quite different from the *Don Quixote* pas de deux. The music of Glazunov was so beautiful that, for me, it went straight to my heart and brought out the lyrical side of my dancing.

The company members started to arrive with all their paraphernalia, and everyone looked young and fresh. Barres were set up for class onstage, and here again I had a dressing room to myself. The theater and its stage were quite large, which meant that one could take really grand steps. It also meant that one had to think ahead about where to recover your breathing versus where you had to make an effort to cover the stage. This was especially the case for the grand pas de deux, where there is just the two of us onstage. The rest of the ballets in our touring repertoire went automatically as by this time we had danced them on all sizes of stages. I walked through my entrances and exits for *Raymonda*, so I was sure of where I would be. Also, after class, we would do a lighting rehearsal as *Raymonda*'s changing moods require different lighting.

Pepe called for the class to begin. He greeted me with our usual kiss on both cheeks and said, "You are too thin." What could I answer? Just a grand pas de deux could make me lose three to five pounds, or two kilos. I would gain it back when I was not performing, as all of us dancers do, and it was not a problem. One has to eat very well on tour to keep up one's strength and weight.

Class proceeded, and after barre, Pepe suggested that we try Cecchetti's quatre pirouettes combination (four turns in every position). Pepe was quite wicked, knowing that besides himself, I was the only person trained in Cecchetti schooling. This combination is also intermingled in the Russian schooling as Cecchetti was for years *the* method in Russia, and he was considered a master teacher by the great dancers there. When I went through the Cecchetti training, I was already highly trained, yet every Thursday I was given the same quatre pirouettes combination. Nobody would step forward to do it as everyone found it so difficult. But finally we grew comfortable with it, and it became a challenge instead of something to be dreaded.

Pepe said, "Janet, please demonstrate." He gave the tempo to the rehearsal pianist, and I asked, "Two or three pirouettes?" As I would be on point, Pepe told me two would do. I prepared and then started. Realizing how strong your back has to be for every preparation *before* the turn is the secret—not the turn itself! Also, the finish after each pirouette involves the whole body and is dependent on how straight you can hold your center and back. Not having done this for a while and not having a mirror to check my positions, it was difficult. However, dancers should not depend on mirrors but be able to *feel* whether they are in the right positions. At last I finished, sweat pouring down my face. The dancers began to applaud, but I stopped them immediately and said, "Pepe, I think if they understood to use the back, it would help." Pepe said "Well done" to me and then asked the girls to step up first. I had a chance to rest as Pepe did the turns beautifully along with the girls while I hollered corrections. This also gave the boys a chance to see a male dancer demonstrate the combination. Pepe was flawless, and it was a joy to watch him do two pirouettes so cleanly and strongly in each position. We repeated the exercise with the boys' group, which I joined. They all attempted one pirouette rather than two, but it was a good try for the first time. We finally completed the combination, knowing it would not be for the last time. Everyone was having a good class, working hard and full out.

We continued with class, but I stopped when we got to big jumps. I knew I needed to do some point work to break in new point shoes. I worked on this in the back, keeping out of the way. When it came time for the girls to execute piqué turns from the corner, I joined in as that would help break in my toe shoes. Class came to an end with the usual reverence.

Ten minutes' break, and we would return to work on *Raymonda* with lights and music. I went to put on my practice tutu; I knew my real *Raymonda* tutu, as it belonged to me, would be no problem to adjust. Pepe would watch from the front of the house to do corrections. Rudi was very attentive as it was a good role for him, and he was more than ready to do it. Rehearsals went well. I never went off tempo; the music was played as it should be, and I adapted to it instead of it being distorted to suit the dancer as it is sometimes done today. A tempo adjustment was allowed only during the tour de force of a grand pas de deux but, even then, ever so slightly. I think today, the music is stretched to a point where the excitement of the original choreography is lost; the steps were designed for the right tempo to show off the dancer's technique at its best advantage. I have suffered as a coach when I have suggested to take *Raymonda*'s variation and coda at the tempo in which the music was written, which for the ballerina becomes faster and faster and not more slowly. I am told "It is not Russian." When I communicated this to my dear beloved friend Jurgen Schneider, formerly ballet master of ABT, he said, "Tell them you are Russian and they are Soviet!" But there is truth to what he said. I worked with the last ballerinas to be trained at the time of the czar, including private coaching of the variations from the classic ballets. One cannot accuse Egorova, Preobrajenska, Nijinska, and so on of not teaching what they knew intimately as dancers. This slowing down started with Nureyev, and everyone else followed.

This rehearsal was to be our last chance before performing it. Our main objective was to work out how to use the whole stage. Pepe made a few corrections after the pas de deux, mainly that we should stay together at the beginning. We continued rehearsing our individual variations and then the coda, which I only marked (not dancing full out) to reserve my strength for the real performance. I felt Rudi was secure in the pas de deux and only by performing it would he improve his variation and the coda. Pepe made a few more suggestions, and Rudi was very quick to accept them. We left content.

We had enough time after the rehearsal to go out for coffee and a small bite to eat. Where we were in Panama was colorful and very busy. Lots of shops tempted us, but we really could not afford spending a great deal of money. Pepe was the worst; he would always buy something for his newly wedded wife. I loved coming along with him and would encourage him, saying she would love each new item that he chose.

When we returned to the hotel, I noticed white envelopes in everyone's key box but did not give it much thought. My box was empty, and I asked for my key. Leaving Pepe in the lobby, I went to my room to rest and do a few things. It had been a good day, and I was looking forward to performing. I still missed Gert and Tatjana and dashed off a note to mail to them. Time passed quickly, and then I needed to return to the theater.

My dressing room was waiting for me, all arranged. Makeup time was prayer time, and that always put me right. Then came warm-up—I put on my leg warmers over my tights and went out to find a place for myself. I had had such a good class and rehearsal but now had to make my body ready to dance. I nodded hello to whoever greeted me, but everybody knew not to disturb this precious moment. Company class was onstage, as usual. Everyone was working hard and doing well. Tatjana would have been very happy to see this. When I finished my warm-up, I went onstage, where Rudi was marking his spacing, and we did some pirouettes together. Then I returned to my dressing room for my usual routine.

Now came toe-shoe hysteria. I had put shoes aside for *Raymonda*, but I had to find the right pair for jumps and pirouettes. My dressing room suddenly looked as if a cyclone had hit it. The first call onstage was announced just as my dresser arrived to put me into my tutu for the *Schumann Variations*. I became calmer with shoes that were just right, tutu on, and, last of all, my shoulders powdered; on went some perfume (Miss Dior), and I touched my good-luck pieces and left for the stage.

Everything went well, and the audience was very receptive. We continued with *Hamlet*, which was very successful and deserved the audience's appreciation. Intermission followed. So far, so good. Dina and Mr. Hoffman came back to say the audience was very posh.

After intermission would be *Raymonda*. This gave me extra time to prepare myself without rushing madly. My tutu for this was an old friend, and I was totally at home in it, whereas had I a new tutu, it would have needed some breaking in. As I left my dressing room, members of the company who passed me said, "Toi toi toi." Reaching the wings with my dresser, I gave her last-minute instructions about where I would come off and so on so that she would be there for me. I also checked our flowers, pulling out one rose a little to be able to take it out to hand effortlessly to Rudi. He appeared, and I gave him a kick with my knee (which for dancers means "good luck") and said, "Merde," likewise. I added, "Enjoy, and all will go well."

There was a brief overture then curtain, and we went out doing a mazurka-like step, which then led into a most beautiful adagio. There were no scary parts for me in this adagio, so I could relax and enjoy dancing it to its fullest, using my back to the end of every line. The music was in my body, and I made use of it totally.

Then came the male variation, which I watched. It went very well. Rudi was good, and his technique was perfect. He received good applause.

Then came my variation, which I really loved. It was so sensuous and dramatic. It built up to the fast music, which I also enjoyed to the last slap of my hands in the finish. I heard great applause from the audience. Then we launched into the coda, which we completed strongly. The pas de deux was a success! I handed Rudi the rose from my bouquet, and he kissed my hand, which the audience loved. We again made our reverence, as the audience made theirs.

After the performance, Jeff came to my dressing room to tell me that the whole company had been invited to dinner at the German consul—except for him and me. I was shocked as it was obvious that, as the two Americans, we were being singled out—and, after all, I was the prima ballerina! Everyone left for dinner, and Jeff and I enjoyed our own dinner at the hotel.

Before going to sleep, I varnished my toe shoes to try to harden them and placed them in a line on the verandah to dry overnight.

During the night, I thought I heard jungle noises, but then the jungle was just a few feet from the hotel. The doors to the veranda had been left open. In the morning, I got up and went out to check on my shoes. To my horror, I found them scattered everywhere, with big teeth marks on them! I threw down the shoe I had in my hand and screamed, ringing all the bells for help. I was ready to change rooms immediately. My first thought was that the little cub had gotten loose, but that was not the case. It was worse; the manager told me that rats had climbed the walls, attracted by the odor of the varnish. He called for my room to be fumigated, and from then on, the management was very attentive to me. That night, all the toe shoes were placed in the kitchen's huge refrigerators!

Meanwhile, I received a note from the German consul general saying that he offered me the use of his driver at any time. In reply, I sent him a note saying that since he had overlooked my presence at his dinner party, I certainly would not accept any other invitation from him for anything.

Instead, I hired a car from the hotel, and Jeff joined me for a spectacular drive along a road that took us partway into the jungle. I saw the most beautiful flowers and asked the driver to stop so I could examine them more closely. He warned me not to go near that beauty as it would be glad to eat me up! So much for my jungle adventure. Jeff and I decided we had had enough and headed back toward the bustle of the city. This was to be our very last performance, which would end with *Signale*.

We thought it best to return to the theater as we had little time left. It had been such a lovely day, and we had spent it well, enjoying Panama's special beauty. We were ready to work plus I needed to start packing out my theater things. Dina and Mr. Hoffman had left a note on the board asking me to dinner after the performance. I thought it was disappointing that they had said nothing about my snub the night before, but nevertheless, tonight would be our last opportunity for dinner together and was not the time to begrudge them this evening's kind gesture.

We had a hard dance program that night. It was sad that the tour was coming to an end. Alone in my dressing room, putting on my makeup, I thought that this would be my farewell to this special time for a while, and so I made it last a little bit longer than usual. Backstage, lots of people were wandering around, which was unusual and normally not allowed. Then first call was announced. Time flew by, and it was intermission time.

After intermission came the *Don Q* pas de deux. No matter how many times you dance it, you always think about the hard parts beforehand, but in the end, you can't do anything more about them. This pas de deux was always special for me. I think that is because I started with my head down, as if in prayer. The curtain opens on this quiet, still scene of you and your partner, before four chords start your movements. Then you dance your heart out. It's full of technique, but also you must reach out to the audience and make them feel joy and exhilaration so that they are really there for those moments with you. Pepe was absolutely carried away with his variation, and that inspired me. I followed with great strength and we both danced our hardest parts in the coda as if they were nothing. We finished to the sound of bravos and stamping feet. Also, many of the company dancers had been standing in the wings watching, so when we came offstage, we received their applause, too. We went out again in front of the curtain, and Pepe and I went to each side to bow and finally to center stage. I made my deepest reverence with my hand over my heart—and that was given with all of my heart. I then turned to Pepe and gave him my final reverence. He kissed my hand, lifted me to standing, and we stood together acknowledging our receptive audience. In my heart, it was all of South America that I was thanking for the love that they had showered upon us.

32

Far East Tour

After what seemed like a long time, we were back in Berlin. Gert and Tatjana greeted us at the airport, and it was really homecoming for everybody, including me. I was now a "Berliner *Kind.*"

I went off with Gert. Tatjana was brimming with things to tell and planned to take me to dinner after I had left my suitcase at my hotel. I was welcomed with great joy by the hotel staff that always saved for me room number 12 with the balcony. I should have felt very tired, but I was wide awake. I dabbed a bit to feel refreshed and changed clothes, which gave me new energy. Then I left to meet Tatjana and Gert for dinner.

There were a few nice restaurants that she frequented, and naturally, they all knew who she was—and also Gert—so whenever we entered, all heads turned and Tatjana walked in as if she was royalty. Gert ordered champagne in my honor, and I was very touched as I knew that our intimacy was very special. At last I told them all that had gone on in South America and how good everyone had been even under difficult circumstances (except for one boy, who had been difficult and who perhaps should have been put on probation). When I told them about Panama, Tatjana was furious. She said nobody should have gone: "The incident was done behind my back or I would have said something to Mr. Hoffman." But it really was so stupid. I let it go, assuring Tatjana that I had taken care of it in my own way.

Gert then gave me the news of the company's plans to go to Asia and said, "We have very good feeling with your Mr. Szilard [Hungarian-American impresario Paul Szilard]. We are now waiting any day for Bonn [the senate seat of West Germany at that time] to give the command and money for such a tour." Gert felt that the senate would approve as no German company of any of the arts had had a chance to go to the Orient. Paul had arranged a guarantee of Hong Kong then Tokyo, where a very big contractor of artistic events would sponsor the entire Japan tour. It was almost too good to be true.

One of the demands by the senate was that we use the name Berliner Ballette Tanztheater Deutschen Oper. Since we would in essence be using our Berlin choreography and dancers, it seemed to me no great change. But Gert said, "Wait." That "wait" sounded ominous. Regardless, I was very happy about the prospect of the tour and asked all kinds of questions, especially about what repertory we would be taking. Tatjana assured me that I would have my own two grand pas de deux for sure on program 1 and program 2. She had heard all about the great success of both. I was pleased that I did not have to ask for this as I felt I deserved it.

I was very happy that things were working out for Paul Szilard as well since he had instigated the whole idea. I knew in my heart that this company would be successful in Asia and expressed as much to Tatjana. The choreography would be absolutely new to that audience. The basis for it was classical, but Tatjana had been the first to deviate from the Balanchine style, in a style one could call neoclassic modern. At that time, John Neumeier in Hamburg, started to choreograph somewhat in this form, but his company was not going East with it. As a company, we were so ahead technically and dramatically that one could say that Tatjana was truly a genius far ahead of her time. I was very grateful to be her prima ballerina.

For the time being, the company was not performing in Berlin and would perhaps do a small tour locally before heading for Japan. Obviously, Tatjana understood that I would want to go home first. I thought it might be the right moment as that would still give me time to come back to Berlin and rehearse for the tour—and, this time, travel to Japan with the company. I had learned my lesson about traveling separately! Tatjana told me that Pepe had some short ballets he would like to choreograph for the company and that in these the soloists would have more opportunities to dance. She assured me that none of my solos would ever be danced by anyone else (I was aware that one person had actually understudied all of my roles, who was not a kind person, who had done it behind my back). Tatjana asked me if I was willing to dance all my solos when I came back so that they could film them. I didn't hesitate to say yes as I knew this way the steps would be kept for the future (alas, this was in the days of 16 mm film, before videotape).

So finally we had things settled. I would leave for San Francisco the very next day. The company would pay for my return flight. I felt this was very fair and generous. Good-bye to everyone being difficult! The next day, I called Constanza, and we met for coffee. We spoke about everything—we always discussed life and love and what we thought about, even our secret thoughts. I would miss her very much as she was so close to me and I to her! We hugged each other, and one would think our separation was to be forever—I would be coming back. After all, I was now a Berliner *Kind*!

I flew on Pan American back to California—over the Pole. In those days, it was always exciting to fly, and the planes weren't jammed with people as flights are now. I kept getting up to exercise and to stretch my legs. My feet would always swell, and I had to stick them straight up in front of me, shocking almost everyone as that was over 90 degrees. I finally devised a system of hiding them under a blanket, though the effect was still the same. At the end of the journey, no matter how many times I had made this trip, landing in San Francisco was always breathtakingly exciting for me. I was so looking forward to seeing my parents; I had had only enough time to phone Peter about my imminent arrival; he forwarded the information to my parents.

At the airport, I was reunited with Peter. I broke into tears, and he likewise seemed very emotional with joy and love. When we were back at our apartment, Peter presented me with roses, and I collapsed into a chair. I started to ask questions when he interrupted me to inform me that that night there was a party for my parents, who were about to leave on a long trip they had planned around the world. Did I have enough energy to surprise them by showing up, he asked. That was too good a challenge; I replied that all I needed was a shower and a pretty dress.

When we arrived, our hostess nearly gave it away as we motioned for her to be silent. She gaily announced that a special delivery had arrived. In I walked, flying into my parents' arms. Now everyone was crying and speaking at the same time. What a wonderful surprise for me as well as for them. Everyone had a glorious time. But there was another surprise in store for me.

By the time I returned to our apartment, I had been awake for twenty-four hours. Peter suggested a cognac. I declined, but he poured one for himself. I have no idea to this day what suddenly made me feel something was very wrong. I asked Peter what was on his mind. He babbled on about how much he loved me and how he would never love anyone as he did me—but that he must have a divorce immediately!

I could not believe what I had just heard. I asked if there was another woman and said that if so, I was prepared to wait until that relationship was over. He said that was not the real reason but could not say anything more. So I was to believe he loved me with all his heart and to yet divorce him? On what grounds? Again, no answer. I was to do the filing.

The next day, I went to see my mother and told her what had transpired. I made her swear she would not cancel her trip over this. She agreed, on the condition that I would tell my father. I remember that day so clearly. Father was waiting for his tea, sitting and reading and watching the ships go back and forth, a magnificent view from our living room window facing the ocean and Golden Gate Bridge plus the mountain ranges across the bay on Seacliff Avenue. I went to him and blurted out what I had to say, falling to my knees beside his chair. I rested my head against him and sobbed. Suddenly I felt a hand at the back of my head. My father's voice loudly and clearly pulled me up: "I never want you to fall on your knees for any man. Do you understand?" He then held me in his arms. I felt safe and loved and slowly understood why he was so angry. He taught me a great lesson that day just as the foghorns started their song. He just held me.

My parents left on their trip as they had promised. I moved back to Seacliff, and in due time, my marriage was terminated.

Happily, I was to return to Berlin shortly to resume my career as Gert beckoned for me to rejoin the company to start rehearsals for Japan. The tour was finally a reality and could not have come at a better time for me. I had my work, and that could never leave me, or so I thought innocently.

I arrived in Berlin to a fresh scandal. Tatjana and Gert met me at Tempelhof. Again, there was the preliminary of depositing my luggage, this time with a tutu I had had made for *Raymonda*. I felt the nervousness in the air, and over coffee at Kempinsky, I thought, "What is going on?" Tatjana then announced that she had refused to take the company abroad without me! It was news to me that there had ever been any question of my belonging, but Gert informed me that the dancers at the Oper had circulated a petition against me—a foreign ballerina—representing the Deutschen Oper Berlin!

Tatjana had stood up for me, saying that I had danced all the difficult tours for five years of touring plus two ballets had been choreographed just for me, and last of all, the invitation for the company to go to Asia had come about because of me! Her position was if I couldn't go, no one would go.

I must say, I couldn't believe what I was hearing. Stunned, I remained silent. Then finally I said to Tatjana and Gert, this tour was too valuable to the company and they must go, no matter what. Tatjana responded, "No Sassoon, no Gsovsky." Gert stayed calm, but I knew him too well—his anger was all inside. He said we would have to wait as that day they had informed Bonn that I would be listed in the roster as prima ballerina and not as guest artist. I had been a ballerina of the Berlin Ballet for all these years, within Germany and abroad, and I would represent Berlin now. Gert was sure that the petition would be dropped. Also, the company had just added four soloists from the Deutschen Oper Ballett, so the company would be well represented with natural-born Germans.

I could not believe dancers would do such a thing as this to another dancer. I truly lived in fairyland! "This was nothing," Gert explained. "They are jealous from the first performance you danced." And I, who loved my colleagues. The best we could do now was to wait for the answer to come from Bonn. Tatjana declared absolutely that we would not go.

Similar incidents had happened before: an offer for Boston Symphony to tour to the Middle East had come up; however, it excluded anyone of the Jewish faith. The symphony had then stated proudly, "We are all Jewish." Another incident had occurred closer to home, when the San Francisco Ballet was to go to the Middle East. If even your grandmother was Jewish, they could not take you! I was the only Jewish dancer in the company at that time, but conveniently I had had other choices. Still, I will never forget or forgive being told by the manager that they could not take any Jew with them!

Now here I was up against opposition coming from the very dancers I worked with. The dancers of the Stadtische Oper Berlin had their own dressing rooms and dressers, with secure jobs all year, never needing to move. They never had to dance three ballets a night! We danced our hearts out for very little money just to dance. We traveled long hours by bus, danced in little villages on bad stages, and changed in cold dressing rooms just so people could see ballet. But we all loved what we did, and you never heard a complaint from one dancer in our company. On the contrary, when we thought we might not continue to exist as a troupe, we told Tatjana that we would only take our money per day, no salaries. Can you imagine what a wonderful atmosphere existed in such a company? We loved one another and were happy to work with Tatjana and Gert.

The best thing for me to do was to continue to work and go for costume fittings. We alsohad to rehearse the new dancers, who were put into Pepe's new ballets. I rehearsed *Raymonda* and *Paquita* with Rudi, as we had never had time before to concentrate on *Raymonda* and I needed to teach him *Paquita*. We rehearsed as usual, expecting the tour to be approved. And we were correct: Gert announced that the tour was on—and that the prima ballerina would be coming along. There was great rejoicing. Rehearsals were now scheduled with understudies, except for *Signale*. I went to Tatjana and asked her why. She said simply, "No one will ever dance your role." I protested as it was a ballet that was always a big success. She nodded and said, "One day, you will understand." I never questioned her further as I respected her judgment totally. And I understood.

Now everyone went to the board to read all the notices as there was a lot to do. All passports were turned in to Ursula Zigurs, our very patient secretary. Next, there was posted a time schedule for all the boys and girls to go to the doctor's office for the shots required for the tour. We each had a yellow card that bore the dates we had been vaccinated for tetanus, cholera, yellow, fever, polio, malaria, and so on. I had already received injections for tetanus, polio, and smallpox.

At the doctor's, the boys went in one at a time as the girls waited, discussing clothes and girl things. Suddenly the first victim came out, pale as death. We sat him down as he really could not go very far. This went on, boy after boy, until the waiting room looked like a hospital ward. Halfway through the boys, the doctor decided to vaccinate a few girls. We went in two at a time—and those ahead of me came out chatting away as before, not understanding what on earth was going on with the male dancers who had previously seemed so healthy and strong. The doctor just laughed and said, "Men are terrible when it comes to shots. Women like you, who are thin and fragile looking, usually just breeze through, suffering only a bit of a sore arm the next day."

We could not help giggling as we left his office. When we told Tatjana about our experience, she laughed yet showed little surprise as Tatjana believed women were much stronger than men when it came to bearing pain. The next day was free, which gave the boys time to recuperate and the girls time for washing their hair and preparing their clothes. Then the schedule was put up on the board, outlining our departure. [insert schedule]

I immediately noticed a stopover in Cairo and knew the name Sassoon would be recognized immediately. Sure enough, the next day, I was called to decide what to do with me while the plane would be refueled in Cairo. Simple, I suggested—I stay on the plane. But there was a rule that no passenger could stay on board during refueling. Now that presented a problem—if I left the plane and my passport was checked, the Egyptian officials might keep me off. The company didn't want to risk handing me over to the Egyptians. A debate began between Pan American Airlines and the company in Berlin. Pan Am decided to break its own regulation and permit me to stay on board. Another battle won, but what next, I wondered. There was still my arrival in Hong Kong to contend with.

At least the more immediate worries out of the way, we boarded our plane to Frankfurt and then changed planes in Rome. We were on a Boeing 720 jet that would make many more stops. Our only sadness was at leaving Tatjana behind; the Oper could not spare her. However, Gert was with us, and we looked good as a company. Everyone then dressed quite well for travel plus in those days people expected to see a kind of glamour about one when one was a dancer. At receptions after performances, everyone was expected to dress elegantly—the girls in cocktail dresses, the boys with ties and jackets. We were all ambassadors who, besides dancing, represented a country.

Now came the first meal. Little did these stewardesses know what was coming. This was Jurgen's cue. He stood behind the cart, and as the stewardess served drinks, he imitated every move. The whole planeload of passengers started to laugh. Every time she stopped to look around, Jurgen pretended to be talking to a person who was sitting down. It was hilarious. His talent for comedy was natural. I must add that when Berlin Ballet ceased to be, Jurgen Feindt became a very famous TV star, until his death by a crash of his private plane.

First stop was Cairo. The announcement came that we would be landing and for all the dancers to return to their respective seats. Boarding cards were distributed for everyone who would be exiting the plane during refueling. Rudi came over to me, and I said I'd do anything for a good Egyptian coffee. He said, "Wait—let's see what the guards are up to, as I have my Luger in my pocket." I nearly died. That's all I needed, a shootout at the airport! Everyone but Rudi left the plane as I watched from the window. The people outside sort of looked like me, except for the Berlin dancers who were all fair with blond or light brown hair. We noticed no one was checking passports. Rudi said, "Let's go—I'll protect you." Off we went, past the guards—and, to my delight, I had my coffee. Then one of the girls was having trouble buying a scarf, and I answered for her in Arabic, which is close to Egyptian. The salesman said, "Where are you from?" As nonchalantly as I could, I answered, "Oh, the same place as you." We now noticed the guards looking our way. Rudi gave me a nudge and said, "Walk very slowly." I obeyed, as we jabbered in German until we were past the guards—and then on cue we ran to the plane! We had been within minutes of being stopped by the guards. Soon, everyone else boarded, and we were on our way.

Over the years, the tale developed, one version being that Rudi had pulled out his Luger and waved it until I had made it back safely. However, what I have just described is the true version. I did get a furious letter from my father afterward, asking me what was I thinking? I had chanced my life or, almost worse, risked being held for ransom! He was outraged. But I chalk it up to my being young and adventurous. Nothing happened, and life went on.

Our next stops were Dharan and Karachi, followed by Calcutta (now called Kolkata), where my father was born (Sir David Sassoon, a relative, had started the incredible Sassoon dynasty in Bombay, now called Mumbai; a great-great-grandson, Sir Victor Sassoon had built many buildings in Shanghai and during the late twenties had owned the Cathay Hotel, where anybody who was anybody stayed. Sir Victor had his own private suite on its tenth floor. The Sassoons were responsible for buildings schools, hospitals, and a synagogue in what was known as the Shanghai Ghetto to where many refugees had fled, escaping Hitler). I was very happy to disembark in Calcutta, to roam the airport, where everyone stared at me. I did not look Indian at all, but the ladies especially noticed me and smiled. And I smiled back. Many years later, I would come back to this country with my darling present husband, but that's another story—a true fairy tale.

We passed through Bangkok and then arrived in Hong Kong, where we would start our tour. We were put in a lovely hotel called Astor Hotel. It was very exciting for me as these were places I knew about. I was now in the area of the world where I had been born—and where the German dancers now looked out of place. I looked just fine there. And I felt at home. We were on the Hong Kong side of Victoria Harbor, and the theater where we were to perform was on the Kowloon side. I decided to leave my hotel room and roam around to see where I was. I met Dritta and Gritta in the lobby, and they were happy to go on an adventure with me.

It was very strange to be there. I felt as if I had been there before. I led the girls to the main street and said, "Let us find the stalls where they sell gold jewelry." Onward we went and found stalls on both sides of the street, selling all kinds of gold jewelry. It was truly fabulous, just as I had imagined it. We then proceeded to window shop. Silks and gorgeous Chinese dresses dazzled our eyes. For me, they were not foreign as my mother always wore beautiful silk jackets for Friday night Shabbat service at home. She had made a trousseau for my sister and for me that included lovely silk lingerie—slips, nightgowns, and lounging pajamas—and had done this long before we were of age to be married. Our lingerie was hand stitched, and even now, I do not see the same quality (I still have mine, and my sister's has just been altered to fit me).

As we walked, we saw some posters advertising Berlin Ballet, with my photo on them. For some reason, everyone would choose the same dance photo even though the company sent out many. We all laughed and decided to return to the hotel to find Gert, whom I knew was asleep, and to dress up to go to dinner. We wanted to eat at one of the many floating restaurants in the harbor. Dritta and Gitta felt lost, but oddly enough, I already knew where we were. I said, "No, we go this way and turn on the main street and walk a few blocks," and sure enough, we entered our own little circle where the hotel was. We were tired from our explorations yet very excited to be in Hong Kong. I could imagine for the German dancers this was such a different, exotic culture. But it was easy for me to be there because I was raised in the English and Oriental cultures. I cherished my elders and respected them; I thought nothing of kissing my grandmother's hand or that of just some older person. Well, this was foreign to my colleagues. They were also surprised that the name Sassoon was known wherever we went. Certainly not from my being in the dance world but from my father's side of the family having been so influential in the Far East.

Back at the hotel, I asked the concierge to make a reservation at the best floating restaurant and to put it under the name Sassoon. That way we'd be sure to get a good table. Then I went up to my room and had a wonderful bath with bath oil and soaked my poor body. We had been flying for two days! I put on a nice dress and my pearls, which my father had given me. The weather was perfect, just as I loved it—warm enough that one didn't need anything more than a light shawl or sweater. I was now ready to go downstairs.

It was Gert who raised the question of my having lived in Hong Kong before. I told him my parents had been there and that I thought I might have been too, but when I was eighteen months old! He was surprised at this, just as the girls were. This could not have explained why everything felt so familiar to me; maybe it was just that my parents had talked about Hong Kong so much. At any rate, we relaxed and enjoyed our night out at the restaurant the concierge had booked for us. It was still hard to believe that this tour was a reality.

The next day would be an orchestra rehearsal. Our conductor had already worked with the symphony ahead of our arrival. As this would be a technical rehearsal, we decided not to stay up all night, tempting as it was.

—

The next morning, I descended to the hotel lobby a little bit early. Some of the dancers were already waiting to be taken to the Kowloon side, where we would dance at the new City Hall. I said, "It is quite easy, why don't we just go?" A few came along with me to board the Kowloon ferry. At that time, Hong Kong belonged to the British; therefore, English was spoken almost everywhere—British English! In 1962, not much had been built up yet on the Kowloon side. The Peninsula Hotel was the largest structure there, and little did I know, it was owned by the Kadoori family, related to the Sassoons. When the ferry crossed the harbor, we proceeded to the theater, where, once inside, we all felt at home.

It was a new theater and was fully equipped with a light board, top-mounted lights, and so on. Our crew had worked hard the day before to put everything in order. All we had to do was find the bulletin board and our dressing rooms. Mine was easy to find, all mine and close to the stage. I was very happy about that as we had three programs, which would involve a lot of changes for me. I unpacked and made my dressing room comfortable: I set out Tatjana's good-luck piece and Gert's *Schlaf Katze* (sleeping cat) that was really worn out plus good-luck notes on the mirror. My three-tiered makeup case was opened. Now, the horror of the shoes. I just dumped the entire shoe bag upside down, took all the new pairs, and arranged them for breaking in during rehearsals, medium in one pile, soft for the jumps. Finally, I changed into practice clothes and headed for the stage. Even though the rehearsal was to be for only the principals, lots of the other dancers came anyway.

A very nice-looking older man was speaking to Gert. I realized it had to be the impresario who was presenting us in Hong Kong. Gert called me over and said, "Janet, this is Mr. Harry Odell, who says his wife went to school with your mother in Singapore!" I gave him my hand and said, "You mean Esther Goodman, who lives in San Francisco, is your sister-in-law?" He said, "Yes, and we insist on entertaining all of you after the opening night." I thought that was a great idea. He said he would arrange everything and have us picked up after the performance. He would have a magnificent buffet dinner prepared for us. And he said his wife was so looking forward to meeting me. I, too, was delighted to find this extraordinary connection. Gert and I then excused ourselves because it was time to begin the rehearsal.

We started with the *Schumann Variations*; no problem, except for Pepe and my variation. We asked the conductor if he could pick it up a bit on the allegro part. The orchestra sounded very good. Then came *Romeo and Juliet* with Marion Cito and Gert. It was the first time I saw it with this choreography; they did not say who had staged it. I thought, *Why not do*

—

McMillan's? It always works. The music is to dance with all your heart, and McMillan choreographs from inside one's soul! I thought it was a mistake to use a completely different choreography. Then we had a ten-minute break. Gert asked me what I thought of the pas de deux. I told him, "We will speak of it after tonight." Then the call was made for *Signale*. The tempos were good for the first jazzy part. Then came my entrance, with Gert to the finish, but we needed to stop. Gert asked if the conductor could take it slower on our big jumps before he kills me. They played it again, and it was perfect. We both went to the edge of the stage and applauded the orchestra.

Twelve-tone music is very difficult to play so well. There was already a nice, professional feeling between us and the orchestra. As it was, it was hard to dance and to hear such music; such composers were protégés of Schoenberg. The realization was obvious that all ballet companies would include neoclassic choreography with twelve-tone music and that orchestra would have to be able to play it.

After this, the orchestra was excused, and we cleared the stage in preparation for doing a technical run-through of program 1. Gert went out in front and asked me to mark places where we needed special lighting. Then Rudi and I marked *Raymonda*. It went very well until my part in the coda, which starts slowly and progressively increases in speed. I wished to have it faster as it is more exciting that way, and I was able to do it.

We were now ready to perform program 1. I returned to my dressing room as by now it was really too late to go out. Mr. Odell had sent over a manager who was kind enough to ask us if anyone needed anything to eat or drink. Gert and I said we would appreciate some black coffee.

I went to Gert's dressing room, where we discussed the lighting for *Signale*. I felt it was too dark at the end and also that the pas de deux with Harold Horn should not be spotlighted. Gert agreed, and would talk to the lighting man. Since the lighting system was so modern, the changes could be made by changing the numbers punched in. The whole conception of what could be done backstage would continue to change for the next ten years: Giselle would fly in the air; she would rise from the grave; anything would be able to seem real. I said as much to Gert, and he laughed and said to me, "And you will dance forever. I will not dance for ten more years, *Gott ist will*."

We'd slipped into Asta and Charlie, a personal joke between us, meaning the famous silent screen star of Germany Asta Nielson and Charlie Chaplin. We ended up laughing as usual, so much that tears

—

ran down my face. When the coffee arrived, the manager found the two principal dancers in hysterics; we could barely stop to say thank you.

Finally we returned to normal, and time was passing by; I had to do a good class. I asked Gert if he wanted to do barre work with me. His answer was, "I would make too difficult." This, too, made me laugh. Gert was unique in his preparation for performances.

I returned to my dressing room, where I put on a pair of toe shoes that needed breaking in. Off I went to do my own class. By now my colleagues had arrived for class. While they started at the barre, I changed my toe shoes to a different pair. Finally when they got to center, I joined them. Maja Beck, our ballet mistress, was giving class. The girls were not permitted to wear soft shoes, only pointe shoes in class. This was normal in Europe, with all teachers that taught professional class: we never wore soft shoes in any of the ballets that we performed, so why do so in class? Also, with the girls, it becomes second nature to just forget about the shoes; one becomes accustomed to doing everything *en pointe* automatically.

The stage was cleared, and then Gert and Marion Cito did some partner work from *Romeo and Juliet*. Rudi and I would have time to rehearse a little during the intermission. There were lots of *merdes* and *toi-tois* and kicks in the rear for good luck.

We opened with the whole company onstage dancing *Schumann Variations*. With the orchestra, it made such a difference to how we danced. It was such fun to let go and enjoy dancing full out without fear; this was pure classical technique that I loved to dance as did many of the others as well. We looked good.

Our curtain calls were well received; the audience was warm but not ecstatic. I explained to Gert that this was a very British audience and that this was about as enthusiastic as they would probably get. Everyone left the stage to change for the next ballet, which I was not in. It seemed odd as I had always danced in every ballet; however, I appreciated the little bit of time off.

I prepared for *Raymonda*, which required a classical hairdo. I was always nervous before a pas de deux taken from a full-length ballet. One did not have the build-up before the grand pas de deux. Plus, it was a big moment in the program, and we were always aware of the responsibility attached to it. If it was danced well, the company would get high marks hopefully for performing one of the well-known classics.

Unlike *Don Q*, we began from offstage after the music started and the curtain opened. We did the original opening from the ballet then the pas de deux followed by his variation, which received good applause. Then I followed, with a very good response from the public, and finally came the coda, as in the other pas de deux, for him and for me and then together. Curtain down, now up, and we took our bows together. Out came a man who handed me a bouquet of roses. I pulled one out and gave it to Rudi, who kissed my hand. Curtain down. Still applause, so Rudi went out in front of the curtain then me then both of us. All I could think of was that I needed to change for *Signale* fast. Finally we were finished, and I kissed Rudi, saying, "Merci." I tried never to forget to do this.

Now to change for *Signale*—hair loose, shoes changed, all props accounted for. The conductor saw I was ready and headed for the pit. Here we go with the twelve-tone music, which I thought the public would not like so much. Anyway, its composer was good, well known, and the ballet is dramatic. Most dramatic ballets, those with a story line are well received.

Gert was inspired by the orchestra and was in very good form. I prayed that he would not use too much force. As the dancers came out as in on a train, there was applause. I have always thought this choreography so original, pure genius. Gert was dancing well from what I could see, and the whole company was giving a good performance. At last came the death scene, with no Tatjana in the wings to hold my hands, which were ice cold. Only my dresser, whom I was making quite nervous! It was catching! I made my last entrance, and Gert came toward me for the slap. Thank God someone remembered to slap backstage as I know otherwise Gert would have gladly done it. We continued until the brutal ending, where I was really dragged off the stage. I was helped up by two of the male dancers and then came the crash and finish. At least here, we were not the first to come out; the corps took their bows, and then the soloist in the jazz part, followed by Harold Horn, receiving great applause. Then Gert and I, walking slowly from the very back of the stage and bowing together. Finally, all of us together. I then brought out our conductor, Heinrich Kreutz. Again, all together, we bowed. The curtain closed, and Gert and I came out together. The ballet was very well received. Gert told all the dancers that they had done very well. Everyone had a happy face.

The next day would be program 2, with Helga Sommerkamp and André Marlière holding down the fort as well as Gert and me. Perhaps our old group so loved Berlin Ballet that we danced as a team, and our newcomers did not yet have the same feeling and danced for their personal success. Either way, it was important to dance well. Well, tomorrow would tell.

We returned to our dressing rooms and rushed to get ready for Mr. Odell's supper party. The nice thing was that we could leave things where they were and not pack up. I did bring a beautiful evening dress with me, and now I had the chance to wear it. I was so eager to meet Mrs. Odell, who knew my mother!

Still, before I left the theater, I didn't forget to go onstage and say (at last) in English, "Thank you, gentlemen to the crew." They all seemed very pleased and said good night. Then we dancers left for the Odells'.

The whole company descended from our bus to be greeted by a rather small lady who had a lovely smile and was very hospitable. Mrs. Odell was so happy to have us at her home. When she saw me, she exclaimed, "Flora's daughter!," and gave me a big hug. She told me I looked like my mother. I answered that I hoped so and wished I also had her sweet, loving, gentle, nature. I asked Mrs. Odell all about going to school with my mother. I also told her that I saw Esther Goodman very often at affairs in San Francisco. She then remembered that I must be very hungry, and so we went into the dining room, where a lavish buffet was laid out for the company. I could smell curry. I told her I could smell our kind of cooking, and she laughed and said, "Have some of it." I saw Gert, plate in hand, and he joined me as I filled his plate as well as mine. Germans don't typically eat spicy foods, so I served him from dishes other than curry. But to me, everything was prepared just like being at home.

Gert and I found a spot to sit and eat and talk. He said he had watched *Raymonda* and thought it was marvelous. He liked my variation the best. He also felt that the audience was most receptive for this. He then asked me about *Romeo and Juliet*. I said to him that I thought the choreography didn't say anything—that it was just steps. He said that this version had been done long ago at the Oper. I still preferred the version done by McMillan just as I prefer pas de deux that have been handed down from dancers who had been with Pepita when he had staged them. That way, they were kept as pure as possible. Since at the moment McMillan's version was so beautiful and danced everywhere with success, it was strange to present new choreography unless it was better than what had passed before. This pas de deux required that great passion be expressed, with many musical climaxes that have to be followed dance-wise. To me, this version Gert was dancing just didn't convey that kind of feeling. He admitted to me that he thought what I said was right. I told him I could show him the McMillan choreography as I had danced it before. He would have loved to take me up on the offer, but Marion Cito had brought it in and tampering with it would have created a problem. I could never understand this—if the situation were reversed, I would jump at the chance to improve it. I had learned *Sleeping Beauty* from Toni Lander, and I cherished every step; likewise, *Don Quixote* from

—

Toumanova and *Raymonda* from Alan Howard with whom I had danced all these pas de deux. He had been in the Ballets Russes, partnering Danilova, Slavenska, Baronova, and Toumanova. But Gert said that there was another mentality at the Oper.

We dropped the subject and enjoyed the party that had been given in our honor. When desserts were announced, the butler took our plates and served the most luscious, forbidding desserts I had seen in a long time. The only reason why I could even look was that by now I was so thin that everyone thought I was too thin. In my mind, I could never be too thin—brainwashed by John Taras and Lew Christensen by the Balanchine image!

Then came time to say good-bye as we had to dance the following day. I did have the morning free, however, and accepted with pleasure Mrs. Odell's invitation to drive to the Hotel Victoria for tea. Then, since it was on the Kowloon side, she would take me straight to the theater. This was to be the company's last day in Hong Kong, and I wanted to see the city from the spectacular view that the drive would offer. And I had heard so much about that hotel; it served as a meeting place for the British, at that time. I thanked the Odells for the lovely evening and so appreciated the dinner and kindness they gave to all of us. Then we were driven back to our hotel. This evening had been a success, and tomorrow would have to be better. That night, I had a hard time falling asleep, as usual. I had wondered what my mother had been like when she was in a girls' school—a convent, no less—in Singapore, and now I was here with one of her friends! The world was indeed very small.

33

Japan

Those last hours of our trip to Tokyo seemed the longest I had ever spent. My legs needed to move, and my body needed a good stretch. We all had dancer's itch by then. Finally we heard "Fasten your seatbelts," first in Japanese, then in English. Now I would be able to understand some things—I had practiced "thank you" in Japanese, and "please"—but other than that, the language was impossible for me to decipher.

We were greeted in English at the airport by our Japanese impresario and his representatives. Gert pushed me forward, and I found myself making the introductions. He was the nicest and most charming man called Tatsuji Nagashima. He was very well educated and explained that he would be with us throughout this part of our tour, along with two members of his staff. He also assured Gert that the technical directions and conductors/dancers' schedules were already posted. He thought we should go to our hotel and unpack and then, if we had the energy after the flight, to join him for dinner. I accepted immediately as I observed Gert's eyes slowly opening and closing (a trick he would do with people—he actually didn't hear a word, as he was asleep with his eyes open!). I nudged his hand, and he said, "Good, ja, no now we go." Amazing—charming as always! I could have killed him. He had no idea whatsoever when I told him later that we had been invited to dinner.

Likewise, when we said our good-byes to Mr. Nagashima and I discussed our rehearsals, Gert appeared absolutely awake and aware, yet he did not have one *clue* of anything that was said. This caused us to roar with laughter to the point that I had tears running down my cheeks. My impossible Schlafe Katze (the name I called Gert, which means "sleeping cat"). He could sleep anywhere, anytime. Sometimes he would actually say to me, "Come to my room in ten minutes. I sleep for five minutes, then we go." This would make me furious because I could never get to sleep so easily.

This would be a very interesting tour, for many reasons. At the time, ballet in Japan was just starting to grow, and ballet was not yet at a professional level. Their classical music was already outstanding as they had a national orchestra. It was exciting to be in Japan in the early sixties (this was 1964) when everything was modern and ahead of us, thanks to the money and help that America gave that country after the war.

We were to stay at the Palace Hotel just a bit outside the center of the city. It had literally been a palace previously and had beautiful grounds. It was quiet and peaceful, with very nice Western-style rooms. I was happy to unpack, shower, and rest. I had my Japanese phrasebook with me and tried to learn a few more words. It was truly difficult because the entire structure of sentences, not just words, was different from English. I was lost, he was lost, she was lost, we were all lost! So much for that. Why can't we have an international language, I thought. Eventually we will have to.

I decided to put the book aside and investigate the hotel. There was a magnificent dining room where one could imagine the guests were really dining in a palace. There was also a shop with exquisite kimonos. It was irresistible for me to go in and look. The trouble was, my parents had already given me lovely kimonos, and even my theater robe was a kimono. Still, it was fun to look at the merchandise. I bought some postcards to send home if I would ever find the time to write them. Then it was time to meet Gert and Mr. Nagashima in the lobby.

Straightaway, I could see that Gert was in good form, speaking out his own special English and being understood. As I'd had to do in Germany, when we traveled outside that country, he would in most cases have to speak in English. I expressed my delight that we had been put in such a peaceful hotel with picturesque grounds. Mr. Nagashima was pleased to hear this and told us that there was a story about the palace, concerning a princess and a man whom she would meet at various places in the garden. They fell deeply in love, but her parents had already chosen a husband for her and she was to be married shortly. On the day of the wedding, there was great preparation in the palace, but the princess was heartbroken. Her hair was done up in a traditional, formal manner with jeweled combs. Then her kimono was wrapped tightly around her, with a great knife at her side. When she was ready for the ceremony, she looked radiant, but her heart was heavy. She moved slowly to meet her chosen one, and they knelt together as the priest came forward. Suddenly, she keeled over. The bride had stabbed herself with her knife rather than marry someone she did not love. Her beloved was among the guests and ran to the bride. He picked her up and carried her out into the garden—and neither of them was ever seen again. Gert and I looked at each other, each thinking what a great ballet that would make. I loved the sensitivity with which Mr. Nagashima had told the story. He also told us that we could call him Tatsi (a shortening of his first name).

He brought us to a restaurant that was known for its famous beef. It was completely packed, but everyone knew Tatsi, and we were ceremoniously shown to what was obviously one of the best tables. Suddenly I realized that Gert and I hadn't eaten anything since breakfast on the plane! It was the perfect place to come to when we were so hungry. We told Tatsi what we liked, and he had the chef prepare the meat with onions right in front of us. Meanwhile, we asked about the local theater. Tatsi explained that it was on the top floor of a huge building. The theater was new; indeed, in most cities we would visit in Japan, we would be dancing in new theaters. I thought to myself, *This is not Europe*, where as in spite of the war, most of the opera houses had survived, and most of them were old. I loved it when the curtain rose to reveal the red velvet seats and gold trim and lovely boxes. But Japan would be a different experience for us—they had lost the war and had rebuilt to look modern; their theaters would lack the atmosphere I had become accustomed to in San Francisco, Europe, and even South America. They didn't even have the same smells, of the scenery, and velvet curtains, and years of being there. Also, touring in Europe and South America had been different because they already had a tradition of symphonic music, classical ballet, and Western drama. Japan had its own classical traditions using other instruments and other dance and acting styles. I, at least, had been to San Francisco's Japanese Town, where I had experienced Japanese food and met Japanese people, but to the German members of the company, this would be very foreign. As for our audiences' reactions to *us*, that would soon be discovered.

We were to dance *Signale* on Japanese TV, so our one day in Tokyo was spent rehearsing at the television studio. After a break, we put on our makeup and costumes, and they filmed the performance. We then packed and left for Osaka, where we were to officially start our tour; we would return to Tokyo as our last stop.

When we arrived in Osaka, Gert asked me to attend a small press conference held in our hotel. We answered most of their questions, Gert directing them most of the time to me as Japanese-accented English was very hard for him to understand. Even I had to listen carefully as many of the questions were surprisingly esoteric; for example, I was asked how Japan compared visually with Berlin. I needed to think of something to answer besides "the traffic." Finally I said something about the trees, commenting on the natural beauty of various colors. Gert wasn't missing a thing; he just smiled away as the reporters said, "Ah, so." Finally it was over, and we had just enough time to unpack in our rooms and get to the theater.

Tatsi asked us to dinner after the performance, and of course we accepted. This was to be the beginning of great generosity bestowed on all of us. What little I saw of Osaka, I thought it must be the most beautiful city in Japan—until I saw Kyoto. Once we were in the theater, we all felt at home doing our usual class and preparation, knowing what to expect. Backstage was a life of its own, no matter what country in the world we were in. We knew it with a familiarity we all understood.

Our first ballet went well, but when we were finished, the applause was barely audible. This made us all very nervous because we thought that they did not like us. Tatsi said, "Wait," and after the entire performance was completed we received a great thunder of applause. We all drew a sigh of relief. At the end, many young people gathered to meet us at the stage door for autographs and photos. Tatsi told us he would have small prints made from some of our photos so that we could sign them in advance— brilliant idea! Which he did do. On occasion, I still run across one in my belongings.

We then proceeded to dinner. We were totally awed as we entered a lovely garden, where we were instructed to take our shoes off before being seated in a private dining room, in Japanese style. We were met by an older woman who bowed very low to Tatsi and then to us. Then incredibly young women—geisha girls—started to do everything, the old lady watching their every move. The room was filled with beautiful carved jade articles that we were told were hundreds of years old. This was where Tatsi's father had brought him when he was younger; Tatsi now came on his own; and although he was not yet married, if he had a son, that boy would continue the tradition.

The food was delicious. While we relaxed together, the old lady gave a signal for the geishas to begin playing music. It all happened quietly and unobtrusively, on instruments even I could not recognize. Life felt very good at that moment, and I knew I would conjure up this scene many times in the future. Sadly, this remarkable experience had to come to an end, however, because we had to be off again the next morning to another tour stop. The new Japanese bullet train would take us to Nagoya, where we would do program A.

This was another incredible experience. Each person aboard had a swivel chair and a table bearing a red rose. It was all supermodern. In Nagoya, we stayed at a small inn, where we were given a great treat. Tatsi had asked permission for us to use the baths although in our case separating the boys from the girls (the Japanese prefer a unisex arrangement). Since it was for late at night, he was given the okay. We changed into robes and, filled with mirth and giggles, proceeded to the baths. It was such a wonderful feeling for our poor bodies to be totally immersed that we sighed with delight. But a few of the inn's guests didn't know about the special arrangement: a man, his wife, and their small child entered the room and got into the bath with us. All the girls dived under except me. I could never get my hair wet in a pool because it would turn to curls. I had to stay upright, knowing my chums couldn't hold their breath that long anyway. We greeted one another in the best Japanese manner, bowing. And slowly, one girl after another came up. I couldn't help having the giggles as one face after another first looked at me as it appeared and I pretended that everything was perfectly normal! Now, getting out of the water was another matter. We kept hoping the baby would fall asleep. Instead, it splashed, cooed, and loved the water, to its parents' delight. Well, the time had come for all good men, as they say, to come to the aid of their party; I wished the couple *sayonara*, looked straight ahead, and got up and out the door. By the time we were through, the boys had already been finished with their bath and had headed to dinner, which that night was in the inn. The promise of food was sure to entice the girls out, but still no action. Finally, the Japanese couple came out, baby in hand, and the coast was clear. In fifty seconds, all the girls were out, looking very sheepish. That night certainly deserved a place in the Berlin Ballet's things-to-remember book!

We next had a tour to Kanazawa, where we did program A. After that, we returned to Tokyo, an important place for us, to do programs A and B with full orchestra (we'd used a high-powered tape recorder elsewhere, run by our conductor and pianist), rehearsing the latter in between performing the former. This time, I stayed in a lovely hotel at the very center of the city. The grounds were again well tended and seemed like a setting for a fairy tale. This, too, had been a palace and had been kept immaculately.

Tokyo, however, was anything but serene. The cab drivers drove like kamikazes. When I entered a taxi upon arrival in the city, I was determined not to show fear as this seemed to add to their delight of conveying nonnatives. When I reached my destination, two Americans waited to get in, and I couldn't help saying, "I hope you have good insurance!"

Our performances went very well in Tokyo. The company seemed to have lifted in spirit, dancing with the best concentration I had seen through the tour. Everyone worked a little bit harder, and it showed. We danced in huge sold-out halls. The audience was not just the older generation but very young people as well. I think the Japanese had been starved culturally, and when the war and its initial difficult aftermath was over, they wanted to fill themselves with everything that they had been deprived of.

One afternoon in Tokyo, I witnessed a fascinating sight. I was taking an enjoyable stroll along the hotel grounds when I saw a young girl who was having her hair dressed in traditional Japanese style. She was then dressed in a formal kimono. Someone asked me if I wanted to watch a Japanese wedding. I said, "If I am not intruding, I would be honored." At this moment, she was being wrapped in her obi—and I saw a knife go into the folds. I questioned this and was told that it was a tradition that if, before she was wed, another man would take her, she would kill herself. I thought this was just too unfair—she should kill the man! And also the tale Tatsi had told us made me hope she wished to wed her bridegroom!

Amid the tranquility of the palace grounds, I couldn't help thinking, *Here I am, watching an ancient art in a country that had been at war with mine during my own lifetime—a war brutal, cruel, and without pity against our soldiers—and now, here I am, dancing in a ballet company again from a country that had also tried to annihilate my people.*

However, I did not delve deeply into those thoughts. The war already seemed to have happened a long time ago.

I was pleased that we danced to filled halls and to people of all generations. This means a great deal to any performer. Our ballets in twelve-tone music seemed to fascinate our attendees, appealing to their sensitivity. I had never thought about it, but their own music contained at times off-scale notes, so perhaps that explained part of their interest in twelve-tone. The musicians were absolutely marvelous. Everything we did seemed to be a success.

In one city that was very small, Tatsi gave the company as a whole another treat. We were told that after a performance there would be a banquet in our honor at our hotel. He added that, in each room, we would find a silk kimono for us as a remembrance of our Japanese tour. He asked us to wear the garments that night to the banquet. This touched me so much that I was close to tears. As we entered where we were to dine, gone was the joking and fooling around, replaced by genuine respect and love. Each person looked so beautiful that night, and I believe it was a way of showing reverence.

Our last stop was Kyoto—unbelievable beauty. We had three days of hard work but were all aware of the approaching end to the tour. Dancing with all our strength and hearts, we were a most unusually empathetic company. None of us knew what was to come, we only thought of now. Gert came to me on the last night, bringing a box. When I opened it, there was a Japanese porcelain doll in elaborate dress with several changeable hairpieces. This was really funny as, for years, the staff at the Oper would make me my hairpieces. The note was simple: "To Asta from Charlie. Love, Gert." The note now bears the signs of many tears that have dropped onto it. I had a feeling then that we would not see each other for a long time, but we would always have this very special love for each other.

The company returned to Tokyo, where Tatsi promised to give the film of *Signale* to Gert when it was edited (it would be shown as an art film in movie theaters in Germany). Then the company went back to Berlin, and I flew to San Francisco with a very heavy heart.

Interludes

Ballet West

One of the engagements I did was for the University of Utah Ballet headed by Willam Christensen, in collaboration with the Utah Symphony Orchestra. At this point, it was not yet Ballet West. This was the seed that William was once again sowing, which would become a full company. I felt honored that he asked me to dance with them and that he had told me to bring my own partner. I think this was his way of saying that someday we would be at the top; and, indeed, the company was eventually renamed Ballet West and performed to great praise, with other guest artists and better dancers generally as time went on. I brought Adriano Vitale, with whom I would appear in my own gala in San Francisco. We were to dance the *Don Quixote* pas de deux, one of my signature pieces, and also one of Adriano's; it suited both of us, with our dark looks and fiery eyes. Adriano was a handsome Italian, and obviously the girls swooned over him in Salt Lake, in the company and out.

We were in a fantastic mood, but nevertheless we needed rehearsal time as I was also dancing one performance of Willam's *Ballet Symphonia*, set to music by Mozart. In addition, I had not danced *Don Q* often recently; it had been some time since I had last worked with Adriano in spite of the fact that we had engagements galore in front of us.

He was the perfect partner for me: masculine, muscular, and with a good height and physique. He always looked into my eyes. I think this is *so* important. A pas de deux means just that—for two. He was dignified and strong in his look to me before my difficult steps. This helps a ballerina to have confidence. You are all alone on the stage, just the two of you, and God! If you take a pas de deux out of a full-length classical work, means the beginning, adagio, male solo, female solo, coda male, coda female, and then together and finish. When the curtain rises, there is no time to build up a sizzling rapport between you as characters in the piece; it has to be in place the moment that you start, as dancers.

In *Don Quixote,* the curtain opens with the last four measures the introductory music and the two of us simply standing—I in front, he behind me, with our heads down. Then, four chords, we bring our arms up abruptly in four counts, lift our heads, defy the audience, look them straight in the eye—applause here, usually. That excites us and tells us we are on our way.

I must tell you, I have done everything in those bars of music before the curtain opens. I have prayed, cried, sworn, wished I was somewhere else, or my heart beats so fast that I think it's louder than the music. I think I can't remember anything, but my legs won't forget the music as is indeed always the case once the curtain opens and our actions begin.

I truly adore this pas de deux. For me, it is absolutely from the inside of me. Technically, I have to concentrate as I immediately balance after the entrance. I tell myself then that if I don't have an exceptionally long balance, don't throw the rest away. I have a chance again for balances later on. This choreography was by Oboukoff, and he was the first to dance it with Toumanova in this version, which is all balance, which she excelled in. I had very good balance. Some nights, the gods gave me phenomenal balance, and we had a way to tease that out; however, no matter what I was taught, I could not play Russian roulette, so to speak: at least a certain balance had to be there nightly—less, never. This is all in the training and coaching. If you use your proper technique, you will always come to a certain mark. Many times, you will stay seemingly forever, but you must *always* stay to a definite mark. You must never just hope for the best or fall short but think, *That will do.* It betrays a lack of discipline and/or bad schooling if you cannot hold to a high standard. The versions I see today of *Don Q* are watered down. My good friend Jurgen Schneider, former ballet master of ABT, would lament with me, saying, "They are doing a Soviet version, and you are doing a Russian version." We used to laugh very much over that. Either version takes strength, but those balances at the beginning—when they come, you are all alone, except for two thousand people in the audience and a few true balletomanes who know what's next. Deep breath, off your hand to your partner, smile into his eyes, mount on pointe, take your attitude, hold eight counts if possible—the audience knows that was not too bad—now repeat four counts again, offer your hand, and again. This time, the maestro is watching you and slowing the music down a little. You are on a good streak, thank God.

This is only the beginning; now enjoy it for a while. Dance under control, but burst them open with all you can give. Technique is in the

—

354

legs, the memory is there, you only have to open up. Now comes the variation, Please, Adriano, one more bow so I can shake out my legs in the wings. No more time. Fan in hand. Here I go right onstage. I walk and circle the stage, placing myself in the rear corner, and then the chord and the fan snapping open have to happen at the same time. The variation is quick, technically difficult, and I must make the fan open and close as I dance. Toward the end come the *pas de chevals* (literally, steps of the horse) that I stampede on the diagonal across the stage, giving it everything I've got until the finish, which really fills one with delight and joy. The reaction of the public gives me the energy to work. They are now there with me.

So sooner have I finished with my solo than Adriano reenters to start his tour de force of the coda, which I pray might last a little longer, but it does not, and so I do back out to do my own tour de force. Then we join to dance our hearts out until the last flying leap and the end.

I must say this version never failed to get a standing ovation anywhere in the world. The choreography is stunning and requires dancers with technique and artistry. It really has to come from inside of the performers: the joy in the moment, the music, and, most of all, the giving of the self back to the audience. I can't speak for all dancers, for each individual is different. I can only say that it is not the applause that I remember after a performance, it is my reverence: I thank God for a gift that I can give to my audience—joy, happiness, sometimes a depth of their own feelings. I hope to touch them in some way, without speech; only through my body and heart can I pass this to them. And even then, it is just for a moment, at best a fleeting one. This is what we live for to perform nightly.

Our first time with the Utah Theater Ballet was lovely. Their angel was Glenn Walker Davis, whose family owned the *Sacramento Bee*. She was a great friend of Ernest Hemingway and invited us to her marvelous home. It was rather like a fairy tale as she had swans floating in a lake that you had to cross on a bridge to enter; there were gardens of flowers and also of vegetables. The guest cottage was Hemingway's hideaway. Everything in it was his—photos, books, and so on. Rather strange, as one expected he would be there for dinner. She had tons of lilies of the valley on the dinner table (my favorite flower, which grows mostly in France) on which I commented as in America one paid dearly for one stem. She was a delightful hostess and certainly a great ballet lover.

The next night, I found a massive bouquet of lily of the valley in my dressing room, with a note inviting me to stay with her on my return for the next season, to which we had already agreed.

I cannot leave this episode without mentioning two people who had been in San Francisco ballet and whom I loved very much. When Willam left, they went with him. One was Bene Arnold, a lovely dancer who was to become his ballet mistress and right hand. I so respected her. She was smart, quick to pick up steps, and most of all, she knew how to transmit to the dancers what they needed to do. She was thoroughly professional, compassionate, and capable. Her manner was what it ought to have been, strict but gentle. I never heard her scream at the dancers. She didn't have to. Her grandmother made all the costumes. She had been the one who had invented a tutu hold for me when I had to bring my own costumes to Europe. I adored her. How lucky they were in Utah to have such a great team.

Adriano and I returned to the company, where this time we had the chance to do the pas de deux from *Signale,* which had been choreographed by Tatjana Gsovsky. Its twelve-tone score obviously had to be taped music. I had every intention to include this in my forthcoming gala in San Francisco.

Again, to take out just a portion from a longer ballet is terribly difficult as the audience has not had a chance to build up to the point. The story, translated from the German, seemed even more banal in English, but the violent ending was something nobody could possibly misunderstand. Since it was always a big success all over the world, it was a surefire inclusion here in the States. This was the perfect place to try it out. Adriano had never danced it; it had always been a tour de force in our repertory of Berlin Ballet. Adriano and I would also dance the *Don Quixote* pas de deux after the intermission, by popular demand. Our week of performances would be a great preparation for my gala.

Maestro Maurice Abravanal was the conductor; he was a wonderful ballet conductor. He always kept to the tempo and understood the breath in the music. Most dancers make mistakes when they discuss music. Having studied music helped me to understand the difference between saying "Slower," meaning "Broader" or "Legato." That does not change the music, only perhaps slightly on the codas. I resent hearing a ballet totally out of the right tempo to accommodate the dancers. We were never allowed to do that in our training. It would also be presuming to be the conductor.

There are three significant difficult parts in *Signale* that could be used as a pas de deux; we chose the last, where the signal man suspects his wife of cheating on him and she doesn't respond (see page XX for a fuller description of the plot).

Adriano and I were both quite nervous before the opening. Onstage, there was the ladder with a red drape intertwining its steps, and a bench. That was it. The lighting was important. The stage crew and lighting people were very good. I sauntered in on cue, and Adriano came toward me slowly, as if questioning where I had been. I nonchalantly tossed off my hat, removed my gloves, and then he glared as I slowly bent away in a huge backbend. He then slapped my face (or appeared to; the sound actually came from offstage), and we began. Frantic and truly difficult steps, lifts, floor slides. Finally, there was a moment when we remembered the love that was once there, but now I was unforgiving of his behavior since his jealousy was all in his imagination. Slowly I began to fear him and try to escape; each time, he blocked the way until he had lost all reason. We then did a huge circle of *grand jetés* until he grasped me by the neck and strangled me. I was then dragged offstage. The lights flickered, and you could hear a crack as he ran back to give the signal to the trains to change tracks. In Utah, we used just lights as he frantically waved his lighted signs. In the complete ballet, the train was comprised of people, some reading, others eating, etc., and at the moment of the crack, they all fall from their seats and die. Blackout, curtain down.

This was an absolute triumph for both of us and, of course, for the company. The audience was on its feet. We made our reverence first together walking slowly and dignified as if I had just come back from the dead. Then Adriano bowed, to great shouts of "Bravo!" Then I was alone, making my most dignified reverence. Finally, we had to go in front of the curtain and do it all over again until I called Adriano to join me and I dropped to one knee to him and he kissed my hand and then we both bowed to the audience.

We were very excited as the company now seemed to have its adrenaline raised. The excitement backstage was palatable. You want that, as dancers do better when they are tested in this way. We wished them *merde* and *toi toi toi.*

We were off to a good start but now wanted to dance pure classical ballet.

Off I go to my dressing room to check my makeup and arrange my hair in a classical hairdo. Now the hysterical moment of the toe shoes. I had already chosen one pair to wear, but one has second thoughts. On, off, fold it and then flat until one foot feels okay and then finally for both feet to agree. On they go, ribbon sewn so the knots don't show. Flower in the hair on the left side. Earrings glued on, sleeves adjusted comfortably. Oh yes, the fan. Last of all, the dresser brings the tutu and you climb in, fighting all the way, pushing it down, squirming your back. Now powder arms, chest, and back while your poor dresser tries to help you and says everything will be all right. At last, you appear backstage.

Adriano's already warming up. Everyone who isn't dancing is gathering in the wings to watch. This is normal; we have all done this. You make idle chatter, but you keep moving like a racehorse waiting at the post. Finally, the ballet that has been on ends, and you are next.

Adriano tries a pirouette with me to get a feel for the tutu and for where his hands will go. I check my diagonal and then time runs out. We go to our corners, Adriano says *merde* to me and I to him as he crosses himself, and I look heavenward and ask God to give us magic so we can give the audience something special.

I am sure you, the reader, ask yourself why does this fear come every time, when they have danced this pas de deux for at least a hundred times, and with different partners, different conductors, different stages, different companies. Perhaps the insecurity of so many differences is part of it, but for most premier dancers, there is always the desire to improve on what you did before. It must not simply continue as before; it has to grow. You must reinvent yourself. That is the real challenge. You are never satisfied with your work. You always feel you could have done better. Technically, you can reach a peak, but what makes this an art is what you do artistically to make it your own. Imagine how many ballerinas and premier danseurs have danced the same pas de deux before you. Think back on how many performances you may have seen. Yet no two dancers give the same performance or even the same couple on a different night. Each time, your body and soul has to speak to the audience, and your nervousness beforehand is over what shall be spoken this time.

Ballet Gala

It was a good time for me to return to San Francisco when the Berlin Ballet was establishing its position with Bonn and its state support. We were in a tricky position; basically, Tatjana was at that time head of ballet in the Stadtische Oper. Gert was first dancer as well, and we were using the name Berliner Ballet, which now became a point of contention. I knew the next few months would be free and I was ready to be home. Parting from Tatjana and Gert was very difficult, but we knew it would be temporary. I left a suitcase with Constanza; aptly, there was a popular song in Germany at the time, *"Ich habe eine Koffer im Berlin"* ("I [always] Have a Suitcase in Berlin"). It was very exciting for me to be going home. One of the boys in the company, an American, wanted to join the San Francisco Ballet. He was a very good dancer, and I was sure they would hire him. So I told him to come to San Francisco with me, and he did get the position.

I was greeted happily by my family after such a long absence. After a week of rest, I needed to keep up my training. Of course, I took class with the San Francisco Ballet company. It seemed as of I had never left, except for the fact that dancers in the lower levels of the classes were now company members. It was very nice being back.

Sadly, nothing was going on dance-wise. I'd thought about using this time in a creative way. I always thought getting together a small group of soloists would be successful as it would be easier to utilize their talents and save on costumes and scenery. A bit of Tatjana had rubbed off on me. I discussed this with Peter, and he encouraged me to do go ahead. I suggested I make a budget of what it would cost. My first concern was that it should be done professionally right there in San Francisco. We had a very good impresario by the name of Spencer Barefoot. Immediately I contacted him, and he agreed to handle what I termed a ballet gala. He liked the idea, and it had really not been done before.

Now my work began. I always imagined that one day I would retire and have a small company, so this was a good trial for me. Obviously, I needed another ballerina who would be known to San Francisco audiences. Jocelyn Vollmar was the perfect choice as to what we could both do dance-wise. I also needed a partner. My first call was to Leon Danielian, who graciously said he was very flattered but that I needed someone younger as he would soon be retiring. What a lovely man he was. He made some suggestions. Then I called Michel Panieff in Los Angeles, and he put me in touch with an Italian dancer from Milan whom he thought would be great for me: Adriano Vitale. I made contact with him and gave him all the artistic side of the project while Spencer made the contract with him. It was agreed that I would go to Los Angeles for a week to rehearse with him and then he would come to San Francisco in advance of the performance. (As it happened, we would dance in Salt Lake City first, in *Swan Lake*, before the gala took place in San Francisco.)

Now I had to think out a program, music, and the other dancers. Everything fell slowly into place. The opening would be the *Schumann Variations*, which, with Tatjana's permission, I set on only three girls and three boys. It worked beautifully, and for this, dear Russell Hartley was doing all the costumes, except for my tutu and Jocelyn's. San Francisco Ballet supplied those. Then the program included the puppet dance from *Petrouchka* and the pas de deux from Tchaikovsky's *Romeo and Juliet*, which I danced with a young man coming up in the company, Roderick Drew, who later joined the Joffrey Ballet. Jocelyn did the *Black Swan* pas de deux, and I danced Cassandra's solo from Tatjana's ballet *Das Tor* (The Gate), which featured twelve-tone music by Heinz Hartig. Willam Christensen choreographed an ending ballet to the music from *Eugene Onegin*, which brought us all onstage in long tutus. This was pure dance.

I tried to make it an interesting evening, but it was very hard indeed. Between Jocelyn and myself, it would be a feat of endurance. We had double pianos for all the classical ballets played by Roy Bogas and Douglas Thompson. There was a tape of the German twelve-tone music as played by its orchestra, and my orchestral tape for *Don Q*. Roy arranged all the music for four hands, which sounded fuller than just using a solo pianist.

Everyone rehearsed very hard. Jocelyn and I set our own times for when we could do our respective pas de deux rehearsals with our pianist. I also had my orchestra tape of *Don Quixote* with my tempos from Berlin plus Cassandra's music and that for *Signale*. In fact, duplicate tapes were made off the master tapes just in case something went wrong. Meanwhile,

Spencer consulted with me as to what date to choose. You can never be sure, but you want to try not to compete with any other big dance or musical event.

We also needed posters and announcements designed. Again I went to Russell and asked him if I might use one of his drawings from his sketches of dancers, which I truly loved. He was so delighted that he gave me permission to use it whenever I wanted. Slowly things pulled together.

Bruce Kelly was my stage manager. He was the perfect person for this, whom I knew I could trust. The theater we chose was the Veterans' Auditorium next to the opera house. It seated nine hundred people. Spencer handled the ticket printing and box office as well as the theater rental and arrangements for rehearsal time. Now came the first blow. The union considered this an international presentation—due to me! Spencer argued that I was a San Francisco ballerina as well. The point was, local performing groups had a break on certain things and other performing groups did not, price-wise. Finally, they settled by giving in a bit but still requiring us to have a minimum of four musicians. This was so outrageous, to think how hard we'd worked to save every penny just to come out even. No wonder nothing happened easily in San Francisco at that time. I finally got them down to three. This third man, by the way, appeared the night of the performance, sat downstairs, did nothing, and collected union wages as if he'd worked.

These were the things that Spencer handled very professionally. He had also managed to gather a great deal of press notices. My return helped enormously as after all, union or not, I had previously been a principal with the San Francisco Ballet.

Jocelyn rehearsed *Petrouchka* and a pas de trois choreographed by Lew Christensen, and I rehearsed the *Schumann Variations* and what I could of the closing piece while making sure that I saw the rehearsals of everything. I soon found out that it was not easy to be director and dance at the same time. My worries were everywhere, mainly for the dancers—some had never danced such principal roles before. What I saw at each rehearsal was amazing. Everyone improved before my eyes. My fears lessened, and I started worrying about me!

At last, Adriano arrived, and I had my partner for a few days, working very hard. Our dress rehearsal was two nights before the performance, only because the theater was not free the day before. Usually, you have the theater all day and night before the actual performance night. Again, somebody up there was looking after me, though little did I know why at the time.

—

Dress rehearsal was music, lights, and costumes. We had run through during the day in rehearsal clothes and practice tutus, but now we needed everything, including our headpieces. We needed to know now how everything worked and what didn't work to be able to fix it. There was a small audience, mainly people connected with the dancers and crew, including all the Christensens: Ruby, Harold, Lew, and Willam.

We were ready and went through it from the beginning. I still tried to see how everyone's variation was, but I soon had to dance; I knew my piece well albeit with a different partner. Good opening ballet. Everything went well. Russell had done a fabulous job, producing red tutus. "Here we are, ready to dance," they seemed to scream out. We ran nicely through the program, stopping only for some light or music corrections.

Jocelyn and I had the burden of doing so much, something that would never happen in a normal dance program. She looked great as I knew she would. Now came *Don Q.* with Adriano. We stopped because he wanted to correct something at the end of the music. He then started back, and I took my preparation for a fly leap, which would finish with my head on the floor. Adriano was going to say something else to Roy when, to his horror, he saw me flying through the air. He made a dive to the floor where he thought I might land. That is what a professional partner would do. He broke my fall, but still my head hit the floor. Everyone rushed onstage. I was dazed but mostly just embarrassed and insisted I was okay. We finished the rehearsal.

Afterward, my father had invited everyone to dinner at the Fairmont Hotel since the next day was free. By then, I did not feel so well and felt I should go home. So as not to break up the plan, I insisted that everyone should go but that my sister would take me home. Everyone was sad that I would miss the dinner, but I knew I was not totally all right. Arriving home, I just made it before I was throwing up several times. I could do nothing but rest as I turned out to have a slight concussion. My sister knew what to do for me and got me into bed and watched me until Peter came home.

The next day, I felt fine and went to class and rehearsed with Adriano. Everything seemed all right. Now was the hardest part: waiting for an important performance. Since I had the responsibility for the entire program, it was a genuine worry; however, I was confident that all the jobs were in capable hands, and I had to think now about what I was going to do. The choreography was in my body, so that was not a problem. I would just have to be on guard a bit. Adriano was experienced and had learned *Signale* quickly; for *Don Quixote*, we did parts from the version he knew. Basically, the coda and ending were a bit more spectacular—that is, if I didn't fly off by myself again and land on the floor! Back at home, time seemed to crawl by. Here is where I do strange things because of the distraction: sugar ends up in the refrigerator while milk sits in the sink. Until I get to the theater, I am not myself.

I arrived at the theater far too ahead of time and was the first one there. Only a stage light was on the curtains fully open. I love that special moment of being in the empty theater, my place of worship.

I cannot say that I was not excited or nervous. First of all, I had been away for a long period, and the ballet audience would surely be there as well as all the dance critics, social correspondents, friends, and enemies. All the Christensen brothers, to my knowledge, had not been together at a performance for a long time. Ruby and Gisella, I adored, so that was wonderful and encouraging for me. I just had too many things to think about. However, I had great people backstage, and I knew everyone was totally professional. I now had to switch off these details and think about dancing.

Everyone arrived slowly, and we attended to our respective preparations. Jocelyn did her barre on one side of the stage, and I hung onto a ladder on the other side; it would be a prop later in the program. There was definitely a special atmosphere backstage. Everyone was busy doing what he or she was supposed to do, and I found myself once more in my ballet frame of mind, concentrating on what I had to dance. After my barre work, I went onstage and checked my entrances and exits, also the spacing to have a sense of where center was. I tried out my *manège* (circle of turns). Everyone seemed okay and excited. We were told that even standing room was selling. I did not really want to know things like that when I was waiting to dance. However, I saw a tremendous amount of flowers adding up in piles backstage. This was a good omen.

Now it was time for me to put on the first costume for the opening ballet. For once, toe-shoe hysterics did not happen. I headed for the stage, and this time, it was my voice that announced, "Take your places, please." I must say at that moment, I saw the tableau of something out of a Degas painting. Everyone had heeded my orders: hair a certain way, clean shoes, and so on. I felt proud to be onstage and said, "This is it—have fun!" I did not add "Love it," except to myself, under my breath.

The curtain lifted, and *Schumann* started. Everyone applauded even before we began. The audience came expecting something from us, and we were not going to disappoint them. I can't say anything else about this first piece, except that I know this ballet had wonderful jumps for me and my partner, and we flew through the air, having the best time. Jocelyn did her pas de deux from *Swan Lake* with Roderick Drew. Beautifully danced; I took a quick glimpse but needed to change. Then there was the *Petrouchka* pas de trois with Fiona Feurnster, Jeffrey Hobart, and Michael Smuin. Jocelyn had set it as we had done the whole ballet with the de Cuevas company. Big success.

Now it was me again with Roderick, in the *Romeo and Juliet* pas de deux. We started out beautifully, and he put his heart and soul into it. It touched me so much, as this was new to him. I, too, danced with all my heart. Youth was on our side, and in that moment, parting was sweet sorrow indeed. We received tremendous applause as we stepped forward to bow. As we backed up, suddenly the whole outer gold curtain started to unfold and tear, missing us by just inches. The stagehands were marvelous and came forth to rip down whatever was left of it. Can you imagine the dust and weight of that curtain! We were very together and just stepped forward of the pile on the floor to make our last bows. We really "brought down the curtain," as one reviewer said.

Next was intermission. Luckily, we had the best stagehands; they told me not to worry, everything would be okay. I went back to my dressing room, where Jocelyn checked in with me.

After intermission was the *Don Quixote* pas de deux with Adriano and me. It was well received by the audience, and also we were totally at home onstage in this piece. I saw happy faces come offstage as the Lew Christensen pas de trois followed *Don Q.* It, too, was a tremendous success and was totally homegrown. I had personally chosen this and did love it, and it was perfect.

I began to feel we were throwing so much at the audience, one could not say the program was not diversified. I was next with the Cassandra solo, to music that was anything but melodious. So far, we felt the excitement from the audience, almost as if at this point they were waiting to see if we were going to make it. It was already a marathon for Jocelyn and me; everything was so difficult to dance. We'd put our heads into the guillotine, and nobody was going to save us.

After the second intermission was the *Black Swan* pas de deux for Jocelyn and Roderick, who were dancing better than ever. We knew that this part of the program must not show the strain or be less than the earlier pieces. It had to be better. I had put the hardest things at the end to make a strong finish to the evening. Now came the pas de deux of the death scene from *Signale.* Adriano put all this strength into this, and it was remarkable how he adapted to its different style. This ballet was one I don't think the audience expected. It took them off guard and showed them such versatility that we had the right to use the word *gala.*

Signale was the biggest success, audience-wise. We were now at the finish line, and now came Willam's closing piece, requiring me to change into a long tutu and headdress. I was so rushed that I had no time, except to try to make it to my entrance. Bruce Kelley, the stage director, was waiting for me and finally said, "Go." The music of Tchaikovsky filled the air as Jocelyn, Fiona, and I came out followed by all the men in a glorious grand finale. I remember people applauding as we came out. I thought, *You thought we couldn't make it.* However, I think they were truly joyful, and we onstage were also. I said to Adriano, "I have a cramp." He answered, "I have two." We were actually laughing as we danced, having a wonderful time.

The curtain closed and opened, tons of flowers everyone brought onstage, and last came Jocelyn and I with our partners, to great bravos. Then, to my surprise, the three of them pushed me forward, and I stood alone in that moment. I dropped to my knees in great reverence.

Flower Drum Song

One of my greatest adventures was dancing in the musical *Flower Drum Song*. I was just recovering from mononucleosis when the offer came for me to dance the part of Mei Li in the dream scene. I loved the idea as I had never been in a musical. The choreography would be a love pas de deux for me and James Shigeta. Jimmy had created his role and was well known as an actor of stage, screen, and television. Because of my illness, I told the doctor I could not miss this chance; he said if I didn't have to stand around a lot, it would be all right to dance. The musical was playing in Berkeley, so it meant driving back and forth across the bay bridge, but I would miss the rush hours, so it would be really easy.

The choreographer was Walter Painter, who worked very much in the style of Jerome Robbins. He was young and very good and excited to have a ballerina for his leading lady. I, in turn, watched the group as I arrived early for my first rehearsal and saw marvelous dancing, very much like that of *West Side Story*. I loved it but could never do that as I was a classical ballerina.

Everyone was dismissed as I changed into practice clothes. Warming up, Jimmy came in, and we were introduced to each other. As he changed for the rehearsal, I did the same steps I had seen onstage in the middle, and turns. Walter was happy to see me already at work and expressed himself with a loud "Great!" I had explained that I didn't have my full force back yet due to my illness, but if he would rehearse me and not let me stand around a lot for one week longer, I knew I would be strong and dance full out and be much better. He said, "You are already dancing way above first-rate caliber," but of course, he would do anything to keep me.

Jimmy was now ready. Walter told me Jimmy had had some dance experience, but he would do easy lifts and leave the solo dancing for me.

We started out, and Jimmy was so professional. He learned quickly, trying very hard to watch where Walter took my hand for a lift or what he should try next. Obviously, it was not a grand pas de deux, so I just needed to understand the role of Mei Li. We danced to the music where Jimmy's character sings to Mei Li that she is the beautiful and shy girl he wishes to marry someday. The actress playing Mei Li and I really did look the same as she was thin and petite. At the end of the pas de deux, Jimmy had to kiss me. It was my first musical kiss, and I quite liked it!

He went to dress, and Walter came to me and said, "Janet, can you go to Capezio and buy Jimmy a dance belt?" I tried not to burst out laughing as—of course, poor Jimmy was attempting to do lifts without a dance belt, which is an absolute necessity for all male dancers to wear. Obviously, it was far too mortifying for him to purchase one for himself. When this little discussion was done with outside his presence, Jimmy came out and asked eagerly when the next rehearsal would be. Walter said, "Tomorrow, after the dancers doing the café scene rehearsal."

We bade each other farewell, and back I went to San Francisco, driving on air. And then I rushed to Capezio to purchase a dance belt. When I got home, I took an indelible pen and wrote on it, "From your first ballerina," then I wrapped it up gleefully.

The next day, I gave it to Walter to do the honors then went to change into my practice clothes. I had a leotard and a long chiffon skirt that just came to the knee. Very Russian and, at that time, not seen here as American dancers followed Balanchine's school of rehearsing in plain leotards, unlike my training in Europe and working with companies there. We used skirts as most ballets had some kind of skirts or practice tutus so you can learn the distance and feel of your partner. When I came out of the dressing room, the dancers were sort of hanging around in hopes of getting a glimpse of us. Then Jimmy appeared wearing a great grin and whispered into Walter's ear. All three of us burst into laughter at the same time.

Walter was very easy to work with, and his skill as a choreographer was precise and backed up technically by a strong schooling in ballet. He started working with Jimmy as he sang the same song as the day before then I entered, and Jimmy had to do a lift. Then we did a bit of dancing together, in which he actually partnered me. That afternoon, we finished learning several lifts and the entrance plus the dream pas de deux. We only had the ending still to finish. Both Walter and I were amazed at Jimmy's ability to learn as quickly as he did as it was not easy choreography. He was just able to concentrate, and at that time, there were a lot of talented actors who had to be good at everything. They were not only pretty faces. Jimmy could not have been more attentive toward me and obviously worked hard at rehearsals. He was always asking if I was all right and whether he was okay. Finally, we finished the scene where he walked toward me and gave me the kiss that ends the dream.

We were very happy with our private rehearsals. Next came the run-through, with orchestra, singers, dancers—the entire cast. Everyone was out front: director, manager, stage people, and so on.

The dream ballet opened act 2, so I watched some of act 1 from the front of the house. It was really a wonderful musical of Rodgers and Hammerstein, and the words were marvelous. Plus it was set right here in San Francisco! I was amazed at how smoothly it all went together. The ballet in the first act looked as good as *West Side Story*, by which I mean the dancers were sharp and moved in a way that suited Grant Avenue. They were good, and I loved watching.

Then there was a break and a lot of commotion. Adjustments to lighting, staging, and tempo were discussed while everyone took that union break. These breaks, called by a union representative, were somewhat new to me and seemed untimely. One could be in the middle of dancing something, discovering at last what to do in just those few seconds, finally almost getting it, and the union rep would call out, "Take ten. Break!" This made me furious as I was not used to this kind of behavior. We had a spokesman in Berlin, but when the principals worked, we never looked at clocks or thought about "taking five" whether we needed to or not. We were treated with dignity and kindness, and if someone showed fatigue, that person was immediately told to take a break besides being offered tea or whatever.

At last the call was "All ready for act 2. Please get ready. Orchestra call." We began the act, which started with the dream scene for Jimmy and me. I honestly think you could have heard a pin drop as we danced our pas de deux. There was such great rapport between us, and Jimmy looked the part. His concentration never faltered, yet his body and face seemed to be totally relaxed. I was, meanwhile, concentrating on being Mei Li. As in our private rehearsals, the scene finished with his putting his arms around me for a kiss. What a lovely ending. When we were done, we were both surprised by the applause. I was very glad for Jimmy as he had danced and partnered perfectly. It went so well for us; I truly think that Jimmy had a great capacity to do anything in the theater.

The dream ballet was a great hit with the play's audiences, who filled the theater nightly and at matinees. The pleasure this gave me was remarkable. This was a new medium for me plus I had a good choreographer and a superb leading man. We totally enjoyed the success

—

we received. And I had a chance to get to know Jimmy as we would go to the fountain shop or a restaurant after the performances to simply enjoy each other's company.

The time flew by as happens with anything that is perfect and easy for one to do. The last matinee is rather a time for pranks. One of the dancers who did outrageous bumps and grinds and who was tall, blond, and sexy let me do that as a joke. Mind you, between makeup and a blond wig, I managed to become a very sexy blonde who could be found in a bar. I didn't tell anybody else about this because I didn't want them to laugh ahead of time. There was a scene where Jimmy and the others were in a café, and that was where I sashayed in. I have to admit I must have looked like a prostitute. Obviously, the trick was to do it so absolutely perfectly that the audience did not see a single thing as being a change as then you would be breaking a theater law. Well, in I went, bumping and grinding! Jimmy could not help but laugh, and actually, everyone onstage was in stitches. The orchestra in the pit started to stand while still playing to see what was going on. Mission accomplished, I exited to go to my dressing room.

Mr. Kaplan, the manager, was at my door as I approached cautiously. He screamed, "How could you do such a thing? Being Mei Li and changing into this totally different character?" I said that that was the point: nobody in the audience knew it was me. I also reminded him of the tradition of last matinees. He couldn't help but break down and smile. I may have come to the company as a ballerina, but I was leaving it a theatrical pro.

Critics

Wonderful is Janet Sassoon who came from San Francisco to Berlin. Complete mixture of dynamic temperament and precision, dramatic power of expression and perfection . . .
To be compared with the Tallchiefs . . .
STUTTGART

••

Janet Sassoon tremendously vital . . . Her temperament often approaches the ecstatic . . . .
KIEL

••

The darkly burning passion of Janet Sassoon's Cassandra gives the tragedy of this character a powerful elan . . .
BERLIN TELEGRAF

••

Excellently trained Janet Sassoon has mastered the highly varied facets of classical ballet technique with remarkable precision . . . The connoisseur recognizes as well the art of her refined line.
NURNBERGER NACHRICHTEN

••

The high point of the evening is Janet Sassoon in whom vitality is harmonically blended with virtuoso brio . . . .
FRANKFURT

••

The phenomenal Janet Sassoon showed in the Don Quixote Pas de Deux she has complete command of the classical style.
KARSRUHE

••

Janet Sassoon is a dancer of unbounded originality . . . .
KASSEL POST

• •

A ballerina of technical virtuosity and beautiful expressive line . . .
SAO PAOLO

• •

Janet Sassoon merits the public acclaim which she received . . . .
CARACAS

• •

Janet Sassoon danced with precision and brilliance—An excellent
ballerina . . .
CHILE

• •

Janet Sassoon—magnificent with an exquisite personality . . . .
BOGOTA

• •

Straight from the classic ballet was the Pas de Deux with Janet Sassoon
and Orrin Kayan . . . And in their hands, feet, bodies, the classic ballet
came to life.
EL DORADO

• •

Janet Sassoon—a strong dancer with an interesting stage presence.
ANATOLE CHUJOY—NEW YORK
DANCE MAGAZINE

• •

It is not for nothing that European critics rave over "Idylle" . . . it has wit,
humor and a delicate charm. Its ballerina, Janet Sassoon, has all these
qualities, also allied to a strong technique. This is a dancers' ballet . . . A
perfect gem . . .
MACON, GEORGIA

• •

The most distinguished dancing of the evening . . . Janet Sassoon,
dexterous and lithesome . . .
TERRI HAUTE

• •

Janet Sassoon an interesting and exotic young lady . . .
ANN BARZEL—CHICAGO

• •

Janet Sassoon danced splendidly . . . . Demonstrates her talent . . . .
NEW ORLEANS

• •

Glazunov's Raymonda gave brilliant opportunities fully exploited by Janet Sassoon. This was a cameo in ballet artistry, in absolute mastery of movement giving the precise edge to every delightful gesture. Sheer abandonment to the joy of the poetry of motion.
CHINA POST—HONG KONG

• •

Quite the best dancing of the evening—Raymonda Pas de Deux—Miss Sassoon reminds me strongly of the Russian dancers of the Bolshoi and Leningrad companies . . . . Unlike so many Western dancers, she had great strength in her back thus enabling the whole body to be involved in the dance . . . .
This was classical ballet at its best, and it was not because of any conservatism among the audience that it was best received.
HONG KONG

• •

B.J Examiner
Sunday, June 4, 1961

Strong Finale for New Pacific Ballet
By STANLEY EICHELBAUM

TWO PREMIERES and an extraordinary display of bravura dancing in the "Raymonda" Pas de Deux made the final performance of the Pacific Ballet at Veterans' Auditorium an especially rewarding event.

THE "RAYMONDA" excerpt magnificently danced by Alan Howard and Janet Sassoon was a gem. Miss Sassoon, an exciting ballerina from San Francisco who has made quite a reputation for herself in Europe, set the stage aglow with the intensity of her dramatic projection and her vibrant pyrotechnics. Together with Howard's thorough professionalism, the showy performance made the evening.

Editorial Page of the SUNDAY EXAMINER
2 Sec. II CCCC
SUNDAY, MAY 28, 1961

Pacific Ballet
Janet Sassoon, of course, was style personified. She is by far the most exciting dancer hereabouts. She has that umja-cum-spiff that is the special radar of the prima assoluta—she imparts that quiver of the scalp, that new shiver. What a pity the young Grand Dukes can't draw her droshky down the Nevsky Prospekt. Absolutely. K.R.

Editorial Page
of the
SUNDAY EXAMINER

2 Sec. II CCC
SUNDAY, JUNE 4, 1961
KENNETH REXROTH
•

A new ballet company—Pacific Ballet, yesterday and Friday. Too late for me to do it this time—it is not yet "yesterday" as I write this, but as of this writing I am looking forward to Alan Howard and especially to Janet Sassoon. She is certainly one of the more impressive young dramatic ballerinas now in America.

Janet Sassoon Classes

After watching Master Classes over a number of years and in particular the series of classes during the last couple of years, one is constantly amazed at the variety of approaches that can be made in teaching. All the guest teachers have stressed the basic technique, which all the students hear regularly from their own teachers, placing, turnout, feet, arms, hands, transfer of weight, line, etc. All pick out the same faults which reoccur year after year, but each teacher has her own vocabulary and it is always interesting to notice how individual students react to the various instructors, and the understanding and rapport that sometimes transpires and the instant improvement in the student as a result. This was never more apparent than at the recent JANET SASSOON two day session.

We knew she had an excellent background in ballet both in training and in performing. We now also know that she is a remarkable teacher. We saw some fascinating glimpses of her as a dancer, and if anyone can instill a "love of dancing" along with a fabulous technique and artistry she can.

She emphasized the importance of "good schooling" and was able to demonstrate the different methods, Cecchetti, etc., while she herself seemed to lean toward the French school, stressing all were correct. She admonished the students, "Keep your schooling simple, don't complicate things, one can't undo forever".

Most of the juniors were at a class of this type for the first time, they were nervous, but touching in their enthusiasm and efforts to please and to do it right! There were several who showed promise, one in particular who worked with such understanding, that she put many of the seniors to shame.

The seniors take themselves more seriously and unfortunately it shows. Who wil forget, Miss Sassoon imploring them—@Come on dance, you should have force to do it to both sides, your faces aren't doing anything for me. It's an incredible honour and priviledge to dance—that is what you are here for".

"Tell me the story with your feet. You love that stage, feel the floor. Now walk—proud—your chest—eyes. Now grow—don't ever stop".

Miss Sassoon on her own volition gave a free class to all who wished to take it in DANCE THERAPY. She said, that not only was incorrect technique the cause of injuries that dancers suffer (the prevailing fault everywhere being lack of turnout from the top of the leg which result in knee injuries) but that they put in long arduous fourteen hour days on their legs, combined with constant touring which result in "wear and tear" of the body which breaks it down. Hence the use of DANCE THERAPY which is medicine and corrective therapy for the dancer.

This class is comprised of exercises on the floor—some of which have been around for sometime, but many of Miss Sassoon's were quite unique. They were demonstrated by her seventeen old pupil and helper Regina Ravella. The suppleness and mobility of her body was beautiful to watch.

There were several teachers in the audience, all busily taking notes and we are always glad to see them. However experienced a teacher is he or she can always learn a new way of saying a familiar thing. We learn all our lives or should.

Chicago Ballet

My efforts in constantly trying to contact Ruth Page paid off, but not in the way I had expected. I very much wanted to dance the main role in a ballet of hers that I had seen many years before, *Frankie and Johnny*. I knew the role would be a good one for me and was sure to have a tremendous success in Berlin and the rest of Germany with it. Tatjana Gsovsky had given me permission to try to obtain the ballet for Berlin. Sadly, no matter how hard I had tried in the past, it never worked out because Ms. Page did not have the time to reset it for us. She had a company of her own called the Chicago Ballet. Her dancers had their own season plus they did all the ballets in the Chicago Opera's season. Instead of offering me *Frankie and Johnny*, she offered me a two-month season of dancing and touring with her company. At that time, I was free and, of course, accepted with great anticipation.

When we drew up the contract, I requested that it would include my dancing a pas de deux of my choice several times a week. Besides that, I was to dance in a ballet called *Idyle*. This had been choreographed for Marjorie Tallchief by her husband, George Skibine, in the Grand Ballet du Marquis de Cuevas. It was a fabulous little showpiece with only three dancers in it. Very difficult because all three dancers never left the stage. Ruth also gave me a leading role in her *Die Fledermaus*.

Ruth called all her guest dancers "stars" and hired very-well-known first dancers for any tour. That meant her own dancers took a backseat although she did alternate the ballerina roles in *Carmen* and *Fledermaus*. I well understood the cold reception I received from the company.

I was to dance *Idyle* with Orrin Kayin, who was to be my constant partner there. This suited me very well. Kenneth Johnson also danced in *Idyle* as he was the first male lead in the Chicago Ballet. Fortunately, once we started to work together, the ice broke as we were professional dancers and they knew Ruth's habit of hiring outside dancers occurred yearly. They could not hold a grudge against us, and in reality, this also gave them the chance to dance with well-known artists. Sonia Arova was also to dance with the company during my time. Besides possessing a great technique, she had style and stage presence. We shared a dressing room, and she was kind and helpful. Later in the season, Josette Amiel and Fleming Flindt joined us. Fleming was originally from Denmark and trained in the Bournonville school. Both had very grand reputations in Europe. They were to dance *The Flower Festival at Genzano,* which was added to the repertoire. Sonia and I would alternate in dancing the classical pas de deux. Another guest star was Melissa Hayden from New York City Ballet, who joined us for a short while. She was one of my favorite dancers, and in spite of all the gossip about how difficult she was, with me she was kind and helpful. The "stars," as Ruth called us, stayed pretty much to ourselves. Perhaps we felt the obvious turmoil of the company's dancers.

Orrin Kayan was my main partner, well suited to me in looks and height. He was very nice to me, and slowly the other dancers came around, as they knew the importation of dancers was Ruth's idée fixe. She always had successful tours due to the fact that she hired the best.

Ruth Page herself had been a good dancer, I was told, as I was too young to have seen her dance. She soon began to choreograph also. I must say that I truly loved her personality. She was a lady, and she certainly treated me very well.

I arrived in Chicago the week before the tour. Basically, I had to learn *Fledermaus* and *Idyle,* which were new to me. *Don Quixote* was a matter of teaching my version to Orrin. Very few differences in the choreography when I had a new partner, but still we had to rehearse as this can't be just thrown together. We started rehearsing *Fledermaus,* and I tried desperately to pick up the steps quickly. My concentration was very intense until suddenly, one member of the company said, "Coffee break." I was furious and turned around, saying, "Wait, please, until this sequence is finished." The dancers stopped, and there I stood with my mouth open. Ruth saw me completely perplexed and explained to me that union rules required a certain length of time that the dancers should work. I said, "Yes, but it breaks your concentration—why couldn't we break in five more minutes?" She then said under her breath, "You are not in Europe now." But in fact, all her stars rehearsed if need be at night at their own request. I was horrified as I had never had someone interrupt while the choreographer was in the middle of a sequence. Nevertheless, the company here had strict union rules.

Ruth asked me if I would come to her home to dinner that night as "Agnes" would be there. I accepted with pleasure but hadn't a clue as to who Agnes was. Ruth was married to an attorney, a wonderful man, Thomas Hart Fisher. It was a lovely cab drive to her very large apartment along Lakeshore Drive. It was very cold in January, and I wrapped my fur coat around me as I entered the main foyer of the building. The doorman directed me to a floor that was Ruth and her husband's entirely. She was extremely kind and showed me the incredible view. The bell rang, and her other guest arrived. She introduced us: "Agnes de Mille, Janet Sassoon." So it was *that* Agnes! My heart skipped a beat as I had read her books during my early years and also loved her choreography. She was truly one of America's treasures. We had dinner served in a very casual manner by a butler, and then Ms. de Mille said that at nine o'clock there would be part of her *Rodeo* on television. Would we be interested in watching it? Of course; that was even more of a treat for me. I had a lovely evening, and Ruth asked her guest if she could drop me at my hotel as I was staying not far from her. Ms. de Mille said it would be a great pleasure. I, of course, thought all of this was a dream and that I would soon awaken, but here I was, sitting next to this great lady of dance in a taxicab. We chatted easily, and I told her that I had once written to her asking for an audition. At that time, she had had a small company, but sadly, it did not continue for very long. Ms. de Mille was kind enough to say, "What a pity, as I have a feeling you would have been very good." We parted company, and I floated to my room and slept well that night.

Rehearsals continued; we had only one week to learn Ruth's ballets. Since the main dancers had brought their own things, it was fine for them, but it wasn't easy for me to have two ballets I had never danced before. Somehow, photo sessions, costume fittings, and so on were also fitted into that week. We were somehow ready for the first performance, which was in Terre Haute. Remarkably, Anna Kisselgoff was there to review it.

The tour was a new experience for me. It took in the Deep South and East Coast. After Europe, touring in America came as a shock, mainly because every little village in Germany had its own state theater with proper stages; some were wonderful theaters with a great atmosphere. Here, we were like a band of gypsies bringing ballet to such towns as Greensboro, Mississippi, and Rome, Georgia. Obviously, Boston, Philadelphia, and Atlanta had proper theaters, but in other places, there was really nothing but a gymnasium floor that we could not dance on. We weren't allowed to put rosin on it to keep us from slipping. It was truly a nightmare, and very often, I wondered why we even attempted it. I felt I

—

had never danced so badly as at most performances I could not give freely or let go for fear of falling.

I remember in one such college auditorium Orrin told me to relévé, which meant to rise on my pointes and move to where he was waiting for me to do an arabesque. I was afraid to come down again for fear of falling on my face, so he let me bourée and then held me in an arabesque pose. We improvised like that through the whole piece as we were truly taking out lives in our hands—and feet! However, the audience was young, college age, with some older people; here, we were bringing ballet to places that had never heard or seen one. Now as I look back on this period in America, I have great respect for all the companies, as few as they were, who toured the Orpheum Circuit. Hard as it was, we were pioneers of our art. It was the Ballet Russe and Ballet Theatre that led the way.

The sacrifices just to dance were so great. But we also had some places that were very sophisticated and adored that we were there. They gave us some lovely soirees after performances, especially in the South. Some houses there seemed to come directly out of *Gone with the Wind.* We also had one or two unpleasant experiences. We danced in Atlanta and then went on to Rome, Georgia, for one night. A few of us decided that rather than spending the night in Rome, we would take the Greyhound bus back to Atlanta, saving us from unpacking for a few days. After the performance, a small group of us went to the bus station, only to find it had no restaurant or food counter. We still had an hour or so before departure, so I went with one of the girls in the corps de ballet, who was really quite beautiful and blond, to find someplace in the area where we might eat. After walking a few blocks, we found ourselves in a very undesirable neighborhood. Suddenly, slowly, one or two men started to walk behind us as at slight distance. A couple more joined them. I, not knowing how to deal with this, was in a sheer panic and ready to run as fast as I could. She coolly held my hand arm and moved to the middle of the street, giving me quiet, calm directions: "Walk normally, keep cool, and don't turn around." I had to admire this girl who had had experience with living in Chicago and knew how to handle this situation. I was maybe three years older than her but in comparison had never had any experience of this kind. We had actually walked in a circle, and the bus station came into view. When we saw it, we made a run for our lives. She was laughing when we arrived at the station—and I was trembling. I couldn't believe how much discipline it took to walk when she gave me that order and how natural she was about it. I must say I was very happy to have been with her. Of course, we told our colleagues about our adventure, and they laughed and said it happened all the time. I realized there how protected I always was, and how different America was at that time from Europe. Of course, I knew that even in San Francisco, if you were in the wrong place at the wrong time, the same thing might occur.

Meanwhile, someone had found a place that had sandwiches, and we were all happy to board the bus with our goodies. To my horror, my sandwich had been fried! I was, indeed, in the South. We returned to Atlanta, and not only did we stay there to dance several performances, but we also had a free day during our stay.

Of all the people on the tour, Ruth Page seemed to enjoy touring the most. She really loved her company and dancers and what she was doing. If we thought touring was hard, think of what an older lady had to endure, especially one-night stands and traveling 500 miles in one direction only to go back 300 miles the next day. This was because of how the theaters were booked; sometimes we had to go back and forth because of the available dates.

And so life passed in this mostly insular way. Often I would ask what there was to see, to be told, "Nothing." Unlike Europe of this time, in the United States, we were going to towns and small cities that had little or no culture.

We began to head toward New York, where Rudolf Nureyev, who had defected a few months earlier, was to dance for the first time with us at the Brooklyn Academy of Music. He evidently was a great friend of Sonia's, and we were all happy to welcome him. Since Sonia was responsible for his appearances with us, the *Don Quixote* pas de deux was going to be danced by Sonia and him. I was to dance in a performance of *Fledermaus*, but in a gesture that was not entirely without thought, I went to Ruth and suggested that her own ballerina dance it, eliminating me from the program as a statement that if I didn't dance in *Don Q.*, I didn't wish to appear in something that did not really suit me or show me at my best. It is sometimes very important in a career to not dance something you know will not show you to your best advantage. You need to understand that some things may be good for you, but others may be brilliant. Most dancers don't think this way and will dance all things, good and bad. New York was not the place for me to be seen in what I felt was not the best I could do. I did, however, dance *Idyle* the next night, to great success.

Rudi arrived the first night, and Sonia and I were, as usual, in the same dressing room. That night, Rudi shared the dressing room with her while I was in and out. He spoke no English and very little French, which is what we conversed in. He was shy, very giving and eager, and I truly enjoyed him. This was his first American performance. He was wonderful, and the audience went mad. Rudi and I wouldn't meet again for a few years, and he would never again be this Nureyev: naive, trusting, and open.

After New York, the season was over, and we all hugged and swore we would keep in touch. Ruth and her company returned to Chicago while the guest dancers dispersed to other continents. As I now look back on this experience, although I feel that for half the tour I danced badly due to the conditions given us, we did bring our art of dance to so many little towns and perhaps helped to expose Americans who did not live in one of the big cities to ballet for the first time in their lives. This I know to be true as often I would be told this, especially by young people. We were indeed ambassadors of dance in our own way. This was in the early 1960s. Now there are hundreds of small regional ballet companies in these same towns and cities, with their own seasons and audiences. I am grateful that I was a small part of that time even though I never did get the ballet *Frankie and Johnny* to take to Berlin.

34

Returning to San Francisco

Now at last I had time to gather my thoughts and stay in one place for a while. I also needed to attend to my knee, which had been getting steadily worse. Since that wrench in Hamburg on a slight mishap during a movement in *Signale* where Gert caught me and pulled me into a split, I had known that something was really wrong.

I was living in my parents' home as my divorce was filed but not final. Unlike today, it took two years after filing for a divorce to be final. I was very unhappy over the situation, but seemingly nobody could speak with Peter, my soon-to-be-ex-husband, to find out the reason for such a drastic action. His response was the same to everyone. He could not or would not discuss it and said that it had nothing to do with me. It was so exasperating because it certainly had to do with me—I was his wife! But he assured everyone that he still loved me. This was so insane that everyone who discussed it with him and then me was as frustrated as I was. On top of all this, I would get phone calls from Peter asking me to lunch or to see him. At first, I did go, thinking I could understand what the problem was, but nothing came forth, only his continued assurance that it had nothing to do with me or that it was no fault of mine. I was angry as I thought marriage was between two people who would love each other forever. Obviously, Peter had made his decision without any regard for my feelings. This was unforgivable and was to hurt me deeply for years.

I was happy that my parents were behind me as always and gave me great support. In my heart, I knew that Peter had hurt them, too, as my mother and father had treated him like a son because he had no parents.

Life soon changed for me, and I started meeting new people and being a bit social.

I took class every day, but finally the knee really locked. I had to see a doctor—and did—and he said it was torn cartilage. Of course, in Germany, unknowingly what they had been injecting into my knee was cortisone. It had kept me dancing, but this had allowed the knee to be damaged even more. I now faced what all dancers dread: surgery. My plans had to be changed as just that week Lucia Chase had asked if I could dance with American Ballet Theater. It was my dream as then I would be able to do roles in a company in America whose repertory was varied in nature, not one sided. ABT did the classics but also had a fabulous repertory for a dramatic ballerina. I think, at that time, it was the only company that did such a marvelous array of the great classical ballets as well as almost every important American choreographer. Sadly, I had to refuse due to the impending surgery, with hopes that I could accept at another time. She left the offer open, and we both hoped that I would soon return to dancing.

Needless to say, it turned into a long series of nightmares. First, I had open surgery on my left knee. I suffered great pain, and although I went back to class eventually, the knee continued to be swollen and painful. The second operation was on both the front and back of the knee. To regain full use and think of dancing again was agony for me. Mentally, I was totally lost. I could not believe I might not dance professionally again. It would be impossible to live a life without dancing, or so I then thought. I knew that one day I would stop, but not at this point in my career or at this age—I was only thirty-three years old. I was brokenhearted, and to make things worse, my father informed my mother that, on a trip to Los Angeles, he had bought a house on Mulholland Drive. My mother was shocked as she did not wish to live in a city without her children nearby. (Unknowing to all of us then, my father had also suffered a small stroke.)

I found an apartment in San Francisco that was suitable and very artistic, and I made it unique. It was in the North Beach area, which at that time was called Little Italy. There were great coffeehouses and markets and bakeries. Everyone spoke Italian, which I loved.

Gert and I would telephone each other almost every week. He was very sad for me and tried to give me courage. I knew he was the one person I could always count on. He was also having problems then, with Tatjana and the Oper. We were both in the position of having to change. Tatjana had the school and made another with Gert; however, he would become director of the ballet for the Stadische Opera, which at that time was in West Berlin (we had always been West and East with the wall and checkpoint Charlie separating us). As I write this, I think that during my time in Berlin, today's Berlin would have been unimaginable—no East Berlin, just one enormous, thriving city. The ballet is now where it belongs, Unter der Linden (in former East Berlin), where it originally should have been. At that time, Gert was involved in a tremendous work. Being director of the ballet in the Stadtische Oper meant finding choreographers for new ballets; hiring dancers from other countries in spite of its being a state theater; dealing with designers, conductors, and finance. I had the privilege of being of some use to him as I helped from afar. I sent several dancers to him, whom he accepted sight unseen. I was very careful about what I did since the responsibility was on me. He sometimes discussed other choreographers or dancers I knew and asked my opinion. I suggested Michael Smuin from San Francisco Ballet, who was choreographing and assistant director with Lew. He was talented and very theatrical and had just done a ballet called *Shinju* that I thought would work well in Berlin. Although I put them in touch with each other, nothing came of it as Michael began to take on the directorship of the San Francisco Ballet and had his plate full. I understood Gert perfectly even though we were so far away from each other. I could help in many ways and was very happy to still be a part of the ballet in Berlin in this strange way.

It also filled in the great sadness as I struggled to gain strength. I would also attempt to phone Tatjana, just to hear her voice, but it was so difficult for her to understand my bad French over the telephone, and I always ended in tears. I was so hopeless that Tatjana also cried. It was better if Gert was there with her as then we both had some self-control. I felt total love for this incredible woman whom I respected so much; I really think she was a genius, ahead of her time as regard to choreography, her choices of music, and so on. She had such imaginative ideas for costumes and masks that she had to create models of them for others to follow. She saw in her head everything before we started a new ballet. She never stumbled; she just knew what went where. To say she was exceptional as a human being is not enough. After all my experience of working with a hundred or more choreographers, she would still deserve placement in a special bracket all her own. Maybe ten years from now, someone will catch up with her. I now see also that Gert had had such strength and had carried the same kind of force to make the Stadische Oper Ballet a very good, technically great company, one that improved and rose during his time as its director.

Trying to find a new direction, I thought of Alan Howard. Whenever I came home in between engagements, I would work with Alan and his company, the Pacific Ballet. Alan had developed a fine school and a nice group of dancers. The star was Alan, the ability to set original choreography also came from Alan. The talent and professionalism was Alan, all because of his many years of dancing as a premier danseur with the Ballet Russe de Monte Carlo (he is featured in the documentary about that company).

Working with Alan was another thing. For example, he never liked to rehearse a great deal when he was dancing. I would arrive on time to rehearse, and he would say, "Let's have a cup of coffee." It was amazing: I needed the rehearsal, and he would warm up with two *grand battiments* and that was it! According to our bible of dance somewhere, it says, "Thou shalt not rehearse without a good barre and warm-up." But Alan proved this to be false. Maybe I was jealous because my body could never dance a grand pas de deux without a proper warm-up. We would go through the adagio, and I must say, he was a perfect partner physically. By that, I mean he was long, and every line we would take seemed to extend us together. His feet, for a male dancer, were more than good. Our pointing together in a pose seemed to pull our two bodies from the pointed toe through the head and arms. It was like butter—everything melted together. His memory was truly remarkable. We were like one physically as we moved across the stage. We both had clean techniques; in fact, at times I would be very cross with Alan because he would dance more like the ballerina, technically. But it was a great pleasure to dance with him. He had a great sense of humor, and I will never forget how much we would laugh and how hard I would make him rehearse. When I rehearsed my solo, he would show me very clearly the choreography if I missed anything because he cared about my performance even while I was not being partnered by him. His solo turns went so easily (even without warm-ups). I think Alan was a rare creature and a wonderful partner. He made it so uncomplicated. Maybe it was his experience dancing with Danilova, Slavenska, and every other ballerina in the Ballet Russe that gave him the ability to just adjust to a ballerina's body—or maybe all this was just something that I had with Alan. What I missed with him that I did have with other partners was eye contact. Not just looking but going deeper through the eyes and enriching what we were dancing. Speaking through our bodies from inside. Emotionally, he was not for me a Gert or Pepe with whom I'd danced dramatic ballets in which my partner and I had to sustain a shared emotion. Nonetheless, according to the critics, there was a certain thrill when Sassoon and Howard danced together.

To this day, I have never seen a male dancer turn in à la seconde three times after two singles in a coda. That is with the free leg extended horizontally to the side as you turn. I also know he had great reverence for the past and tried to hand it down to the present, which I think he did very well indeed. For example, Alan taught me many versions of choreography that were slightly different from mine. In this, he was very generous.

As a teacher, he was completely relaxed and joked a great deal while he pushed a student forward. I don't think I ever heard him scold or raise his voice while teaching. He gave the illusion of not working very hard, but that was not true. He was organized and somehow managed to find the right person to do the work he needed done. Alan also had a collection of dance memorabilia that was extraordinary. His love and respect for the past was obvious, but he lived in the here and now, using the past as examples of what had certainly left a great tradition for all of us dancing at that time. Especially for those of us in America, where ballet was almost in the pioneer stage.

With all these thoughts in mind, I contacted Alan at his school, the Academy of Ballet. Under his direction, the school was thriving. He made me a proposal, which was for me to teach in the school and that I, in turn, would contact Gert to ask him to arrange for Alan to teach in Berlin. This would be on a trial basis for both of us. I was not at all prepared to take on a school permanently. But we both agreed that we should try this, and in a funny way, the decision had already been made for me. My father had subsidized the renovation of this studio for Mr. Del Oro, who had designed it and made it into the Academy. My father had had nothing to do with the ballet; he just gave the money for this project, thinking it would keep his daughter home! Well, at last he got his wish—one year after his death.

And so I started to teach, but the problem knee intruded. When I used it, it would puff up with fluid that the doctor had to remove with a syringe and elevate to reduce the swelling. I could not demonstrate in class full out as I had initially begun doing. This degree of restraint was extremely difficult for someone who had always danced full out and who was forced to stop at that age. It was a matter of discipline. I had to learn the hard way, which was to not dance everything myself but to come up with ways to present my knowledge for others to follow.

Gert had come through, and Alan was thriving in Germany. He taught a few classes for the company at the Stadische Oper, but Gert felt he belonged in a school. He eventually found a place that he liked and was offered a professorship at the Hochschule for Dance in Hanover.

—

Alan left me with one children's class only as his main income back in San Francisco came from the adult class in the morning, which was a hodgepodge of nonprofessional adults and some serious dancers. The afternoon was another class and then, in the evening, adult beginners and adult advanced. From the start, Mark Wilde taught the adults, and I had the morning and evening advanced girls. Those classes had many girls and some boys, at the perfect age, who were interested in a career in dance.

In the class, I had some beautiful material and talent. Two girls in this group, I truly raised and became very fond of. One was Regina Revilla, a talented and bright young girl with a keen sense of humor and a very down-to-earth work ethic. I adored her even though I eventually sent her away for a while because she needed the experience of dancing in a ballet company. I was able to make an entrée for her with the San Diego Ballet, then run by my great colleague Sonia Arova. She made the audition and danced with the company, which gave her self-esteem and also the experience and prestige of being in a ballet company. The other, Marina Hotchkiss, was a girl who had a perfect body—long and thin—and the face of an angel. She had a Russian back, which I pushed very much. Her long back and neck were extraordinary. I had her as a pupil since she was fourteen years old. I worked with her very carefully and was very pleased that she kept her own style. Because I saw in her a rare talent, I thought Gert in Berlin could help to mold her into doing the kind of neoclassical ballets that I thought would suit her. I eventually sent her to Berlin, where she advanced within the Stadische Oper as they looked after her.

At any rate, this class was my great joy, and I really produced some fine dancers. Every teacher has one class that he or she works with for years until the students are ready. This class was really special. I felt they inspired me as I hope I did them. I always talked theater to them in class. I believe you must do this to let them become excited about dancing onstage. They must be aware of why they are working and where it will eventually end: on a stage with an audience. They must never lose sight of that as it is their raison d'être.

Mark informed me that he wasn't really interested in teaching as he was a truly talented choreographer. I was in a dilemma as I really needed another teacher. Alan suggested Marjory Bressler from New York City Ballet. He knew her and thought, between us, we would bring in people. Arrangements were made, and there she was at my door. She, too, had had an injury and had given up on dancing but was willing to teach. Her personality was completely "New York," which the adults seemed to like.

My idea of a school was not just to teach adults for exercise and fun. To me, a school meant children, and I needed to build it up from almost zero. I remember two little girls, both seven years old (which to me was the earliest age to start) who arrived for my grade 1 children's class. Both were daughters of friends. However, better two than nothing. One was the child of my dear friend Denise Hinckle, and she brought a friend with her. That is what I started with. I stuck to my ideals, determined to make this a professional ballet school. I lost a lot of points with the adults, but I knew that I had not danced all those years to teach ballet to adults who had no interest in ballet as a career. I needed to give back my knowledge to the next generation of dancers as I had promised my teachers I would do someday.

Eventually, Marjorie wanted to leave as she missed New York and her friends. I could understand that totally. She had been very good and popular with the classes she taught. I was sorry to see her go. Now I had to find a professional dancer who had semiretired and who could commit to being a partner who shared my vision for the school. My prayers were answered. Howard Sayette came into my life. He had danced with the American Ballet Russe de Monte Carlo. We had both danced the classics, and our schooling was compatible. And, more important, we agreed on what kind of school we wanted it to become. I had a children's class—grade 1—of sixteen to twenty children, about ten of whom would progress to grade 2, and we went all the way to a class of advanced girls that Alan had already established. From that class came Kyra Nichols, who was just about ready to be kicked out of the nest. She was beautiful and rare.

Slowly, we kept pushing and adding curriculum. Howard and I alternated giving the advanced class as it is great to have a male dancer and a ballerina teaching the same group. I then put the advanced girls on point. I gave pointe and variation class, and Howard gave pointe for the last fifteen minutes of the advanced class when he taught it. My intention was that that my advanced students would never wear flat (soft leather) ballet shoes. Deshanked toe shoes were made a must, at first, and then, eventually, toe shoes. But I did not believe in keeping students off pointe in regular class for advanced students. In Paris, we never took class without being in toe shoes as you don't use flats anyway in any ballet company except in character work. Actually, we then put in a character class as both Howard and I could teach the essentials needed for such ballets even though neither of us had worked as character dancers. We taught czardas, polka, polonaise, and, of course, the waltz. Eventually, boys started coming so that we could give adagio classes.

Dancers from the San Francisco Ballet began to attend my morning class: Anita Paciotti, Nancy Delmar, Jim Sohms (who I sent to Berlin to Dance for two years), Val Canaparoli, Alexander Filipov, Tom Rudd, Madeline Bouchard, Damara Bennett, and many others.

The school went very well. I had tremendous respect for Howard, and we never really had a problem. However, sadly, he received an offer from Oakland Ballet. Ron Guidi was really developing that company, and it was a great opportunity for Howard. I hated to lose him as a partner but understood totally that he had to do more than teach. Oakland would give him the opportunity to do much more, and under Ron Guidi, they went forward to develop dancers and repertory ballets. Once again, I had lost a perfect person for the school.

However, the one great event was in the summer. Every year, about twenty girls aged fourteen to nineteen would arrive from Vancouver, British Columbia, with a chaperone. This eventually grew to two groups, juniors and seniors. Many were on scholarship. I prepared a summer program for them that was quite exciting and full. They had ballet class every day plus pointe class and variations from the ballets. They also did a floor class twice a week (taken literally on the floor to gain further turnout and flexibility). They also took a character class as well as learned from a makeup artist from the San Francisco Opera Company how to put on stage makeup. Then, once a week, they had lectures on various subjects such as nutrition, injuries, and dance history, presented by dancers as guest instructors. All of these professionals donated their time and expertise. It was quite something and I think one of the best summer sessions for dancers anywhere. At the end, we always gave a performance in which they were shown off as a group, and their progress was seen by an audience and appreciated enormously. It was always hard work for me, but I loved doing this program. My fondness for these girls was very special. Some returned for several years. I had a great lady as a chaperone, Donna Furneaux, whose daughter Dorea I sent eventually to a ballet company.

On my last summer session with my Canadians, we had a wonderful news reporter by the name of Robert McKenzie, then at channel 7 in San Francisco, do a piece about the program, from bits and pieces about the training right through to the end performance. The two cameramen popped in at all hours to get footage on all the classes, catching everyone off guard. Therefore, the show captured what it was truly like at the school. Robert did a great job. We viewed it together prior to the broadcast, cutting a great deal of footage. At last it became a television special, presented during the last half hour of channel 7 news. It was very well received and, to this day, a great memory for me of the Canadian girls.

When Howard left the company, that summer was very hard on me. I taught three to four classes a day plus my own ladies' exercise class that I gave four times a week. My schedule was full, and besides all the normal problems of running a school, I had my own problems of hip pain that was progressing rapidly. Meanwhile, I was invited to Munich to teach, where my dear friend and colleague Constanza Vernon was then head of the Heinz Bosle Foundation, a school named after a lead male dancer who had died of cancer and who had partnered Constanza when she was ballerina of the Munich State Ballet. I accepted. By now I had acquired enough teachers for the school, and we closed the children's division in the month of August in favor of doing the Canadian summer program.

We had a wonderful time as we had been very close during my Berlin days. Although we worked very hard, we could always laugh together. I find that when one is brokenhearted, one can only cry with someone one can laugh with. We shared our loves and dreams together. On my arrival in Munich, we felt as if we had never been away from each other. We soon picked up from where we had left off. I was staying in a guest apartment directly across the way from Constanza and her wonderful husband, Fred. This was very convenient as we could come and go to the school together.

She took me to the school, and I watched the advanced girls and boys who had been working with Olga Lepenshinskaya from the Bolshoi. Her classes were truly marvelous and very familiar to me. Many of the things I, too, had learned sparked my memory. One was forbidden to watch her classes, but she allowed me to do so. She gave center barre and a very long adagio to build stamina. Her classes were long and hard for the students. At this particular time, she was just about the only teacher that the Soviets had allowed to leave the USSR to teach as a guest artist. Her husband had been a general close to Stalin.

I became devoted to her, and we exchanged books in English. I had just finished reading a biography of Golda Meir, and she was very happy to read that as she had already seen the film about her. Even in San Francisco, we had not had a screening of that. It amazed me how well Russians of her unique sphere were kept informed.

She knew of my hip problem and offered to take me to the USSR, where she could arrange for surgery at no expense to me; I could even stay with her after the surgery. I was overwhelmed but did not think that I could again be so far from home.

I had a good time in Munich. Constanza and Fred were wonderful to me. Connie, as I called her, was very ambitious and thrived on creating and planning future programs for her school. She was already certain to become the next director of the Munich State Ballet. She had the great luck to have a husband who took over the business side of the school so that she could be free artistically, not burdened with all the mundane details that go into such projects.

But I knew the time had come when I couldn't stave off the inevitable anymore as concerned my hip. I had started to compensate and overuse my feet and other parts of my body, which is the danger when working with any injury. It becomes a round robin; you just end up injuring other areas. I left Munich with hopes of working again with Constanza on a summer program in Saint Moritz, Switzerland, the following year.

I returned to San Francisco, where I was x-rayed and shown my left hip was quite bad. Somehow though the ballet grapevine, Pat Wilde—a former principal of New York City Ballet and a wonderful dancer— was now teaching, and she gave me Edward Villella's phone number. Seemingly, he had had the same surgery but in London, where they were using a new technique that was far better than what was being done in America. The American Medical Association knew of this surgery but had not passed on it yet. I thought, *Not again—can I afford drastic surgery only to have it not be successful?* I called Edward Villella, and he gave me the name of his doctor, Mr. Freeman, in London. His surgery had been a great success with Villella.

I immediately called Mr. Freeman, and his office was marvelous. They told me exactly what to expect and what the entire cost would be for a three-week stay in the hospital. They told me that Mr. Freeman would need me to stay in England for three more weeks before returning home. It so happened that my very best friend, Lisa (Popper) Weiss, had settled in London with her husband, Stanley, and their two children, Lori and Anthony. It was a great chance for me as I felt completely at home with them, and she was very happy to have me stay with her. I made the decision to do it, and now I had to make sure that the school was in good hands.

It was still summer, so the classes were mostly in the small-adult division. I had several teachers and a very trustworthy young woman who had run the school in my absence in addition to teaching some classes. She was more than capable of taking charge, and I knew everything would go smoothly.

Camden Lloyd was my student at fourteen and had stayed on after working with Rosella Hightower's school in Cannes, which I sent her to with a special letter to Rosella. After Rosella and a short stay in Paris, she returned to me and made the decision to teach. She was given the management of the school and also started teaching the beginner childrens class. She assisted me in the running of the school.

At that time, my private life was very happy as I had been seeing the same young man for four years. He was so exceptional a person who loved ballet, music, theater, and all the things I thought I could never find in a man. He came from a good family, and although we came from opposite sides of the world, our upbringing had been very similar. I had met John through a very dear friend of mine, Veronica di Rosa.

She was an artist originally from British Columbia, who had come to the Napa Valley. She was divorced with two children from a previous marriage. Her children were in their teens and were still living part-time in British Columbia. Veronica had married another friend, René di Rosa, whom I had known for years. He, too, had been married and divorced twice. He was a great character and an extraordinary person. We saw a great deal of each other.

Veronica and I made jam together, something we had been doing since she began living with René. It was of course easier for two people to do this than for one on her own. We enjoyed it, and even entered the results in the county fair. On this particular occasion, Veronica told me to come and to bring along a dress to wear or something else nice to change into after our jam-making as she had invited a friend for dinner. In other words, our jam-smeared jeans and T-shirts would not have been adequate that evening. I brought a simple dress to change into. It was wonderful to be totally absorbed by strawberries and sugar that afternoon; somehow, seeing those jars lined up and listening to the sound the lids make when they pop-sealed was what one loved to see and hear while canning. Veronica would always bake a small brown bread while we worked, and at four o'clock, we would take a tea break. René would stroll in and out of the kitchen, content to watch us use the large pots in front of us, sterilize the jars, and smash the fruit in enormous bowls.

Toward the end of this particular jam-making session, Veronica started putting things in the oven for dinner. She suggested that I go and change in the guest room. While I was changing, I heard a car pulling into the driveway and peeked out the window. I had not really given it much thought, but Veronica obviously had. The guest was John Upton Jr., who owned and worked a vineyard, 3 Palms, with his brother, near Calistoga. John spent the weekend in San Francisco at his parents' home on Pacific Avenue. When I finally made my entrance, Veronica introduced us. John said, "I am happy to at last meet the Black Pearl of the ballet world." I was stunned. Toumanova was the ballerina originally called the Black

Pearl. She was now retired, and some critic wrote of me, "We now have a new young ballerina who is our Black Pearl." That was not at all well known; not even dancers necessarily knew this—only someone who was a balletomane would have come across that information. So imagine my surprise at meeting a person from outside the profession who mentioned this very nonchalantly.

During dinner, our conversation was quite lively. At one point, Veronica asked me to come to the kitchen with her, supposedly to bring out the cheese. When we were alone, she said to me, "At last I introduce you to a man, and you are arguing with him!" It quite shocked me as I saw us being happily immersed in a passionate conversation about something. I was certainly not arguing as this man knew what he was talking about, and I was enjoying myself immensely. I convinced Veronica to her satisfaction, and we both returned to the table to finish our lovely meal. After some time, René announced that he was going to bed. Veronica and I cleared the table, and then we packed up my jam and put it in my car. She bade John and me good night and left the two of us alone together. The time had come for my departure back to San Francisco. John escorted me to my car. When I was seated, I said my good-byes and by chance asked him if he would like to go to the Joffrey Ballet the following week. He accepted with pleasure and said he would call to arrange fetching me and to suggest where we could eat after the performance.

That was the beginning of our very long relationship. We had so much in common, the more I knew him. Time passed very quickly because I was so happy with John. During those four years, I continued to teach and work hard in the school. I also produced a demonstration called "Dancer's World" at the Veterans Auditorium, using dancers from the San Francisco Ballet and my own pupils. John attended with his mother and aunt. His father was by then unable to go out.

Now, four years had passed. I felt that now perhaps we should part as I wanted to be married again and still have a child. John had not proposed marriage, but we were very comfortable together. I knew in my heart that if I did not break off the relationship during my absence, in London I would not be allowing myself to meet another man, my chances being very limited age-wise. John was forty-three and had never been married. So my decision was to go to London, have the hip surgery, and put some distance between us. It would be easier to do, simply to not be in the same country! Drastic, but I felt it necessary for any kind of future besides being married to my profession.

I had started coaching professional dancers. My life was what it should have been as I was accepting slowly that I would never dance as a prima ballerina again. But now, threatened with hip surgery, I feared losing my profession altogether. This was not fair, and life was unfair! I now needed all my strength, physically and emotionally, to get me through this new ordeal.

All the arrangements were made in London, and my mother had returned to San Francisco after the death of my father. It was also a tremendous blow to me, losing my wonderful father. I was still grieving, and now came having to deal with my hip and John.

Better to go and do what I must, and hopefully, things would look brighter if I was not in so much pain. I remember flying out from San Francisco airport after John put me on the plane for London. This was one unhappy lady leaving in despair. I felt as if I was saying good-bye to everything—and never look back.

Ten hours later, I arrived in London's impossible airport of 1983. One could see every aircraft of almost every country on its airfield. Immediately, I was in some ways coming home as London had already been an important part of my life. As usual, the customs agent asked me if I planned to work, and I said no. Then he noted, "Sassoon is British, is it not?" I said yes; however, I explained that I had dual citizenship and was now living in the United States. He passed me through with a "Hmmph."

Somehow I managed to clear the airport and arrive at 17 Tregunter Road in Chelsea, which would be home to me for the next weeks. As usual, Lisa greeted me with hugs and happiness just as I, too, had been yearning to see her. That alone was the one good thing in this ordeal: I would see and have some time with my lovely best friend. I burst into tears, and she quietly embraced me, understanding everything I was going through. What could I have had at this moment as a better friend than Lisa? Her love would give me strength. I had a few days before the surgery, and Lisa made sure that they were filled with exciting and fun things to do. She was like a thunderbolt, always arranging my schedule from my first cup of coffee to my last pill for the night. I always told her, if she ever had to work, she would have made a fortune arranging itineraries. However, she only did this for those she loved, and it was obvious that everything was filled with care and love. We were so happy to see each other that I actually stopped thinking about the horror of surgery.

Lisa had my room ready and had even rented a TV for it in case I needed to stay in bed and could not go upstairs to watch TV. Books and even nighttime candy (a must for us!) were there. Lisa would be away for three weeks of my stay, which period fell during the time I would be in the hospital and for a little bit afterward. To make up for that, she had invited all our mutual friends for dinner in the days before I was to check in, and I loved seeing the familiar faces. I loved her children as if they were my own; they, too, were a part of my life, very precious to me. We held gab sessions at night, sitting on her bed, and Stanley would actually sleep through them—as long as we never said his name! Sure enough, if a "Stanley" did come out, to our amusement, he would say, "What?" and we would roar with laughter. It was Stanley's good nature that he endured the two of us! How he could even sleep was incredible as Lisa and I were insomniacs. We envied people who could fall asleep easily. But we used that time to catch up.

Lisa was sorry to hear of my intention to leave John as she knew I really loved him but that there was no future for us, or so I thought. For now, my surgery was overwhelming enough for me. I went to see Mr. Freeman at his Harley Street office that was almost directly across the street from the hospital where I would be staying, called the London Clinic.

This seemed the best place for me. Mr. Freeman was very good and explained exactly what to expect and how I was to manage after his surgery. His technique would only change the socket, not put steel down my whole leg. Oddly enough, years later, my mother was to have this same surgery as was my future mother-in-law soon after her. However, both mothers were in their late seventies when they required it.

For some reason, the thought of this operation made me rather hysterical as I felt something was being placed in my body the same way someone might replace a tire. The thought of a foreign object encasing my hip, and at that age, seemed to fill my mind with horror. I thought, *Where was that body that could do anything, flying to the heavens if need be?* Lisa understood my mental agony and total fear. She had a friend (not a dancer) who was about the same age as I was and who had had a hip replacement, who was doing marvelously. She asked her friend to speak to me about how happy she was with her surgery. The friend even said she wished she could have had it done sooner. This helped, but I thought to myself, *She is not a dancer, therefore she doesn't use her hip in the same manner as I do.* However, for Lisa's sake, I calmed down and tried to enjoy my few last days of freedom.

Finally, the time arrived for me to enter the London clinic. I took a cab there, as Lisa had left for her holiday. Upon my arrival, the doorman took my suitcase and escorted me to a woman, who said that we would go directly to my room. I felt as if I was checking into a first-class hotel! We proceeded to my room, which was private, of course; it was a cheerful and large space with even a fireplace. The woman sat down with me and explained that I could order anything I wanted and it would be there for me. Also, a secretary was available and she would be happy to deposit into their safe any money or valuables I had with me. I told her immediately that I would like to use her services. I had ten thousand dollars with me. Mr. Freeman had told me that the entire cost for the surgery, the anesthesiologist, and so on, as well as the hospital and a regular GP who would check me frequently would be $8,000 for the three weeks that I would be there. Unbelievable, compared to even one week in an American hospital. And this included a night nurse and a day nurse plus the head nurse who was a "sister." The nurses were not changed for others; I had the same people day after day. My day nurse turned out to be absolutely the best; she not only took care of me but also overprotected me. She adored my beautiful nightgowns and took them home after I had worn them to wash and iron them herself. She would not allow the hospital laundry to touch them!

They knew I was a ballerina, and Mr. Freeman saw to it that I was being cared for and made comfortable in my room. The next few days after the surgery were not pleasant, but pain medication was administered on a regular basis whenever I needed it. My room was filled with flowers sent by Lisa and ordered from home—even though I was in London, everyone made sure I knew they were thinking of me. I soon became a celebrity at the hospital. Mr. Freeman ordered red wine for me and suggested I have a glass with dinner. My physical therapist was a young girl whom I enjoyed very much. She was good and not surprised by my quick progress. I was walking with Canadian crutches, which were easier for me to handle as I could use my hands to push down on them rather than having crutches against my armpits as I'd had in the knee surgery. We soon made a pouch so I could take something with me as I walked. By then, I felt almost no pain, except at night. Whenever I rang, the head sister would arrive and suggest that I have a nice cup of tea first, and then she would take care of my pain. My life at the clinic was not as horrible as I had imagined, and I was soon released.

Lisa had arranged for permanent help living in and had given her full instructions before leaving for her trip. Lori was also there and in her teens, so I could communicate with her. Also, Lisa had arranged for a lady to drive me if the need arose plus a young dancer would accompany me (much later) to ballets and theater when I was better. I was quite content but naturally looked forward to Lisa's return. During this time, Anthony came home with a cast on his foot. Then Lisa also had something that required a walking cast, and so there we three were!

I had met a darling man named Maurice Blinder who did all the special effects for the 007 movies. With Lisa back, things picked up in the

—

house, and we once again had a lot of things going on. One of the most amusing incidents was being taken to lunch by Maurice with the two of us on crutches—and entering the restaurant Lorenzo's, where everyone knew everyone. We certainly made an entrance. Our situation sometimes made Lisa and me have a *fou rire*—we could not stop laughing until tears poured from our eyes. Often, we would just look at each other suddenly when we were somewhere, and we understood exactly what had come into our minds, which started off gales of laughter. We were hopeless.

Lisa was small and thin; I was also small and thin. I could wear her clothes, except her waist was small and mine was not, as dancing also develops one's ribcage. I loved changing clothes and adored wearing those of Lisa's marvelous things that suited me. Not everything did, as her tastes ran to tailored clothes whereas mine did not.

At her home, breakfast was always served to me in bed; Lisa and I had lunch and dinner in the dining room. I liked what we ate as it was very healthy and good. I was thin enough after the hospital, so gaining weight was not a problem.

I began to receive phone calls from John, and even little packages arrived. Lisa would remark on this and told me that I had never seemed so in love before. John's sudden attentiveness to me was a mystery. This did not help my decision to leave him. I just let what was happening happen as my struggle to get physically strong again was my first and foremost priority.

At long last, my time in London was over: Mr. Freeman dismissed me and gave me the go-ahead to leave. However, he estimated that I had six weeks more of using one crutch. I was now pain-free and no longer felt as if I had a foreign object in me.

I said my good-byes to Lisa at the end of May. John had called to say he would pick me up at the San Francisco airport in his mother's 1949 Packard limousine.

I was very happy to see John and did not care now about the future. I was just grateful that the worst was behind me. John brought me home and helped me get my things in order, and said he would ring me later. I had someone there to help me unpack and get settled as I was still handicapped by needing a crutch.

The next day, John called and asked if I was free. I said I was having tea with Mother but that the next day would be okay. Obviously, my mother was very happy to see me and to know that the surgery had been a success. I also called the school to check; everything had run smoothly in my absence. Summer vacation was upon us, and the children's classes had ended.

John came the following day to fetch me, and we just drove around the embarcadero and the piers. I remember saying my father once had to go through a worker's strike line when George Killion, who was head of the steamship company APL (American President Lines), was trying to help my father get his goods off a ship via which he was importing them from the Orient. John stopped the car on the old railroad tracks as we looked at all the empty piers that had once been the main docks for all of San Francisco's ships. Now, because of politics, all the ships were docked at Oakland. Suddenly, John turned to me and said something I didn't quite get. I said, "I beg your pardon?" He then said again, "Would you marry me?" I think I was so stunned that I just burst into tears, until John asked, "What is your answer?" I realized I'd never answered and blubbered out a yes. That was the last thing I'd expected to hear. Needless to say, I was so happy that I couldn't' stop crying.

John gave me a choice between marrying before his grape harvest and delaying a long honeymoon until late in the year or waiting until after the harvest. He said we could take off a week and go to Mexico. I asked him if I could give him my answer in a few days. I was elated.

I asked my mother to meet me for lunch the next day, where I intended to tell her. We went to the lovely restaurant upstairs at Neiman-Marcus. After we were seated, I ordered a half-bottle of champagne. Mother hardly ever drank anything, and I certainly would not normally have done this. We chatted away, remembering when Neiman-Marcus had opened where the great old store City of Paris had been. I had spent many lunches with my mother there and thought this was the place and the moment to tell her. I encouraged her to raise her glass of champagne as I had something to tell her. Finally, I told her of my intentions of marriage to John. She burst into tears discreetly out of happiness for me. She told me that she knew I cared deeply for him and was very happy for me. She liked John very much and felt we were well suited for each other. There was one question that was her only concern, not on my side but on John's, and that was religion. John was Roman Catholic, and I was Jewish. Mother knew John's mother would be very unhappy because of this. I felt it was John I was marrying and that it was, at this moment, his problem. Knowing John, I was sure he had thought all of this out and was obviously capable of handling it. The problem out of the way, Mother was truly happy, and I was beaming.

Now we discussed dates. I told her the reasons John had given. My mother was so wise and said I should marry him in August as his father was still living, and she feared that if I chose to wait, John's father might die, and that would be very sad for John. As usual, my mother's reasoning was right on the button. That left us six weeks before the wedding. We both knew that this was the least of my troubles. Now she understood the bottle of champagne and my choice of places to tell her.

I still had to consider the school as well, and it seemed that for all reasons, August was perfect. I could start back to work in September when the school reopened. I also had my coaching, which I was anxious to get back to. In addition, Natasha Makarova would be home, and for several years, I had had the great job of coaching her daily after the birth of her son to get her back into shape and to work, and then every time she came home between her engagements. I was one of many coaches she worked with, but the most important time for me was when she was in my hands. Coaching was my greatest love, and after Natasha, I really started getting more people, in brief periods, when they were guesting with San Francisco Ballet or when American Ballet Theater was here. I had once worked with Cynthia Gregory and Fernando Bujones. (It was Fernando I was working with, but Cynthia joined him.)

Meanwhile, my life at the school was incredibly busy, and people from everywhere dropped by to work with me or get in touch with me if they were in San Francisco. During such a period, I had developed a great friendship with Terri Westmorland from London's Royal Ballet. We were very much alike. He would come and have dinner with me in my little house, and time would fly by. He loved great cooking, and I loved to cook. But also I loved his teaching and approach to his work. He was teaching company class for the San Francisco Ballet. Every two months, Michael Smuin would invite a "name" teacher or dancer to give a class to the company. This way, the dancers in the company had the opportunity of not getting stale with one person and also trained with people in different styles. Terri had asked me if I would join him in France, where he had a house, to teach in the summer. We discussed his taking some dancers to give classes to, who would board there. I would give pointe class and cook. We were hatching plans, but then I received a letter from Michael Smuin asking me to teach at San Francisco Ballet, and I accepted gladly.

The school and company were now at Eighteenth Avenue off Geary Boulevard. I knew some of the dancers, but on the whole, it was a fairly new group of company members. I did my work daily, getting to know more of what I thought I could give to help them. I worked a great deal on their upper body and porte de bras. Those areas seemed lacking to me. The dancers all appeared to work very hard and well. When there was an incident with a young man's preferring to do his own thing, I simply suggested that he use another studio so as not to disturb me or the class. There were some beautiful dancers among them: Evelyn Cisneros, Betsy Erickson, Daniel Simmons, Tino Santos, Robert Sund, and more too numerous to list. I enjoyed working with the company, and I believe the feeling was mutual. On my last day, after class, the dancers presented me with a bouquet of flowers. I was very touched by their lovely gesture. As I returned to my dressing room, I bumped into Michael on his way up the stairs for rehearsal. He gave me a big smile, saying, "That's some bouquet—they will miss you." I grinned back, saying, "Thank you."

I had come full circle, and my heart was full.

35

Coaching

The honorable thing for a ballerina to do when she retires from dancing is to coach. My first constant coaching of a single ballerina was when I worked with Natalia Makarova after the birth of her son. Armen Baliantz—a one-time restaurant owner and great friend of Nureyev, Baryshnikov, and many other Russian dancers—had recommended me to Natasha. I remember that she called me to come to her house in San Francisco, where she had a small studio in which to work. I arrived, and there stood Makarova, very small and eager to resume her training.

I tried doing a proper barre, but at the end of one hour, I stopped and told her I would arrange time to use my studio the next day, where we could work properly, as her own studio was very small. I would also arrange for a pianist to play for class. Afterward, we could do variations, using the pianist or using tapes that I had of almost everything in her repertoire, except *Bayadère*. If she had tapes of her own, we could play them in my studio, where I had a good sound system. I told her I would keep the doors closed to provide her with the utmost privacy. She could use my dressing room, which was always kept locked. She needed to be in a professional studio with its advantages; if I were doing my job correctly, I too needed to have her work properly and keep her well protected.

My children at the school were well disciplined but nevertheless very excited at the thought of just seeing this great ballerina walk in the studio. They were told that they were never to disturb us or open the door when she was working with me. And so our work began.

I gave Natasha a well-rounded barre, allowing for her slower pace. She needed time to feel all of her muscles. Giving birth is hard on the back

–

especially. I put her on the floor with a floor barre of Boris Kniaseff that I had learned when I was dancing in Paris. I taught it twice weekly and had taken it further, using various degrees of advancement. For Natasha, it was a very good way to start. She took to it like a fish to water. On the floor, the stomach muscles are the first to come into full use, allowing for the strengthening of the back as well. We did this daily at the beginning. Flexibility, she had by nature. We needed to strengthen her natural suppleness.

We commenced slowly but thoroughly. It was a great joy to at last see someone who used her arms throughout my barre work. I showed her how to do it once, and she proceeded to work completely full out. Yet we were both trying to find our way. At one point, I showed her a bit of footwork and she watched, but after I did it, she did not get the combination. I asked her what was wrong, and she said she was looking at my feet, which were in a pair of old toe shoes. I said, "After this, I will wear teaching shoes." Teaching shoes are of soft leather, with a small heel. I realized that my job was to give the combination, not to dance it. After that, I would mark each exercise for her, not perform it myself. I remembered how I had been coached by Egorova, who wore shoes with a small heel. At the age of seventy-two, she made us understand the steps. This was my first lesson to learn now that I was a coach myself!

We needed to be patient with each other. I needed to sniff out the best way to work with her. I found out soon enough that she was extremely intelligent and the coach working with her had to have a reason for presenting combinations and to pay attention to the order in which they were given. For example, Natasha had a marvelous back, and one saw this in her training at the barre. I tried always to make a clean ending for the entire body. Sometimes explaining it in English didn't work, nor did my demonstrating it, and so I would take her body and make it do what I wanted. After one week of working together, I knew what to do, and she was now ready to work every day building up the strength in her entire body. It was really miraculous to see her go from day to day regaining everything she had had before and now making it even better.

I gave her a combination that was Cecchetti's quatre pirouettes (four turns). It is a well-known sequence of turns in every position. This combination was familiar to her, and she started doing it with two turns—or doubles, as we called it. Extremely difficult for any dancer to do correctly.

Sometimes I noticed that she needed to work more slowly as some dancers need more center preparation and warm-up exercises at the beginning of a center barre. I felt she wanted more combinations for her feet than were normally given in class. She needed more time at this than I was giving. Since the class was only for her, we started doing much more preliminary work for her center barre; as the term implies it, is barre work repeated in the center of the floor. Again I tried to tailor the class to her needs. This is something one must do when working with a dancer the caliber of a Makarova.

We began work on the variations she would dance. We started with the one from *Swan Lake*, act 2. The quality of her first steps was good (*rondes de jambe*; circles of the leg), nice and high. I asked her to do this the same way but to follow through to the end of the next movement, breathing with the top of the *ronde de jambe* but not stopping it. We worked on this until she could do it without effort. This is the true mark of a great dancer: body, arms, legs, eyes, face all together, never one thing without the other. We proceeded to the ending, which she did seemingly with complete abandonment. Again we did this, over and over many times. I made corrections, and she repeated it again. I felt it was now time to move on.

We took a small break as she changed shoes. Changing shoes is a continual process; it never stops. The shoes for one variation were perhaps not good for another. We then commenced the *Black Swan* variation, which starts with a very big movement using the back. Not many ballerinas do this with flexibility. Again, we repeated this solo many times, until Makarova's back was bent almost halfway over in a movement that required she do it from the rear corner moving forward on the diagonal. She never stopped working until she got it right.

Sometimes a minor correction would give her the right clue. It wasn't all about technique; it was what she needed to put into it as far as strength and endurance while always making it look easy. Her arms were always beautiful, but sometimes I would correct their spacing as being too close to her face or distracting in their movement. Unlike the American schooling, the arms of a Russian-trained ballerina are always softly rounded at the elbow, never straight. (I think this quality is also God given as well.)

We continued to work every day for five to six hours. We often would go out to dinner together and had wonderful times discussing other things than her work in class.

I knew that it would be useful to do some adagio work with a partner. I asked Natasha if I could arrange for one of the first male dancers of the San Francisco Ballet, if that would be agreeable. She was happy to do this. My good friend Jim Sohm, with whom I had worked at my school, was one of the company's principal dancers at that time. I phoned him, and we found a mutually acceptable time for us to get together and rehearse. It was great for Jim as he was dancing with the greatest ballerina of that period. Now the corrections flew out of me as he and Natasha did the pas de deux in *Swan Lake*. Working like this made sense to me as now we didn't have to stop; we could do the pas de deux variations right through to the coda.

It takes a great deal of stamina to attain the endurance for an entire pas de deux. Natasha was magnificent and was doing triple turns in the *Black Swan*. I was very content, and my corrections became more and more precise. We had our moments; for example, when I said, "Well, this is always difficult," after giving her a combination that was a struggle for her. She turned to me and said sharply, "I don't need you to tell me how difficult it is, I need you to tell me how to do it!" She was absolutely right. I went home rather dejected as I took this very seriously. The next day, I mentioned it to her, and she had forgotten it totally and scolded me for giving it so much importance. She was now in perfect form, and I also became more at ease and totally involved in her. I think as a coach, you must give up yourself completely. Forget how *you* did it. Look at the person and see what she cannot see for herself about how *she* needs to do it.

I remember one afternoon toward the time when the light changes in my large studio, when we were coming to the end of our rehearsal. I was sitting on my high director's chair as I too was very small. After thinking *This is the greatest ballerina in this moment of time in front of me,* I made the request for her to do the variations from *Swan Lake,* act 2 to end our session. Natasha did, and when she finished, she said, "Well?" I told her, here I had the most beautiful ballerina in front of me and I had decided I would like to watch her dance for me just to enjoy the sight of her. I had had the audacity to sit back in my director's chair and have her dance for my pleasure. She looked at me, and I didn't know if she would be angry or not. Suddenly, we both burst out laughing and couldn't stop. We understood each other perfectly. For once, I hadn't looked for corrections or anything: I'd simply enjoyed this most beautiful and very beloved creature in front of me. This was the start of a long and loving relationship. I would coach her every time she was in San Francisco, and also eventually Gert invited her to dance in Berlin. But that's another story.

I have coached many dancers since, and this I find my true love. I worked with Karen Averty, who became a ballerina for the Paris Opera. I watched her grow and develop into a wonderful ballerina. Jean Charles Gil was another dancer I coached; I had no problem with him in spite of his reputation for being difficult. He was anything but. A very beautiful dancer who came to me because he needed more than he was receiving from regular rehearsals in his solo in act 1 of Swan lake—where Siegfried's tutor leaves him and where he is now alone with his own thoughts—we worked on over and over again until I was happy with what poured out of him. I have rarely seen anyone dance with such poetic beauty.

My next big challenge was working with a young and rising choreographer of the San Francisco Ballet, Val Caniparoli. He had choreographed abstract ballets for the company during various seasons, and then soon he was choreographing everywhere. He choreographed *Lady of the Camellias* for the Cincinnati ballet, based on a story by Alexandre Dumas, for Cincinnati Ballet. Victoria Morgan was director of the company, and I was asked by Val to come along. We had a very successful collaboration. The dancers were good, and the principals were marvelous to work with. I worked with the latter while Val worked with the corps. When I was free, I would sit with Val and help make corrections during his rehearsals. We were always under pressure as we would have perhaps all of two weeks to come in and teach, perfect, and perform. Really less, as the last days were with orchestra rehearsal and last of all, complete dress rehearsals in the theater. Val had so much to attend to, including the lights, timing, scenery, dancers, and their spacing on the actual stage. This is where I found myself really working the hardest. I basically made dancers' corrections. Val was totally immersed in what he was doing, yet he was never temperamental or moody. The dancers responded to him with great respect and adored him. He belonged to another generation of choreographers than what we were raised with. He was far more accessible and much younger than were the choreographers were in my young days, when the choreographers were already very well known and far older than the dancers. He was seemingly always prepared; he moved easily and sometimes even choreographed the work out of sequence to accommodate which dancers were available, sure of what he wanted and that it would all come together.

I worked again with Val at Boston Ballet. Mikko Nissinen was the ballet director and an old friend, again from San Francisco Ballet. Val was doing his *Lady of the Camellias*; Robert de la Rose was designing the costumes. The decor was an entirely new design from what was used in Cincinnati. I must say the sets were stunning.

I worked with three groups of principals, one being Larissa Ponomarenko and Yuri Yanowsky—exceptionally beautiful dancers and also very easy for me to work with. I also had the Cuban ballerina Larissa Feijoo, another true artist. I spotted another dancer Sarah Lamb, who was doing mainly solos but had great potential. I started giving her my time directly after class, putting her through Egorova's turning combinations. As was somewhat ballet tradition, after class, the pianist plays music from ballet codas and the boys have the floor first to do their turns and practice leaps and "tricks." The girls go on next to perform the famous thirty-two fouettés, and so on. During this period, when I suggested combinations to Sarah, she really bowled everyone over. Every day, she got better and better, doing brilliant steps that ballerinas must perform. She was definitely ballerina material. Not surprisingly, she joined England's Royal Ballet directly after the Boston season and became one of their principal dancers. Coaching Val's ballet in Boston was wonderful; I enjoyed watching three very different couples dancing the same roles.

During ABT's visit to San Francisco, Natasha was appearing with them. Lucia Chase, the director, was using my office with her staff. At that time, Jurgen Schneider was the company's ballet master and a good friend. John Lanchberry was conducting, and besides admiring Sir John, as I called him, I found him to be a wonderful person, always reminding me that he was *not* a "sir" yet. I just beat the Queen to it. We had great fun together, lots of good times as well as good work.

Natasha and I were working in the studio when someone came through to go to Lucia's (my) office. I left Natasha and went over; Lucia explained to me that Anthony Dowell would not dance. *Swan Lake* had been was scheduled the next evening or matinee. It was a small disaster as every ticket was sold. Lucia's decision was to call Nureyev to come and dance rather than risk receiving rejection from the public. She asked me if I could convince Natasha to dance with him. I went back to my studio and explained the situation. This was not so easy as Rudi and Natasha were not at that time on perfect terms. However, this would certainly be a disaster for the company if they did not do it. She agreed, and I was to do the coaching. It was now five o'clock in the evening, and the plan was to get Rudi from the airport and rehearse at eleven that same night. We all agreed happily, for Lucia's sake.

I sent Natasha home, and I went to dinner with my family. I also had a few moments to call and tell friends to get tickets at any cost as there was a great surprise coming.

At eleven o'clock, we were all assembled at the studio, and in came Rudi on his best behavior. Natasha was totally prepared. Rudi asked for a towel, and my secretary went to get one from a Walgreen's that was still open close by. We did the pas de deux, and all went well.

The next day, it was announced in the theater that Anthony Dowell would not appear due to an injury. One could hear a groan from the audience. However, the announcement continued, Rudolf Nureyev would be dancing instead. Audibly great excitement. After the ballet ended, I sped to Natasha's dressing room to give her the corrections that she always wanted. I told her that it had looked very good from the front of the house. She then told me to go to Rudi, which I hesitated to do. However, I did go and see him and told him it looked good. His response was, "Your towel gave me luck." I smiled and said, "Let's see after the next performance!" I had no trouble with him, and I must say it was truly one of the best performances of *Swan Lake* I had ever seen.

When I go to a ballet now, when I am part of the audience, it is sad for me to see things that are not necessarily noticeable to the public but that we coaches would spot and correct. It is not the responsibility of a ballet mistress or master, as the case may be, as they are out front to watch the corps for straight lines and to make corrections upon the production as a whole. I also observe that, but also I am trained to see if the individual dancers are speaking to me—the audience. They may have a wonderful body and line, and of course, in America, these are the qualities that might make a dancer's career. The body's line and language are beautiful, so people accept these aspects as being the most important. It is not so for me and, in reality, not for an audience either.

To this day, we still cannot define what Pavlova had that made her a heroine to so many; the people who actually saw her could not explain why. My mother, who is now long deceased and who saw Pavlova as a child, always said, "Pavlova was unforgettable." Was it technique that made her memorable? My mother, who knew ballet and had seen everyone dance from the time I was a child to the year 2000, did not think so. What is the essence that Pavlova had and yet which eludes the remarkable dancers of today? Technically, they are far beyond Pavlova or, for that matter, Margot Fonteyn, my great love when I was growing up. I can't speak for Pavlova as I have only seen films of her which never capture her true personality. I can only say, when Margot Fonteyn came out as Aurora, she was that young girl in abandonment ready to fall in love with total naïveté. She immersed herself in love when she danced with her Prince Charming. While she danced with the four princes which were presented to her, her balances with each prince seemed effortless as she gave her hand to each, enjoying the moment—or so it seemed to me. I never saw a shaking hand or a quick letting go. There was never a change to her wonderful young girl's face as she danced that role, or Juliette, into her forties.

I now sit glued to my chair as I watch the dancers of today do the same movements. One is relieved when it is over, not exhilarated. It is a mistake for them not to be observed and then instructed by a coach while they dance like this. But there are no coaches for these dancers as the companies can't afford to hire an adequate one. And so the dancers must conjure up the conception of what they are dancing on their own.

Luckily for me, I have had the privilege of coaching many ballerinas and also a number of male premiere dancers, who have come to me and asked for help. I do so with great pleasure and love, for I know those moments where we work together can make the difference of making their performances artistically totally better. They become more secure in those harrowing minutes that make you better than you even knew. This I knew from the great ballerinas who coached me long ago. To honor Egorova and Leo Staats, Preobrajenskaya, and all the others who put their time and hands upon me, I humbly do the same—passing down my experience to the next generation—and I do so with great reverence.

Index

Q

Queen Elizabeth, 151, 153-54, 157, 170

R

Raphael, 313-14, 316-17, 319-22
Raymonda, 176, 290, 324-25, 327, 333, 335, 341, 344, 375
Recife, 291-95
Reinholm, Gert, 236-37, 240-41, 251-52, 255, 258, 261, 264, 296, 304, 307, 345, 361, 385-86, 388
Robinson, Henry, 149, 151, 154, 156-57, 159, 161
Rome, 294, 336, 380-81
Romeo and Juliet, 187, 339, 341, 343, 362, 366
Royal Ballet, 99, 167
Rudi. *See* Weise, Ranier

S

Sandloff, Peter, 235-36, 261, 332, 361, 364, 384
San Francisco, 15, 26, 29, 33-34, 42, 44, 55, 59-62, 65, 68, 79, 81-82, 96, 101, 103, 132, 147, 151, 155, 158, 160, 167-68, 171, 178, 228, 234, 236, 239-41, 290, 292-93, 296, 302, 312, 332, 339, 343, 347, 351, 355, 358, 361-63, 369-70, 372, 375, 382, 384-85, 389, 391-96, 399-401, 403
San Francisco Ballet, 18, 21, 25, 41, 45-46, 50, 60, 63, 93, 291, 386, 390, 395, 401, 405, 407
San Francisco Ballet School, 17, 61
San Francisco Civic Ballet, 41, 44-45, 49-50, 56, 60
San Francisco Opera Company, 391

São Paulo, 296, 298-99, 301, 304
Sayette, Howard, 375, 390-92
School of American Ballet, 18, 107
Schumann Variations, 315, 318, 327, 339, 362-63
Signale, 242, 247, 250, 256-57, 290, 295-97, 299, 306, 328, 335, 340, 342, 358, 366-67
Sommerkamp, Helga, 273, 292, 297-98, 301, 309, 342
Staats, Leo, 63, 81, 101, 410
Swan Lake, 51, 58, 87, 98, 112-13, 115, 124, 127-28, 141, 148, 362, 365, 405-9
Switzerland, 100, 118-20, 133, 159, 163, 165-66, 279, 287, 393

T

Taras, John, 47-49, 55-56, 62, 81, 108, 112-13, 116, 127, 139-40, 143, 145, 161, 378, 383
Tatsi. *See* Nagashima, Tatsuji
Toby, Harriet, 117, 132
Tokyo, 331, 345, 347, 349-51
Toumanova, Tamara, 51-60, 222, 257, 344, 356, 394
turnout, 19, 76, 376-77, 391

U

United States, 62, 64, 96, 100, 253, 255, 382, 396
Upton, John, Jr., 394-97, 399-400
Urbani, Pepe, 246, 253, 268, 273, 284-86, 288, 290-91, 294-95, 297-301, 305, 307, 310-11, 314-15, 318, 323-26, 329, 331, 334, 339, 387
Utah Theater Ballet, 357

Edwards Brothers Malloy
Thorofare, NJ USA
December 27, 2013